CORREC

Numbers in first column refer ... *sh"*

See also Key to ...

21	**sp**	Spelling, pp. 372–79
23	**ss**	Sentence sense, pp. 417–19
24b	**sub**	Subordination, pp. 422–23
4	**SV**	Subject-verb agreement, pp. 290–94
9b	**t**	Tense, p. 314
31e	**tr**	Faulty transition, pp. 476–82
24	**un**	Sentence unity, pp. 422–24
9	**v**	Verbs, pp. 310–16
22	**w**	Word use, pp. 383–411
22h	**wdy**	Wordy, p. 396
22i	**ww**	Wrong word, pp. 396–411, or consult dictionary
16	**x**	Unnecessary punctuation, pp. 348–50
	√	Check for obvious error
28	**∧**	Faulty omission, pp. 439–44
27	**//str**	Paral
10	**./?/!/**	End
11	**∧̦**	Com
12	**;/**	Semic
13	**∨̓**	Apostrophe, pp. 330–32
14	**"/"**	Quotation marks, pp. 334–38
15a	**:/**	Colon, pp. 342–43
15b	**/—/**	Dash, pp. 343–44
21d	**/ = /**	Hyphen, pp. 377–79
15c	**(/)**	Parentheses, pp. 345–46
15d	**[/]**	Brackets, p. 346
31	**par**	Paragraph structure, pp. 458–82
	¶/no ¶	Start paragraph/No paragraph

[redacted]

College Writing

College Writing
A Rhetoric and Handbook

J. Harold Janis
New York University

Macmillan Publishing Co., Inc.
New York

PRINTED IN THE UNITED STATES OF AMERICA

Macmillan Publishing Co., Inc.
866 Third Avenue, New York, New York 10022

Collier Macmillan Canada, Ltd.

Library of Congress Cataloging in Publication Data

Janis, Jack Harold, (date)
College writing.

Includes index.
1. English language—Rhetoric. 2. English language
—Grammar—1950- I. Title.
PE1408.J43 808'.042 76-6903
ISBN 0-02-360230-9

Printing: 1 2 3 4 5 6 7 8 Year: 7 8 9 0 1 2 3

Preface

This is a rhetoric and handbook for a first course in composition. It is designed to meet the need for a textbook founded on literary principles yet pragmatic enough to aid all students, only a few of whom will ultimately find themselves in literary practice.

My experience in university teaching and in conducting writing classes in government and business has convinced me that, for talented and ambitious individuals, the need to write effectively is as compelling as the need to excel in the other facets of their work. In *College Writing* I have therefore treated composition not as an introduction to literature or to Composition as Art, although under certain conditions it surely deserves to be so treated, but as a necessary tool for getting things done.

This concept I have tried to carry through without doing violence to those features of the composition course that have, over time, proved their worth—the emphasis on expository writing, the adherence to established rhetorical principles, the reliance on the weekly theme as a vehicle for writing performance, and the inclusion of the library paper, through which the student is put to a major test of scholarship and rhetorical skill.

I have, on the other hand, made some additions and some shifts in emphasis. The opening chapters put writing in a broad communication context. The extensive chapter on argument and persuasion—a nod in the direction of the competition of ideas that characterizes our society—can serve the student in both the role of persuader and that of an aware citizen to whom, increasingly, persuasion is directed. The several chapters on business and technical writing, including a chapter on job applications, may be used independently by the student or included in the course work. In either case, they stand as illustrations of the writing demanded outside the academic world and show, more concretely than would be possible in a strictly literary approach, the applications of rhetoric to job performance.

The two parts of the book complement each other. Part I, the rhetoric, takes up not only the basic elements of structure and style, but also, in separate chapters, particular types of writing. The progression is from the fairly simple subjective forms, like the personal letter and the diary entry, to the more complex tasks of analysis and advocacy. Other theme types treated in the text include the familiar essay, description, and narration.

Part II, the handbook, is planned to ease the instructor's task of correcting papers and the student's task of revising them. Students can also look to it for guidance in drafting their themes when questions arise regarding grammar, punctuation and mechanics, word use, and sentence and paragraph structure. Current standards are observed throughout. With respect to grammar, the treatment is limited to those aspects most directly affecting composition, and the terms used are those most likely to be understood by the nonspecialist. Even so, a brief review of grammar and a glossary of grammatical terms have been included. Ease of reference has been a guiding principle in the organization of the handbook section, and the indexing of symbols and rule numbers in the endpapers provides additional convenience.

In both parts of the book, the users will find examples to go with every important statement of principle. These, in conjunction with the text, are intended to help students form ideas and find effective ways of expressing them on paper. Although I have relied mainly on current or established literary sources, I have also taken examples from business, government, law, science, and similar pursuits to show, at least by suggestion, that good writing is not entirely the property of "literature," as the term is commonly understood. Exercises to be discussed in class or done outside class will be found at the end of each chapter in the rhetoric and after each section in the "Handbook of English." The specific theme topics offered at the ends of most chapters supplement the comprehensive list of theme subjects in Chapter 2.

Like any author of a book such as this, I owe a great deal to those writers and publishers whose materials I have sampled; their contributions are formally acknowledged in the footnotes. Additional help came from the work of my students and the suggestions of colleagues both at New York University and elsewhere. Specifically, I want to thank Richard J. Conway for permission to use his library paper "Charles Macklin's Shylock," as well as students Mary Dwyer, Jo Ann

Friia, and Stewart York Greenberg, who have allowed me to use their writing for illustration and analysis. Finally, let me thank D. Anthony English, my editor at Macmillan, for his perceptive reading of the manuscript and his many valued suggestions.

J. H. J.

Contents

Part I: College Writing

GETTING STARTED

EXPOSITORY WRITING

Part I
College Writing

1
The Craft of Writing

"Writing is drudgery."

"Writing is fun."

"Writing makes me nervous."

"Writing is for creeps."

Whatever you think of writing, you are destined to do a great deal of it. In college there are exams to take and papers to write, and—in your composition course—themes, themes, themes.

After college, there is more writing—writing *for* a job, and then writing *on* the job. For if you fulfill your ambitions at all, you *will* have something to say, or you will *have* to have something to say, and no medium is better for formulating thought than—writing.

Of course, you are no novice to writing. You have been studying and practicing it for most, if not all, of your academic life. So what can you learn about writing that you have not learned already? What can you do about your writing that you haven't already done? Let's begin with several assumptions.

First, you want to be able to write well. You may tell yourself that you already do; but hardly anyone does well enough. Even if you never thought about it seriously, the fact is that writing is not just a means of expression; it is also an important criterion of competence in any field, and an avenue to self-respect and self-realization. Few things in our society are done without preparatory writing, or without written documentation afterward. Not to be able to put one's thoughts on paper—with facility—is to invite frustration and, at times, personal embarrassment and economic penalty.

Second, to write you must have something to say. Words do not rush in to fill a vacuum; they cannot even materialize until thoughts or feelings, however formless, begin to seek expression. Thus, if you suffer from "writer's block," if you have trouble getting started, if you gaze prolongedly and emptily at a blank sheet, your problem is probably not how to write, but what to say.

Third, society imposes certain standards of expression on those who wish to enjoy its favors. True, there is no universally accepted standard of English. On the other hand, some words and language patterns are more suitable than others for particular audiences and particular circumstances. Further, some institutions—the law, the church, business, government, education, the sciences—maintain standards that suit their own needs. The same person may use, on different occasions, language as dignified as a bishop's or as crude as a marine sergeant's after a bad day. But one must not, on penalty of ridicule or worse, confuse one's role.

In your composition course, you will probably be held to fairly strict standards of English. A close analogy is the emphasis on draftsmanship in the schooling of artists. The reasoning is that having a mastery of certain fundamentals, the writer and the artist can then, with greater confidence and assurance of success, make those departures in treatment that their creative purposes dictate. As a student of writing, you should have enough words at your command so that you can make the choices required for accuracy. You should be able to spell those words or obtain their correct spelling from the dictionary. Grammar? Sentence structure? Punctuation? Let's say that there are certain amenities that both literacy and sentence sense require. You no doubt have a knowledge of the basic grammatical phenomena—verbs agree with subjects, pronouns with antecedents, and so on—and are able to exercise some informed judgments in constructing sentences and punctuating them so that your meaning is clear. With care in writing and proofreading, you will further assure that the reader sees what you intend him to see.

So much for an elementary but necessary discipline that good writing will exact from you. Fortunately, that discipline is peripheral to the main task before you—the act of composition itself. As you will see, there are many ways in which you will be permitted to develop as a writer. Whatever ways you choose, it is important that you have an intimate acquaintance with the craft of writing. To treat writing as a craft is not to preclude its emergence as art. Attention to craft will, however, help you meet the compelling need—one shared by all serious writers—for a mastery of the principles, techniques, and skills through which you may express your thoughts and feelings. In prose composition, the elements of craft are well established. They include a generous background of knowledge and experience in the subject to be treated, a sense of order, a taste for language, and an endless striving for clarity, precision, conciseness, and interest. If you add to these virtues a dash of originality and enthusiasm for your subject, then you may well find that you have produced not merely a craftsmanlike work, but an aesthetically pleasing one as well.

Expository Writing

The medium most often used to teach the writer's craft is expository composition. So that you may better understand the term, it is necessary to distinguish between expository writing and creative writing.

Creative, or imaginative, writing includes—most prominently—poetry, fiction, and drama. Such writing is original in concept, inventive in its details, and usually more dependent on mood and symbolic meaning than on fact or literal truth. Its aim is to entertain, amuse, challenge, or otherwise stir the emotions.

Expository writing, on the other hand, is strongly rooted in fact, observation, and experience. It includes all prose works that can rightfully claim to be nonfiction—for example, biography, philosophy, history, and scientific and technical treatises, as well as such shorter forms as essays, letters, and reports. Expository writing, like creative writing, may entertain, amuse, or excite, but those effects are usually only incidental to its principal functions, which are variously to inform, instruct, analyze, reason, dispute, and at times move the reader to action.

The Theme as a Vehicle

If the expository writing course is the medium for teaching expository composition, the expository theme is the vehicle. The use of the word *theme* in the sense of an essay or written exercise is itself unique to the course in composition. In essence, it is a short practice piece that permits the student to use whatever literary treatment he is required to demonstrate. The modes of expression run the gamut from narration and description to analysis, reasoning, and overt persuasion; and the styles range from the familiar, the humorous, and the satiric to the matter-of-fact, the formal, and the poetic. Opportunities are thus provided for the expression of all sorts of factual material and ideas in a manner that best suits the mood and purpose you want to achieve. You can use the expository theme as a conveyance for your personal experiences, your views on current issues, your pleasure in a hobby or other extra-academic activity, your special knowledge of some little-known subject, your perception of people, places, and things, and your observations on the culture and environment in which you live.

With success in writing themes, it is but a short step to proficiency in other types of writing requiring similar skills—examination papers, course reports, laboratory reports, job applications, business letters, business and technical reports, papers for professional journals, literary criticism and—who knows?—perhaps news stories, feature articles, press releases, and advertising copy. Mechanical requirements and vocabulary may be somewhat different for each of these tasks, but the verbal skills and structural principles you must apply are the same as those you use in your themes.

So there is utilitarian value in writing themes. But there is also a big bonus in the personal satisfaction you can derive from your effort. In an age of mass production, mass consumption, mass culture, and—yes—mass education, it is comforting to have a medium in which you are free—in fact, encouraged—to be yourself. True, you probably will not engage in the kind of invention you would experience in writing fiction or poetry, but within the broad boundaries of the expository theme, you may impose your own thoughts and styles and moods on almost any subject. You need no classroom, no laboratory, and no tools or materials except a pad of paper and a writing instrument. For a research paper, you have the freedom of the library.

The work is hard; you may not always be able to find the words and word patterns that precisely express your ideas, but with writing, rewriting, correction, and counsel, you should become more proficient as the term progresses. As you gain facility, your confidence in yourself will grow and so, too, will your pleasure in your ability to make words work *for* you. You may never like to write—not all writers do—but with increasing success in your efforts, you will most assuredly, as an experienced author once put it, "like to have written."

Characteristics of Writing

Man first expressed himself by signs and noises, and then by spoken words. Writing began as pictorial representations of familiar objects.

A significant advance was made when the pictures began to stand for the sounds of spoken words. Later it was discovered not only that spoken language used very few different sounds but that these sounds could be represented by a set of simple abstract symbols which in turn could be used to record any word or combination of words. Thus was the alphabet invented.

This brief history is not without significance for would-be writers, for it helps to point up one of several characteristics that give writing its uniqueness. Fundamentally, speech is the prototype of writing, but in the transfer of language from one medium to another, adaptations have had to be made. In consequence, writing is not so much recorded speech as it is a representation of speech. The difference is important in a number of ways.

Absence of Feedback. As any reader of transcribed and unedited conversations knows, impromptu speech—even that of educated people—tends to be wordy and at times illogical, disorganized, or unconnected. If the listener does not notice these faults in the speaker, one reason is that the spoken language is immediately dissipated in the air. Another reason is that the speaker's intonation, gestures, and facial expressions supply meaning or emphasis that the words themselves may not. Less apparent is the fact that the speaker simultaneously receives signals from the listener—a comment, a question, a nod, a smile, a shake of the head, a slackening of attention. Through these signals, called *feedback*, the speaker is reinforced, guided, and even permitted to correct himself as he talks.

As a writer you do not enjoy such advantages. Unable to use your voice or your "body language" to carry part of your meaning, you are forced to rely solely on your skill with words. Without feedback as you write, you can only guess what the response to any part or all of your message will be. Fortunately, you have a whole line of defenses to compensate for these disadvantages: You can take the time to select and organize your material; you can cut or add as the need arises; you can examine, rewrite, and edit the draft before you expose your thoughts to others. Thus, if the spontaneity of speech is sacrificed, order, clarity, and precision are enhanced. And if writing is not speech, it can in a craftsman's hands give an excellent imitation of the texture of speech.

Linearity. Writing is unique not only in its relation to speech, but also in its relation to the objects and events it attempts to describe. Writing is *linear;* that is, it cannot say anything except through an orderly sequence of word after word and line after line. This limitation contrasts with the simultaneous nature of objects and events in the real world and in pictorial representations of them. An individual run down by a car will experience a number of sensations—noise, pain, confusion—all at once, but when he later recovers and is required to make out an insurance report, he finds that he cannot record those sensations all together, as they occurred, but must relate them one after another. So, too, a writer, in describing a scene or picture, is confronted with what might best be described as a mosaic—a patchwork of lines, curves, and colors; yet in writing of them, he must organize his impressions so that one follows another.

The linear characteristic of writing poses no special burden to the writer detailing a purely chronological sequence of events, but it creates a problem in description and in the exposition of ideas. The problem is often difficult, but never insoluble. When, for example, you see such phrases as "The most important reason is," "On the other hand," and "Despite these advantages," you are seeing evidence of the writer's attempt to show the relationship of ideas that exist outside a time frame.

Inherent Advantages. Apart from the techniques they impose, the unique characteristics of writing also afford certain opportunities and advantages. The basis for this statement is the peculiar virtue of writing as a medium of reason and responsibility. The linear characteristic of writing, as we have seen, requires that the writer consider not only the sequence of thoughts, but the logical relationships among them. Indeed, logic as a discipline did not exist until writing opened the way. Writing is private. It is composed in private and may be read in private. Being private, writing invites the expression of the writer's most intimate thoughts and feelings, whether in letters, diaries, or other forms. Writing is also permanent, with traditional official status; thus it is the medium of all sorts of documents, including formal procedures, statutes and laws, and legal papers; family, church, school, business, and government records; and the results of scientific investigation. For these purposes, especially, the convenience of writing for reproduction, storage, and reference is not to be overlooked. Writing, finally, is an accountable medium. Barring fraud or propaganda, it customarily bears the name of the author or publisher to whom responsibility can be traced; and in any event it is in a form that permits ready examination and, if necessary, corroboration.

Goals for the Writer

So far we have been discussing the nature of writing, especially expository writing, and its characteristics as a medium of expression. Now, before we get into the writing process itself, let's direct our attention to the writer's objectives. If you are going to express yourself in a worthwhile way, you will have to give some thought to your reason for writing, your audience, and the best use of your writing skills. Viewed in this context, expository writing has at least three legitimate goals: (1) task performance, (2) communication with the reader, and (3) rhetorical effectiveness.

1. Task Performance. It has been said that you "can't write writing." Writing needs, above all, a task to perform. You may think that the aim of writing is self-expression. For practical purposes, however, think of self-expression as the means to the end, not as the end itself. Thus self-expression is inherently part of the process of writing a theme, but your immediate task is to demonstrate your proficiency in some form of discourse as, for example, description or explanation. In a similar way, the task of a job application is to obtain an interview, and the task of an editorial is to win adherents to a particular cause or point of view.

When you set a definite objective for your writing, you can measure your success by the extent to which the objective was met. Did your instructor respond favorably to your theme? Did writing meant to enlighten, amuse, or entertain do just that? Did your job application result in your obtaining an interview? Did your editorial urging the installation of a soft-drink machine in the student lounge enlist the support of others? The point is that writing can seldom, if ever, be treated as an abstract exercise; it is not to be regarded as "make-work." Like analyzing an organism under the microscope, or devising a mathematical model, or researching consumer habits for a prospective advertiser, writing has practical objectives with definable and realizable goals. In each instance, you must determine the goal and try to reach it.

2. Communication with the Reader. If the first objective of the writer is the performance of some task, the second is establishing a connection with the reader. We might picture the process in this way:

In this representation, the message may be considered the link between the interests of the writer and those of the reader. If the reader does not already have an interest in the subject, it is the function of the writer to arouse that interest. Where interest exists, the writer must feed it and make it grow. Let us say that you have a strong interest in the cinema and I have but a casual interest. You know Hitchcock's work thoroughly; I have merely seen some of his pictures and enjoyed them. If you can share with me, through your writing, some of your enthusiasm for Hitchcock and some of the details evidencing Hitchcock's mastery of his medium—details of which you are aware and I am not—then I will be richer for the experience. When your writing has such a result, you are not just writing, not just expressing yourself; rather, you are engaging the reader—you are communicating.

The writer's attempt to engage or interact with the reader is more apparent in some kinds of writing than in others, but ideally all writing should consider the intended audience and enlist its interest and sympathy. In a letter, the interaction between writer and reader is most direct. For example, an apprehensive eighty-one-year-old policyholder reports to the New York Life Insurance Company that she has lost the account book in which her insurance agent has recorded her monthly payments. She is fearful that unless the book is recovered, her husband will be deprived of the funds he is entitled to as her beneficiary. The correspondent who replies openly shows her concern for the reader when she begins her letter:

> I am sorry you lost your book, but do not let it worry you any longer, for I am sure I can help you.

The opportunities for adapting to the reader are less apparent in other kinds of writing, but they do exist and need to be utilized. Most students, for instance, would fare much better than they do if they would look upon their examinations not just as a way of telling what they know, but of giving the instructor the particular information he is trying to elicit from them. A closer study of the examination questions would help materially in the selection of content and the framing of the answers.

In other kinds of writing, such as essays, which are intended for a wide and not always easily identifiable audience, the problem of communication is admittedly harder. True, your natural empathy—your ability to experience the feelings of your readers—is always an asset. Beyond that, the best advice that can be given is that you learn as much as possible about people in general and your chosen audience in particular, and then adjust your content and language accordingly. In the end, you must view your readers not merely as passive receivers, but as active guides to your own expression. Only then can communication, in the best sense of the word, take place.

3. ***Rhetorical Effectiveness.*** You now have, let us say, a writing task to perform and a reader with whom you are going to communicate. Your next objective is to frame the message as well as you can. We will call this objective rhetorical effectiveness—the word *rhetorical* having reference to the ways you use language to accomplish your purpose. Your attempts to gain such effectiveness will take two directions.

First, you will want to be sure that you organize and formulate your ideas so that your objective in writing is fulfilled. Second, you will want to use English in ways that are consistent with current standards. The first aim depends for its successful accomplishment on your mastery of your subject and your ability to think clearly and use language artfully. Which details will you include? Which will you leave out? What specific choice of words will you make? What allusions, illustrations, comparisons, and other literary devices will you use to help you make your point? How will you apportion your space among the subordinate ideas? What order will you follow in the whole composition and in its various divisions? How will you begin and end? These are only some of the questions you must answer if you want to communicate your ideas accurately and forcefully.

With respect to the second aspect of rhetorical effectiveness—using words in acceptable ways—you should bear in mind that good usage is generally determined by the consensus of literate people. No one is going to make an issue of the plural of *man* (*men*), the past tense of *walk* (*walked*), or the spelling of *achieve* (not *acheive*). Other usages, however, are not so firmly established and there may be legitimate differences of opinion. Should one say, for example, "recurrence" or "reoccurrence"; prefer one thing "to" another or one thing "rather than" another? The choice may depend on the taste of the writer or on the kind of message and the degree of formality. Nor is it only individual words and idiomatic expressions that are involved. Take the sentence, "A review of the testimony revealed a number of discrepancies." A less careful writer might say, "In reviewing the evidence, a number of discrepancies were discovered," maintaining with some justification that the two statements mean the same thing. (But see Rule 26a in Part II, "Handbook of English.") Such problems of language can be resolved, but some fine lines must often be drawn, and that is why your knowledge of usage and the development of sound judgments about usage are so important.

Your First Paper

Theme assignments in the course will probably begin immediately. If you are permitted to choose your own topic, you may welcome the suggestions at the end of this chapter. Look ahead, also, to Chapter 2, where you will find advice on limiting your topic and suggestions for organizing the theme.

Most teachers have their own preferences with regard to the manner in which papers are to be prepared. Where no contrary instructions are given, follow these directions:

1. Use medium-weight 8½-by-11-inch paper, unruled for typing, wide-ruled for handwriting.
2. Put your name and section in the upper right of the first page.
3. Give your theme an appropriate title.
4. Typing should be done only by the author. Double-space throughout, leaving an inch margin all around.
5. If you write by hand, be sure to write legibly. Leave a one-inch margin on the left and right sides. Use black or dark blue ink.
6. Write on only one side of the sheet.
7. Number all pages and fasten them with a clip.
8. Proofread your work carefully before handing it in.

Methods of correcting papers vary among instructors. In the following pages, a section of a student's theme is shown, first, as marked by the instructor and, second, as revised by the student. Your instructor may also want you to rewrite papers. Keys to the symbols and rule numbers used by the instructor will be found in the endpapers of this volume, and the rules themselves are explained and illustrated in Part II, "Handbook of English."

In revising a theme, always use a lead pencil, a thin crayon, or an ink that will afford a contrast in color with the one you used in writing the original theme and with that used by the instructor in marking it.

My friends ask, "What makes a person like
ww yourself want to devote their entire lives to pron
lc/p Motion Pictures. I answer, "Its a feeling, a ✓
feeling inside you when you're on a movie set that 25b
doesn't happen anywheres else in any other way. w/wdy
✓/nw Its waking up at 5 o'clock in the morning in
wdy some part of the country you've never been to to K
nw be at work at 6 and look forward to the work of the //str
day ahead. Going to work with a busload of people
who feel exactly the same as you do about what 2
13c their doing with their lives.

26a Arriving at work, the set begins to come wdy
alive. The actors are being made up while going K
over their lines once more. The people from ward-
22e robe bring in all the clothes. The generator truck
is warming up the cables are being laid. The 3
director goes over the scene with the actors on
^ the set while no one is there then the actors go 3
sp/wdy back to their moble home vans to put on their costumes as the director talks to the heads of each PV
p department explaining what he wants in the scene.
sp Then he goes to his moble van and thinks about the 27e
scene before shooting.

p Meanwhile back on the set the prop men bring
in the props and arrange everything the way it was
the day before from photographs they take, some- 25b
what like a detective takes pictures of a crime prop
scene.

No ¶/lc The Grips (stage hands) bring in the equip- K
lc ment. The Director of Photography decides the
camera angles and calls for the stand-ins (These overused ()
22e are people who stand and move in the actors places ✓
p so the actors don't have to be there) They know wdy
t where to stand because they had watched the actors
7 run through it before.

Theme Section Marked by the Instructor

My friends ask, "What makes a person like you~~rself~~ want to devote ~~their~~ *his* entire ~~lives~~ *life* to *m*otion *p*ictures?" I answer, "It's a feeling, a feeling ~~inside~~ you ~~when you're on a movie set that~~ ~~doesn't happen~~ *don't get* anywhere~~s~~ ~~else in any other way~~ *but on a movie set*."

It's waking up at ~~5~~ *five* o'clock in the morning in some *strange* part of the country ~~you've never been to~~ to be at work at ~~6~~ *six* and ~~look~~ *looking* forward to the ~~work of the~~ day ahead. *It's* going to work with a busload of people who feel exactly the same as you do about what ~~their~~ *they're* doing with their lives.

~~Arriving~~ *When they arrive* at work, the set ~~begins to~~ come~~s~~ alive. The actors are ~~being~~ made up while *they* go~~ing~~ over their lines once more. The people from wardrobe bring in all the ~~clothes~~ *costumes*. The generator truck is warming up; the cables are being laid. The director goes over the scene with the actors on the set while no one *else* is there; then the actors go back to their ~~moble home~~ *mobile* vans to put on their costumes as the director talks to the head~~s~~ of each department, explaining what he wants in the scene. Then he goes to his ~~moble~~ *mobile* van ~~and~~ *to* think~~s~~ about the scene before shooting.

Meanwhile, back on the set, the prop men bring in the props and, *guided by photographs,* arrange everything the way it was the day before. ~~from photographs they take, some-~~ ~~what like a detective takes pictures of a crime~~ ~~scene.~~ The ~~Grips~~ (stage hands), *called "grips",* bring in the equipment. The *d*irector of *p*hotography decides the camera angles and calls for the stand-ins. (These are ~~people~~ *substitutes* who stand and move in the actors' places. ~~so the actors don't have to be there)~~ They know where to stand because they ~~had~~ *have* watched the actors run through ~~it~~ *the scene* before.

Marked Theme Section Corrected by the Student

EXERCISE

A. The theme below was written by a student early in the term. What do you think of the writer's ability to "communicate"? How would you rate the theme for rhetorical effectiveness? What changes, if any, would you suggest in content and language? Be prepared to answer these questions in a classroom discussion.

IN NEED OF CHANGE

After serving some thirteen years in America's public school system, I am now ready to make some comments and criticisms on my past experience and present beliefs.

First of all, if school is to be a place of maturing and growing up, students should be treated in that manner. I don't give much credit to the school system that treats high school students like floundering children, capable only of mischief. You are treated as if you cannot make decisions for yourself, and need a teacher's guidance every step of the way. I'll relate one of my experiences to give you an idea of what I mean. Picture this—I am sitting in class and have to go to the bathroom. In order to leave the room I have to get the teacher's written permission that I can go to the bathroom. How would you feel, being 18 years old, and having to ask a teacher to write you a note saying that you can go to the bathroom? To me, this type of discipline defeats the whole purpose of education.

Secondly, the whole educational system is too rigidly structured. Public school, like many other government institutions, allows little room for change or creativity, which I'm sure many administrators and teachers would like to engage in. In order for any change to come about, miles of "red tape" has to be gone through. This procedure, which is an American way of life, is very lengthy, and takes long periods of time, over which many people lose interest. If, finally, a change comes about, it is often too late, and of no value to the people or situation it is meant to remedy. For example, in my high school there was only one English course you could take each year. A number of new courses were proposed by creative and interested teachers so that the student would have more of a choice to meet his particular interests. Not exaggerating, it took about four years of review by committees and board of education members to get those new courses instituted into the curriculum. There is obviously some need of radical change in school structure if things take that long to get done.

Finally, the period from when a child enters kindergarten to graduation of high school is too long. I think very easily, many years could be cut off from a public school education. Grammar school could certainly be shortened, and high school easily condensed into three years. In most third world countries children are forced to leave school at about age 12 because of their commitment to supporting their families. Here, because we are more affluent, or lack of anything else useful to do with children, should not be a factor in prolonging an easily shortened curriculum. A shortened curriculum would enable more children to pass through our educational system at a faster rate, and would solve the problem of "overcrowded classrooms." It would also allow more students to go onto higher education or maybe in the future, a higher public school university. A shortened curriculum would also benefit those students not suited for higher education. These students are usually the disciplinary problems in schools and get little out of the school system. They would be able to learn a trade or find work ameniable to them instead of subjecting them to extra years of unachievement.

These are just a few of my beliefs and experiences concerning education in America. If there is to be any change brought about in the educational system, people in high educational positions, teachers, and students are going to have to do something. Teachers most of all have to speak out and demonstrate the need for change; because they are part of the system, and change comes from within the system.

THEME TOPICS

1. Write a theme on one of the following topics or on a close adaptation of one of them.

(a) My favorite reading—and why.
(b) Are English teachers too fussy about English?
(c) How "practical" are fiction and poetry?
(d) Advice to writers of textbooks from a student who has suffered through them.
(e) How writing influences me—some concrete examples.

2. Develop a theme on one of the topics below. Provide your own title.

(a) My first impressions of college
(b) My pet peeve
(c) My favorite season
(d) My career objective
(e) My hobby

FOR REFERENCE

BERLO, DAVID K. *The Process of Communication: An Introduction to Practice and Theory.* New York: Holt, Rinehart and Winston, 1960.

JOHNSON, WENDELL. "You Can't Write Writing." *ETC.*, 1 (August 1943), 25–32. Reprinted in *The Use and Misuse of Language,* edited by S. I. Hayakawa. Greenwich, Conn.: Fawcett, 1962.

MCLUHAN, MARSHALL. *The Gutenberg Galaxy: The Making of Typographic Man.* Toronto: University of Toronto Press, 1962.

2 Topic and Plan

A perennial question of the student writer is, "What shall I write about?" Another question—just as important, but often little considered—is, "What plan will I follow?" Here we will try to provide help both in the selection of a topic and in the development of a plan that will permit you to present your thoughts most effectively.

Finding a Topic

It is probably no exaggeration to say that a student will often spend more time in choosing a topic than he spends in the actual composition of the theme. Thinking about a topic is by no means a waste of time, but the sooner a suitable subject is chosen, the sooner the planning and writing can begin.

When you are given a theme assignment, the instructor will probably suggest some topics, but your receptivity to any given subject will depend on how clearly you can relate it to your interests and experience. Interest itself, however, is not a sufficient reason for choosing a topic; you must be willing to pursue that interest to the point where you learn enough to make writing about it possible. Often it suffices to be able to call forth from memory a particular set of experiences, ideas, and feelings. At other times it is necessary to do some related reading or other kind of research. But here another problem enters. With a week in which to write a theme, the time for research is obviously limited; hence, if you choose a topic outside your own experience, you must choose one that will not put an undue strain on your ability to get the information you need in time to write your theme and meet your deadline.

Fortunately, whether you realize it or not, you have a huge stock of experience on which to draw—experience gained in the home, in your neighborhood, in your travels, in the pursuit of your hobbies, in your relations with your parents, relatives, and friends, and in the reading and thinking you have already done. On pages 36–38 you will find a list of suggested subjects intended to jog your memory and stimulate your thoughts. More specific theme topics will be found at the end of this and following chapters.

In addition to the areas of interest mentioned here, you will want to rely at times on topics currently under discussion in the classroom and outside. If reading is a regular part of your course work, you will find many themes suggested by the anthology or other materials you are studying. You might, for example, compare the points of view of two authors, offer a critique on the work of one of them, or use a particular story or essay as a point of departure for your own thoughts on the same subject.

Newspapers and periodicals are another important source of ideas. Those listed below are easily available and are noted for their high editorial quality:

The New York Times (especially the daily "Op-Ed," opposite the editorial page, and *The New York Times Sunday Magazine*)
The Washington Post
The Los Angeles Times
The Christian Science Monitor
The Wall Street Journal
Time
Newsweek
Atlantic
The New Yorker
Saturday Review
Harper's Magazine
Scientific American
Fortune

Should you need specific data to help with any part of an informative theme, you may turn to a dictionary, an encyclopedia, an almanac, or another reference work. For a list of such sources of information, see Chapter 9, "Researching and Organizing the Library Paper."

In using material obtained from a printed source, you should be aware of the need to give proper acknowledgment and to avoid using the exact words of your source unless you enclose them in quotation marks. Such direct quotations should be used sparingly. For the most part, you should assimilate your source material so well that you can put the original aside while you write your first draft. You can thus select the arrangement and language that suits your needs, putting your individual stamp on the work. References to your sources may be incorporated informally into the text of your theme or put more precisely in footnotes. Formal methods of documentation (footnotes and bibliography) are explained and illustrated in Chapter 10, "Writing and Documenting the Library Paper."

Requirements of a Good Topic

To any topic you choose, you should apply a number of criteria to help improve your chances for an effective theme. A good topic is (1) unique, (2) limited in scope, and (3) appropriate.

1. Uniqueness. A unique topic is one that stands apart. It is distinctive, or different from others, in its content or in its point of view. Even the most ordinary subject can be made distinctive by the way you treat it. For example, the subject of urban crime is not unique in itself, but a theme describing the decay of a single small neighborhood and the terror of living there is unique in that it provides a particularly concrete and dramatic point of view. A family's Christmas celebration is another topic that seems fairly commonplace until a student of Italian ancestry writes about the long hours of feverish work in the kitchen by all the members of the family as they prepare a Lucullan feast consisting of mountains of savory Sicilian dishes. If you search your memory or examine closely your past activities or your special interests, you will probably find similarly unique writing opportunities.

2. Limited Scope. Unlike a book, a good theme topic is severely limited in its coverage. You could, of course, write about life on a farm, but a single boy's or girl's experience in raising a colt would make a better theme. The reason is that in a relatively short composition the broader subject forces you into generalization and a loss of detail. The more limited topic, on the other hand, promises a concentration of attention and a more purposeful selection of particulars and incidents. A comparison of the paired topics below should suggest the superiority of the more limited treatments in the second column.

General Topic	Limited Topic
Music as a Sideline	The Night I Played Bass in the Wedding Band
Vegetarianism	A Meatless Meal

Saving the Earth	The Threat to the Ozone
Keeping Physically Fit	What Jogging Does for Me
The Importance of the Arts	A Saturday Crowd at the Museum of Modern Art
Divorce	Life Without Father
The Meaning of Culture	The Wisest Person I Ever Knew

3. ***Appropriateness.*** Almost any subject is appropriate if you have an interest in it and sufficient authority to write about it, and if you treat it in a way that does not offend the sensibilities of the reader. It is always a mistake to choose a topic about which you are unenthusiastic. If you are well into a theme and find you are not saying anything significant, consider dropping the topic and searching for another that will be more interesting to you and the audience. As an alternative, you might also try to take a fresh look at the initial uninspiring subject by seeking more information about it or by tackling it from some other point of view. If, for example, you are floundering about as your attempt to relate your personal experiences with the strict discipline of your high school, you might consider switching to a sketch of one of the more authoritarian teachers whose methods of punishment seem in retrospect to have done little to reform his students, but much to reveal his own character.

With respect to taste, you should consider the effect of the theme on your instructor and on your classmates to whom your writing may be exposed. A theme that depends for its humor on a physical infirmity like stuttering is not only inappropriate but cruel. In bad taste, also, is the use of the theme as a medium for the writer's boasting, exhibitionism, or approval of antisocial behavior. Taste in the choice of words is another concern in this day of uninhibited expression. Be guided here by a sense of fitness for audience, subject, and occasion, regardless of the fashion of your contemporaries.

Forms of Discourse

In addition to meeting the criteria already mentioned, your selection of a theme topic will also depend on the kind of expository writing—the "form of discourse"—you propose to engage in. Are you going to narrate a personal experience or some other actions or events of which you have knowledge? Are you going to explain a point or otherwise convey the results of your observation or study? Are you going to describe a person, a place, an object, or an idea? Or, finally, are you going to engage in argument, that is, use facts, opinions, and reasoning to put forward or gain acceptance of a particular point of view? Narration, explanation, description, argument—these are the customary forms of discourse.

Explanation is part of all expository writing, but many expository compositions lean just as heavily toward description, narration, or argument. There is almost invariably some mixture. Decide at the start what form of discourse will predominate, and then select and cast the material accordingly. Let us say, for example, that a writer's subject is his hobby, portrait photography. He might develop a number of themes in each of the several forms of discourse, as the following titles suggest:

NARRATION

How I Got General Halton to Sit for His Portrait

A Chance Meeting with Jill Krementz [a professional portrait photographer]

How I Got Started on Portrait Photography

The Day My Studio Was Wrecked

EXPLANATION

Posing a Subject for a Camera Portrait

How to Choose a Portrait Camera

Lighting—A Key Factor in Portrait Photography

DESCRIPTION

Steichen's "A Woman in White"

The Ideal Photographic Model

The Best Camera Portrait I Ever Made

ARGUMENT

Portrait Photography Is an Art

Don't Believe Camera Salesmen

Every Face Is Beautiful

Why the Serious Photographer Must Develop His Own Pictures

Although a title is listed here under one form of discourse, it could also qualify for another, depending on the treatment the theme received. For example, "A Chance Meeting with Jill Krementz" is listed under narration, and it *is* narration if the writer develops a chronicle of his meeting with this well-known photographer of literary figures. The same title, however, may also be developed as a characterization of the artist herself, and the result will be a descriptive theme. Similarly, the titles "Portrait Photography Is an Art" and "Every Face Is Beautiful" can also be treated as description or explanation rather than as argument.

Structural Guidelines

Having decided on the topic and the kind of discourse you will favor, you can now begin to think of the structure your theme will eventually assume. Only with a solid framework can you hope to manage all the details. The alternative is confusion for both you and the reader. Fortunately, you may rely on principles that have been recognized as valid ever since the art of rhetoric was formalized. These principles are (1) unity, (2) coherence, and (3) emphasis. Unity relates to the pertinence of ideas, coherence to their order and connection, and emphasis to the relative stress ideas receive.

Unity

Good writing stays on track. The subject you have chosen is the one you must stick to. A first step to ensuring unity is to put in writing both the title of the theme and a brief one-sentence statement of the central idea. A good title is usually short; it piques the curiosity and suggests the content of the theme. The statement of the central idea, which is formulated for your guidance alone, should not only summarize the content, but also provide clues to its development. Here are some examples:

TITLE: Guitar Making—The Martin Way

CENTRAL IDEA: The guitars favored most by America's leading "pop" music stars have been made since 1833 in the small town of Nazareth, Pennsylvania, by descendants of a German guitar maker, Frederick Martin.

TITLE: Where Will Fido Go?

CENTRAL IDEA: With New York City's cat and dog population numbered in the millions, pets are being abandoned wantonly because their owners give too little thought to their responsibilities.

TITLE: I Celebrated My First Christmas When I Was Fourteen

CENTRAL THEME: Because I come from a family of orthodox Jews, Christmas was always an uncelebrated time for me until I was allowed to spend the holiday with one of my gentile friends.

TITLE: The Driving Lesson
CENTRAL THEME: One way to test your father's patience—and bravery—is to have him teach you to drive.

As you develop your theme, you must test each point for its relevance to the central idea and discard those that are irrelevant. You can also use the central idea as a guide to the kinds of material you will need to flesh out the theme. For example, the theme on Martin guitars, as described in the statement of the central idea, suggests the development of these points:

(a) The names of some of the "pop" stars who use Martin guitars
(b) A history of the makers
(c) A description of how Martin guitars are made

It might occur to you, during some phase of the planning, that the reader might also be interested in the economics of the pop music field or in a discussion of the other, sometimes odd-looking instruments used by pop musicians. You will be wise, however, to discard these ideas as not relevant to your main point, which has to do with the "most-favored" status of Martin guitars.

Coherence

To "cohere" is to stick together. A composition consists, as we have seen, of a variety of data relating to the central idea. These data must be grouped and arranged effectively, and they must be connected in ways that clearly show their relation to each other.

For good reasons most compositions have an introduction, a body, and a conclusion. The introduction and the conclusion set the limits of the paper, the former helping to build up the reader's expectations and the latter reinforcing his impressions of the message. The essence of the message is contained in the main part, the body, within which a further division must take place. Such a division will result in a number of related topics, as we demonstrated above in the instance of the theme on Martin guitars, or it may consist of a simple balancing of elements as, for example, advantages and disadvantages or causes and effects. In addition, some logical arrangement of the material within individual parts of the theme must be achieved. For instance, a historical survey permits a chronological order of events, reasons lend themselves to a ranking based on their relative importance, and description invites an order that progresses from the general first impression to the less conspicuous details.

Organizing Ideas

As the preceding examples suggest, the writer has available a number of well-established literary orders. Several orders are usually combined to form the pattern of the whole composition. How this integration of orders takes place is demonstrated in the essay excerpted on pages 128–129. In the next several chapters you will be shown how particular forms of discourse favor particular orders, and in Rule 31d in the "Handbook of English" (Part II), you will see specific applications of many of these orders to the paragraph. Meanwhile let us summarize the principal orders as they apply to composition generally.

1. Time. Events are usually related in the order of their occurrence. Applications of such chronological order are found in the narrative composition and in the description of a process, in which the various steps are described in the order in which they are performed. In some instances an inverse chronological order is used, as when a storyteller begins with a particular time period and then fills in prior events by flashback. In a job résumé, an applicant also uses the inverse chronological order when he lists the last school attended or the last job held and moves progressively backward in naming previous schools or jobs.

2. Space. Spatial order is used when the description of a place or object moves, for example, from east to west or north to south, from top to bottom or bottom to top, from the center to the periphery, from the outside to the inside. Thus a home might be described in the order in which one might take a visitor through it: front lawn, entrance hall, rooms on either side of entrance hall, rooms upstairs, then downstairs again to utility room and garage, and out the back exit to the garden. Writing on the problems encountered in the laying of a transatlantic cable, an AT&T engineer begins by delineating the order he proposes to follow:

> A convenient way to cover our subject is to begin at the cable terminal building (near where the cables come ashore—or put to sea, if you will), and continue down to the shore and on through the water to the deep ocean floor, stopping to consider each of the possible hazards we find along the route.

3. General-to-Specific/Specific-to-General. Suppose you were to begin with the generalization, "In the turmoil and fierce competitiveness of the stockbroker's office, Mr. Wesley's inoffensiveness commanded respectful attention." This statement provides a number of cues for specific development of the theme or paragraph. There is, for example, the opportunity to show by detail and example the "turmoil and fierce competitiveness" of the office. There is also the opportunity to contrast this atmosphere with the "inoffensiveness" of Mr. Wesley. In what ways was Mr. Wesley inoffensive? By his dress, his bearing, his manner, his voice, his actions, his philosophy of life? How did these qualities command respect? As you zero in on Mr. Wesley's personality, you again use a number of details and specific examples to demonstrate the truth of the generalization you started with.

The antithesis of the order of general-to-particular is that of particular-to-general. The latter is especially useful as a way of arousing interest when the particulars are more engaging than the generalization they lead to. Starting with the particulars may also be helpful when the generalization is too abstruse to be understood if stated beforehand.

4. Inductive/Deductive. Here we have the application of the particular-to-general (and general-to-particular) order to situations involving argument and analysis. When evidence and reasoning lead to a conclusion, the conclusion may either follow the supporting data (inductive order) or serve as an introduction to it (deductive order). The inductive order usually appears more objective. It is also useful when the reader is likely to be more interested in the data than in your inferences, or when acceptance of the conclusion is conditional on acceptance of the evidence. The deductive order, on the other hand, appeals to the reader who is impatient to know the meaning of the evidence and is willing to wait for the supporting details until later. A busy reader may skim through the supporting details, comfortable in the knowledge that they are available for reference if necessary.

5. Importance. Whenever an arrangement of facts or reasons is required, the problem of the order of these details will arise. In most instances, the order of decreasing importance will suggest itself because that order ensures that the reader will obtain the most important points while his interest is still fresh. However, it is better to use the climactic order (order of increasing importance) when you are using the details to build up a strong case for a following conclusion or recommendation.

6. Comprehension or Interest. If the parts of your subject have various degrees of complexity, it is often possible to begin with those that are easiest for the reader to understand and lead into those that are more difficult. In dealing with the selection of a camera, for example, an article advocating photography as a hobby would take up first the simplest types of cameras and then move on to the more sophisticated. If the cameras requiring more technical knowledge were dealt with first, the amateur might soon be discouraged and stop reading. Similar to the order of comprehension is the order of interest. Here the author engages the attention of the reader by beginning with matters of primary interest to him and proceeds from those to matters that are less compelling but still pertinent. Following this order, a theme on the marked increase in suburban burglaries might begin with a narrative about one family's experience, lead from that to facts and figures about the incidence of such crimes, and finally end with suggestions for the homeowner's protection.

7. ***Alternation.*** For comparison and contrast, as well as for other rhetorical purposes, the alternation of ideas appears to provide the most orderly arrangement. To demonstrate this order, let us assume that we are comparing two sports cars, A and B. The particular respects in which they are going to be compared are (1) physical appearance, (2) mechanical features, and (3) cost and upkeep. The comparison can be made in either of the two ways that follow:

EXAMPLE NO. 1

I. Sports car A
  (1) Physical appearance
  (2) Mechanical features
  (3) Cost and upkeep
II. Sports car B
  (1) Physical appearance
  (2) Mechanical features
  (3) Cost and upkeep

EXAMPLE NO. 2

I. Physical appearance
  (1) Sports car A
  (2) Sports car B
II. Mechanical features
  (1) Sports car A
  (2) Sports car B
III. Cost and upkeep
  (1) Sports car A
  (2) Sports car B

In the first example the cars are treated successively, feature for feature; and, in the second example, the features are treated successively, car for car. The first method seems better in this instance because it provides for more compactness and less shifting back and forth. Alternation, or a similar correspondence of parts, is also possible in such pairings as these:

Causes/Effects
Problems/Solutions
Advantages/Disadvantages
Questions/Answers
Needs/Methods of Fulfillment
The Way Things Were/The Way They Are Now

*8. **Functional Order.*** This order is dictated by the writer's purpose and the use to which the composition is to be put. Although it may encompass any of the other orders as well, the term *functional order* is useful in explaining arrangements of material that may otherwise be hard to classify. The order of introduction-body-conclusion is functional in that it provides a useful way to deal with almost any expository topic. In persuasion, the steps of attracting attention, motivating the reader, and stimulating action are also functional in that they lead progressively to the desired outcome. Business letters and reports are arranged functionally, as are laboratory reports and answers to examination questions. In the last instance, for example, questions can usually be broken down into their parts, with each part being answered in turn. This process, as we shall see in a later chapter, is called analysis, but it can also be viewed as an application of the functional order because it ideally serves the needs both of the student and of the instructor who reviews the answer.

Connecting Related Ideas

In addition to the choice of the appropriate methods of arranging your material, coherence also requires that related ideas be joined, not separated by intruding ideas. Suppose, for example, that one is writing a theme in which he proposes to take up first the advantages of dormitory living, and then the disadvantages. He has just written a paragraph describing the first advantage, the opportunity to be a full-time member of the college community. Now he continues:

Another advantage of living in a dormitory is the independence you develop. Of course, there are some exceptions. A friend of mine—I'll call him Joe—has the misfortune of sharing a room with a student who is constantly taking advantage of their relationship. The roommate leaves his bed unmade, fails to clean up, expects Joe to be his errand boy, and depends on him for help with his French.

As you can see, the writer has abruptly switched from a discussion of the advantages of dormitory living to an example of one of the disadvantages. He should have completed the paragraph with the thought he began with and continued with any other advantages he had in mind. A place for the example cited could then be found later in the theme where the disadvantages are discussed. The best way to ensure a logical and uninterrupted arrangement of ideas is to develop an outline, a topic discussed on pages 31–36.

The connection of related ideas is shown not only by their proximity to each other, but also by connecting words and phrases and similar rhetorical devices. Thus in the theme on dormitory living, the break between the advantages, on the one hand, and the disadvantages, on the other, could be sealed with the statement, "The advantages of dormitory living undoubtedly have wide appeal, for there is always a waiting list for living quarters on campus. However, the same students who enjoy the advantages must also put up with the disadvantages." Transitional statements like this are not part of the initial plan or outline of the composition, but must wait for the actual writing. For specific methods of connecting ideas, see Rule 31e in the "Handbook of English."

Emphasis

With a central idea and a plan for its development, you face still another problem in structuring the theme. If all your points get the same weight, there is a diffusion of emphasis, with the result that no point stands out. The solution is to decide what parts of the theme need emphasis and then to find ways to give them that emphasis.

You can achieve some degree of emphasis, of course, through effective sentence structure and choice of words. Since our concern at the moment, however, is with the whole composition, we need to look for other means. These involve the position of ideas and the apportionment of space.

From a psychological point of view, the most important places in a

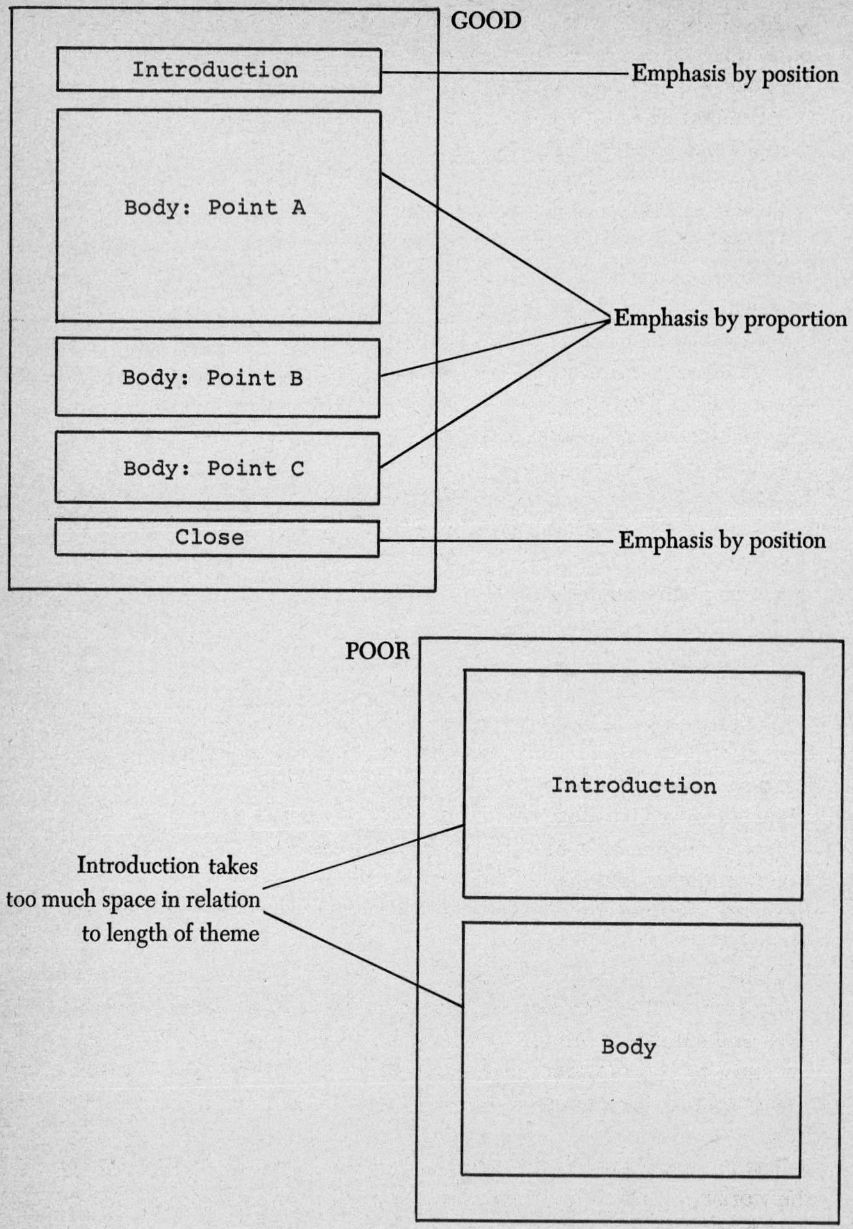

RELATIVE EMPHASIS

composition are the beginning and the end. The beginning receives emphasis because it is the part that is seen first (the principle of primacy). The end is important because it is the part that is read last and is therefore likely to be retained in the reader's consciousness (the principle of recency). If you wish to take advantage of these principles, you will give special attention to the opening and closing of your theme. This point is developed further in the next chapter.

In the apportioning of space, good sense decrees that the more important ideas should get more space than the less important ones. Thus you may devote several paragraphs to a key point, but combine a number of lesser but related points into a single paragraph. The way to enlarge on important points is to reinforce them through the use of details, examples, comparisons, analogies, and the like, and not simply to take one hundred words to say what can be said in fifty. (For methods of development, see Rule 31c in the "Handbook of English.") You will also see to it that the introduction, important as it is, takes full advantage of its position, but does not occupy so much space that it dwarfs the main part of the composition or tries the patience of the reader.

Outlining

Although a short, informal theme can sometimes be written from a few brief jottings, most papers require a more disciplined outline. Usually, an outline is prepared for the writer's use exclusively. At times, however, it must be exhibited to others—a teacher, an employer, a client—as evidence of work done or as a kind of blueprint for examination and discussion before a report is completed. In some instances, outlines are distributed to an audience as a formal written record of a speech or lecture.

To be most useful, an outline must be formally constructed, it must fairly represent the proposed contents of the paper, and it must be clear and consistent. Adherence to these specifications will be helpful not only to the outsider who sees your outline, but to you as the writer as well, for a good outline is the precursor of a good composition.

The outline from which the draft of your paper is written is called the working outline. As you write, you will be constantly testing the soundness of the working outline, and you will make whatever changes in content and order you feel are necessary to produce the desired outcome. At the same time you should try to avoid the stiffness that results from adhering too closely to the enumerated phrases or sentences of the outline, and try instead to achieve a natural flow of thought and language. The final outline, if one is required, is the outline of the finished paper.

In starting to construct an outline, you will do well to assume that your composition will have an introduction, a body, and a conclusion. The main parts of the outline may not actually bear these names and, in fact, the "body" may well encompass not one but a number of major divisions. Still, the initial tripartite scheme forms a concrete base for the development of a more specific structure. How this development takes effect is demonstrated in the outline below. The outline also shows how the methods of organization already described can be manipulated to form a logical structure for the whole theme.

Relieving Traffic Congestion on Main Street

Central Idea: Traffic congestion on Main Street requires that some remedial action be taken.

I. Introduction: The problem described
   A. Effects — Order of
   B. Causes — interest

II. Methods of dealing with the problem
   A. Banning private cars during business hours
      1. Advantages
      2. Disadvantages

Functional
order

   B. Limiting Main Street to one-way traffic — Order of
      1. Advantages — ascending
      2. Disadvantages — importance

   C. Developing off-street parking facilities
      1. Advantages
      2. Disadvantages

III. Recommendations
   A. Develop off-street parking facilities — Order of
   B. Reroute through traffic — descending
   C. Permit private cars and two-way traffic on Main Street — importance

An outline for a subject requiring a different treatment is shown below. Here the chronological order is used to take the reader through the principal stages in the process described. You will note, however, that for the convenience of the reader, the basic steps are grouped under not one, but two main heads (III and IV).

THE WAY WITH CLAY

Central Idea: Earthenware and stoneware owe their origins to clay and the art of "clay-throwing."

I. Introduction
   A. Clay—the beginning of pots and bowls
   B. The debt to the potter's wheel
II. The potter's wheel
   A. What it is
   B. How it works: lower and upper disks
III. First steps
   A. Preparing the clay
   B. Starting the wheel
   C. Fusing the clay to the upper disk
IV. Shaping the pot
   A. Centering the clay
   B. Raising the clay
   C. Opening the vessel
   D. Controlling the width
   E. Shaping the rim
V. The finished product

Conventions of Outlining

For clarity and consistency, an outline should conform generally to the following conventions. Try to observe them with the common sense that must be applied to all rules if you are not to become their victim.

1. See that the outline fulfills the promise in the title and the statement of the central idea. If it does not, either include the missing parts or change the title and thesis statement to conform to what you propose to cover.

2. Allot space in the outline so that it is roughly proportionate to that in the final theme. If one third of your outline is taken up with the introduction and another third with the conclusion, you are probably giving too little space to the body material, which should be by far the dominant feature. The solution is either to cut the amount

of space your outline gives to the introduction and conclusion, or to add to the details in the body.

3. Choose between a topic outline and a sentence outline. The topic outline, which consists of phrases rather than complete sentences, is generally favored because it is relatively simple, saves time, and displays the parts of the report in a way that makes them easy to examine and rearrange if necessary. Some writers feel more secure with the sentence outline, which is also more useful as a summary of the final composition. Examples of topic outlines have already been given. A sentence outline is shown below.

Divorce Insurance

Central Idea: Divorce insurance would ameliorate the consequences to marriage partners in the event of divorce.

I. One out of four marriages ends in divorce.
   A. Lives are wrenched.
   B. Alimony and child-support worsen the trauma.
   C. Current laws protecting spouses and children are inadequate.

II. Divorce insurance provides a rational method of dealing with the consequences of a failed marriage.
   A. The terms of settlement would be decided when the man and woman are happy with each other.
      1. The proposed settlement would benefit both parties.
      2. Reasonable terms, set in advance, would replace the vengefulness that occurs later.
   B. Enforceable terms of agreement would replace awards not now enforced by the courts.
      1. Thousands of the victims of divorce are deprived of alimony and child-support within one year.
      2. The welfare rolls are swelled.
   C. The terms would provide funds for a divorced spouse to enter a job-training program.
      1. The spouse could eventually be self-supporting.
      2. Alimony could be dropped after a reasonable period.

III. The social advantages are numerous.
   A. Awareness of the consequences of divorce will promote better and longer marriages.
   B. Public funds used to support divorced persons and their dependents could be devoted to other uses.

IV. Conclusion: Divorce insurance bespeaks not the expectation of failure in marriage, but a sensitivity to the consequences of failure.

4. Follow a consistent numbering scheme to show the relationship between the parts. Main, or first-degree, heads usually carry Roman numerals. Succeeding orders of headings are identified by capital letters, Arabic numbers, and lowercase letters respectively. A period follows the number or letter.

5. Be reasonably consistent in phrasing the parts of the outline. In general, topics of the same rank should be expressed in parallel structure.

INCONSISTENT

II. Qualities of Darnay polyester
  A. High tensile strength (noun phrase)
  B. Won't lose its color (verb phrase)
  C. Moisture resistant (adjective phrase)

CONSISTENT

II. Qualities of Darnay Polyester
  A. High tensile strength (noun phrase)
  B. Color fastness (noun phrase)
  C. Resistance to moisture (noun phrase)

6. Do not give unequal ideas the same rank when their relationship is better shown by subordination. Avoid, also, topics that over-

TOPIC: INCOME TAX DEDUCTIONS FOR COLLEGE TUITION

	Faulty Coordination	Improved
	I. The need	I. The need
Overlapping heads	II. The proposed solution	II. The proposed solution A. Eligibility B. Tax allowances
Overlapping heads / Subordinate ideas shown as equal	III. Features of the proposed solution	III. Anticipated results
Subordinate ideas shown as equal	IV. Eligibility	IV. Conclusion
Subordinate ideas shown as equal	V. Proposed tax allowances	
	VI. Anticipated results	
	VII. Conclusion	

lap; that is, coordinate topics that are worded differently but include the same substance. Be suspicious of any outline that does not provide a good mix of main and subordinate heads. Compare the outlines at the bottom of the preceding page.

7. Eliminate single subheads. The division of a topic logically presumes two or more subtopics. If you cannot create a second subtopic, consolidate the main topic and single subtopic by some modification of phrasing. A single subtopic is permissible when it is used to signify an example.

Not	But
I. Number of machines in operation A. Five	I. Five machines in operation
II. Trouble reported A. Frequent breakdowns	II. Trouble reported A. Overheating B. Cycle uncompleted C. Damaged electrical connections

ACCEPTABLE

I. Institutional advertising
  A. Example: Xerox Corporation

Suggested Theme Subjects

Listed below are subjects in several different categories. All but a few of the subjects are too broad for satisfactory treatment in the confines of a theme, but they should suggest topics with a more limited perspective.

Hobbies, Recreation,
and Personal Life

1. Friends
2. Dating
3. Getting along with parents
4. Childhood experiences
5. Vacations and travel
6. Holiday celebrations
7. Trouble
8. At the beach
9. Collecting
10. Music
11. Dancing
12. Acting

13. Sports
14. Gardening
15. House plants
16. Woodworking
17. Interior decorating
18. Raising fish, animals
19. Museum-going
20. Movies
21. The theater

School and Career

22. Teachers
23. Teaching methods
24. Curricula
25. The grading system
26. Choice of a college
27. Choice of an occupation
28. Dormitory life
29. School politics
30. College fraternities
31. Clubs
32. College sports
33. Summer jobs
34. The working student
35. The cafeteria
36. The student lounge
37. The library
38. Getting into graduate school (or law school or dental or medical school)
39. College costs

Cultural Phenomena

40. Fast-food restaurants
41. "Singles" bars
42. Convenience foods
43. Modern merchandising
44. Packaging
45. Shopping malls
46. High-rise buildings
47. On the road
48. Motels
49. Tipping
50. Leisure clothes
51. Mysticism
52. Rock concerts
53. Television programming
54. Television commercials
55. Home movies
56. Home sound systems
57. The news magazine
58. Pornography
59. Paperback books
60. The cult of self-improvement
61. Christmas shopping
62. Apartment living
63. Suburbia

Government, Economics, and Politics

64. Controlling inflation
65. Measuring economic growth
66. Government snooping
67. Government spending
68. Taxation
69. Getting elected
70. Campaign gifts
71. The abuse of office
72. The profit motive
73. The "American way"
74. Government's role in social progress
75. Making money grow
76. The United Nations

77. Foreign relations
78. Labor unions
79. The labor market
80. Monopolistic industries
81. A national policy on energy
82. Encouraging agriculture
83. Foreign trade

Social Conditions

84. Drug abuse
85. Crime
86. Gun control
87. Deteriorating neighborhoods
88. Welfare
89. Unemployment
90. Trailer homes
91. Urban transportation
92. Air pollution
93. Housing for the poor (or middle classes)
94. Public day-care centers
95. Caring for the aged
96. The quality of medical care
97. Hospital costs
98. Malnutrition
99. Prison reform
100. Strikes by public employees
101. Changing sexual standards
102. Consumer protection
103. Strip mining

Health and Family

104. Prolonging life
105. Wonder drugs
106. Relieving tension
107. Pill-popping
108. Doctor and patient
109. Food labeling
110. "Natural" foods
111. Vegetarianism
112. The working mother
113. Fatherless homes
114. Entertaining relatives
115. Visiting a relative
116. A favorite relative
117. Getting along with parents
118. Parents as teachers
119. Sibling rivalry
120. A family reunion
121. The family home
122. The family car

Science and Nature

123. Undersea exploration
124. Exploring the planets
125. Space stations
126. Endangered species
127. Earthquakes (and other natural disasters)
128. Vanishing land resources
129. Modern armaments
130. The gas-efficient car
131. The future of the SST
132. Science in agriculture
133. Animal behavior
134. Developing sources of energy
135. Controlling oil spills

EXERCISES

A. Applying the criteria given at the beginning of the chapter, generate a specific theme *topic* from each of *ten* of the suggested theme *subjects* listed on pages 36–38. Before each of your topics, put the subject number in parentheses.

B. Max Neuhaus, the author of the following essay, is a composer.

1. To what degree does the essay conform to the requirements of a good topic, as stated on pages 20–21? What do you think of the title?
2. In your opinion, what form of discourse—narration, description, explanation, or argument—predominates? To what degree are the other forms of discourse used?
3. What is the central idea of the essay? Express it in a single sentence.
4. What evidences of unity, coherence, and emphasis do you find in the essay?
5. What is the principal order used in the essay? If your instructor requires, make a topic outline of the paper, using first- and second-degree heads only.
6. To what degree do you find the essay interesting? well developed? persuasive? Do you have any suggestions for improvement?

BANG, BOOooom, ThumP, EEEK, tinkle[1]

The popular concept of "noise pollution" is a dangerously misleading one. In reality, dangers to hearing do exist in prolonged, excessively loud sound levels. However, the residue of the idea that has ended up in the mind of the public because of misleading publicity is that sound in general is harmful to people.

A brief examination of a pamphlet, "Noise Makes You Sick," published by the Department of Air Resources of the city's Environmental Protection Agency, is typical of the literature and clearly illustrates the problem.

The first sentence, "Sound is instantly transmitted from your ears to your brain and then to your nerves, glands and organs," is of course literally true. Actually the reaction doesn't normally go as far as the glands and internal organs.

[1] Max Neuhaus, "BANG, BOOooom, ThumP, EEEK, tinkle," *New York Times*, 6 December 1974, © 1974–75 by The New York Times Company. Reprinted by permission.

However, we are left with the impression that we have absolutely no defense against unwanted sound. This is untrue. The body has automatic reflex barriers, both physical and psychological, to deal with sounds it does not wish to react to.

The pamphlet goes on, "Any loud or unexpected sounds put your body on alert." This is true with a newborn child or in primitive societies, both of which need this reaction to survive, but certainly the modern urban dweller is not put into a state of fright (except of course when there is actual danger) very often by the sounds around him.

A human being conditions himself fairly quickly to what is "loud or unexpected" in his particular environment.

Once having "established" the impression that we are constantly in a state of "fright" though, the brochure goes on to extrapolate in august pseudo-medical terms: "Adrenalin, an energy-producing hormone, is released into your blood stream. Your heart beats faster, your muscles tense, and your blood pressure rises. Sudden spasms occur in your stomach and intestines." This finally gives the impression that every honking horn brings us a little bit closer to death.

The law defines noise as "any unwanted sound." Surely several hundred years of musical history can be of value: At the very least, they can show us that our response to sound is subjective—that no sound is intrinsically bad. How we hear it depends a great deal on how we have been conditioned to hear it.

Through extreme exaggeration of the effects of sound on the human mind and body, this propaganda has so frightened people that it has created "noise" in many places where there was none before, and in effect robbed us of the ability to listen to our environment.

Admittedly it may be necessary to oversimplify an idea to bring enough public pressure to bear on the producers of ear-damaging sounds in our environment to stop this victimization of the public. This degree of misrepresentation is not only unnecessary, but irresponsible and ultimately negative.

This present concept of noise pollution condemns all sounds by leaving, in the public mind, the impression that sound itself is physiologically and psychologically harmful.

It is this exaggerated and oversimplified concept that is doing most of the damage, not sound—damage that can and should be rectified by curtailing misleading propaganda and showing people other ways to listen to their surroundings.

Obviously we need to be able to rest from sound just as we do from visual stimulation, we need aural as well as visual privacy, but silencing our public environment is the acoustic equivalent of painting it black. Certainly just as our eyes are for seeing, our ears are for hearing.

THEME TOPICS

1. Write a theme on a topic generated from one of the subjects listed on pages 36–38. (See Exercise A, p. 39.) Following the style of the outlines in this chapter, submit a topic outline with your theme.

2. Study the orders discussed under "Organizing Ideas" (pp. 25–28); then select a topic and develop a theme that lends itself particularly well to one of the orders. In one sentence, below your theme title, state the central idea and, in another sentence, name the principal order you have used in developing the theme.

3
Drafting the Paper

By whatever route you arrive at the plan of the paper, the actual writing is best accomplished successively from beginning to end. Now you must meet the challenge of transferring thoughts into words and—more than that—creating interest, developing a mood, and giving your paper character.

The Beginning

A good beginning not only engages the reader's interest, but leads him into the central idea. It also reflects the tone of the whole composition. It may consist of one paragraph or several, but the need to attract attention creates a bias toward relatively short paragraphs. The content of the opening will vary with the subject, the purpose, and the degree of formality you want. As a rule, it is better to begin with specifics than with generalities. You may state some little-known facts about your subject, provide an example or instance, offer a pertinent quotation, ask a question, or relate some anecdote or experience that serves as a lead-in to your central idea. These and other methods are examined below.

1. Narration. In this kind of opening, an incident is chosen both for its inherent interest and for the introduction it provides to the main idea. The beginning that follows is part of the same narrative account that occupies the whole story. The MHT of the narrative is the Manufacturers Hanover Trust Company of New York, in whose employees' magazine the article appeared.

> The bulky ferryboat slid out of its lower Manhattan berth into New York Bay. Ordinarily it would be headed southwest to Staten Island.
>
> Not this time. Its destination was an undefined spot about a quarter mile out in the Bay. There the captain would cut the engines, and for the next five hours the boat's location would be determined by the vagaries of the swirling current.

Including well-known TV-producer-writer Rod Serling, the pilot and a skeleton crew—less than 50 people were aboard. All were there to help film a 30-second MHT television commercial. Subject? Command Credit.[1]

In the example below, the brief anecdote in the first paragraph is used independently to introduce the main subject, Rome's Via Condotti.

Herman Melville, visiting Rome in 1857, noted with gustatory and fiscal approval in his *Journals:* "I dined on 19 cents at Lepri's."

The old Trattoria Lepri, which catered to Rome's foreign colony, sprawled then through a series of rooms for different nationalities—English, French, German, American—and stood directly across from the Caffè Greco on Via Condotti. Its hospitable premises are now divided between the emporiums of Gucci and Bulgari. Nineteen cents will no longer buy more than the time of day, if that, but Via Condotti is still a great street and a continuing magnet for visitors to Rome.[2]

2. ***Facts.*** Sometimes specific facts and figures make an interesting beginning to an informative article. Sometimes more general assertions are sufficient to arouse curiosity.

The United States, according to some estimates, pays a health bill of $30 billion annually for illnesses related to faulty nutrition. "Junk" foods account for more than 35 percent of a typical American family's food budget. Sugar consumption has risen close to an annual 120 pounds per person. Food additives are proliferating on the grocer's shelves. Cholesterol-rich diets, perhaps in combination with other factors, are taking an ever larger toll of men in their prime years. Nutritional deficiencies are not confined to the poor; they are rampant among the privileged and affluent, and particularly the young in this group—though the young have lately been in the avant-garde of the health-food movement.

Millions of children have no difficulty finding money to spend at soda-and-candy counters. They grow up with a built-in sweet tooth, a vice further encouraged by the estimated five thousand commercials a year the American youngster watches during childhood. Many teen-age girls ruin their health with one fad diet after another. A decade ago the soft-drink-and-pizza mania was considered a stage in growing up, along with pimples and acne. Today junk, snack, and pop food—high in calories, high in fats and sugars, low in nutrition—bulks large in the daily diet of Americans from cradle to grave.[3]

[1] "At Sea with MHT: Shooting with Serling on New York Bay," *Topics*, June 1974, p. 3.

[2] Al Hine, "Rome's Via Condotti," *Travel & Leisure*, March 1974, p. 37.

[3] Clara Pierre, "The Nutrition Dilemma," *Saturday Review*, 18 May 1974, p. 53.

The opening below, though less statistical and more assertive, still has enough particulars to arouse the reader's interest.

Of all our fellow-mammals, the most remote and the most difficult to understand is the great whale. Its size and the alien element it inhabits cut it off from us both in imagination and as an object of study. It is more nearly possible to feel kinship with a mouse, and a mouse is also immeasurably easier for a scientist to observe. Men have pursued whales for centuries, and killed them with unbounded cruelty and in staggering numbers, without learning much more than the simplest facts about their anatomy and their habits. Most of our knowledge of whales, in fact, has been derived from dead whales. Their giant corpses have been dissected, and scientists have charted their astonishing insides: arteries with the circumference of stovepipes, hearts weighing a thousand pounds, and large, complex brains suggesting extraordinary mental powers.[4]

3. ***Analogy or Contrast.*** A juxtaposition to show the relation of dissimilar things (analogy) or differences in similar things (contrast) can make an effective lead, as shown in the respective examples below.

Faces, like fingerprints and snowflakes, come in virtually infinite variety. There is little chance of encountering two so similar they cannot be distinguished, even on casual inspection. Unlike fingerprints and snowflakes, however, faces can be recognized as well as discriminated. It is possible not only to tell one from the other but also to pick one from a large population and absolutely identify it as something previously known, just as in reading one not only can tell that an A is different from a B but also can identify and name each letter.

Why are faces so readily recognized?[5]

Twenty years ago the first regional shopping centers started a retailing revolution that played a major role in the dramatic growth of the nation's suburbs. Today another revolution is taking place in which many of these sprawling, one-story complexes will gradually disappear. Replacing them will be high-rise "omnicenters" that offer a range of community facilities as well as merchandise.[6]

As the last example shows, contrast is a useful device for pointing up a trend. The contrast there involves a kind of yesterday-today

[4] Faith McNulty, "Lord of the Fish," *The New Yorker,* 6 August 1973, p. 38.

[5] Leon D. Harmon, "The Recognition of Faces," *Scientific American,* November 1973, p. 71.

[6] Lathrop Douglass, "Tomorrow: Omnicenters on the Landscape?" *Harvard Business Review,* March–April 1974, p. 8.

sequence that helps to dramatize the change. The example that follows employs a similar technique, but in a more spirited manner.

Children are a relatively modern invention. Until a few hundred years ago they did not exist. In medieval and Renaissance painting you see pint-size men and women, wearing grown-up clothes and grown-up expressions, performing grown-up tasks. Children did not exist because the family as we know it had not evolved. In the old days most people lived on the land, and life was a communal affair.

Children today not only exist; they have taken over. God's Country has to an astonishing degree become Kids' Country—in no place more than in America, and at no time more than now. Once more 'tis the season, holiday time has begun, the frantic family skedaddle from pumpkin to holly when Kids' Country runs in its jumpingest high gear.[7]

4. Questions. The interrogative beginning must be used with care, lest the questions sound trite or obvious. Good questions pique the curiosity.

Can one take seriously the proposition that Boston was once part of Africa, separated from western Massachusetts by an ocean? Or that New York is farther from London than it was a year ago? Or that Los Angeles will some day nestle alongside San Francisco?

Until recently, such propositions would have seemed preposterous, but today a revolutionary new understanding of the planet on which we live has made them plausible. . . .[8]

5. Contrary Idea. An interesting beginning can be made of an idea that runs counter to the conventional wisdom. The questions in the opening immediately above suggest such an idea. Here, an opening expresses a contrary idea in a different vein.

You hear a lot these days about speed-readers. But we can tell you from experience that nowadays the problem isn't really speed-reading at all—it's speed-stopping. The fact is that there is so much published today, the art of knowing when to stop reading not only can increase your literary life but also can, literally, save it. Anyway, here are some examples of what we mean. . . .[9]

And here is another opening expressing a contrary idea—this time with a touch of humor.

[7] Shana Alexander, "Kids' Country," *Newsweek*, 11 December 1972, p. 37.

[8] Walter Sullivan, "The Restless Continents," *The New York Times Magazine*, 12 January 1975, p. 12, © 1974–75 by The New York Times Company. Reprinted by permission.

[9] Cleveland Amory, "Curmudgeon-at-Large," *Saturday Review*, 4 May 1974, p. 8.

There are a great many people who really believe in answering letters the day they are received, just as there are people who go to the movies at nine o'clock in the morning; but these people are stunted and queer.

It is a great mistake. Such crass and breathless promptness takes away a great deal of the pleasure of correspondence.[10]

6. Description. Occasionally description is sufficiently interesting in itself to provide an effective lead to a descriptive topic.

Sloths have no right to be living on the earth; they would be fitting inhabitants of Mars, where a year is over six hundred days long. In fact, they would exist more appropriately on a still more distant planet where time—as we know it—creeps and crawls instead of flies from dawn to dusk. Years ago I wrote that sloths reminded me of nothing so much as the wonderful Rath Brother athletes or of a slowed-up motion picture, and I can still think of no better similes.[11]

7. Example. When a paper treats some condition, social or otherwise, that needs attention, an interesting beginning may be made from a concrete example. In the following opening, a single family is used to exemplify the general plight of middle-class Americans. The figures cited obviously predate the recent inflationary trend.

Joe Taylor is one of the "Forgotten People" of America's working class. He is forty-one years old, has been married for twenty-one years, and is the father of three children. His grandfather, a tailor, came from Poland with the name Zbroszczyk. An immigration official could not pronounce it; so, from that moment on, the American branch of the Zbroszczyk family has been known as Taylor.

Joe works in a factory, belongs to a union, and makes $9,600 a year. He dropped out of high school, went to work at the factory where he has worked ever since, and married a girl, Mary, he had known since childhood. Their twenty-year-old son, Michael, a Vietnam veteran who cannot find work, lives at home. Another son finishes high school this year, is bright, and has been encouraged by his teachers to go on to college. But Joe does not know where the money will come from. Their daughter, Doris, is twelve. She wants to go to college, too, and Joe does not know where the money will come from for her, either.

The Taylors live in a two-story, twenty-five-year-old, four-bedroom, $17,000 home near the downtown section of a middle-sized city. Their home has one bathroom. Mary has a clothes washer but not a dryer. She

[10] Christopher Morley, "On Unanswering Letters," *Mince Pie* (New York: Doran, 1919, 1947), p. 35.

[11] William Beebe, *Jungle Days* (New York: Putnam, 1925), p. 92.

would like a rollaway dishwasher. But that is a luxury they cannot afford now. She would also like a garbage disposal. Joe would like to buy a color television set.

The Taylors are always short of money. Joe makes $800 a month, but his take-home paycheck is only $635. Grocery bills amount to about $200 a month. From the remaining $435, mortgage, telephone, electricity, and gas bills claim $210, life insurance $12, and car expenses including insurance and payments $75. Their church receives $2 a Sunday, or $8 a month. Joe spends $20 out-of-pocket a month. Mary about the same. Clothing, personal care, and other family expenses take up as much as $50. They stubbornly save $30 a month whenever possible. Therefore, if they are lucky—if the sink doesn't stop up, if the children don't catch the flu, and if everything else works okay—the Taylors end up each month with about $10 to spare.[12]

The specific example cited leads to a generalization and a direct link to the body of the article.

There are eighty-two million working-class Americans like Joe Taylor—many of them in similar economic straits. They are quite literally broke all the time. Any serious illness requiring prolonged hospitalization could wipe them out financially. It is often impossible for them to send their children to college. Retirement presents the threat of virtually guaranteed impoverishment. They read about their being the most highly paid working people in history, but when they compare their lot with that of their more well-heeled contemporaries they sense that the gap between rich and poor is just as great as ever. They feel that their government has brushed them aside, that politicians and social service agencies are preoccupied with the problems of blacks, youths, and other more troublesome minorities, and that, in short, the working class is a forgotten class.

And they are right. Working families comprise the largest single group in the United States; yet as a society we have ignored their increasing difficulties and needs. America can no longer afford to do so. It is time to define the problems and propose solutions. As a first step we should take pains to examine the feelings behind working-class grievances.[13]

One can now see fairly clearly the purpose of the article and the shape it is assuming.

The Ending

A formal ending is not always necessary, but it is often useful as a summary or as an echo of the central idea. In any case, the ending

[12] Abraham Ribicoff, "The Alienation of the American Worker," *Saturday Review*, 22 April 1972, p. 29. Reprinted by permission.

[13] Ibid.

must provide a fitting conclusion; it must not leave the reader with the feeling that more should have been said.

The straight narrative is the form of discourse most likely to dispense with the conventional summary. Thus the close of the story on the making of a television commercial (the beginning is on pages 42–43) is simply the end of the narrative.

It was about 2:30 P.M. when all the pieces fit together—background, timing, the Serling monologue. Even the usually faultless Serling wasn't immune to "fluffing" his lines—probably because he had to deliver them in precisely 28 seconds.

But on each occasion he apologized to the crew with something like: "I'm sorry, I blew that one. But bear with me, I'll get better. Maybe by tomorrow morning."

He did get better. Half an hour later (about 3 P.M.), after the 23rd take, the director triumphantly exclaimed, "Okay, wrap it up. That should do it."[14]

The use of a summary is exemplified at the end of a critique on the work of the American artist Robert Motherwell.

Motherwell is a very uneven artist because, I think, he also wants to be tough. Probably he has the same doubts we all feel when confronted with charm, even one's own. Certain paintings that seem to me flabby, to him probably point toward other possibilities, to the phrasing of a more objective, historically progressive content. Meanwhile, we should be grateful to him for being so concerned with tender feelings—with their transposition into sensual correlatives of line, color, and texture—and with the poignant implications of the metaphor.[15]

When the proposition is expressed in the beginning, an effective close can be fashioned from an echo or refrain of the same idea. Here, for example, is the close of the article on "Kids' Country," the beginning of which is shown on page 45.

Certainly as a people we thrive. By the time they are 16, most American kids today are bigger, stronger—and smarter—than Mommy and Daddy ever were. And if they are not precisely "happier," they may well be more "grown up." But being a civilization with no genuine rites of passage, what we are experiencing now seems in many ways the exact opposite of medieval and Renaissance life. If, in the old days, children did not exist, it seems equally true today that adults, as a class, have begun to disappear, con-

[14] "At Sea with MHT," loc. cit.

[15] Thomas B. Hess, "Vanity Fare," *New York* Magazine, 29 April 1974, p. 69.

demning all of us to remain boys and girls forever, jogging and doing push-ups against eternity.[16]

Still another way to end is to propose some action or provide some way to cope with the problem to which the paper is devoted. Here is the ending of the article on nutrition begun on page 43.

In a word, an enormous number of us suffer from faulty nutrition, even amid affluence. We don't need to take *all* the blame onto ourselves personally. Irresponsible food producers, dangerous diet books and eating fads, a plethora of TV and other advertising, a largely uninformed medical community—all these have to be faulted. On the other hand, we *do* have some individual choice in the matter that *can* make a difference. By eating sensibly we may cut heart and vascular disease by 25 percent and diminish diabetes and infant mortality by half. If we can do this, our national health costs for diet-linked illness will be spectacularly reduced.

Precisely because poor diet is an old story that we've all heard before, our inclination is to shrug and forget it. It *bores* us. But unless we *keep remembering it* and see that it holds our interest long enough and stubbornly enough, then nutrition as a national health problem will never go away.[17]

And here is the ending of an article on coping with the fear of poverty. The quotation, as useful at the end of a paper as at the beginning, provides a final fillip.

I am now capable of taking a few measures, mainly to demonstrate that social action is possible. Some are trivial, others—a meatless day, a thermostat turned down, a car pool—if widely adopted may have considerable bearing on the situation. Let us not take WIN buttons in lapels for deeds. Let us continue to care for the truly poor, here and abroad.

The final answer may be beyond our reach, and here even economists may agree. For want of something rational, let us turn from the newspapers to The Book of Common Prayer. "Lift up your hearts"—that just might do it.[18]

Tone and Style

Although the beginning and ending mark the extreme positions of the composition, they must form a structural unity with the body. The preceding chapter dealt with the elements that help promote

[16] Alexander, loc. cit.

[17] Pierre, p. 55.

[18] Hans Rosenhaupt, "The No-Holes-in-the-Shoes Blues," *New York Times*, 24 November 1974.

that unity. Now we will deal with the elements of language—specifically tone and style—which give the unity of structure a complementary force.

Tone is the attitude the writer shows toward his subject, his reader, and himself. He may treat his subject formally or informally, seriously or facetiously. He may be matter-of-fact with respect to his reader, or possibly condescending or even insulting. If he refers to himself at all, he may do so with a certain degree of objectivity, or he may show, intentionally or not, a high or low opinion of himself.

The style of the work encompasses the tone and is evident as well in the originality of expression. Any special aptness with words or figures of speech, any special interest given to the composition by the inventiveness with which the author turns a phrase or fashions a sentence, will contribute to the total impression. It is an impression that is usually best achieved when the author is so at ease with his subject and the use of language that his individuality comes through freely.

Good writers invariably develop a style that is characteristically their own. The following paragraph by Walter Lippman, the noted journalist, is typical of his formal approach to a subject and his depth of thought.

> For the most part we do not first see, and then define, we define first and then see. In the great blooming, buzzing confusion of the outer world we pick out what our culture has already defined for us, and we tend to perceive that which we have picked out in the form stereotyped for us by our culture. Of the great men who assembled at Paris to settle the affairs of mankind, how many were there who were able to see much of the Europe about them, rather than their commitments about Europe? Could anyone have penetrated the mind of M. Clemenceau, would he have found there images of the Europe of 1919, or a great sediment of stereotyped ideas accumulated and hardened in a long and pugnacious existence? Did he see the Germans of 1919, or the German type as he had learned to see it since 1871? He saw the type, and among the reports that came to him from Germany, he took to heart those reports, and, it seems, those only, which fitted the type that was in his mind. If a junker blustered, that was an authentic German; if a labor leader confessed the guilt of the empire, he was not an authentic German.[19]

In this passage Mr. Lippman's style is evident not only in the seriousness of the tone, but also in the felicitous way he expresses his

[19] Walter Lippman, *Public Opinion* (1922; rpt., New York: Penguin, 1946), p. 61.

ideas. The meaty generalization in the first few sentences quickly gives way to a specific illustration. The language is precise, but not ponderous. The phrase "the great blooming, buzzing confusion of the outer world," which in an earlier reference Lippman attributes to William James, is an apt use of alliteration; and the series of questions later in the paragraph, as well as the final sentence with its balanced structure and contrasting ideas, succeed in providing variety and interest.

A less distinctive but still serviceable style is demonstrated in the following example. It might be called the corporate style because it is the kind of writing regularly found in business and government. It is clear, matter-of-fact exposition, deliberately impersonal, but useful in communicating and interpreting information for an interested audience. Note especially the orderly classification in the first paragraph and, in the second paragraph, the reasoning used to explain an oddity of the employment figures.

The labor force can be divided into those workers who are strongly committed participants and into another group for whom participation is one option in a choice of life styles. The first group is composed largely of family breadwinners while the spouses and teenaged children of those breadwinners make up a goodly proportion of the second group. When a member of the first group is laid off or otherwise out of work, he or she joins the ranks of the unemployed until a new job is found. Some members of the second group, however, leave the labor force when jobs are lost and potential members don't enter the labor force when jobs are scarce.

Since the adult women and teenage segments of the labor force comprise a larger proportion of people in this second category, this helps to explain why unemployment rates for these groups don't rise proportionately as much as they do for adult males when recession strikes. The converse is that, at such times, participation rates for these groups are subject to wider variations from trend than the rates for adult males.[20]

In contrast, Richard Condon, writing about his life as an author, uses an informal style marked by a highly personal point of view and a sense of humor. Here the purpose is not so much to inform or interpret as it is to reflect and entertain. The paragraph quoted below follows a passage dealing engagingly with the persecution publishers inflict on writers untrained in business.

[20] First National City Bank, "Unemployment—The Worst Is Yet to Come," *Monthly Economic Letter,* June 1974.

I work on a ten-hour-a-day schedule, writing about six hours but staying within the vicinity of the typewriter for the whole period, playing solitaire and writing threatening letters to maintain an even level of the same daily motor habits. If lucky, I work seven days a week. My family skims across my field like gaily-colored papagayo birds. Vacuum cleaners hum, radios play. Teen-age girls plot the salvation of teen-age boys. I hear them only when the noise stops. I tap away, girded with the righteous knowledge that writers should write, loafers should loaf, and that a novelist must try to be harsh about the practices of those who disagree with him—for novels are nothing more than opinionated views of emotion and consequence expressed in character and action. One needs muscular prejudices for the novelist's work, and on that score I am a very, very rich man.[21]

Condon's flair for language is shown in a number of ways: the lively change in pace provided by a burst of short sentences following the initial long one; the odd juxtaposition of words, for example, "playing solitaire and writing threatening letters"; and the lovely picture created by the simile "My family skims across my field like gaily-colored papagayo birds." In the selection of numerous specific details, the author also communicates his industry and his serious attitude toward his work, even while jocularly defending his "muscular prejudices." Thus tone and style are joined to form our view of the author as an individual.

The broad humor of Woody Allen's style derives from its whimsicality and the surprising twists the reader encounters as he moves from one sentence to the next. In the following paragraph Allen introduces his review of the hypothetical book *Boo!* by Dr. Osgood Mulford Twelge, "the noted parapsychologist and professor of ectoplasm at Columbia University."

There is no question that there is an unseen world. The problem is, how far is it from midtown and how late is it open? Unexplainable events occur constantly. One man will see spirits. Another will hear voices. A third will wake up and find himself running in the Preakness. How many of us have not at one time or another felt an ice-cold hand on the back of our neck while we were home alone? (Not me, thank God, but some have.) What is behind these experiences? Or in front of them, for that matter? Is it true that some men can foresee the future or communicate with ghosts? And after death is it still possible to take showers?[22]

[21] Richard Condon, "Adventures of a Middle-Aged Novelist," *Holiday*, January 1962, p. 10.

[22] Woody Allen, "Examining Psychic Phenomena," *The New Yorker*, 7 October 1972, p. 32.

Several more examples will serve to show how authors express their attitudes in their writing. In *The American Way of Death*, Jessica Mitford satirizes American funeral practices in a number of ways, but her style is epitomized in this single sentence poking fun at the undertaker's niceties of language and using a cliché of her own as a mark of derision.

The body is first laid out in the undertaker's morgue—or rather, Mr. Jones is reposing in the preparation room—to be readied to bid the world farewell.[23]

Franz Kafka often turned his gift for language against himself. To his fiancee, Felice Bauer, whom he never married, Kafka wrote, "You are a girl and want a man, not a flabby worm on earth."[24] Nor was he more kindly disposed to his father, whom he blamed for his difficulties. In a letter addressed to his father, but never sent, his bitterness and morbid sufferings are hardly concealed.

It is also true that you hardly ever really gave me a whipping. But the shouting, the way your face got red, the hasty undoing of the braces and laying them ready over the back of the chair, all that was almost worse for me. It is as if someone is going to be hanged. If he really is hanged, then he is dead and it is all over. But if he has to go through all the preliminaries to being hanged and he learns of his reprieve only when the noose is dangling before his face, he may suffer from it all his life. Besides, from the many occasions on which I had, according to your clearly expressed opinion, deserved a whipping but was let off at the last moment by your grace, I again accumulated only a huge sense of guilt. On every side I was to blame, I was in your debt.[25]

James Baldwin is another writer whose bitterness is ill-concealed. The following is an excerpt from a letter to his young nephew.

This innocent country set you down in a ghetto in which, in fact, it intended that you should perish. Let me spell out precisely what I mean by that, for the heart of the matter is here, and the root of my dispute with my country. You were born where you were born and faced the future that you faced because you were black and *for no other reason*. The limits of your ambition were, thus, expected to be set forever. You were born into a society which spelled out with brutal clarity, and in as many ways as

[23] Jessica Mitford, *The American Way of Death* (New York: Simon & Schuster, 1963), pp. 68–69.

[24] Franz Kafka, *Letters to Felice* (New York: Schocken Books, 1973), p. 288.

[25] Franz Kafka, *Letter to His Father* (New York: Schocken Books, 1966), p. 47.

possible, that you were a worthless human being. You were not expected to aspire to excellence: you were expected to make peace with mediocrity. Wherever you have turned, James, in your short time on this earth, you have been told where you could go and what you could do (and *how* you could do it) and where you could live and whom you could marry. I know your countrymen do not agree with me about this, and I hear them saying, "You exaggerate." They do not know Harlem, and I do. So do you. Take no one's word for anything, including mine—but trust your experience. Know whence you came. If you know whence you came, there is really no limit to where you can go. The details and symbols of your life have been deliberately constructed to make you believe what white people say about you. Please try to remember that what they believe, as well as what they do and cause you to endure, does not testify to your inferiority but to their inhumanity and fear. . . .[26]

Concreteness

The style of a work is invariably affected by the degree to which the writer employs either abstract or specific terms in dealing with his subject. The quality in writing which makes it specific, realistic and, colorful is called concreteness. Relevant to this point is the report of a student who had asked the porter in her dormitory what he liked about the tabloid newspaper he was reading. His eyes brightened as he answered, "It makes everything come to life."

Concreteness is a quality not confined to tabloid newspapers—it belongs in all writing—but it carries more interest and is more easily understood than general, or abstract, writing; and one is more likely to find it in, say, reportorial or narrative writing than in philosophic writing. In the following passage, the historian Arnold Toynbee skillfully combines the abstract and the specific. On the whole, though, he seems more concerned with the broad philosophical principle than with the particulars.

What is the essential difference between the primitive and the higher societies? It does not consist in the presence or absence of institutions for institutions are the vehicles of the impersonal relations between individuals in which all societies have their existence, because even the smallest of primitive societies is built on a wider basis than the narrow circle of an individual's direct personal ties. Institutions are attributes of the whole genus 'societies' and therefore common properties of both its species.

[26] James Baldwin, *The Fire Next Time* (1963; rpt., New York: Dell, 1969), pp. 17–19.

Primitive societies have their institutions—the religion of the annual agricultural cycle; totemism and exogamy; tabus, initiations and age-classes; segregations of the sexes, at certain stages of life, in separate communal establishments—and some of these institutions are certainly as elaborate and perhaps as subtle as those which are characteristic of civilizations.[27]

A marked contrast in style is afforded by the following example of journalistic writing, the beginning of an account of the reporter's experience as a contestant on a television quiz show. In the personal narrative at the beginning and in the specific and colorful language of the second paragraph, the whole graphic experience of watching daytime television is evoked.

The first time I was ever a contestant on a quiz show, it was on radio, in 1949, and I was 6 years old. I was unable to answer the question, "What is a baby tadpole?" (I knew a tadpole was a baby frog, but what was a baby tadpole?) I didn't win the $25 U.S. savings bond, and was taken home in tears. The next time I played a game show was this summer, when I became a contestant on *The Dating Game* to find out what it's like to be a performer in television's daytime game show carnival.

Like a mutant phoenix, the TV game show has risen from the ashes of *The $64,000 Question* and has proliferated, filling the hours between Mr. Greenjeans and the afternoon news, challenging the ratings supremacy of those once all-channel champions, the soap operas. For those of us who spend our days in offices, daytime TV game shows are a sometime thing, accompaniment to chicken soup and cold pills. A week of watching them in good health, head clear and sneezeless, left me awed by their monumental, impossibly magnificent, *brontosaurian* vacuity. They are games of mental tiddledywinks, snake oil to embalm dead midafternoons.[28]

A more restrained example of specific writing is found in the excerpt below from the testimony of Nelson A. Rockefeller when he appeared before the Senate Rules Committee for confirmation of his appointment to the vice presidency by President Ford. You will note that even this brief section is not without its generalizations, which are useful and necessary in summarizing facts and establishing their significance.

By the time my grandfather was 14 in 1853, his family had moved to Cleveland, Ohio, where he went to high school. At 16, my grandfather left

[27] Arnold Toynbee, *A Study of History*, abridged by D.C. Somervell (New York: Oxford Univ. Press, 1947), p. 48.

[28] Judy Fayard, "How I Won Bruce, Ruth, and Acapulco," *Life*, 10 November 1972, p. 53.

school and after weeks of diligently searching for the kind of work that would give him experience in business, he found a job as an accountant at $3.50 a week with a firm of commission merchants and produce shippers, where he remained for three and a half years.

At the age of 20, with $900 savings and $1,100 borrowed at interest from his father, he and a young Englishman organized Clark and Rockefeller in a new commodity commission business with $4,000 capital to deal in grain, hay, meats and miscellaneous goods. The business prospered, and four years later, he and his partner joined three others in forming a second company, called Andrews, Clark and Company, to go into the oil refining business.

Two years later, when he was only 26, he and Andrews bought out the three Clark brothers for $72,500, and formed a new oil company under the name of Rockefeller and Andrews.

This was the beginning of the Standard Oil Company. Their refinery was already the largest in Cleveland and one of the largest in the country. During the ensuing years, the company grew rapidly into a totally integrated industry, handling oil from the wellhead to the consumer on a worldwide basis.

To a degree far beyond anything my grandfather had dreamed of, the oil industry tapped the immense resources of oil, affecting every home and machine shop, starting a revolution in transportation and becoming a spectacular part of world commerce.

"Thus," as Allan Nevins has said, "the size of his fortune was an historical accident."[29]

A useful way to avoid an excess of generalization—apart from the use of specific details—is to introduce an example. In the instance below, the writer offers a tip to home-movie enthusiasts, with a specific example following the more general advice. At the end of the example, the author returns to a generalization.

Short shots (2–4 seconds) are preferable to longer shots, although some shots, like those with lots of action, are sometimes best left uncut. Shots with very little action should be short, or the viewer might get bored too easily. It sounds heathen to say things like that, but editing often requires decisions that don't "go down so well," yet are best for the good of the film. If the film still does not flow well several things can be done to help it along.

One helpful technique to aid flow, and to break up what might be an otherwise monotonous shot, is the "cutaway." For example, there is a 20 second shot of cars racing around a speedway—a pretty boring and overlong shot. To liven things up a shot of the crowd cheering in the stands

[29] Nelson A. Rockefeller, Statement Submitted to the Senate Rules Committee, 23 September 1974, quoted in the *New York Times*, 24 September 1974.

could be inserted into the middle of the speeding cars. But cut out about five seconds of the race and insert only two seconds of the crowd cutaway. The pace of the scene picks up dramatically, yet the entire scene is shorter in length than the original shot of the speeding cars. This cutaway technique is very useful in a variety of situations and should be used frequently.[30]

The use of example in a more literary context is offered in a brief excerpt from the review of a book by English novelist Margaret Drabble. Referring to "Drabble's understated but poisonous wit," the reviewer continued:

The driving force of the novel is Frances's love affair with Karel—they are apart at the beginning of the book and do not come together until the end—yet they show little affection, let alone passion for each other. A scene that Frances and Karel perceive as a moment of romantic bliss—lunch in a roadside tea shop—Drabble records as polite English drivel: " 'I love you, Karel,' she said. 'I really love you,' 'Do you, my darling?' he said. 'Shall we have cheese and tomato?' 'There's nothing like a sandwich, is there,' said Karel, after a pause, 'when it's what one really wants.' " Drabble has a keen ear for the nuances of talk; her characters reveal themselves most blatantly when they speak.[31]

In descriptive writing, the opportunities for concreteness are always present. The main challenge to the writer is to observe sharply and communicate in vivid detail what is seen and felt. Aldous Huxley displays these skills admirably as he describes the Mayan ruins in Honduras, Central America.

Time and its allies in destruction, vegetation and weather, play curious tricks on the works of man. A city left to their tender mercies is generally destroyed as an architectural and engineering whole, but spared in its decorative details. The great masses of masonry are buried and disrupted; tend, if the vegetation is strong, to vanish altogether, dissolved into their component parts; the statues, the reliefs, the fragile pots and jewels survive, very often, almost intact. At Copan, for example, a few mounds covered with trees, a wall here and there, some rubbish heaps of tumbled stones, are all that remain of the great complex of pyramids, of platforms, of walls and terraces, of sunken courtyards, which once occupied the site. Buried and, under the mould, disintegrated by the thrusting roots of the tropical vege-

[30] Steven T. Smith, "Editing Will Improve Every Home Movie," *New York Times*, 22 June 1975.

[31] Lore Dickstein, reviewing *Realms of Gold* in *The New York Times Book Review*, 16 November 1975, p. 5.

tation, a sacred city of pure geometrical forms once stood here. Its sharp-edged planes of hewn stone, of white or painted stucco, shone smooth, like the surfaces of a crystal, in the perpendicular sunlight. But toiling up and down through the scrub, among the fallen stones, I found it all but impossible to reconstruct in my imagination the Mayas' huge embodiment of a mathematician's dream. I had read the writings of the archaeologists and knew what sort of monument had been raised at Copan. But these almost shapeless barrows supplied my fancy with no visible foundations on which to rebuild the Mayas' prodigious works. Only the plastic decorations with which their mountains of solid geometry have been incidentally trimmed were still there, in unequivocal existence, before my eyes. The whole had gone; but a few of the ornamental parts remained. In a maize field at the foot of the wooden mounds—the mounds were the acropolis and principal pyramid, the maize field had been a great forum—stood a group of magnificent stelae, floridly carved in such deep relief that the stone was sometimes pierced from side to side. Using neolithic tools, the Maya sculptors had displayed an almost contemptuous mastery of their material; they had treated their twenty-foot monoliths as a Chinese craftsman might treat a piece of ivory. One is left bewildered by the spectacle of so much technical accomplishment displayed by people having such inadequate technical resources.[32]

You have now seen by example many different styles, many different modes of expression. Most writers develop "a style"—one uniquely their own—after much experience and experimentation. It is not unusual, though, for a writer to have many styles. Certainly in college, and perhaps in positions you will hold later in life, you will have to adapt to different subjects and different audiences. Thus your lab report will hardly follow the same style as a theme urging students to get out and vote for their class officers. In the same way, you would have to make adjustments in style if you were writing a legal brief, a letter home, or a commercial for a laundry detergent.

Probably the best way to cope with the problem of style is to learn to write with such facility that you don't have to think about it. Style, you will then come to realize, is not a gift, but the result of hard work—thinking and planning, writing and rewriting, editing and polishing. Just give all your energies to what you have to do, never forgetting your purpose and your reader, and your style will take care of itself.

[32] From pp. 190–191 in *Beyond the Mexique Bay* by Aldous Huxley. Copyright 1934, 1966 by Aldous Huxley. By permission of Harper & Row, Publishers, Inc.

EXERCISES

A. Below are the beginnings of five student themes. Comment on the interest and concreteness of each, as well as on any other factors that influence the impression they make. Take the *two* openings of which you are most critical and rewrite them to make them more effective.

1. ADVICE ON CHOOSING A COLLEGE

Choosing a college might be one of the most difficult things a young adult has to do at that time in his life. The student must decide what basic direction, in terms of careers, he wants to head towards. Once that decision has been made, the actual task of choosing a college is not too difficult.

2. CHRISTMAS, A TIME TO CELEBRATE

In recent years Christmas seems to have become more of a chore than a holiday. There are various reasons for this change in attitude, according to each individual. One reason may be that religious forces don't play a large role in our lives any more. Another may be that Christmas has become overcommercialized and we, the consumers, have become fed up. The high cost of living dampens the "holiday spirit." We aren't able to celebrate the way we used to. Whatever the reason, Christmas has lost some of its sparkle. Something must be done to change this.

3. DIVORCE INSURANCE

One out of every four marriages now ends in divorce. Millions of people have their lives wrenched by this unfortunate event. The emotional trauma which so often accompanies divorce is made worse when the subject of alimony and/or child support is introduced.

The current laws relating to alimony and child support and the enforcement of those laws are totally inadequate. I believe a whole new method for coping with the financial problems accompanying divorce, alimony, and child support is called for. The method I propose is divorce insurance.

4. IS YOUR BODY IN SHAPE?

Do you often lose your breath climbing up the stairs? Do you prefer to wait for the elevator than walk up three or four flights of stairs? Do you usually drive your car to a nearby grocery instead of walking a few blocks? When you go to the beach, do you prefer to relax and bask in the sun rather than jump around and swim in the ocean? Is physical exercise a dreaded and difficult exertion for you?

5. IN DEFENSE OF STARFISH

"Whatcha got in the container?" asked Nick, a heavy, rough man who enjoys fine cuisine when it does not interfere with his game of horseshoes and who smokes huge cigars whose stench fouls up the air around the cabana court. "A few things I collected at the shore," I answered, and showed him the crabs, starfish, and other shore animals I had gathered into this container. Nick spotted the starfish and asked what I planned to do with it. When I told him I planned to put it in my marine aquarium for study and then set it free, he gasped and then coughed acrid smoke into my face, saying, "Are you crazy? Those things destroy the clam beds and I love clams. They aren't good for nothin'." I was red and ready to give him an ecologist's tirade, but controlled myself so as not to cause a scene. I went inside the cabana grumbling and wondering how anyone could be so narrow-minded. Yet Nick is not alone, in fact, he is probably one of a majority of people whose lack of understanding of our world's ecological system could destroy that system.

B. Write a closing paragraph to complement each of the two openings you have selected for revision in Exercise A. You may make any reasonable assumptions about the content of the themes.

C. Comment on the content, tone, and style of each of the following statements. Try to relate these characteristics to what you believe to be the purpose of each message.

1. ON THE REFINEMENTS OF CITY LIVING:

Up to the seventeenth century, at least in the North, building and heating had hardly advanced far enough to permit the arrangement of a series of private rooms in the dwelling. But now a separation of functions took place within the house as well as within the city as a whole. Space became specialized, room by room. . . . Privacy was the new luxury of the well-to-do. . . . The lady's chamber became a boudoir, literally a 'sulking place'; the gentleman had his office or his library, equally inviolate; and in Paris he might even have his own bedroom, too, as husband and wife pursued their separate erotic adventures. For the first time not merely a curtain but a door separated each individual member of the household from every other member.

Privacy, mirrors, heated rooms: these things transformed full-blown love-making from a seasonal to a year-round occupation: another example of baroque regularity. In the heated room, the body need not cower under a blanket: visual erethism added to the effect of tactile stimuli: the pleasure of the naked body, symbolized by Titian and Rubens and Fragonard, was part of that dilation of the senses which accompanied the more generous dietary, the freer use of wines and strong liquors, the more extravagant dresses and perfumes of the period.[33]

2. FROM A TV CRITIQUE:

The fact of the matter is that CBS, one of the three major networks to turn down "Space 1999," turned up "Bronk." The splendid thing about being a major network is that you can hire an actor of genuine talent, like Jack Palance; surround him with writers who must be doing their typing at the laundromat, inside the machine, during the spin cycle; sentence him to directors who would have a hard time organizing a slice of buttered toast; concoct a fiasco; put it on in prime time and still be a major network. As a network, you should be "whipp'd with wire, and stew'd in brine,/ Smarting in ling'ring pickle"—that's Shakespeare, who is not, alas, one of "Bronk's" writers—and yet the only one likely to be punished for "Bronk" is Jack Palance.

What bad luck this man has. He is a professional. He will do his best in the worst of parts, and the worst of parts is too often what he gets. To have been marvelous as Alan Ladd's satanic adversary in "Shane" has meant being typecast as a menace-on-wheels ever since, with the exceptions of a neat turn in "The Big Knife" and a preposterous turn in "Che!" I think playing Fidel Castro in "Che!" was his last fat part in a big-budget Hollywood movie. Omar Sharif was Che Guevara in this shambles, hooted at by most audiences. It is typical of Palance's bad luck that he should get mixed up in an enterprise that was moronic even for Darryl Zanuck.[34]

[33] Lewis Mumford, *The City in History: Its Origins, Its Transformation, and Its Prospects* (New York: Harcourt, 1961), pp. 384–85.

[34] John Leonard, "So Who Picked 'Bronk' over 'Space 1999'?" *New York Times*, 19 October 1975.

3. FROM A MEMORANDUM TO THE FACULTY AND STAFF OF A LARGE UNIVERSITY:

We recognized that the whole purpose of the allocation and management of the University's resources is the support of its various educational programs at whatever levels of quality we might propose for them. The design and control of program, and the selection of personnel, with their development and assignment in teaching and research, are the most critical processes of management in the closely interrelated elements of university administration. Budget development, space planning and assignment, and business services must undergird the requirements to develop and maintain excellence in program and faculty. The long-range allocation of resources to build and maintain a given quality in program and staff can be brought about only by a unity of purpose and method of management in which the faculty, schools, and central administration share information, plan jointly, and act in concert in their respective areas of responsibility.[35]

4. REMARKS OF A MEMBER OF CONGRESS, AS REPORTED IN THE CONGRESSIONAL RECORD AND CIRCULATED TO HIS CONSTITUENTS:

Let us make no mistake. The problems of America today are immense and they are complicated beyond belief. There are no easy solutions before us. There is no guarantee that our party has better ideas than their party, or that any of us are wise enough to choose the right path. All we can do, those of us who have been chosen by the people to represent them, is to hope that our best instincts prove correct. We can work ourselves as hard as possible, seek every available bit of information before locking ourselves into a fixed path and we can respect other points of view, because, as we begin, it is just possible that they might be right and we may be wrong . . . .

As the President indicated in his speech last night, the role of Congress will be greatly expanded this year and next. I firmly believe the Congress has the obligation to act boldly and responsibly, whether it be in agreement with, or in opposition to, the proposals set forth by the President. No longer is it a simple case of partisan

[35] "Task Force Report," (Office of the Executive Vice President, New York University, October 1958), p. 1.

politics: it can literally become a matter of the Nation's survival as the most important free Nation in the world.[36]

5. ON CLASSROOM LEARNING:

So, what students mostly do in class is guess what the teacher wants them to say. Constantly, they must try to supply "The Right Answer." It does not seem to matter if the subject is English or history or science; mostly, students *do* the same thing. And since it is indisputably (if not publicly) recognized that the ostensible "content" of such courses is rarely remembered beyond the last quiz (in which you are required to remember only 65 percent of what you were told), it is safe to say that just about the *only* learning that occurs in classrooms is that which is communicated by the structure of the classroom itself. What are these learnings? What are these messages? Here are a few among many, none of which you will ever find officially listed among the aims of teachers:

Passive acceptance is a more desirable response to ideas than active criticism.

Discovering knowledge is beyond the power of students and is, in any case, none of their business.

Recall is the highest form of intellectual achievement, and the collection of unrelated "facts" is the goal of education.

The voice of authority is to be trusted and valued more than independent judgment.

One's own ideas and those of one's classmates are inconsequential.

There is always a single, unambiguous Right Answer to a question.

English is not History and History is not Science and Science is not Art and Art is not Music, and Art and Music are minor subjects and English, History and Science major subjects, and a subject is something you "take" and, when you have taken it, you have "had" it and if you have "had" it, you are immune and need not take it again. (The Vaccination Theory of Education?)[37]

D. The following theme was written early in the semester by a first-year student. By specific reference to the text, comment on its structure and style. What techniques help to make the

[36] Remarks of Hon. Joseph P. Addabbo, House of Representatives, 14 January 1975.

[37] Neil Postman and Charles Weingartner, *Teaching as a Subversive Activity* (rpt., New York: Dell, 1969), pp. 20–21.

theme as interesting as it is? Where does the writer falter? What corrections or changes would you suggest?

WHY DO I DO IT?

Oh, how I dread it! Why am I up at 8 A.M. on a cool, lovely autumn Saturday? Why do I allow myself to be so persecuted? Why? Because I need the money!

It isn't enough that I chose an expensive university, but I long for the finer things in life—like a movie on Saturday night or a new pair of jeans. As it stands now, Mom and Dad pay half my tuition. I don't really think they mind—they're fine, loving parents—but I still feel it's an unnecessary burden for them. So, for this reason, and very little else, I will maintain this part-time job in the supermarket.

My job. I don't know whether it's bad or worse since I've been "promoted" from the checkout counter to the office. At least at the counter I didn't have to put up with *them;* just ring up, collect, and bag. Boring and tiresome, but simple. Now, in the office, even with an increase in pay, it doesn't seem worth it. All those additional responsibilities, and I have to put up with *them!* That little man, for instance, that strange little creature with sandals and an old shopping cart. He approached the desk window slowly and quietly. "May I help you, sir?" Thrusting a brown paper bag in my face, almost breaking the glass separating us, he screeched, "Here—take it! I don't want it! It's disgusting! I pay good cash for things, expecting to get a fair deal, and what I do bring home—!" "Well, sir, if you'll tell me exactly what the problem is, maybe—." Reaching into the brown bag, he produced an eight-ounce container of sour cream. "Open it," he continued, "it will shake hands with you!"

They're crazy! Those consumers are nuts! To think I have to take it with a smile! "Yes, sir, here's your money." "No miss, that item isn't on sale this week." "Was that one lottery ticket or two?" "I'm sorry, ma'am, but I can only cash one check a week." "I understand he's house trained and very lovable, but a great dane cannot go shopping—Department of Health rules!" Sometimes I simply have to laugh.

And the condition of this office! It's like being buried alive with gray file cabinets, manila envelopes, rainchecks, lottery tickets, coupons, adding machines, and a "hot line" telephone! Not bad, laid to rest with a hot line—"Hello, mommy, it's a little cold here. . . ." That's terrible! But I'm not alone; there is always Igor, our charismatic manager. When things are bad, I can always count on him.

"Mary Lou."

Yes, sir."

"I have to make a deposit at the bank and fill a few order forms. Would you please stay in the office and work through your lunch hour?" How cruel! "I'll make sure you'll get paid for the extra hour." Well that's a horse of a different color—olive green!

"Yes, I'll stay. Sir? Do you mind if I send out for a sandwich and a cup of coffee?"

"All right, but don't let the customers see you eating or drinking."

Time! When I'm working I don't have a minute to myself. I never check a mirror to brush my hair or straighten my uniform. I look and feel like an S.O.S. soap pad: "If you love me, you'll use me." How embarrassing when those few male shoppers come to my window! "Yes, may I help you? Please, I know I can be of help." They don't even notice. Why should they when I resemble a kitchen cleanser?

What! It's five o'clock! Impossible! I still have to do the register readings, store books, next week's schedule. . . .

THEME TOPICS

1. Develop two short themes (about 350 words each) describing a particular student type, for example, the intellectual, the politician, the playboy, the glamor girl. In the first theme describe the subject facetiously, and in the second, treat the same subject seriously. In both instances strive for an effective beginning and ending, and use specific details and instances to achieve concreteness.

2. Take a college subject you are interested in and, starting with a short narrative or example, write a theme showing the career possibilities offered by the subject.

3. Choose one of the topics below or a subject they might suggest. Where necessary, narrow the scope of the topic to avoid overgeneralization and permit the use of concrete details. Let the tone of the theme reflect a special point of view toward the subject, for example, approval, disapproval, openmindedness, skepticism, disillusionment. Provide your own title.

(a) The trend to small cars.
(b) What you can learn from television.
(c) College is for everyone.

(d) Welfare reform.
(e) Urban worker—suburban dweller.

4. From the suggested theme subjects on pages 36–38, develop a theme topic of limited scope and write a theme that accords with the principles discussed in this chapter. Pay close attention to beginning and ending, be concrete, and try to achieve a distinctive style and tone. Work over the theme carefully, making several drafts if necessary.

4 Informal Discourse

If you have ever stared at a blank sheet of paper you had to fill with part of a 700-word theme, you know how intimidating the sea of white space can be. But put today's date at the top of the page and begin "Dear Gerry"—addressing a friend—and the task immediately seems less formidable. For the theme now has a physical shape and a target audience. Even more important, the fact that you are writing a personal letter reassures you; you can relax and express yourself naturally as one individual to another.

The personal letter is one of several kinds of writing to which the name informal discourse can be applied. Another is the diary or journal. A third is the familiar essay. Although somewhat different from one another in mechanics, these forms give you a broad choice of literary treatments. Any letter or diary, for example, is enhanced through the use of description, exposition, and narrative, as well as such modes of expression as satire, humor, and unashamed sentiment. If you keep a diary, you want to enjoy the experience of reading it at a later date—and you will if it represents you at a high point in feeling and verbal proficiency. Similarly, if you write a letter, you want it to be as interesting as you can make it—a delight to receive and read.

Literary Treatment

Published examples of informal discourse show styles of writing as diverse as the personalities and moods of the authors. In letters to his editor Max Perkins, F. Scott Fitzgerald exhibits the earthiness one expects of the author of *The Great Gatsby*. The misspelling in the first excerpt is Fitzgerald's.

I think all the reviews I've seen, except two, have been absolutely stupid and lowsy. Some day they'll eat grass, by God![1]

and

I thought Elizabeth Lemon was charming—I wonder why the hell she never married.[2]

George Bernard Shaw's conceit, wrapped in self-deprecation, is evident in lines from a letter to Ellen Terry, whom he had never met.

Up to the time I was 29, actually twenty-nine, I was too shabby for any woman to tolerate me. I stalked about in a decaying green coat, cuffs trimmed with the scissors, terrible boots, and so on. Then I got a job to do and bought a suit of clothes with the proceeds. A lady immediately invited me to tea, threw her arms around me, and said she adored me. I permitted her to adore, being intensely curious on the subject. Never having regarded myself as an attractive man I was surprised; but I kept up appearances successfully. Since that time, whenever I have been alone in a room with a female, she has invariably thrown her arms round me and declared she adored me. It is fate. Therefore beware. If you allow yourself to be left alone with me for a single moment, you will certainly throw your arms round me and declare you adore me.[3]

A more modest note is struck in a letter from William James to his Radcliffe students who, at a college ceremony, had presented him with an azalea plant. When James's graciousness begins to seem almost overdone, the sincerity of the closing paragraph puts his appreciation in its true perspective. The phrase "my Psychology" is a reference to his *Principles of Psychology*, the work that made him famous.

Cambridge, Apr. 6, 1896

Dear Young Ladies,—I am deeply touched by your remembrance. It is the first time anyone ever treated me so kindly, so you may well believe that the impression on the heart of the lonely sufferer will be even more durable than the impression on your minds of all the teachings of Philosophy 2A. I now perceive one immense omission in my Psychology,—the deepest principle of Human Nature is the *craving to be appreciated*, and I left it out altogether from the book, because I had never had it gratified till now. I fear

[1] From *Dear Scott/Dear Max: The Fitzgerald-Perkins Correspondence*, ed. John Kuehl and Jackson Bryer (New York: Scribner, 1971), p. 106.

[2] Ibid., p. 203.

[3] From *A Treasury of the World's Great Letters*, ed. M. Lincoln Schuster (New York: Simon & Schuster, 1940), p. 445.

you have let loose a demon in me, and that all my actions will now be for the sake of such rewards. However, I will try to be faithful to this one unique and beautiful azalea tree, the pride of my life and delight of my existence. Winter and summer will I tend and water it—even with my tears. Mrs. James shall never go near it or touch it. If it dies I will die too; and if I die, it shall be planted on my grave.

Don't take all this too jocosely, but believe in the extreme pleasure you have caused me, and in the affectionate feelings with which I am and shall always be faithfully your friend,

Wm. James[4]

From the vanities and gratifications of age, we now turn to the longings of youth. The wistfulness of the following autobiographical passage in no way mutes our enthusiasm for the highly original and interesting presentation.

A long Fourth of July weekend. The city is oppressively humid. I am without work, without emotional funds, and longing for a girl named Leslie. Leslie is 23, I am 22, and we have endured the following correspondence:

Me to Leslie: "I think you're smitten with the affectation of professional solitude. No one wants to be 'alone with their books' any more. That's for Stevenson girls named Susan. My God, which books do you have in mind? 'This Is My Beloved' perhaps? Or 'First Love and Other Sorrows'? Your essence is all over my apartment. Please."

Leslie to me: "This would have been our second summer. You are too hot, I am too nothing. Forgive me. It is time to grow separately."

And so I am in Grant's drinking Piels beer. It is 10 o'clock at night and I have seen five movies on 42d Street on this Independence Day. One, at the Apollo, has eroticized me. Another, with William Bendix, has not. The Yankees have swept a doubleheader, and I am waiting for the city edition of The Times. I own one subway token and a dollar bill.

I walk to Leslie's apartment, through the sadness of Eighth Avenue, across the oasis of Columbus Circle, along the ominous park side of Central Park West. I am soaked through and through. 116 West 88th Street. Leslie is home, alone with her books.

"You must go now," is what she tells me.

"Why?" I respond, reasonably.

"The truth?"

"Of course!" The power is hers. My forceful "of course" is a last-ditch effort to regain some standing in our minuscule community.

"I've fallen out of love."

I lie in the park until daybreak, huddled by the base of the wall of

[4] Ibid., p. 430.

Central Park West near 70th. The traffic seems miles above me. Its distant whoosh is reassuring. In that torrid night it is all I have.[5]

One of the most touching accounts of the trials of youth is that of Anne Frank. Anne was a teenage Jewish girl who, with her parents, was secreted from the Nazis in the loft of a Dutch warehouse during the Second World War. Her now famous diary showed her literary flair in a number of ways, including a perceptive analysis of character, an extensive use of narrative and dialogue, and, as in the brief excerpt that follows, an irrepressible optimism in the face of tragedy.

Since Saturday we've changed over, and have lunch at half past eleven in the mornings, so we have to last out with one cup of porridge; this saves us a meal. Vegetables are still very difficult to obtain: we had rotten boiled lettuce this afternoon. Ordinary lettuce, spinach and boiled lettuce, there's nothing else. With these we eat rotten potatoes, so it's a delicious combination![6]

The Personal Letter

With the advent of the telephone, personal letters have become less important than they used to be as a way of keeping in touch with family friends. The widespread—perhaps regrettable—social acceptance of greeting cards has also cut down dramatically on the use of personal letters written for special occasions. Despite these developments, however, the letter is still an important medium for conveying personal news, as well as thought and feeling, from one literate person to another. A good letter is always as much appreciated for its style as for the news or sentiments it carries. Its individuality is shown in its wit or humor, its felicitous turns of phrase, and its aptness of expression. These are qualities you should strive for in your own letters, whether they are written to your friends or as a class exercise.

Even if he lived today, Henry Adams would probably still be a prolific correspondent simply because he had such an affinity for language. The paragraph that follows, part of a letter he wrote at the age of twenty-one to his older brother, Charles Francis, Jr., reveals something of his early life and his literary flair.

[5] Jonathan Schwartz, "Summer," *The New York Times Magazine*, 22 June 1975, p. 63.

[6] *Anne Frank: The Diary of a Young Girl* (New York: Doubleday, 1952), pp. 236–37. Reprinted by permission.

Berlin, January 18, 1859.

My Dear Fellow:—Don't crow too quick about the pleasures and pains of life. To prove to you that I am not inclined to change my position, I will merely remark that I should decline for the present any offer of increasing my allowance, if any such offer were made. The deficit must be made up if, or when, it comes, but that is all. I received a short enclosure from the Governor on this subject in a letter dated the 13th December. He says that he means to send a hundred pounds more, after New Year's, and his concluding passage was incomprehensible to me till I received your last. He says: "On the general subject" (that of money affairs) "I shall have some ideas to suggest hereafter which may have the effect of arranging the affair more satisfactorily." Meanwhile he seems to think that I'm "putting up with privations of all kinds," and he's right too, but I'm happy and what's the odds. All the privations I see won't hurt me, except going without a good breakfast in the morning and having to run to school so fast that I can't enjoy my cigar.[7]

The poet Rainer Maria Rilke used a letter for a more didactic purpose when he wrote to a young poet who had sent him his verses for criticism. Note, in addition to the frankness of this brief excerpt and its philosophic depth, some of the earmarks of style, especially the use of parallel structure and the length and variety of the sentences.

You ask whether your verses are good. You ask me. You have asked others before. You send them to magazines. You compare them with other poems, and you are disturbed when certain editors reject your efforts. Now (since you have allowed me to advise you) I beg you to give up all that. You are looking outward, and that above all you should not now do. Nobody can counsel and help you, nobody. There is only one single way. Go into yourself. Investigate the reason that bids you write; find out whether it is spreading out its roots in the deepest places of your heart, acknowledge to yourself whether you would have to die if it were denied you to write. This above all: ask yourself in the stillest hour of your night: *must* I write? Delve into yourself for a deep answer. And if this should be affirmative, if you may meet this earnest question with a strong and simple "I must," then build your life according to this necessity; your life even into its most indifferent and slightest hour must be a sign of this urge and a testimony to it. Then draw near to Nature. Then try, as a first human being, to say what you see and experience and love and lose.[8]

[7] *Letters of Henry Adams, 1858–1891* (Boston: Houghton Mifflin, 1930–1938), I, 11.

[8] Rainer Maria Rilke, *Letters to a Young Poet,* rev. ed. (New York: Norton, 1954), pp. 18–19.

Despite the telephone, it is quite possible that most of the letters being written today by college students are the letters they write home. The letter that follows falls into this category. It is given special interest by the fact that it was written more than a century and a quarter ago by a teenager named Emily Dickinson, who was yet to show her talent as a poet.

Mt. Holyoke Seminary
Nov. 6, 1847

My Dear Abiah,

I am really at Mt. Holyoke Seminary and this is to be my home for a long year. . . .

As you desire it, I will give you a full account of myself since I first left the paternal roof. I came to S. Hadley six weeks ago next Thursday. I was much fatigued with the ride and had a severe cold besides, which prevented me from commencing my examinations until the next day, when I began. I finished them in three days and found them about what I had anticipated, though the old scholars say, they are more strict than they have ever been before. As you can easily imagine, I was much delighted to finish without failures and I came to the conclusion then, that I should not be at all homesick, but the reactions left me as homesick a girl as it is not usual to see. . . .

I will tell you my order of time for the day, as you were so kind as to give me your's. At 6 o'clock, we all rise. We breakfast at 7. Our study hours begin at 8. At 9 we all meet in Seminary Hall for devotions. At 10¼ I recite a review of Ancient History in connection with which we read Goldsmith and Grimshaw. At 11 I recite a lesson in "Pope's Essay on Man" which is merely transposition. At 12 I practise Calisthenics and at 12¼ read until dinner which is at 12½. After dinner from 1½ until 2 I sing in Seminary Hall. From 2¾ until 3¾ I practise upon the Piano. At 3¾ I go to Section, where we give in all our accounts for the day, including absence—Tardiness Communications—Breaking Silent Study hours—Receiving Company in our rooms and ten thousand other things which I will not take time or place to mention. At 4½ we go into Seminary Hall and receive advice from Miss Lyon in the form of a lecture. We have supper at 6 and silent study hours from then until the retiring bell, which rings at 8¾ but the tardy bell does not ring until 9¾, so that we don't often obey the first warning to retire.

Unless we have a good and reasonable excuse for failure upon any of the items that I mentioned above, they are recorded and a black mark stands against our names. As you can easily imagine, we do not like very well to get "exceptions" as they are called scientifically here. My domestic work is not difficult and consists in carrying the knives from the 1st tier of tables at morning and noon, and at night washing and wiping the same quantity of knives. . . .[9]

The Diary or Journal

Both the diary and the journal are written essentially for oneself, but there is no reason why they, like letters, cannot also be written, at least hypothetically, for some other audience. Ordinarily, a diary needs no salutation at the beginning of each day's entry, but the common use of "Dear Diary" suggests a need to treat the diary as a person, a confidante. This small fiction gives the writer someone to write to, a seemingly more useful exercise than just writing to oneself, and the words may as a result flow more freely.

Anne Frank's diary, which has already been mentioned, was addressed to "Kitty," a friend Anne invented during her long spell of loneliness and fear. One of the entries in the diary reports a discussion with her father, to whom she has written a letter regarding her relations with Peter, a boy living on the floor above. The father had objected to her "necking." Apart from the poignance that comes from our knowledge of Anne Frank's ultimate fate—she died in the Bergen-Belsen concentration camp in March 1945—the entry tells much about Anne's character and her talents as a writer. Note especially her use of direct quotation; her way of addressing herself as Anne, as if she were another person; and, despite her self-reproach, her youthful optimism as she evaluates her own qualities—all in all, a versatile display of style in a very short space.

SUNDAY MORNING, 7 MAY, 1944

Dear Kitty,

Daddy and I had a long talk yesterday afternoon, I cried terribly and he joined in. Do you know what he said to me, Kitty? "I have received many letters in my life, but this is certainly the most unpleasant! You, Anne, who have received such love from your parents, you, who have parents who are always ready to help you, who have always defended you whatever it might be, can you talk of feeling no responsibility towards us? You feel wronged and deserted; no, Anne, you have done us a great injustice!

[9] Letter of Emily Dickinson, in Arthur C. Cole, *A Hundred Years of Mount Holyoke College* (New Haven: Yale Univ. Press, 1940). Reprinted by permission of Mount Holyoke College Library.

"Perhaps you didn't mean it like that, but it is what you wrote; no, Anne, we haven't deserved such a reproach as this!"

Oh, I have failed miserably; this is certainly the worst thing I've ever done in my life. I was only trying to show off with my crying and my tears, just trying to appear big, so that he would respect me. . . .

It's right that for once I've been taken down from my inaccessible pedestal, that my pride has been shaken a bit, for I was becoming much too taken up with myself again. What Miss Anne does is by no means always right! Anyone who can cause such unhappiness to someone else, someone he professes to love, and on purpose, too, is low, very low!

And the way Daddy has forgiven me makes me feel more than ever ashamed of myself, he is going to throw the letter in the fire and is so sweet to me now, just as if he had done something wrong. No, Anne, you still have a tremendous lot to learn, begin by doing that first, instead of looking down on others and accusing them!

I have had a lot of sorrow, but who hasn't at my age? I have played the clown a lot too, but I was hardly conscious of it; I felt lonely, but hardly ever in despair! I ought to be deeply ashamed of myself, and indeed I am.

What is done cannot be undone, but one can prevent it happening again. I want to start from the beginning again and it can't be difficult, now that I have Peter. With him to support me, I can and will!

I'm not alone any more; he loves me. I love him, I have my books, my storybook and my diary, I'm not so frightfully ugly, not utterly stupid, have a cheerful temperament and want to have a good character!

Yes, Anne, you've felt deeply that your letter was too hard and that it was untrue. To think that you were even proud of it! I will take Daddy as my example, and I *will* improve. *Yours, Anne*[10]

Very different in mood is the diary kept by a third-year medical student during his hospital internship. Under the pseudonym of John MacNab, he later published his journal with the thought that his experiences would be interesting to others. Here is one entry made during his service in the pediatrics ward.

June 11

I was given some responsibility today and blew it. The resident asked me to draw a blood sample from Derek (the pt [patient] on anticoagulants) for a clotting time. I wisely made sure his parents and grandmother were not around, assembled my equipment, put on a gown, and went into his room. There I was confronted with a tangle of intravenous solution tubes and pumps whose complexity called for a consult with a master plumber. I "traced the wires," closed valves, and detached some lines, drew some

[10] *Anne Frank*, pp. 240–42.

blood out from a line in the ankle, placed it in the test tube. But on reconnecting the system, I broke a coupling. I asked the student nurse (they should never put two students together alone) to get me another. She went and told the head nurse, who yowled in disbelief. I was informed that there might not be another replacement part in the whole medical center. She started calling other wards, trying to track one down. Time was moving, and this was a time-dependent test. Luckily my roommate happened onto the ward. I gave him the tubes to do the test fast. A nurse came up from another floor with the wrong part. I called the head nurse in and she saw that the part required was actually a simple one and fetched it from a closet. By this time the resident came in (on my "May-Day") and we worked on the repairs. My roommate reported a clotting time of 5 minutes. This was much faster than we wanted or expected. (We were aiming at 20 to 30 minutes.) At my suggestion we tried to draw some more blood to repeat the test. But I couldn't get any blood to flow with either pressure or a vacuum in the syringe. "You know, we may be in trouble," said the resident. If the blood in the catheter had clogged, we would have to pull it out and get a surgeon to insert another (a process that had taken the surgical resident over an hour last night). Luckily the resident was able to get the flow restarted by pushing in some saline with a syringe. The resident was nice about it, and criticized not my mistake but my reluctance to reinsert the new coupling (I was trying to ward off the second bolt of lightning in the same place). I have a new respect for plumbers.[11]

As you can see, a great deal of action is crowded into this single paragraph. The dramatic opening statement creates suspense, and the short sentences help to move the action forward very quickly.

The Familiar Essay

Informal discourse is used most flexibly in the familiar essay. This form of composition has the informality of the letter and the diary, but it addresses itself from the start to a public audience rather than a private one. It is also not restricted by the limited interests of the reader, as in the instance of the letter, nor to the events in a brief time frame, like an entry in a diary or a journal.

The familiar essay thus permits a great variety of subjects and treatments. Yet it does have an important distinguishing characteris-

[11] John MacNab, *The Education of a Doctor: My First Year on the Wards,* entry of June 11, 1969. Copyright © 1971, by James MacNab. Reprinted by permission of Simon & Schuster, Inc.

tic in that it is written in a light, personal vein. That does not mean that the essay cannot have a serious underlying theme; it usually does. What matters is that the writer express some attitude toward the subject, so that by wit, sarcasm, mock seriousness, gross exaggeration, or other literary device, the point is made—entertainingly and with greater force than if a more conventional approach were used.

In the familiar essay, the writer is free to use a conversational style, with its characteristic contractions; refer to himself as *I*; and choose an occasional nonstandard word for its freshness or humor. The organization of ideas may be as obvious and well ordered as in straight narrative or as mixed up as in stream of consciousness. The subject matter and treatment are limited only by the writer's interests, imagination, and verbal facility. Not easy to master, the familiar essay is still a most satisfying form for both the novice and the experienced writer; and, well done, it is a most pleasurable experience for the reader.

Perhaps the informal essay is best explained by illustration. Below are two examples which you can examine and analyze for yourself (though some guides are provided in the exercises at the end of this chapter). The first is by Russell Baker, a modern master of the form. His short pieces, written for the *New York Times*, are almost invariably humorous and always thoughtful, whether they relate to politics, family life, or popular culture. And the care with which he develops his ideas shows in the effects he achieves.

NEGATIVE THINKING[12]

There is a secret drawer at our house which has not been opened for years. Some years ago, all of us tacitly agreed that we would simply not open the drawer anymore. Its contents were quietly, without a word being said, sealed out of our lives like friends of long ago who have drifted away on the eddies of life and become strangers. They were of a time that had passed.

What the drawer contains is snapshots. A zillion snapshots. I opened it the other day and hundreds of them came tumbling out. They were terrible, most of them. Out of focus. Double exposures. Overexposed. Underexposed. Fading away.

And the subject matter! What kind of person could have thought it interesting to photograph a 1956 Chevrolet parked at a hot-dog stand? The

[12] Russell Baker, "Negative Thinking," *The New York Times Magazine*, 14 July 1974, p. 6, © 1974–75 by The New York Times Company. Reprinted by permission.

answer is painful. Here is a blurred black cat skulking under a red metal lawn chair, a close-up of what appears to be a small fish tank but might be the underside of a sink, a rowboat at the edge of what could be either a lake or an empty parking lot.

We used to take these snapshots with a zeal that must have warmed many a heart at Eastman Kodak. It was considered important to preserve your life's great moments so you could relive them in the serenity of your dotage, and I suppose this is still done by persons of a certain age, some of whom may even take good pictures. It is a mistake.

Looking at these people standing around in oceans, having their diapers changed, blowing out birthday candles, gazing at the Tower of London, cutting the wedding cake, dozing at the New Year's Eve party—one sees that they are all wrong, even on the rare occasions when they are in clear focus and well-lit.

The men have too much hair and are too lean and hard. The women's eyes lack wisdom. The old people look middle-aged and dynamic and the babies look so alarmingly alike that it is hard to tell one from another.

You remember most of these people well enough to know they never, never looked like these representations in the snapshots. Or did they? A sad possibility, that. Too sad to be acceptable, regardless of the photographic industry's claim that the camera doesn't lie.

These are not life's great moments preserved, but only life embalmed, all the juices drained, the glory gone to dust. The picture of an arrow snapped in flight, frozen forever against the sky, conveys nothing of this great moment in the arrow's existence, and it is just as useless to try to capture life in the frozen instant of the camera shutter's blink.

Fine photographers who are artists occasionally succeed, but most of us, when we get behind the camera, are doomed to be embalmers. What we can do, however, is take great pictures in our heads, and not only take them, but store them so that they improve with the years.

We can add color, movement, emotion, feel, taste, sound and even smell. What's more, as the years go by we can, and usually do, edit and improve them. I have one of these snapshots taken years ago of some hollyhocks in my grandmother's yard. Not only does it show the pink of the flowers in tints at least as lovely as they were on that distant summer day, but it also contains the incredible blue of the sky—sometimes the sky is filled with glistening cumulus clouds, other times it is the purest blue—as well as the hum of a bumble bee, the distant rumble of a threshing machine, the smell of wild roses on the fence, the purple outline of the mountains in the distance and, behind me, for this camera can also photograph through 360 degrees, the lordly porch of my grandmother's great house.

This is a splendid snapshot. Am I to believe that this is the way it really was, or should I accept this more recent camera version which tries to tell me that my grandmother's house was only a small gray dilapidation and her front yard a small plot overgrown with weeds?

So we put the cameras away after a while and closed the drawer. I opened it the other day only because of a momentary urge to neaten things up by sorting out the pictures and throwing away all but a few.

The job would have taken all day and I quit after 20 minutes. An entire day spent with pictures that treat people as those snapshots do would have been intolerable, so I went to the back yard, sat down and took some beautiful scenes of the sunlight filtering through the elm tree, and felt better right away.

Without any serious design at all, but personal and entertaining, is this informal essay by Rhoda Koenig.

SENSUOUS MONEY[13]

A teen-age girl I know informs me that her friends are very interested in money these days—"not for its own sake," she assures me, "but for what it can buy." To me, this is like eating all the artichoke leaves and throwing away the lovely green heart.

Americans, it seems, have always been extremely moralistic about money, trying to confine its sensual power within manageable limits. The flamboyant gentleman who wishes to show his contempt for money uses a bill to light his cigar. The boutique shopper can buy a roll of toilet paper on which every sheet is printed to look like a dollar bill. And there are all those sanctimonious people who enjoy the sight of money embalmed in Lucite paperweights—no doubt the same people who like their butterflies nice and dead.

I like my money nice and live. Every two weeks I cash my paycheck and walk the two blocks to my bank with a bulging wallet, feeling sexy, accomplished, and invulnerable. Sometimes I take it in $100 bills, and one happy day I walked the distance with a single, elegant $500 bill. I felt like a combination of Mae West, Consuelo Vanderbilt, and Calamity Jane. I wanted to tuck the $500 bill in my waistband, like a handkerchief. I wanted to seduce a traffic cop. I wanted to go into a drugstore and buy a package of gum.

For money, in thick, green, susurrous clumps, confers undeniable sensual attraction on the person who owns it. Lorelei Lee knew this, and so did Santayana. When that eminent man was asked to name the best book of philosophy written by an American, he replied, *"Gentlemen Prefer Blondes."*

[13] Rhoda Koenig, "Sensuous Money," copyright 1973 by Harper's Magazine. Reprinted from the November 1973 issue, p. 90 by special permission.

Most of us, however, are shy about admitting to what seems like such a dry and cheerless lust. So That *Cosmopolitan* Girl goes on smearing hot fudge on her erogenous zones and ignoring other, tidier, sensual experiences. Lovers of money for its own sake are usually imagined as wizened little men, unwashed and dressed in ill-fitting suits of bombazine.

In this unpromising erotic climate, I am happy to report on a friend of mine, an author of one of the rare grand gestures. My friend decided to present his mistress with a condominium (I think it was her birthday) and arrived at her apartment with the purchase price of $65,000 in bills of small denominations. Finding the lady in bed, as he expected, he flung the bills upon her—and himself after them.

Still you say "crass," "unromantic," "cold"? You want to retire from this mercenary world and read poetry to your one and only? Well, don't forget the poet who called money "the sinews of love." And, if you've always admired the *Rubáiyát*, you might look past verse twelve—right, the one about book of verses, bread, wine, etc. In the first line of verse thirteen, that ultra romantic Persian poet exults: "Ah, take the Cash, and let the Credit go!"

EXERCISES

A. Be prepared to discuss the Russell Baker essay, "Negative Thinking," on pages 76–78. Consider especially the following questions:

1. What is the central idea? Do you find yourself in sympathy with it?
2. Is there any discernible order to the essay? If so, what is it? Could you make a brief outline?
3. What words or expressions would you choose as being particularly original or characteristic of the familiar style?
4. How would you evaluate the effectiveness of the beginning and the end?

B. Comment on Rhoda Koenig's "Sensuous Money" on pages 78–79. In what ways does it compare with or differ from Russell Baker's "Negative Thinking"? Consider especially the author's use of language. What impression does she give of herself? To what kind of audience does she appeal? What is your own attitude toward money? Could you write an amusing essay about it? Try it, if your instructor approves.

THEME TOPICS

1. Taking your cue from the letter by Emily Dickinson on pages 72–73, write a letter dated a month or two after your arrival at college and addressed to your parents or a brother or sister; describe in your own idiom your experiences and your feelings about your new environment.

2. Write a letter to a friend, real or imagined, relating in some detail a particular experience you have had.

3. Will Rogers, the comedian and social commentator, traveled abroad for a time as an unofficial ambassador, writing "confidential" letters to President Calvin Coolidge. The letters were widely published. Here is an excerpt from one of them written from London during a general strike that crippled Britain.

My dear President:

Say, I told them about you over here. During all this calm and no excitement, everybody asked me, "How would you Americans take this if it were happening over there?"

So I told them: "We would have all been cuckoo and crazy and shooting and rioting, and everybody up in the air—all but one man. He would have been just like your House of Lords. He might every few days ask, 'Is the strike over yet?' But he would have been the sole individual that would not have turned a hair."

They all would ask, "Who is this remarkable man that you speak of?"

I remarked, "Calvin Coolidge."

I wish you had been there. It was just your kind of stuff. . . .

I will go and see if London Bridge is falling down. I have heard somewhere that it was.

Yours as ever,
W.R.

P.S. Watch the farmers. They are tricky.[14]

In a similarly facetious vein, write a letter to the President or some other high public official, reporting on your observations and offering your advice as "unofficial ambassador."

[14] From *A Treasury of Great American Letters*, ed. Charles Hurd and Eleanor Hurd (New York: Hawthorn Books, 1961), pp. 253–54.

4. Keep a diary for a day or a week for submission as a theme. Be selective in your choice of material, trying to preserve some semblance of unity and continuity. Feel free to express your thoughts and feelings as they are affected by the events you chronicle; and, without straining, let your language reflect your uniqueness.

5. Pay a visit to a local store that specializes in greeting cards. Examine the variety and character of those cards, then write a familiar essay on the subject. Try to make your points in a light, perhaps amusing, way. If you want to include some informal social comment, do so. What, if any, for example, is the relation between the growth of the greeting card industry and the growth of mechanization generally and the impersonalization of our society? Is the use of the cards a sign of laziness? of lack of confidence in one's own ability to express one's feelings? What special human need do the cards fulfill?

6. The telephone, like the greeting card, has had much to do with the decline of the letter as a medium for personal communication. Write a familiar essay on telephone use by young people. What is the appeal of the instrument? Does it really encourage nonstop talking? Or is the portrait of teenage telephone chatter overdrawn? Perhaps you can add some concrete details from your experience and observations.

7. Extract a topic from one of the following suggestions, and write a familiar essay incorporating your thoughts and feelings.

(a) Most of us, when we are young, have a "crush" on an older person. Have you had such a crush? Can you describe the experience and your view of it in retrospect?

(b) Every student body has its athletic heroes, its social lions, its politicians, and its intellectual "geniuses." Have you been any of these or aspired to some special niche among your peers? Is there someone or some class of student you number among your idols? Or do you have a jaundiced view of such leaders?

(c) Cars have a special attraction to youth. Can you describe the causes of this attraction and its particular manifestations?

(d) The "work ethic" appears to have taken strong hold in our society, including the school system. You are told that work, quite apart from its material rewards, is good for you, that it builds character and guarantees happiness. Is there anything good that can be said for idleness? Perhaps you could offer some ideas on the subject and perhaps, even, help to give idleness a good name. Try to treat your subject in concrete terms.

(e) Do you know a very methodical person? Are *you* such a one? Would you like to be one? What does order in one's personal affairs mean to you? Have you any taste for it? In writing this theme, perhaps you could describe the evidence of your love of order or your lack of it.

5 Narration: Personal Experience

Narrative writing is, in effect, the description of a related sequence of events. When the events are altered or wholly imaginary, the writing becomes fiction. When the events are observed or experienced, the writing becomes history, biography, or autobiography. It is the latter type of narrative, particularly personal experience, that we shall be concerned with here.

Some Suggestions

The range of material from which topics can be drawn for a personal narrative extends over a broad area: relations with parents or friends, an incident at school, a vacation trip, a summer job, a family crisis, a social gathering, an adolescent romance. The treatment of such subjects can vary, too, from high seriousness to rowdy comedy, from deep emotion to a gentle philosophic stance.

Problems in the organization of material are usually minimal in narration because the sequence is, with few exceptions, chronological. The exceptions are made when, for the purpose of heightening interest or suspense, the writer describes events out of sequence, often beginning with some central or concluding incident.

Since you will be writing about your observations and experiences, it is important that they be interesting enough to share with the reader. So they will be if they represent turning points in your life or if they have in some way contributed to your character, your view of life, or your knowledge of the world. If your theme is to be given such significance, do not simply move from one event to another, but rather focus on some particular incident from which you have gained new wisdom. Thus a theme on a summer at camp, if it is unselective, will ramble from experience to experience; but if it deals with a more limited aspect of the subject—an unauthorized midnight swim that nearly led to disaster, or the first realization of success as you receive applause for your part as a tree in the camp play—then that single event may be used to expose the deeper meaning of the narrative and give it interest. Of course, there is room in such a narrative for background description or for a brief account of minor events, but such material must be closely related to the main point of the story and not distract the reader from it.

Along with the inherent interest in the experience you are relating, there must be a corresponding interest in the telling. The opening must engage the reader, the body of the narrative must be written in language that is fresh and colorful, character and place must be carefully delineated, and, to the extent the narrative allows, the expository passages should be relieved by passages of dialogue. If you need help with the mechanics of paragraphing and punctuating dialogue, see Rule 14a(1) in the "Handbook of English."

"The Turning Point"—An Example

A fine example of personal narrative is offered by Sherwood Anderson's recollection of an event that proved a turning point in his relations with his father. He begins:

> You hear it said that fathers want their sons to be what they feel they cannot themselves be, but I tell you it also works the other way. A boy wants something very special from his father. I know that as a small boy I wanted my father to be a certain thing he was not. I wanted him to be a proud, silent, dignified father. When I was with other boys and he passed along the street, I wanted to feel a flow of pride: "There he is. That is my father."
>
> But he wasn't such a one. He couldn't be. It seemed to me then that he was always showing off. Let's say someone in our town had got up a show. They were always doing it. The druggist would be in it, the shoe-store clerk, the horse doctor, and a lot of women and girls. My father would manage to get the chief comedy part. It was, let's say, a Civil War play and he was a comic Irish soldier. He had to do the most absurd things. They thought he was funny, but I didn't.

For several pages Anderson details his father's penchant for telling "tall stories," and often going off for weeks at a time "visiting around at farmhouses" while the boy's mother had to work to feed the family.

> And then there came a certain night. He'd been off somewhere for two or three weeks. He found me alone in the house, reading by the kitchen table.

It had been raining and he was very wet. He sat and looked at me for a long time, not saying a word. I was startled, for there was on his face the saddest look I had ever seen. He sat for a time, his clothes dripping. Then he got up.

"Come on with me," he said.

I got up and went with him out of the house. I was filled with wonder but I wasn't afraid. We went along a dirt road that led down into a valley, about a mile out of town, where there was a pond. We walked in silence. The man who was always talking had stopped his talking.

I didn't know what was up and had the queer feeling that I was with a stranger. I don't know whether my father intended it so. I don't think he did.

The pond was quite large. It was still raining hard and there were flashes of lightning followed by thunder. We were on a grassy bank at the pond's edge when my father spoke, and in the darkness and rain his voice sounded strange.

"Take off your clothes," he said. Still filled with wonder, I began to undress. There was a flash of lightning and I saw that he was already naked.

The boy stepped into the pond with his father. A powerful swimmer with broad shoulders, the father guided the son silently across the pond and back to where they had left their clothes. And then, in an occasional flash of lightning, the son could glimpse his father's face; it was a face filled with sadness. "It was as though I had been jerked suddenly out of myself, out of the world of the schoolboy, out of the world in which I was ashamed of my father."

As the story ends, they return home to be greeted by the mother.

"What have you boys been up to?" she asked, but my father did not answer. As he had begun the evening's experience with me in silence, so he ended. He turned and looked at me. Then he went, I thought, with a new and strange dignity out of the room.

I climbed the stairs to my own room, undressed in the darkness and got into bed. I couldn't sleep and did not want to sleep. For the first time I knew I was the son of my father. He was a story teller as I was to be. It may be that I even laughed a little softly there in the darkness. If I did, I laughed knowing that I would never again be wanting another father.[1]

Narrative with Description

By definition, narrative represents events in motion, yet good narrative also requires enough background description to give events

[1] Sherwood Anderson, *Sherwood Anderson's Memoirs,* ed. Ray Lewis White (Chapel Hill: Univ. of North Carolina Press, 1969) pp. 78–85.

depth and realism. Weaving the description into the narrative—"on the run," so to speak—is usually more effective than stopping the narrative flat and taking time to describe the scenery.

The following paragraph shows how the narrative can be kept moving while the descriptive details are sketched in. The author, having been accepted for admission to Harvard, has just arrived in Boston and is on his way to his first meeting with the Dean. Between the two events, we learn a lot about the physical environment in which the new student finds himself.

I had never seen Boston and did not see much of it on arrival as I shot through on the subway to what the guard called "Harvard Squaair." My first impression, as I surfaced, was of a drab, congested shopping center, noisy with traffic and, as this was the opening day of college, thronged with students. I got my breakfast at the Waldorf, a white-tiled, one-armed lunch, more remarkable for speed than taste, and left my suitcase in its care until I had found a room. To cross the street and enter the gate into Harvard Yard, a distance of fifty feet, was to forget the clanging trolley cars as one felt the quiet of a timeless place: the architecture was the mix of centuries, but what I would always remember were the old colonial buildings, square-ended, red brick, white trim, once used as a barracks by Washington's Continentals; the wine-glass elms, with their pools of shadow on the sunny turf; and, in the center, the classical granite façade of University Hall, where I had a ten o'clock appointment with Dean Chester Greenough.[2]

Dialogue

As a standard feature of most good narrative writing, dialogue adds visual interest by breaking up patches of exposition and, more important, heightens the dramatic interest. Here, complete, is an incident from an autobiographical sketch by Richard Wright, who was working at the time as a hotel hall-boy.

One night, just as I was about to go home, I met one of the Negro maids. She lived in my direction, and we fell in to walk part of the way home together. As we passed the white night-watchman, he slapped the maid on her buttock. I turned around, amazed. The watchman looked at me with a long, hard, fixed-under stare. Suddenly he pulled his gun and asked:

"Nigger, don't yuh like it?"

I hesitated.

[2] From *My Green Age* by Edward Weeks, by permission of Little, Brown and Co., in association with The Atlantic Monthly Press. Copyright © 1973 by Edward Weeks.

"I asked yuh don't yuh like it?" he asked again, stepping forward.

"Yes, sir," I mumbled.

"Talk like it, then!"

"Oh, yes, sir!" I said with as much heartiness as I could muster.

Outside, I walked ahead of the girl, ashamed to face her. She caught up with me and said:

"Don't be a fool! Yuh couldn't help it!"

This watchman boasted of having killed two Negroes in self-defense.

Yet, in spite of all this, the life of the hotel ran with an amazing smoothness. It would have been impossible for a stranger to detect anything. The maids, the hall-boys, and the bell-boys were all smiles. They had to be.[3]

The interlayering of exposition and dialogue is also shown in the following excerpt from Maxim Gorky's recollection of his childhood. After witnessing the burial of his father, he has been taken on a boat with his mother and grandmother, and his smaller brother lies dead in the cabin. Note how well the simplicity of the dialogue conveys the impression of childhood.

A broad-shouldered, gray-headed individual dressed in blue now entered, carrying a small box which grandmother took from him, and in which she proceeded to place the body of my brother. Having done this she bore the box and its burden to the door on her out-stretched hands; but, alas! being so stout she could only get through the narrow doorway of the cabin sideways, and now halted before it in ludicrous uncertainty.

"Really, Mama!" exclaimed my mother impatiently, taking the tiny coffin from her. Then they both disappeared, while I stayed behind in the cabin regarding the man in blue.

"Well, mate, so the little brother has gone?" he said, bending down to me.

"Who are you?"

"I am a sailor."

"And who is Saratov?"

"Saratov is a town. Look out of the window. There it is!"

Observed from the window, the land seemed to oscillate; and revealing itself obscurely and in a fragmentary fashion, as it lay steaming in the fog, it reminded me of a large piece of bread just cut off a hot loaf.

"Where has grandmother gone to?"

"To bury her little grandson."

"Are they going to bury him in the ground?"

"Yes, of course they are."

[3] Richard Wright, *Uncle Tom's Children* (New York: Harper & Row, 1940), pp. 12–13.

I then told the sailor about the live frogs that had been buried with my father.

He lifted me up, and hugging and kissing me, cried, "Oh, my poor little fellow, you don't understand. It is not the frogs who are to be pitied, but your mother. Think how she is bowed down by her sorrow."[4]

Personal Feeling

Autobiographical writing invariably presents an opportunity for the expression of personal views and feelings, and an attempt to explain their origins. Marya Mannes, a senior member of the feminist movement, writes:

Some of my ideas . . . are bound to be unpalatable, if not repellant, to the majority of our citizens who believe that prosperity and procreation—in wedlock, of course—are the only valid goals of man and woman. I happen to think that there are other goals as valid, and as valuable, for both man and woman.

She goes on to explain the evolution of those feelings.

How did I get that way? Well, I saw it around me when I was a small child. My mother and father were both concert musicians and both teachers, my mother of the piano, my father of the violin. There was nothing strange whatever to me in the fact that my mother, a woman, spent much of each day practicing or giving lessons, that she often went off on tour with my father, and that she couldn't boil an egg. She didn't have to. In the early part of the twentieth century even people of very modest means had cooks and nurses, and it was taken equally for granted by my brother and myself that if our mother was away, the cook, the nurse, or the great-aunt who lived with us, would take care of us. There was no sense of rejection, no shocks at being "motherless" for a period of weeks. Life went on fully; we studied, ate, and slept, and when our parents did come back we were delighted to see them. . . .

It was therefore quite natural that I should grow up believing that all was possible for a girl or woman. Certainly, both my father and brother made it seem so. Both spoke to me as equals of many things that girls are not supposed to be interested in. My brother passed on to me the first principles of physics, the relativity of time, and how to throw a curve with a baseball. My father discussed with me, from the age of ten years onward, such things as the nature of melancholy, how to get a vibrato on a violin, and how

[4] Maxim Gorky, *My Childhood* (Garden City, N.Y.: Garden City Publishing Co., 1926), pp. 10–11.

sickness could be caused by states of mind. I lived, therefore, for over seventeen years in the world of imagination and discovery, going steady not with the boy next door but the men out of range. I was passionately in love with Julius Caesar, Hamlet, Henry V of England, and John Barrymore of Hollywood. I did not start transferring my affections to more attainable men until I was nineteen, at which point I threw away the books along with self-restraint.[5]

In the following paragraph, Ben H. Bagdikian, a critic of the mass media, amusingly describes his love affair with one of them.

I love newspapers. I was a teen-age dirty old man with indiscriminate lust for every newspaper in sight. I made indecent advances in public places to any paper that came along, whether it was the *Boston Daily Record*, Hearst's hip-swinging little hooker, or the *Boston Transcript*, a little old lady in high choker collar. It sounds depraved but confidential studies show that this is a common adolescent experience and society must stop imposing feelings of shame. Besides, I grew up in a suburb of Boston whence came more bad newspapers than most cities and I read them with the same feverish appetite that I lavished on the copy of *Spicy Adventure Stories* hidden under the stairs.[6]

Sexual attraction of a more conventional kind is shown in a brief passage from the work by Edward Weeks cited on page 86. The close is especially wistful.

Since last summer Cornelia's slender figure had filled out in the right places; she did her blond hair in a high crest and the pastel shades she dressed in set her off. We took undemonstrative pleasure in being together; we challenged her father and older sister, "Tommy," at tennis, read poetry aloud, drove up to Buena Vista in the moonlight or down the mountain to picnic on the Gettysburg battlefield, parts of which—the two Round Tops, the Devil's Den, the Peach Orchard, Seminary Ridge and the High Water Mark—we would long remember; and at supper parties in Charmian, we danced well and often. I delighted in catching her by surprise, making her laugh, and in all of this, save once, was the unspoken understanding that I should come no closer than when we loitered in the car or in her Gloucester hammock, my arm casually resting on the back of the seat. Why did we hold back? In her case, I think, because she was unsure and wanted no beau to have

[5] Marya Mannes, *But Will It Sell?* (Philadelphia: Lippincott, 1964), pp. 53–54. Copyright © 1962, 1964 by Marya Mannes. Reprinted by permission of Harold Ober Associates Incorporated.

[6] Ben H. Bagdikian, *The Effete Conspiracy and Other Crimes of the Press* (New York: Harper & Row, 1972), p. 3.

priority before her debut; in mine, because I was penniless with a long future at Harvard. But desire feeds on denial. For every undergraduate there is a road not taken, a girl not taken, and Cornelia was mine.[7]

Anecdote and Adventure

Two types of dramatic writing that lend themselves well to student themes are the anecdote and the dramatic experience. The anecdote is a brief account of an amusing or otherwise interesting experience. Here is an example, a recollection by Arnold Sundgaard, of an incident of many years ago.

Whenever I see the name Bauer & Black on a roll of adhesive tape, I invariably think of New Year's Eve, 1936.

I was living on the top floor of a shabby hotel on North Wabash and East Erie Street in Chicago. On New Year's Eve, I had exactly thirty-two cents with which to ring out the old and ring in the new. I decided to go to a bar called Ballantine's on North Rush Street and buy two beers and nurse them along from eleven o'clock to midnight. Beer was a dime a glass, and it would leave me a third dime for a somewhat prodigal tip.

As I took my first carefully measured sip, someone slapped me on the back and greeted me like a long-lost friend. He proved to be a familiar face and not all that long lost. About five years before, we had sat next to each other in a history-lecture section of some three hundred students in Bascom Hall, at the University of Wisconsin.

He insisted that I be a guest at his table and meet his friends—three salesmen from Bauer & Black and their wives. They were drinking an eclectic array of the house's sugary specialties and not nursing a thing but potential hangovers.

When I got up to leave—it was two hours into 1937—my by now intimate college chum implored me to get in touch with him soon for another glorious night on the town.

"Call me at the office anytime," he said. "Bauer & Black. When you think of me, think of bandages."

As we walked toward the door I took him aside and said, "I can remember Bauer & Black all right, but the fact is, for the life of me I can't remember your name."

He roared with laughter and told me his name. And then he added, "I got to admit—it's been bothering me all night—I can't remember *your* name, either."

I told him and went out to face the winds of East Erie Street, where I hoped the Hotel Delano (since torn down) was still standing.

[7] Weeks, p. 101.

Once in a while I try to conjure up his name but to no avail, and to compound the obsession I now think of him when I see a Band-Aid, which is made by Johnson & Johnson. I can't even remember the name of the history course.[8]

The dramatic experience is longer and usually, but not necessarily, serious in tone. As an autobiographical piece, it may deal with some involuntary predicament in which the author finds himself or with some adventure he sets out on by himself or with others. Below is an account of a particularly hazardous weekend pursuit.

Up here it's all grotesquely magnified. On the ground—in that other world—I was never aware of how thick my fingertips were, how mushy soft my body was, how useless my vision, how vast the distance between right middle fingernail and left heel, how muscles could stretch, how loud my heart could thunder, how wet sweat could be. Gray speckled/hard/silence/pull/cling/ache—are the only realities now. And the only escape is up.

Move! Fingers scan the rock, over tiny nubs, useless cracks, delicate flakes, grit, crumbles, feeling for a safe place to lodge in the strain upwards. They claw a crack to bring my left leg to a wider ledge, where all of us—my arms, legs, and I—can rest for a moment.

This umbilical cord existence with my leader is reassuring. But fall and I dangle like a fly in a spider web until the right flailing of arms and legs brings me back to the rock. Deny fear. It panics, paralyzes, closes the door to that ground-floor consciousness I came from. And I do want to get back.

Strain convulses my legs—"sewing machine legs," they call them. "Legs, mind commands you to stop." But legs have a mind of their own. *Move!* But how? Which limb to move first, where, to allow which limb to follow? How many body pounds can my right toe support? How far past the piton can I climb and still be able to reach down to hammer it out of the crack? How many hammer hits will make me lose my balance? It's a chess game, with many possible right moves, or only one. I'm two hundred feet from earth, aching, shaking, sweating, contorting my body to keep a delicate balance, and angry at myself for not staying on the ground when I still had a chance.

Curse the rock, curse my clumsy body, curse my brain for failing to compute, sort, and evaluate the rock's possibilities. Not even getting back to nature, except for the prospect of a wasp's nest crammed into the next inviting crevice, or making myself remember to reject "vegetable holds," those crazy, unreliable clumps of grass spurting out of cracks. Repent. Yes, repent. Never again, I swear, if I can get to the top just this once. Please, God, show me a bucket hold . . .

[8] From "Reruns of the Mind" by Arnold Sundgaard. Reprinted by permission; © 1973 The New Yorker Magazine, Inc.

V wedge just above my waist. Inconvenient as hell, but my left leg flies to the wedge, stomach arches for balance, and my right arm hugs a small overhang. Leader in sight now. A quick narrow traverse to the right and here the rock miraculously forms stairsteps.

At the top I stretch possessively on the warm soft earth, swearing never to forsake its security again. Miles out and down, what was threatening to look at an instant ago now is soothing. What an escape rock-climbing is—escape from personality, profession, past, future, into texture, space, adrenalin. What total exhaustion is—muscle fibers stretched to snapping point, joints twisted abnormally. What fear is. I replay it, dissect it, and eventually even laugh at it.

We're tripping down the grassy side of the mountain for a knapsack lunch with other climbers at the base of the cliffs. Down the shrubby path, picking sun-warmed wild blueberries. Giddy, ego-bursting, I did it! Tonight we'll slosh down beer at Emil's, compare holds, ledges, and narrow escapes, crawl bone-tired into sleeping bags. Sunday's sun will expose the bruises on the best of us, but by nine we'll be at the cliff base again, tying bowlines around our waists and clanging pitons over our shoulders. Like idiots.[9]

EXERCISE

A. Comment on the effectiveness of the narrative theme below. Consider especially these elements: narrative flow, descriptive details, word use, sentence structure, and beginning and ending. Do you have any specific recommendations?

RENEWAL

I sat cross-legged on my bed as the radio softly played, the red light of the lamp casting shadows on the wall. The faint scent of incense surrounded me. I felt warm and peaceful.

I took a box from my desk, held it in my hand for a moment, and then carefully removed the contents—old letters, a part of an envelope with a poem scribbled on it, a ragged paper Cupid with the words "Love me" scrawled across its chest. At the bottom of the box lay a silver crucifix, attached to a red rope instead of a chain. I picked it up and held the rope between my two hands, watching the cross dangle helplessly from side to side. The figure of Christ lay prostrate on one side of the cross. The face betrayed no emotion. The body

[9] Nancy Lyons, "Rock-Climbing: Tripping on Adrenalin," *New York* Magazine, 1 April 1974, p. 54. Copyright © 1974 by the NYM Corp. Reprinted with the permission of *New York* Magazine.

appeared lifeless. The other side bore the inscription, "Christ is counting on you."

The metal felt cool against my chest as I hung the cross around my neck. I had not worn it in a long time and it felt strange and foreign. At the same time it comforted me because it made me think of David, the boy who gave it to me.

I met David through my brother, Edward. Religion had started to play an important part in Edward's life. A friend introduced him to David, who was deeply involved in the same religion. Their acquaintance grew quickly into love and brotherhood. I watched my brother change. He was filled with the spirit of David and the spirit of Jesus, and he never seemed happier. I was glad for the intensity with which he was now living, but I also felt apprehensive. I hoped he would be influenced by his own soul rather than what he described as David's fervent spirit.

Edward wanted me to meet David, so we found ourselves traveling to Lincoln Center on a freezing cold night. We were to meet David there and then go to a concert. Nervous, expectant, uncertain—this is how I felt waiting for this young man whom I already knew so much about. Would he like me? How would I impress him? Does he look the way I imagined him to look? I could not stop these questions from running through my mind. Edward had once spoken about David's mystical quality, and I just did not know what to expect of such a person.

Before I could resolve any of my uneasiness, David appeared. He walked quickly and quietly toward us, a shy smile on his face. He and my brother embraced, exchanged some words, and then he turned to me. I was immediately struck by the strange quality of his face. He was very handsome, and he wore a beard. But his eyes were childlike; soft, warm, and filled with anticipation. He smiled shyly again and hugged me tightly. The scent of patchouli filled my head as I hugged him in return. I felt that this stranger was a close friend, and in a sense he was.

The three of us sat down and talked. I spoke hesitantly at first, because I wanted to hear Edward and David talk to each other. David was so warm and so animated, however, that I soon found myself in the midst of a conversation I can remember nothing about. But I remember that we talked, and we talked, without ever running out of words. We almost forgot about the concert!

Now I could understand Edward's feeling for this boy. David captured my heart immediately, along with my love. Strangely, or maybe not so strangely, we never became "close friends." I did not miss him when he was not around and rarely did I feel the need to confide in him. We shared certain things, however, that created love and trust between us. We shared my brother, we shared the pain of once being hurt by unrequited love, the pain of being misunderstood. We shared the fright of being uncertain about things we wanted to depend upon. He shared with me his intensity for living, and I gave him, hopefully, the ability to understand those who seemed impossible to understand.

I am grateful to David for one reason above all others. He showed me the goodness of giving. A friend had once given me a pendant, and it was a gift I was very fond of. David knew I always wore it, and one day he asked if I would give it to him. I did not know what to say, but I knew I didn't want to give it to him. He waited a few moments in silence, and then he repeated his question. I felt hurt and annoyed, and then he asked me again if I would give it to him. I would have gladly given him something else! But then, almost without thinking, I quickly took the chain from my neck and placed it around his. He smiled slowly and then removed from his neck a silver crucifix attached to a red rope. This he gave to me.

Wearing the crucifix now, I remembered all that was attached to it. I felt happy and also a bit sad. I have not seen David in a very long time and I would like to. But he is still with me—his gift keeps me with him and him with me.

THEME TOPICS

1. Write about a personal experience that proved to be a turning point in your life.

2. Describe an adventurous trip or other personal experience, interweaving the narrative with descriptive details and, if possible, some dialogue.

3. Write an autobiographical theme in which you embody your special view of life and of yourself, and attempt to explain its origins and development. Support any generalizations with specific detail and incident.

4. Choose topic (a) or (b) below:

(a) Assume that you have applied for a part-time or summer job. At the job interview you are asked to take some time to write an autobiographical statement with special emphasis on your career aspirations. Write the statement.

(b) Assume that you are applying either for transfer to another college or for admission to some graduate or professional school. An autobiographical statement of 750–1,000 words must accompany your application. You are asked to tell why you have chosen your intended field of specialization and why you selected the particular school to which you are applying. Write the statement.

5. Write a narrative theme on one of the following topics:

(a) A driving lesson (or other learning experience)
(b) A job experience
(c) Your first exposure to college
(d) An encounter with a teacher, adviser, or dean
(e) An encounter with a stranger
(f) A personal feud, rivalry, or physical encounter
(g) A punishment meted out at home or at school
(h) A celebration
(i) A trip or vacation
(j) A death in the family
(k) A reminiscence of childhood
(l) A first date
(m) A personal goal achieved after initial difficulties
(n) Your first lesson in self-reliance
(o) A natural phenomenon or a disaster of which you were an observer
(p) A fire or crime you witnessed or were victimized by
(q) A movie or play review, with emphasis on plot, and character or locale

6 Description

Some description is incidental to almost all writing, and in some instances it is the main form of discourse. If you have difficulty in separating description from, say, narration or explanation, description is probably only an incidental part of the passage. Where description is the principal mode, however, it can usually be identified as either *technical* or *affective.*

Description is *technical* when it provides factual information—information uncolored by your personal feelings—about a procedure, process, object, place, or condition. How does a clerk record a sale? How does the picture tube on the television set work? How is glass made? What are the physical characteristics of a proposed building plot? What is the anatomy of a bee? What are the symptoms of alcoholism? These are some of the kinds of questions that informative description answers. Description is *affective*, on the other hand, when the information it provides is influenced by your personal feelings and when, correspondingly, it influences the feelings of the reader. Examples would include a character sketch of a family friend, your impressions of a visit to the Grand Canyon, your observations on a Chinatown New Year's festival, a childhood reminiscence of the stands at Candlestick Park on Bat Day.

Technical Description

Technical description requires, perhaps more than any other quality, a faithful recounting of the phenomenon or object with which you wish to acquaint the reader. What matters is that you achieve the kind of precision you would get if you were recording your subject in a drawing, photograph, or motion picture. You will be guided by what you know and perceive, but you will filter out any personal impressions or prejudices that may distort the image. Consider also the following suggestions.

1. Organize your description in a way that contributes to the reader's understanding. The description of a task—making a lithographic plate, for example—will first acquaint the reader with the purpose of the task, the results aimed for, and the tools and materials needed. It will then proceed to divide the task into its principal parts and to describe those parts in the order they are performed. The description of an electronic digital clock, on the other hand, will acquaint the reader, first, with its external appearance, and then with the works inside. [Any division of a subject into its parts is a function of *analysis*. For a fuller treatment, see Chapter 7, "Analytical Methods."]

2. Pay close attention to specific details. The reader has no knowledge of what you are describing except through your selection and description of the particulars. In technical description this point is especially important, because if you omit a step or part of a procedure, the reader may be prevented from performing the task the description is supposed to teach; and if you fail to specify a precise quality, like a color, shape, or size, the reader may be unable to identify or construct, or buy intelligently, the article under consideration. Language plays an important part here. Terms must be specific. Words like *large, bright,* or *metal* are not nearly so informative as *5.0 by 24.5 centimeters, 100 lumens,* or *copper-clad aluminum.*

3. Adapt the description to the purpose and the reader. Technical description serves many uses, but it cannot do its work effectively unless the writing is on a level the reader can understand. It should be apparent that description that serves the needs of the expert cannot also serve the needs of the layman. The sentence that follows was intended for aerospace engineers.

Most refractory coatings to date exhibit a lack of reliability when subjected to the impingement of entrained particulate matter in the propellant stream under extended firing durations.

The same passage, rewritten for the layman, might read:

The exhaust gas eventually chews the coating off existing ceramics.

Even among specialists, there is some question as to whether much of the technical writing they read is not more abstruse than it needs to be. This point, in fact, was made by the editor of *Jets and Missiles,* which carried the two examples cited above. The editor expressed a preference for the second phrasing, even in writing for the engineer.[1] In this and similar instances, the only question is whether the simplification results in the blurring or omission of data important to the reader.

Some Examples

With a few simple principles of technical description behind us, we can now look at some examples for study.

In the following introduction to a description of hide curing, the author of *Two Years Before the Mast* follows established practice by telling how the subject is to be organized. Then the step-by-step description of the process is begun. The clarity resulting from this method is apparent.

The morning after my landing, I began the duties of hide-curing. In order to understand these, it will be necessary to give the whole history of a hide, from the time it is taken from a bullock until it is put on board the vessel to be carried to Boston. When the hide is taken from the bullock, holes are cut around it, near the edge, by which it is staked out to dry. In this manner it dries without shrinking. After the hides are thus dried in the sun, and doubled with the skin out, they are received by the vessels at the different ports on the coast, and brought down to the depot at San Diego. The vessels land them, and leave them in large piles near the houses. Then begins the hide-curer's duty.

The first thing is to put them in soak. This is done by carrying them down at low-tide, and making them fast, in small piles, by ropes, and letting the tide come up and cover them. . . .[2]

For the modern reader, instructions for building a compost heap are given, in part, in the following passage. Note the specific details, the natural order of the steps described, and the simple, direct language especially evident in the shorter sentences.

The usual way to build a compost pile is to put the material down in layers, the thickness depending on the coarseness or fineness of the material; leaves, for example, should be put in layers about 6 inches deep, grass clippings 3 or 4 inches deep. Spread out each layer on the pile, making sure the center is slightly concave to catch rain water, and sprinkle about a pint of fertilizer and a dusting of limestone on top. To make sure there is enough

[1] "Letters," *Jets and Missiles*, 21 December 1959, p. 40.

[2] Richard Henry Dana, *Two Years Before the Mast* (New York: Dodd, Mead, 1946), p. 125.

moisture to aid decomposition, dampen the pile for a few minutes with a hose, then top it off with a 2-inch layer of soil from your garden. This soil layer will help to settle the pile, seal in the heat generated during decomposition and add bacteria to speed decay. Continue sandwiching alternate layers of soil and organic material sprinkled with fertilizer and limestone until the pile is 3 to 4 feet high. It will take about three to six months for the composting process to be completed. If rainfall is light, hose down the pile from time to time to replace evaporated moisture. Turn the pile over with a spading fork after four to six weeks so that the outer material becomes incorporated into the center and has a chance to decay. A second turning in another four to six weeks will help to speed the process, but it is not mandatory. The compost will be ready to use when it is dark in color and the material from which it was made either loses its original form entirely or crumbles when touched. A 2-inch application of compost each year will make any soil enormously productive.[3]

A far different subject—the geologic drifting of the continents as theorized by the German explorer Alfred Wegener—is put into focus by Walter Sullivan, a science writer with a gift for organizing complex ideas for easy comprehension.

The theory today sees the earth's rigid surface as broken into six or eight huge plates, of irregular shapes, with smaller ones filling gaps between them. Some, like the Pacific plate, are almost entirely formed of ocean floor. Some are made in part of ocean floor and in part of continental land mass; for example, North America and the western half of the North Atlantic constitute a single plate stretching from Iceland to San Francisco.

The earth's interior can be likened to that of an apple. Inside is the core, probably made of nickel and iron, with a liquid outer part but a center that has been compressed into a solid by the weight of material pressing around it. The crust of the earth is hardly thicker, relatively speaking, than the skin of an apple. It is divided into two quite distinct "provinces," as Wegener recognized when he first set forth his theory: the deep-sea floors and the continental blocks. The deep-sea floors are typically two or three miles below sea level. The continental blocks are either higher than the sea or no more than a few hundred feet below sea level.

Between the crust and the core lies the mantle, which, like the pulp of the apple, is the greatest part. Most of the mantle is relatively rigid and dense. However, thanks to new, sophisticated methods of earthquake analysis, it has been demonstrated that the top 100 miles or so of the mantle are relatively soft—a lubricating layer that makes possible the plate movements and may itself be in motion, carrying the plates on its back.

[3] *Time-Life Encyclopedia of Gardening* (New York: Time-Life Books, n.d.), VIII, 35.

One of the primary movements of the plates is a spreading apart of the ocean floor along ridges such as the one running down the north-south centerline of the Atlantic—it is this that increases the distance to London every year. As the plates on either side of the ridge are carried away from each other, hot, semimolten rock rises beneath them to fill the cracks. New sea floor is being manufactured along a global network of such ridges, which resemble the cracks in a hard-boiled egg and constitute the "seams" of the plates (other branches extend into the Indian Ocean and virtually all other ocean areas).[4]

Some elements of this descriptive passage are especially worth noting. First is the division of the earth into surface and interior, with the surface described as consisting of a number of huge "plates" forming the ocean floor and the continental land masses. The earth is then likened to an apple, with a *core;* a center, or *mantle;* and a skin, or *crust.* This analogy helps the reader form an organized picture of the subject in readily understood terms. Finally, the author explains the interaction of the surface movement with the interior.

The descriptive paragraph below, dealing with a much more limited subject, is made interesting by the use of facts so specific and so unexpected that one can only read it with a sense of awe.

Scientists have calculated the weight of one huge redwood at 1,700 tons or far in excess of 3,000,000 pounds. To reach the upper twigs of such a tree, the sap requires a pressure of nearly a hundred pounds to the square inch. Such a mammoth of the forest begins, as do all the redwoods, with a seed so small that it takes nearly 5,000 of them to weigh one pound. The great trees that develop from such tiny beginnings have unique qualities that help them endure. No other cells known to botany have as high a ratio of length of life to growing period as the cells of the redwoods. They live as long as 4,000 times the period required for them to reach their full growth. Furthermore, according to two American research scientists, D. T. MacDougal and G. M. Smith, redwood trees have strips of living cells in the heartwood of their trunks. No other tree known possesses living cells in its heartwood.[5]

[4] Walter Sullivan, "The Restless Continents," *The New York Times Magazine*, 12 January 1975, pp. 13, 15. © 1974–75 by The New York Times Company. Reprinted by permission.

[5] Edwin Way Teale, *The Lost Woods: Adventures of a Naturalist* (New York: Dodd, Mead, 1945), p. 129.

Affective Description

Like technical description, affective description is informative in its use of specifics, but to the purely objective details there is added a creative dimension, for now you can describe things not only for what they are, but for how they affect you personally. The subjective character of such description immediately broadens the field from which you can select your material and gives you further opportunities to achieve interest and variety of expression. The techniques advocated here are especially pertinent.

Sense Impressions

Good description requires that you use all your senses. Perceive not only with your eyes, but with your nose, ears, and the faculties of taste and touch. The more alert you are to what goes on around you, the more sense impressions you can incorporate in your writing and the more fully you can share your experience with the reader. Note how sight, sound, smell, taste, and touch are all incorporated in this one paragraph:

The Italian *festa* is one of New York's most colorful summer perennials and certainly its most exuberant. From now until early October, open-air carnivals will blossom forth in various parts of the city, and whether it is a one-block, one-day mini-fair, or the knock-down-drag-out super-*festa* that is San Gennaro, each assaults the senses with its sights, sounds, smells, tastes, and touches. Arcaded streets spanned by garlands of colored lights are veiled in the hazy smoke rising from deep-fat fryers and charcoal grills. Curbs are lined with open stalls offering temptation by way of food and drink, games of skill and chance, a glimpse of the future with a computerized handwriting analysis, or salvation for a dollar bill left at the gladiola-banked, gold-leafed shrine of the local patron saint. On jam-packed weekend nights one is carried up- or down-stream by a river of humanity, with lots of good-natured pushing and indifferent trampling. The combined aromas of hot oil, grilling meat, frying onions, oregano, garlic, sugar, vanilla, lemons, coffee, beer, wine, and the cool sea-breeze scent of iced clams and icier watermelon *almost* obscure the passing whiffs of sweat, tobacco, and a dozen cheap perfumes gone wrong in the humid night air. The backdrop is a solid wall of noise, with barkers' cries, the cracking of air rifles at target games, the ratcheting of number wheels, the sizzling and sputter of sausages on the griddle, and the screams and shouts of children and their exhausted, frantic parents. ("Come here so I can kill you," I once heard a mother yell in anger and relief, as she found her small son who had wandered away.) Most characteristic of all are the recordings of Neapolitan love songs blaring out of storefront P.A. systems, sung by tenors who hope to be next season's Sinatra.[6]

In the following passage about a visit to Bali, the sense description concentrates on color.

Physically, it is the most beautiful place I have ever seen, with trees and plants so luxuriantly and magnificently green that at first glance one can see little else; rice terraces draining artfully from high to low but so very gradually that the fall must be calibrated in fractions of inches; volcanic peaks whose slopes are as green as jungles; flowering trees and carved stone temples everywhere, and above it all a dazzling sun in a blue sky. But as though discontented with the natural beauty, the Balinese have applied their own colors to the canvas, the brilliant magenta, yellow, blue and pink of their clothes, the golden brown hue of their bodies, and the wild mixture of colors in the fruit and vegetables they carry. In Bali, the eye is under constant and violent assault.[7]

Personal Feeling

You may describe both the physical attributes of things and your own feelings toward them. In all instances, the description will be more effective if you take a particular stance or emphasize some special characteristic of your subject. Your choice of details and use of language are then determined by the point of view you have chosen.

William Golding finds the neck to be the center of interest in the following description of one of his preparatory-school teachers.

Mr. Houghton was given to high-minded monologues about the good life, sexless and full of duty. Yet in the middle of one of these monologues, if a girl passed the window, tapping along on her neat little feet, he would interrupt his discourse, his neck would turn of itself and he would watch her out of sight. In this instance, he seemed to me ruled not by thought but by an invisible and irresistible spring in his nape.

His neck was an object of great interest to me. Normally it bulged a bit over his collar. But Mr. Houghton had fought in the First World War alongside both Americans and French, and had come—by who knows what

[6] Mimi Sheraton, "An Eater's Guide to Italian Street Fairs," *New York* Magazine, 27 May 1974, p. 92.

[7] Caskie Stinnett, "Bali," *Travel & Leisure,* March 1974, pp. 21, 24.

illogic?—to a settled detestation of both countries. If either country happened to be prominent in current affairs, no argument could make Mr. Houghton think well of it. He would bang the desk, his neck would bulge still further and go red. "You can say what you like," he would cry, "but I've thought about this—and I know what I think!"

Mr. Houghton thought with his neck.[8]

In another instance, Mary McCarthy describes the combative nature of her grandmother. Note how the details have been chosen to support that characterization.

Combativeness was, I suppose, the dominant trait in my grandmother's nature. An aggressive churchgoer, she was quite without Christian feeling; the mercy of the Lord Jesus had never entered her heart. Her piety was an act of war against the Protestant ascendancy. The religious magazines on her table furnished her not with food for meditation but with fresh pretexts for anger; articles attacking birth control, divorce, mixed marriages, Darwin, and secular education were her favorite reading. The teachings of the Church did not interest her, except as they were a rebuke to others; "Honor thy father and thy mother," a commandment she was no longer called upon to practice, was the one most frequently on her lips. The extermination of Protestantism, rather than spiritual perfection, was the boon she prayed for. Her mind was preoccupied with conversion; the capture of a soul for God much diverted her fancy—it made one less Protestant in the world. Foreign missions, with their overtones of good will and social service, appealed to her less strongly; it was not a *harvest* of souls that my grandmother had in mind.

This pugnacity of my grandmother's did not confine itself to sectarian enthusiasm. There was the defense of her furniture and her house against the imagined encroachments of visitors. With her, this was not the gentle and tremulous protectiveness endemic in old ladies, who fear for the safety of their possessions with a truly touching anxiety, inferring the fragility of all things from the brittleness of their old bones and hearing the crash of mortality in the perilous tinkling of a tea cup. My grandmother's sentiment was more autocratic: she hated having her chairs sat in or her lawns stepped on or the water turned on in her basins, for no reason at all except pure officiousness; she even grudged the mailman his daily promenade up her sidewalk. Her home was a center of power, and she would not allow it to be derogated by easy or democratic usage.[9]

[8] William Golding, "Thinking as a Hobby," *Holiday*, August 1961, p. 8.

[9] Copyright, 1948, by Mary McCarthy. Excerpted from "Yonder Peasant, Who Is He" in *Memories of a Catholic Girlhood* by Mary McCarthy by permission of Harcourt Brace Jovanovich, Inc.

Movement

If you think of description as static, you should consider interlacing narrative with your description. This suggestion is simply a corollary of the advice given in the preceding chapter to weave description into narration. An anecdote, an incident, or a bit of dialogue, for instance, will do much to bring out the character of an individual. The description of a vacation locale has built-in narrative possibilities, including the use of historical background. Even when your writing is concentrated on a fixed area, you can achieve a narrative effect by describing the scene as you move about. Thus you might describe the Capitol in Washington from a number of vantage points; or you might describe Fifth Avenue by taking the reader for a walk from the fashionable plaza at 59th Street south to Washington Square, meanwhile noting the changes as you pass through one district to another.

The following excerpt from an article by Bruce Jay Friedman combines narration and character description. A New York City detective, identified only as John, calls at the author's apartment preparatory to taking him along on one of his daily rounds. John's paranoia is quickly established.

I keep an office apartment in Manhattan's East sixties and it was agreed that we would get our project under way at my place. John showed up punctually at eight one night, almost as though he'd been crouched at the door to make sure his arrival was right on the dot. As advertised, he turned out to be a dapper young man with a constant look of incredulity on his face, as though all his life someone had been whispering a long, amazing story in his ear. At times he seemed handsome, at other times quite snotty-looking; on appearance alone, it would not be surprising if he was revealed to be yet another Kennedy brother, long hidden away in some obscure religious order.

Halfway through the door, John began to fiddle with my lock, asking if it was the original one assigned to me by the building. I had to admit it was, and John, with a sad shake of his head, said that not changing it was a bad move on my part since the contractors had doubtless sold the basic key pattern to the rackets people, making my flat a pushover for burglars.

I told John that the building seemed to have pretty good security, with squadrons of attendants guarding each of the entrances. But John said they would all be sitting ducks for Argentinian husband-and-wife teams who would cut through a building of this sort like locusts through a wheatfield. "They are very fine-looking people who can walk through the front door on dignity alone. The husband breaks-and-enters and the wife's skirts are the stash. They have schools for these people in Argentina, training them in assorted con games."

John patted his breast pocket and said, "Here, incidentally, is the best place to carry your money." Tapping his backside, he said, "Here's the worst." Moving deeper into the apartment, John spotted the wraparound glass windows and said, "A voyeur's paradise, I see. I'd like to lock up nine perverts in a place like this. What you'd wind up with is one fat man and a bag of bones." Like other detectives I've known (and many Air Force officers) John is obsessed with the subject of homosexuality. Given the slightest conversational opportunity—or none at all—he will work in a fag reference or girlish imitation of some sort.[10]

Force

Descriptive words should be chosen for their vividness—their capacity to evoke strong images—and they should be combined into sentences that are fresh and varied in structure. Note the force in the following description from an article tracing the course of the Rebel River. In addition to his use of picturesque words, especially verbs, the author varies the sentence patterns with considerable skill. Beginning with a series of declarative statements, he switches to two questions at the beginning of the second paragraph and continues with several statements in parallel structure ("Yes, because . . ."). The whole effect is one of sharp, colorful pictures and swift movement. (See also Rules 22g and 30 in the "Handbook of English.")

Under a table of rock in a gorge deep in the brown, corrugated flanks of Mount Lebanon, a trickle of water flows into a still blue pool where wary trout cruise in chill shadows. After a moment's hesitation the stream spills northward, its course lined with willows, tamarasks and trailing greenery. Veering out of Syria's Lake Homs, the stream carves a path to aristocratic Hama, a green pocket at the edge of the great Syrian Desert, oozes through what was recently a reed-choked marsh, then wheels west toward Turkey and there, amid desolate beaches, slips quietly into the Mediterranean. This is the Orontes, the river called "Rebel."

Rebel? This unprepossessing stream, in places scarcely more than a creek ambling quietly, sometimes invisibly through the Fertile Crescent? Yes,

[10] Bruce Jay Friedman, "Lessons of the Street," *Harper's,* September 1971, p. 86. Reprinted by permission of Candida Donadio & Associates, Inc. Copyright © 1971 by Bruce Jay Friedman.

because in its twisting journey to the sea, it obstinately refuses to permit the high sills of mountain stone to block its passage and steadfastly husbands its waters against the thirst of swamp and desert. Yes, because it refuses to be one thing or another. It spurts into rapids, idles in ponds, races through spillways, seeps into red-brown farmland and cools shady villages clustered close to the thin green line that marks its course. Yes, because unlike all other rivers in the Crescent, which flow south, the Orontes flows north—an oddity explained by the slope of the Great Rift. A volcanic cleft in the earth running from the Great Lakes of East Africa via the Red Sea to Lebanon, the Great Rift tips imperceptibly at just the point where the Orontes begins to move and spills the small stream northward on a course 300 miles long and crowded with geological as well as historical paradoxes.[11]

The remainder of the article follows the course of the river, describing life along its banks and recounting the significant historical events that occurred there as far back as 1500 B.C.

EXERCISES

A. Write a paragraph describing objectively the most distinctive feature of one of the following:

1. Your family's home
2. Your car, cycle, stereo set, or other mechanical object you know well
3. A laboratory or classroom
4. A college building or the college campus
5. A route you frequently travel by foot

B. Write a paragraph in which you describe in affective (subjective) terms the same feature you described objectively in response to Exercise A.

C. Each word that follows names a pronounced characteristic of a person or place. Take *one* of the characteristics in each column and, for each, write a single paragraph in which you fill in the details relating to an actual person or place possessing the characteristic named.

[11] Joseph Fitchett and McAdams Deford, "A River Called Rebel," *Aramco World Magazine*, May–June 1973, p. 14.

Person	Place
Vulgar	Naturally wild
Peevish	Crowded
Enthusiastic	Noisy
Intelligent	Odorous
Cautious	Historical
Industrious	Quaint
Brave	Urbanized
Loving	Neglected
Physically attractive	Beautiful
Well-dressed	Nostalgic

D. The two passages that follow deal with essentially the same phenomenon—the sediments on the sea floor. The first is from a textbook on earth science; the second, from Rachel Carson's *The Sea Around Us*, a work which, upon its publication in 1950, marked the beginning of popular concern with damage to the environment. Compare the two for content and descriptive style.

1. The type of deposit found on the ocean floor is determined largely by the depth and distance of the floor from the land. On the continental shelves are found gravels, sands, clays, and shell deposits. Gravels, sands, and clays are found on the continental slopes, too.

Beyond the continental slopes most of the deep sea floor is covered with soft, fine *oozes*, or muds, composed largely of microscopic shells of dead sea organisms; but bits of volcanic dust, meteorite dust, and dust blown from the weathered rock of the lands are also included.

The sea-floor oozes are of two kinds. Calcareous oozes, made of lime, are formed chiefly from the remains of single-celled animals called *Globigerina*. Siliceous oozes, made of silica, are formed from the remains of one-celled animals called *Radiolaria*, or one-celled plants called *diatoms*.

However, there are some interesting exceptions in ocean-floor deposits. In the Pacific Ocean west of Central America and South America thin beds of almost pure volcanic ash have recently been discovered by Lamont scientists in waters miles deep. In polar regions even deep-water sediments contain large quantities of coarse sediments—gravels, sand, and silts—which were carried out to sea by icebergs.

In the very deepest waters of the ocean, on the floors of the great trenches, deposits of fine *red clay* are often found. This clay consists almost entirely of weathered rock, volcanic dust, and meteorite dust whose rusted iron is believed responsible for its brown or red color. The absence of shells is explained by the fact that at these depths the sea water contains so much carbon dioxide gas that it is able to dissolve most of the shell minerals. Both red clay and oozes accumulate at a very slow rate.[12]

2. Every part of earth or air or sea has an atmosphere peculiarly its own, a quality or characteristic that sets it apart from all others. When I think of the floor of the deep sea, the single, overwhelming fact that possesses my imagination is the accumulation of sediments. I see always the steady, unremitting, downward drift of materials from above, flake upon flake, layer upon layer—a drift that has continued for hundreds of millions of years, that will go on as long as there are seas and continents.

For the sediments are the materials of the most stupendous "snowfall" the earth has ever seen. It began when the first rains fell on the barren rocks and set in motion the forces of erosion. It was accelerated when living creatures developed in the surface waters and the discarded little shells of lime or silica that had encased them in life began to drift downward to the bottom. Silently, endlessly, with the deliberation of earth processes that can afford to be slow because they have so much time for completion, the accumulation of the sediments has proceeded. So little in a year, or in a human lifetime, but so enormous an amount in the life of earth and sea.

The rains, the eroding away of the earth, the rush of sediment-laden waters have continued, with varying pulse and tempo, throughout all of geologic time. In addition to the silt load of every river that finds its way to the sea, there are other materials that compose sediments. Volcanic dust, blown perhaps half way around the earth in the upper atmosphere, becomes waterlogged, and sinks. Sands from coastal deserts are carried seaward on offshore winds, fall to the sea, and sink. Gravel, pebbles, small boulders, and shells are carried by icebergs and drift ice, to be released to the water when the ice melts. Fragments of iron, nickel and other meteoric debris that enter the earth's atmosphere over the sea—these, too, become flakes of the great snowfall. But most widely distributed of all are the billions upon billions of tiny shells and skeletons, the limy or silicious

[12] Samuel N. Namowitz and Donald B. Stone, *Earth Science: The World We Live In*, 3rd ed. (Princeton, N.J.: D. Van Nostrand, 1965), p. 248.

remains of all the minute creatures that once lived in the upper waters.[13]

E. Study carefully the following descriptive passages and be prepared to discuss in class the distinctive characteristics of each. Consider especially the selection of details, the language used, and the author's attitude toward his subject.

1. It is not that Los Angeles is altogether hideous, it is even by degrees pleasant, but for an Easterner there is never any salt in the wind; it is like Mexican cooking without chile, or Chinese egg rolls missing their mustard; as one travels through the endless repetitions of that city which is the capital of suburbia with its milky pinks, its washed-out oranges, its tainted lime-yellows of pastel on one pretty little architectural monstrosity after another, the colors not intense enough, the styles never pure, and never sufficiently impure to collide on the eye, one conceives the people who live here—they have come out to express themselves, Los Angeles is the home of self-expression, but the artists are middle-class and middling-minded; no passions will calcify here for years in the gloom to be revealed a decade later as the tessellations of a hard and fertile work, no, it is all open, promiscuous, borrowed, half bought, a city without iron, eschewing wood, a kingdom of stucco, the playground for mass men—one has the feeling it was built by television sets giving orders to men. And in this land of the pretty-pretty, the virility is in the barbarisms, the vulgarities, it is in the huge billboards, the screamers of the neon lighting, the shouting farm-utensil colors of the gas stations and the monster drugstores, it is in the swing of the sports cars, hot rods, convertibles, Los Angeles is a city to drive in, the boulevards are wide, the traffic is nervous and fast, the radio stations play bouncing, blooping, rippling tunes, one digs the pop in a pop tune, no one of character would make love by it but the sound is good for swinging a car, electronic guitars and Hawaiian harps.[14]

2. When a modern comedian gets hit on the head, for example, the most he is apt to do is look sleepy. When a silent comedian got hit on the head he seldom let it go so flatly. He realized a broad license, and

[13] Rachel Carson, *The Sea Around Us* (New York: Oxford Univ. Press, 1951), pp. 71–72.

[14] Norman Mailer, *The Presidential Papers* (New York: Putnam, 1963), pp. 32–33.

a ruthless discipline within that license. It was his business to be as funny as possible physically, without the help or hindrance of words. So he gave us a figure of speech, or rather of vision, for loss of consciousness. In other words he gave us a poem, a kind of poem, moreover, that everybody understands. The least he might do was to straighten up stiff as a plank and fall over backward with such skill that his whole length seemed to slap the floor at the same instant. Or he might make a cadenza of it—look vague, smile like an angel, roll up his eyes, lace his fingers, thrust his hands palms downward as far as they would go, hunch his shoulders, rise on tiptoe, prance ecstatically in narrowing circles until, with tallow knees, he sank down the vortex of his dizziness to the floor, and there signified nirvana by kicking his heels twice, like a swimming frog.[15]

3. Sophie was not just the unmarried cousin who had always lived with us; her unmarriedness, her need of a husband, of some attachment, was our constant charge and preoccupation. To this my mother gave as much thought as she did to us, and at the center of our household, whether she was off in her room under the picture of two lovers fleeing from the storm, or in the kitchen with her friends from "the shop," drinking tea, eating fruit, or playing at the mandolin, one always saw or felt the vividly resentful figure of Sophie—Sophie beating at the strings of that yellow-shining, deep-bosomed, narrow-waisted mandolin, Sophie standing in front of the great mirror in the kitchen combing up her black black hair. As I watched with amazement, she kept one plait of hair suspended in her hand and then unceasingly and rhythmically, with the curved comb glistening in rhinestones, drew it with her long bony fingers through her hair, back and forth, until, when she had sifted and coiled and piled it up again, she would gather out the last straggle-thin threads in her hand as if it were a claw, and with a last sidelong look, manage with one gesture to throw a little ball of hair away and to give herself one last approving glance in the mirror. How natural it had always been to stand behind Sophie and to watch her combing her hair; or to steal into her room to smell the musk, the patchouli, the stingingly sweet face powder, the velvet skirts whose creases seemed still to mark the pressure of her body, the slips whose straps seemed just to have slipped off her shoulders. In the sepia dusk of the old prints, the lovers still ran rapturously before the storm, *Hope* held up her harp, and the bony gnarled wicker bookstand was filled with romantic

[15] James Agee, *Agee on Film: Reviews and Comments* (New York: Beacon Press, 1958), p. 3.

English novels like *The Sheik* and Russian novels in stippled blue bindings which Sophie alone could have brought into the house. And as if the difference had not already been made sufficiently clear between a mother who always seemed old to me and Sophie forever sultry and vivid, it was brought closer by the fact that my mother was at home all day and that Sophie appeared only in the evenings; when she was home, she was often elaborately sick in bed, with a bed jacket, while my mother brought her soft-boiled eggs and toast. The difference in their status was established by the way my mother worked, and waited on her, and told us to be quiet when Sophie was ill; we knew from my mother's constant expression of anxiety over her, from her anguished sulky looks of demanding love, that Sophie lacked something that everyone else in the world possessed.[16]

4. The Passenger Pigeon, or, as it is usually named in America, the Wild Pigeon, moves with extreme rapidity, propelling itself by quickly repeated flaps of the wings, which it brings more or less near to the body, according to the degree of velocity which is required. Like the Domestic Pigeon, it often flies, during the love season, in a circling manner, supporting itself with both wings angularly elevated, in which position it keeps them until it is about to alight. Now and then, during these circular flights, the tips of the primary quills of each wing are made to strike against each other, producing a smart rap, which may be heard at a distance of thirty or forty yards. Before alighting, the Wild Pigeon, like the Caroline Parrot and a few other species of birds, breaks the force of its flight by repeated flappings, as if apprehensive of receiving injury from coming too suddenly into contact with the branch or the spot of ground on which it intends to settle.

I have commenced my description of this species with the above account of its flight, because the most important facts connected with its habits relate to its migrations. These are entirely owing to the necessity of procuring food, and are not performed with the view of escaping the severity of a northern latitude, or of seeking a southern one for the purpose of breeding. They consequently do not take place at any fixed period or season of the year. Indeed, it sometimes happens that a continuance of a sufficient supply of food in one district will keep these birds absent from another for years. I know, at least, to a certainty, that in Kentucky they remained for several years

[16] From *Starting Out in the Thirties* by Alfred Kazin, by permission of Little, Brown and Co., in association with the Atlantic Monthly Press. Copyright © 1962, 1965 by Alfred Kazin.

constantly, and were nowhere else to be found. They all suddenly disappeared one season when the mast was exhausted, and did not return for a long period. Similar facts have been observed in other States.

Their great power of flight enables them to survey and pass over an astonishing extent of country in a very short time. This is proved by facts well known. Thus, Pigeons have been killed in the neighbourhood of New York, with their crops full of rice, which they must have collected in the fields of Georgia and Carolina, these districts being the nearest in which they could possibly have procured a supply of that kind of food. As their power of digestion is so great that they will decompose food entirely in twelve hours, they must in this case have travelled between three and four hundred miles in six hours, which shews their speed to be at an average of about one mile in a minute. A velocity such as this would enable one of these birds, were it so inclined, to visit the European continent in less than three days.

This great power of flight is seconded by as great a power of vision, which enables them, as they travel at that swift rate, to inspect the country below, discover their food with facility, and thus attain the object for which their journey has been undertaken. This I have also proved to be the case, by having observed them, when passing over a sterile part of the country, or one scantily furnished with food suited to them, keep high in the air, flying with an extended front, so as to enable them to survey hundreds of acres at once. On the contrary, when the land is richly covered with food, or the trees abundantly hung with mast they fly low, in order to discover the part most plentifully supplied.[17]

THEME TOPICS

1. You probably have a degree of skill in some special field. Perhaps you can draw or paint, participate in a sport or game, or perform some domestic chore. Whatever the skill, write a theme telling what it is and describing it in such terms that your readers can either gain a good understanding of it or learn to pursue it for themselves.

2. Write a theme consisting of a technical description of some phenomenon in science or nature that you have studied or personally observed.

[17] John James Audubon, *Ornithological Biography* (Philadelphia: Judah Dobson and H. H. Porter, 1831), I, 319–20.

3. From first-hand experience write a theme in which you describe one of the following:

(a) A place, preferably some limited geographical area which you have a special interest in and fondness for
(b) A journey (combine description with narrative)
(c) A street bazaar or some other colorful scene or event
(d) A family get-together, preferably on some special occasion like an anniversary, a birthday, or a national, religious, or ethnic holiday
(e) An unusual person—perhaps a relative, a friend, a neighbor, a teacher, an employer, or a street character
(f) A busy lunchtime in a restaurant, coffee shop, or cafeteria
(g) An air, railroad, or bus terminal
(h) A hotel lobby
(i) The poolside activity at a resort on a sunny, warm afternoon
(j) A theatrical performance

7 Analytical Methods

Any study of expository writing must include those papers, and parts of papers, concerned primarily with the clarification of ideas and concepts. We are referring here not to the attempt to persuade the reader of the rightness of any point of view—a kind of writing we shall take up later—but only to the process of explaining, analyzing, and interpreting what we know.

For this function a number of expository methods are available. Terms and concepts can be defined and illustrations given; causes and effects can be explored; ideas can be compared or contrasted, grouped or divided, so that relationships can be shown. This chapter will demonstrate these methods. For the application of corresponding methods to paragraph development, see Rule 31c in the "Handbook of English."

Definition

When you must use a term unfamiliar to the reader or a familiar term in a special sense, the need for definition becomes evident. In its simplest form, the definition is a synonymous word or phrase:

> One of the simplest basic ingredients is *phenol*. Perhaps you know this product better as *carbolic acid, an old-time household disinfectant.*

> In electric furnaces huge sticks of *graphite, a highly refined form of carbon,* are suspended from the top of the furnace into the hearth.

Definitions that must be technically accurate take a more organized form. This consists of (1) naming the thing defined, (2) putting it in its class, and (3) distinguishing it from other things in the same class. Here, for example, is a definition of a "model," as the term is used in science and technology:

> In the broadest sense, *a model* [name] *is a systematic presentation of an object or event* [class] *in idealized and abstract form* [distinction].

As you can see, such a definition by itself lacks not only interest, but clarity as well. Fortunately, however, the author has used a preceding paragraph to provide some idea of the need for models and the forms they take (charts, diagrams, mathematical equations, etc.). He now adds to the definition the explanation of a particular restriction of models (their abstractness) and an example of how that restriction is imposed in a specific application.

Models are somewhat arbitrary by their nature. The act of abstracting eliminates certain details to focus on essential factors. For example, an engineer may wish to build one type of model, namely a replica, of a prototype airplane. His aim is to test the effect of wind on a radical concept of wing design. Therefore, he must decide what factors bear most directly on the question at hand and then incorporate them into the model. He must at the same time ignore those items he considers extraneous. He thus finds it unnecessary to replicate all details of an actual airplane. The number of seats and the arrangement of wheel housing units are less important than obtaining a precise model of such key factors as weight distribution, speed, and heat resistance.[1]

After many pages of analogy, details, illustrations, and comparison and contrast, the reader has a considerably more informed idea of the advantages, limitations, uses, and classes of models, especially those relating to the study of communication, the author's primary interest. Other definitions are, of course, more suited to general audiences. In his notable study, *The American Language*, H. L. Mencken begins his examination of slang:

Slang is defined by the Oxford Dictionary as "language of a high colloquial type, considered below the level of educated speech, and consisting either of new words or of current words employed in some special sense."

Tracing the origin of the word *slang*, Mencken again refers to the Oxford Dictionary and calls on additional authorities, including Edward Weekley's *Etymological Dictionary of Modern English*, German philologian O. Ritter, and *Webster's New International Dictionary*. Mencken then settles down to his own analysis, including a division of slang into two classes.

Everyone, including even the metaphysician in his study and the eremite in his cell, has a large vocabulary of slang, but the vocabulary of the vulgar is

[1] C. David Mortensen, *Communication: The Study of Human Interaction* (New York: McGraw-Hill, 1972), pp. 29–30.

likely to be larger than that of the cultured, and it is harder worked. Its content may be divided into two categories: (*a*) old words, whether used singly or in combination, that have been put to new uses, usually metaphorical, and (*b*) new words that have not yet been admitted to the standard vocabulary.[2]

What fills out the chapter are numerous examples of both kinds of slang, instances of the movement of slang into the standard vocabulary, and a distinction between cant and argot, two low levels of language associated with slang.

Although the definition of technical terms has its place in expository writing, you may find more ample opportunities to use definition to clarify an idea or mental concept, which you can treat subjectively. Thus you may write a theme on an abstract quality like love or courtesy; or you can take a fairly common term like *gentleman*—or, for that matter, *public relations*—and show by the application of a distinctive point of view and the use of specific examples or similar devices what the term means to you.

Herbert Gold's essay "The Bachelor's Dilemma" is, in essence, a definition of the unmarried man. He begins:

The confirmed bachelor can be defined as the man who has the courage of his lack of convictions. Once he hasn't made his mind up, he really sticks to it. Swinging more and more wildly from his loosening trapeze, he is another reeling acrobat in the disorganized circus of American love and marriage.

Let us look at him with magical omnipresence from a privileged station in the air above a big-city party. It could be anywhere in America—New York, Cleveland, Chicago, St. Louis, Houston, Denver, San Francisco. There is a crowd—busy, talkative, curious, and anxious—of human creatures hoping for amusement. Chink of glasses, gaggle of laughter, roll of eye. The bachelor enters alone.

What does the wife see? Sometimes she sees him as a bad example for her own husband, but more often she has tender feelings for him. She sees forbidden possibility: a handsome, perfect cavalier, perhaps, mysterious and challenging—unlike her all-too-real, all-too-known, heavy, snoring husband. (The bachelor never snores in the fancy of this lady.) Or she knows he is lonely and she sees a sweet lost lad to be comforted. Or she sees a combination of challenge and need. She wants to feed him, ease him of sorrow, perhaps—she tucks a tooth into her thoughtful lip—perhaps find him someone. Or, in some cases, if she and he are crowded into a corner with

[2] H. L. Mencken, *The American Language*, 4th ed. (New York: Alfred A. Knopf, 1936), pp. 555, 557.

their drinks in their hands, she finds herself whispering those strange, hasty words in that bizarre language of invitation: "Call me. Call me. Hang up if a man answers."

Part of the rest of the essay is taken up with a description of the bachelor as viewed by other members of the party: a husband, a girl, another bachelor, and the bachelor himself. The author then continues with his own concept of the bachelor and his mode of life, especially his desperate search for love. The essay ends:

Usually he does not find the girl of his dreams. That ladder to the stars lies folded in a closet somewhere. Another evening has been spilled away with a swell kid whose name he will soon forget.

We do not see him during those moments when he is alone in his apartment, wondering why. *Alone.* Back home alone to his cold bed, his vacant hopes, and his Dacron shirt drying in the bathroom.[3]

The use of example in definition is well illustrated in Max Eastman's classic essay, "The Definition of Wit." Early in the essay the author makes the point that all famous wits have had a sense of the ludicrous, but that the mere prankster pretends to lead us toward a certain meaning and then abruptly lets us down. The wit, on the other hand, plays jokes that have meaning for the person who is expected to laugh. Eastman then explains the method he proposes to use in developing his point.

As this is a novel proposition, I am going to prove it by exhibiting a series of practical jokes, starting with a gross physical prank, and gradually moving in and speeding up, until we arrive at those instantaneous tricks with pure meaning which are commonly described as wit.

Herewith, some excerpts from Eastman's illustrations, which he numbered from one to thirteen:

Eight. Speaking of his marriage to his Eskimo bride, Hugga Much, Ring Lardner said:

I wanted the ceremony held at Old Trinity; Hugga said it was below her station—she usually got off at Columbus Circle.

There you do arrive at a meaning, but how much is it worth? How funny would it be to learn that Hugga usually got off at a certain subway station,

[3] Herbert Gold, *The Age of Happy Problems* (New York: Dial Press, 1962), pp. 34–35, 41.

if you had not been led away on the thought of a very different kind of station?

Nine. Josh Billings said:

There iz two things in this world for which we are never fully prepared, and them iz—twins.

Here the meaning at which we arrive has a little more dignity. It is at least a sensible and true remark. Twins, moreover, if you can get just the right attitude to them, are a trifle ludicrous to the imagination. Yet no one will contend that the meaning of this remark when it is finished—the truth, namely, that we are never prepared for twins—is what makes us laugh. We laugh because when we heard the words "two things," we expected the two to come separately, although we had no very good reason for it, and we got fooled. We laugh because our uncle Josh Billings has played a good joke on us, and we like it.

Eleven. . . . To be witty is to spring a neat practical joke upon a playful mind. That is the whole story. The function of your real meaning may be merely to make the sentence plausible, and the trick a success; your real meaning may be the weightiest in the world; or you may have no meaning at all. From the standpoint of producing comic emotion, it does not matter. The trick is what produces the emotion. For all Freud's abstruse labors on the various techniques of wit, we can substitute the single statement that wit employs every conceivable device by which a mind can be led on and then fooled.

Josh Billings printed the word *over* on his lecture program and left the other side blank. Joe Cook prints at the top of a page: "Below you will find a list of New York night clubs where a marvelous time can be had for little or nothing," and leaves the rest of the page blank. The jocular technique is the same. The only difference is that Joe Cook's joke means something. What it means, however, is no joke![4]

Comparison and Contrast; Analogy

Closely related to definition as an expository form is comparison and contrast. Comparison is an examination of things to discover in what ways they are similar or dissimilar. Contrast, on the other hand, is concerned only with the differences. Margaret Mead, writing several decades ago, compared third-generation Americans with antecedent generations and found many similarities in the way they

[4]Max Eastman, *The Enjoyment of Laughter.* Copyright © 1936 by Max Eastman. Copyright renewed © 1963 by Max Eastman. Reprinted by permission of Simon & Schuster, Inc.

adapt to their environment. One way, she noted, is their habit, when traveling, of establishing identity by asking, "What's your home town?" Others are the purposeful forgetting of European ancestry, their habit of forming ties by joining fraternal and civic organizations, and "the expectation that the child will pass beyond his parents and leave their standards behind him."[5]

The element of contrast is strong in Charles S. Brooks's "On the Difference Between Wit and Humor." Brooks's distinction is especially interesting in the light of Max Eastman's "Definition of Wit," cited on pages 117–118.

I am not sure that I can draw an exact line between wit and humor. Perhaps the distinction is so subtle that only those persons can decide who have long white beards. But even an ignorant man, so long as he is clear of Bedlam, may have an opinion.

I am quite positive that of the two, humor is the more comfortable and more livable quality. Humorous persons, if their gift is genuine and not a mere shine upon the surface, are always agreeable companions and they sit through the evening best. They have pleasant mouths turned up at the corners. To these corners the great Master of marionettes has fixed the strings and he holds them in his nimble fingers to twitch them at the slightest jest. But the mouth of a merely witty man is hard and sour until the moment of its discharge. Nor is the flash from a witty man always comforting, whereas a humorous man radiates a general pleasure and is like another candle in the room.

Following some additional exposition on the differences between wit and humor, Brooks offers examples of his experiences with two acquaintances, one notorious for his sharp wit and the other appreciated for his gentle humor. A later paragraph provides a summary statement and another example.

Real humor is primarily human—or divine, to be exact—and after that the fun may follow naturally in its order. Not long ago I saw Louis Jouvet of the French Company play Sir Andrew Ague-Cheek [a character in *Twelfth Night*]. It was a most humorous performance of the part, and the reason is that the actor made no primary effort to be funny. It was the humanity of his playing, making his audience love him first of all, that provoked the comedy. His long thin legs were comical and so was his drawling talk, but the very heart and essence was this love he started in his audience. Poor

[5] Margaret Mead, *And Keep Your Powder Dry* (New York: Morrow, 1942), pp. 27–29.

fellow! how delightfully he smoothed the feathers in his hat! How he feared to fight the duel! It was easy to love such a dear silly human fellow. A merely witty player might have drawn as many laughs, but there would not have been the catching at the heart.[6]

Contrast of another sort—that involving historical perspective—is employed in the essay "Country Music." In the following excerpt, the author points out the differences between the country music of the 1950s and that of the 1960s—taking the two decades through which his own experience with country music extended.

To hear country music, live, in and around a city like Boston was not easy in the 1950's. But it was there. One had to enter the night-town world of the city's "combat zone" to find it, at a place like the Hillbilly Ranch where, amid hookers, sailors, derelicts, and lonesome Southerners, both modern electrified country bands and a group like the old-timey and bluegrass Lilly Brothers played to appreciative audiences. In my experience nothing was more expressive of the meaning of country music in a changed world than Bea Lilly singing "Barbara Allen" in this crowded bar. His impassive face belied the impassioned, high-pitched nasal voice that sang the song's continuing truth, while across the street and around the corner the instruments and voices of Greek and Middle-Eastern music caught one's ear. Something unmeltable still survived in the city; perhaps just an echo, a reverberation, but it was assuredly not a sign of mass-produced music or innocuous love songs.

The folksong revivalists of the 1960's scorned this music, though they gradually accepted the old-timey and bluegrass strands. Modern country music was not traditional enough and those singers besides had the tastelessness to employ electrified instruments. I, like thousands of the urban and college-educated, followed the folksong revival with enthusiasm, but it was tempered in my case by uneasiness at the snobbery and misunderstanding that led to the neglect of country music. Predictably, the folksong enthusiasts soon discovered the Lilly Brothers but shunned the modern country styles heard in the same bar.[7]

As the essay continues, the author extends the perspective beyond his own experience, taking the reader back to the commercial beginning of country music in the 1920s and relating it to the rise of the recording industry.

As a form of comparison, analogy deals with only partial similarities. For example, one may draw an analogy between a heart and a mechanical pump; although the two things are emphatically unlike,

[6] Charles S. Brooks, *Chimney-Pot Papers* (New Haven: Yale Univ. Press, 1919), pp. 128, 133–34.

[7] Frederick E. Danker, "Country Music," *Yale Review*, Spring 1974, p. 393.

it is possible to show similarities in the way they operate. A fine example of analogy in a more humanistic vein can be found in Ruth Benedict's much admired work, *Patterns of Culture.* In a long passage describing the basic difference between the Pueblos of New Mexico and other North American Indian cultures, Benedict sees an analogous contrast between two ancient Greek cultures, the Dionysian and the Apollonian. The paragraph that follows catches the essence of the analogy.

The basic contrast between the Pueblos and the other cultures of North America is the contrast that is named and described by Nietzsche in his studies of Greek tragedy. He discusses two diametrically opposed ways of arriving at the values of existence. The Dionysian pursues them through 'the annihilation of the ordinary bounds and limits of existence'; he seeks to attain in his most valued moments escape from the boundaries imposed upon him by his five senses, to break through into another order of experience. The desire of the Dionysian, in personal experience or in ritual, is to press through it toward a certain psychological state, to achieve excess. The closest analogy to the emotions he seeks is drunkenness, and he values the illuminations of frenzy. With Blake, he believes 'the path of excess leads to the palace of wisdom.' The Apollonian distrusts all this, and has often little idea of the nature of such experiences. He finds means to outlaw them from his conscious life. He 'knows but one law, measure in the Hellenic sense.' He keeps the middle of the road, stays within the known map, does not meddle with disruptive psychological states. In Nietzsche's fine phrase, even in the exaltation of the dance he 'remains what he is, and retains his civic name.'[8]

Classification

All subjects, to a greater or lesser degree, lend themselves to division into their components. When those components consist of *classes* or *kinds,* the division is called "classification." When they consist of *parts,* the division is called "partition." Let's look into classification first.

You are, we'll assume, writing a theme about your experience with teachers. You can conveniently divide the subject by noting that there are authoritarian types, permissive types, and middle-of-the-road, or moderate, types. This classification is based on a teacher's behavior

[8] Ruth Benedict, *The Patterns of Culture* (Boston: Houghton Mifflin, 1959), pp. 78–79.

toward the class. There are, however, other bases for classification. Thus you may classify teachers by sex, comparing or contrasting your experiences with male and female teachers. Or you may classify your teachers on the basis of their teaching methods—for example, lecture, recitation, discussion—and try to establish a connection between the method used and the effectiveness of the teacher.

The need for consistency in such classification should be apparent. You should not, for example, classify teachers as authoritarian types, permissive types, and those over fifty years old, for then you would be confusing classification by behavior with classification by age. On the other hand, it is possible, in a classification based on behavior, to note a relationship between behavior and age and between behavior and sex.

In the following paragraph, the author offers a simple classification of trees as softwood and hardwood. Note the use of definition and incidental details to keep the exposition clear, informative, and interesting.

Although there are more than 1,000 kinds of trees in the forests of the United States, only about 100 have commercial value; that is, they are suitable for manufacturing into lumber, paper, and other products.

About 40 of the commercial species are softwoods, and the rest are hardwoods. Softwood trees are usually evergreen; that is, they keep their leaves the year round. Another name for softwoods is conifers. The word refers to the cones in which the seeds of most softwood trees develop. Coniferous, or softwood, trees also have needle-like or scale-like leaves.

Most of our building materials and wood for pulp and paper come from Douglas fir and white fir, hemlock, cypress, redwood, western cedar, larch, and spruces and 11 different kinds of pine trees—shortleaf, longleaf, loblolly, slash, ponderosa, northern white, Idaho white, sugar, lodgepole and jack pine.

Hardwoods have broad leaves and with few exceptions are deciduous trees; that is, they shed their leaves every autumn. Oak is the most important commercial species. Others are gum, yellow poplar, maple, tupelo, beech, cottonwood, birch, basswood, aspen, ash, hickory, walnut, sycamore, magnolia, willow, pecan and cherry.[9]

The next example shows the use of enumeration (first, second, third) in detailing the various kinds of subterranean traps from which oil is obtained. Such enumeration is valuable in connecting coordinate elements in many types of composition. Stylists, however, con-

[9] Press release of American Forest Institute, Washington, D.C.

sider the device somewhat mechanical and reserve it, as in this example, for formal or technical explanations, where the element of spontaneity is not a primary consideration.

Much oil and gas came to the surface of the earth ages ago and was lost. But not all escaped—much of it was caught in subterranean traps formed by the buckling and folding of the earth in early geologic time. These traps are of three major kinds. All of them consist of layers of porous rock covered by layers of nonporous rock.

For example, porous rock into which oil originally moved may have been folded upward, producing a subterranean formation shaped like an upside down bowl or saucer. Oil and gas may collect at the top of such an inverted bowl and be kept from escaping by an overlying nonporous layer. This kind of trap is known as an anticline.

A second kind of oil trap [called a fault, is formed at a] break in layers of rock. The rock on one side of the break has slipped up or down so that an uptilted end of a porous layer is thrust against a nonporous layer and thereby sealed.

In a third type of oil trap, buried sandstone that may once have been an old beach tapers off like a wedge, ending between layers of rock that are not porous. Here the oil moves through the sandstone until it can go no farther and collects to form an oil field. This type of accumulation is called a stratographic trap.[10]

In his sociological study, *White Collar*, C. Wright Mills classifies salesgirls in large stores into a number of types based on research attributed to James B. Gale. The types include the Wolf, the Elbower, the Charmer, the Collegiate, the Drifter, the Social Pretender, and the Old-Timer. The paragraph dealing with the Elbower is typical of Mills's use of specifics in dealing with all of the types.

Intensified, the wolf becomes *The Elbower*, who is bent upon monopolizing all the customers. While attending to one, she answers the questions of a second, urges a third to be patient, and beckons to a fourth from the distance. Sometimes she will literally elbow her sales colleagues out of the way. Often she is expert in distinguishing the looker or small purchaser from the big purchaser. 'I had to develop a rough-house technique here in order to make the necessary commissions. I just couldn't waste time with people who didn't want to buy but who were just killing time. And, after all, why waste time? Why should I bother with the pikers? Let the new clerks cut their teeth on them. Why waste good selling time with the folks who can't

[10] Stewart Schackne and N. D'Arcy Drake, *Oil for the World*, rev. ed. (New York: Esso Standard Oil Company, 1955), p. 32.

make up their mind, the ones who want to tell you their life-history, the bargain wolves, the advice-seekers, and the "I'm just looking" boobs? I want the women who buy three pairs of shoes at a time, stockings to go with them, and maybe slippers, too. I believe I can satisfactorily wait on five at a time, and keep them happy, so I wait on five! Look at my salesbook and note the total for the first five hours today. Traffic is good . . .'[11]

Partition

Partition has already been defined as the division of a subject into its parts. In technical fields, partition lends itself ideally to the writing of instructions, procedures, and the description of objects and processes. A car, for example, may be described in terms of its parts, as

Body
Frame
Engine

The commercial canning of fruits and vegetables may be described in terms of the steps taken in processing them:

I. Preparation for canning
II. Blanching the raw food
III. Filling the cans
IV. Hermetic sealing
V. Heat processing
VI. Cooking
VII. Labeling and casing

As the partitioning continues, further divisions of these steps can be made, so that, for example, the first step—preparation for canning—may be broken down as follows:

I. Preparation for canning
   A. Cleaning the raw food
   B. Sorting and grading
   C. Trimming and cutting
   D. Inspection

Partition is just as useful for dealing with nontechnical subjects. Here, for example, it is used by Bertrand Russell in a brief statement he made at the end of his long life as a mathematician and humanist.

[11] C. Wright Mills, *White Collar* (1951; rpt., New York: Galaxy Books, 1956), p. 175.

WHAT I HAVE LIVED FOR[12]

Three passions, simple but overwhelmingly strong, have governed my life: the longing for love, the search for knowledge, and unbearable pity for the suffering of mankind. These passions, like great winds, have blown me hither and thither, in a wayward course, over a deep ocean of anguish, reaching to the very verge of despair.

I have sought love, first, because it brings ecstasy—ecstasy so great that I would often have sacrificed all the rest of life for a few hours of this joy. I have sought it, next, because it relieves loneliness—that terrible loneliness in which one shivering consciousness looks over the rim of the world into the cold unfathomable lifeless abyss. I have sought it, finally, because in the union of love I have seen, in a mystic miniature, the prefiguring vision of the heaven that saints and poets have imagined. This is what I sought, and though it might seem too good for human life, this is what—at last—I have found.

With equal passion I have sought knowledge. I have wished to understand the hearts of men. I have wished to know why the stars shine. And I have tried to apprehend the Pythagorean power by which number holds sway above the flux. A little of this, but not much, I have achieved.

Love and knowledge, so far as they were possible, led upward toward the heavens. But always pity brought me back to earth. Echoes of cries of pain reverberate in my heart. Children in famine, victims tortured by oppressors, helpless old people a hated burden to their sons, and the whole world of loneliness, poverty, and pain make a mockery of what human life should be. I long to alleviate the evil, but I cannot, and I too suffer.

This has been my life. I have found it worth living, and would gladly live it again if the chance were offered me.

In this passage, the partition consists of the division of the three passions mentioned in the topic statement. Each of the next three paragraphs develops one of them, and the final paragraph offers a brief conclusion. This organization, both simple and effective, is applicable to many analytical themes. If any caution is to be observed, it is that, not having Russell's reputation for concrete achievement, the student writer is expected to be far less abstract in the treatment of his subject.

A more specific treatment of partition is provided by Melford E. Spiro's exposition of the underlying ideas of the kibbutz, a type of commune characteristic of many Israeli agricultural villages. Beginning with the most important ideal, the moral value of labor, the

[12] *The Autobiography of Bertrand Russell, 1872–1914* (New York: Harcourt, 1942), pp. 3–4.

author explains and demonstrates by example and contrast each of six such principles, including communal ownership, social and economic equality, and individual liberty. A short abridged excerpt will show how, through the use of example, the author is able to develop his theme with a minimum of generalization. Here Spiro tells of an experience in Kiryat Yedidim, the fictitious name he gives to the kibbutz which he had, for a time, joined.

Probably the single most important ideal upon which the entire kibbutz culture is based is what might be termed the moral value of labor. . . .

The importance attached to work is in constant evidence in Kiryat Yedidim and almost everyone responds to it. Work has become almost a compulsive habit, so that absence from work, even for good cause, elicits feelings of guilt. For three months, for example, the author had been working in the fields with a chavera whose work was characterized by drive and great energy, and who seldom took a break. He was amazed to discover somewhat later that this labor was torturous to her; she could not tolerate the heat, and she suffered constant pains in her arms and hands. Again, a chavera of the kibbutz donated one day a week to work in an immigrants' camp. She became quite ill, and was ordered to bed by the doctor. She complained, however, that she must return to her work, and when she heard that there was no one to take her place in the camp, she insisted on rising from her sickbed and returning to the camp. It is interesting to note in this connection that, according to the kibbutz nurse, there are no cases of malingering or of "goldbricking." . . .[13]

Cause and Effect

A common type of analysis states a condition and sets forth in detail its causes and effects. We have an economic recession. What caused it? What are its manifestations? Crime is rampant. Why? And where and among whom is it felt most? Drought grips the midwest. What meteorological conditions brought it on? What will happen to crops, to farmers, to farm prices, and to the consumer if the drought continues? In the following paragraphs, playwright Arthur Miller treats one cause of delinquency and some of its effects, but not before he establishes the point that deliquency is not entirely confined to the American urban poor.

[13] Melford E. Spiro, *Kibbutz: Venture in Utopia* (Cambridge: Harvard Univ. Press, 1956), p. 17.

Unlike most problems which sociology takes up, delinquency seems to be immune to the usual sociological analyses or cures. For instance, it appears in all technological societies, whether Latin or Anglo-Saxon or Russian or Japanese. It has a very slippery correlation with unemployment and the presence or absence of housing projects. It exists among the rich in Westchester and the poor in Brooklyn and Chicago. It has spread quickly into the rural areas and the small towns. Now according to Harrison Salisbury, it is the big problem in the Soviet Union. So that any single key to its causation is nowhere visible. If one wants to believe it to be essentially a symptom of unequal opportunity—and certainly this factor operates—one must wonder about the Russian problem, for the Soviet youngster can, in fact, go right up through the whole school system on his ability alone, as many of ours cannot. Yet the gangs are roaming the Russian streets, just as they do in our relatively permissive society.

So no one knows what "causes" delinquency. Having spent some months in the streets with boys of an American gang, I came away with certain impressions, all of which stemmed from a single, overwhelming conviction—that the problem underneath is boredom. And it is not strange, after all, that this should be so. It is the theme of so many of our novels, our plays, and especially our movies in the past twenty years, and is the hallmark of society as a whole. . . .

Other people, of course, have known boredom. To get out of it, they go to a bar, or read a book, or go to sleep, or turn on TV or a girl, or make a resolution, or quit a job. Younger persons who are not delinquents may go to their room and weep, or write a poem, or call up a friend until they get tired talking. But note that each of these escapes can only work if the victim is sure somewhere in his mind, or reasonably hopeful, that by so doing he will overthrow his boredom and with luck may come out on the other side where something hopeful or interesting waits. But the delinquent has no such sense of an imminent improvement. Most of the kids in the Riccio and Slocum book have never known a single good day. How can they be expected to project one and restrain themselves in order to experience such joy once more?

The word rebel is wrong, too, in that it implies some sort of social criticism in the delinquent. But that would confuse him with the bourgeois Beatnik. The delinquent has only respect, even reverence, for certain allegedly bourgeois values. He implicitly believes that there are good girls and bad girls, for instance. Sex and marriage are two entirely separate things. He is, in my experience anyway, deeply patriotic. Which is simply to say that he respects those values he never experienced, like money and good girls and the Army and Navy. What he has experienced has left him with absolute contempt, or more accurately, an active indifference. Once he does experience decency—as he does sometimes in a wife—he reacts decently to it. For to this date the only known cure for delinquency is marriage.[14]

Combining Analytical Methods

With few exceptions, one cannot engage in any extended exposition without combining a number of analytical and other expository methods. It is not unusual, for example, for a definition to be followed by a comparison or for a comparison to be followed by contrasting examples and specific details. Causes and effects also require details and sometimes a narrative line as well. In some instances, it is incorrect to say that one method *follows* another; rather, the methods are so intertwined that it is hard to tell where one leaves off and another begins. The few paragraphs that follow will illustrate the point. As the marginal notes suggest, the pattern of analysis is quite intricate. Still, the passage reads smoothly, and one is hardly aware of the rhetorical shifts.

Brain Size and Language

Several lines of evidence suggest the possibility that, at least in mammals, there may be a critical absolute brain size below which language as we know it is impossible and above which language as we know it is possible and even probable.

The topic statement relates brain size to language ability.

In saying "language as we know it," I am referring not to a literal, slavish view of the human languages as they currently exist; I am referring, rather, to the ability of these languages to transmit, store, and carry from one mind to another certain kinds of information and certain degrees of complexity of information.

A critical term is defined and a comparison of two interpretations is made.

14 Arthur Miller, "The Bored and the Violent," *Harper's,* November 1962, pp. 50–51. Reprinted by permission of International Creative Management. Copyright © 1962 by Arthur Miller.

This information can contain data related to the past, present, and future; it expresses to the mind of the receiver, however imperfectly, the state of mind of the sender, his plans, actions, and problems.

The author's meaning of the term is further explained.

In the case of the adult human, the critical brain size seems to be of the order of 900 to 1,000 grams. Detailed, microscopic examination of other mammalian brains of lesser and greater size than that of the human have shown the cerebral cortices of all to be remarkably alike. However, there are definite differences among brains of different sizes. Some areas are not involved in the immediate input-output computations. These are silent areas, the so-called associational or interpretive or "uncommitted" cortex, present in larger brains and not in smaller ones.

The silent areas are those that add computational abilities to the brain in such a way that language as we know it can be generated. Children born without these areas of cortex (microcephalics) are incapable of learning language as we know it.[15]

Running through the passage is an analogy between the functions of a computer and those of the brain.

The author returns to brain size and compares the human and animal organs.

The effects of different brain sizes on language ability are contrasted.

EXERCISES

A. Write a paragraph in which you define one of the following qualities. Find some concrete way—details, example, contrast, etc.—to make your point.

1. Taste
2. Courtesy
3. Ignorance
4. Perseverence
5. Courage
6. Ambition

[15] John C. Lilly, "Brain Size and Language," *Harper's*, December 1975, p. 117.

B. Develop a topic outline offering a methodical way to go about preparing a theme. Treating the task of composition as a process, divide it into its components, beginning with the selection of a topic and ending with the proofreading of the finished work.

C. Write the first paragraph of a theme on one of the following topics. In that paragraph develop a classification of your subject that would lend itself to development in the body of the paper. Within the limitations imposed on you, write as interesting a paragraph as you can.

1. High school teachers you have known
2. Student types
3. Dining out
4. Learning opportunities outside the classroom
5. Vacation choices

D. Develop, through the method of cause and effect, a paragraph dealing with some limited facet of one of the following subjects. Begin, preferably, with a concrete illustration.

1. The welfare problem
2. The housing shortage
3. Shoplifting by juveniles
4. Traffic congestion in the inner city
5. Poor-quality television programs
6. Low-caliber elected officials
7. The decline of the family farm
8. Small-town decay
9. The shrinking family
10. The rise of the nursing home "industry"

E. Be prepared to name and discuss the analytical methods used in each of the following passages. To what degree do you consider each passage effective? Support your answers by specific references to structure and language.

1. In the media era there are three functions that are worth distinguishing. One is the media as a transmitter of continually breaking news. The press transmits it at a brief time-remove but gives it some permanence. Radio and TV transmit it instantly, with TV as the supreme dramatic form.

The second is the media as a prime mover, digging out news,

starting and tracking down leads, not only responding to a news situation but taking an investigative hand in creating it. Whether we use the old phrases (the "expose" or "muckraking" role) or the new one (investigative journalism) the media cannot forego or neglect this function of theirs. It is difficult, sometimes dangerous; it requires both brashness and courage; it is often open to abuses. But it is there, as part of our time.

The third is the media as critic and assessor of people and events, whether through columnists, commentators, editorial writers, or (don't underestimate them) the Letters to the Editor, where people function in a critical do-it-yourself role. This, too, is part of the adversary function of the media. But to be done responsibly it must be done with a fairness the media have not always notably shown.[16]

2. According to the National Petroleum Council, the total United States output is projected to increase from about 57,000 trillion B.T.U.'s in 1971 to about 92,000 trillion B.T.U.'s in 1985—an increase of about 60 per cent. This would require annual capital expenditures for energy production to rise from about $26.5 billion to $158 billion over that period.

This trend coupled with the growing inefficiency in energy use means that energy production will consume an increasing amount of the total capital available in the United States for investment in new enterprises—in the factories that use energy and produce energy-using goods, not to speak of homes, schools and hospitals.

One projection based on present maximum estimates of energy-demand indicates that energy production could consume as much as 80 per cent of all available capital in 1985. This is, of course, an absurdly unrealistic situation in which the energy industry would, in effect, be devouring its own customers.

Thus, the compounded effects of a trend toward enterprises that inefficiently convert capital into energy production threaten to overrun the system's capacity to produce its most essential factor—capital.[17]

3. Most people can control what they do with arms and legs, with eye, face, or other muscles, using the kind of body control called voluntary. But until recently, medical science has believed and taught that nearly all other body functions, such as blood flow, body temperature, brain waves, or even residual muscle tension itself, were

[16] Max Lerner, "A Media Era," *New York Post*, 24 August 1973.

[17] Barry Commoner, "As the West Sinks Slowly into the Sun," *New York Times*, 20 November 1974.

under automatic regulation and beyond voluntary control. Almost without warning this dictum has collapsed. The new research has shown that people can learn to control even these kinds of body function.

The discovery of this ability of mind is abbreviated in the term *biofeedback*, an ideograph that describes the phenomenon of control over internal biological functions occurring when information about the function is "fed back" to the person whose biologic activity it is. It is a compound of a technology and a training procedure, using specially designed electronic instruments to detect and monitor physiologic activities (such as heart rate or brain waves). The individual practices to control the action of the monitor by manipulating his mental and internal activities, and the result is a learned, voluntary control over the physiologic functions monitored. It is a technique for extending the capabilities of the mind to control the body—and the mind.[18]

4. What is it, then, about Tanguy and Matta [surrealist artists] that at once mystifies and enchants me, that carries me beyond the specifics of either technique or theme, into a world totally their own creation, peopled with unidentifiable shapes, lit with a strange radiance? It's a world in which the life force seems to have been replaced by something else. It's not the death force, in spite of all Tanguy's gleaming parched white bones painted in a panorama of infinite space where sky and earth meet and are inseparably fused, or Matta's infernos, in which the "bones" have been levitated to some nameless sulphuric space where they burst in explosions of fire and brimstone.

What it is, rather, is the force of that world in between we know as dream. And that, of course, is Freud's world, which I've no intent or special knowledge to deal with here beyond mentioning that Matta himself once referred to it as a place where the search is for equilibrium between life and death.

It's also the world of surrealism, a word so long in currency it has become part of the language, though it still defies easy definition. What's clear about surrealism is only that its exponents draw their images out of fantasy and the subconscious, rather than the real and visible world, and that they depict them, generally, with great precision, even as dreams themselves, free of the "bondage" of reality and reason, may come to the dreamer in images as stunningly clear as they are irrational.[19]

[18] Barbara Brown, "Biofeedback: An Exercise in Self-control," *Saturday Review*, 22 February 1975, p. 22.

[19] Emily Genauer, "Art and the Artist," *New York Post*, 16 November 1974.

5. Politicians are pragmatists. They deal with specific events in the outer world, with this harvest or that economic crisis, this war or the next war. Their concerns tend to be short-term and topical—as we know all too well—and, although we *want* them to deal with specifics, from past experience we *expect* them to talk in generalities. More astonishingly, we expect politicians to distort facts, misrepresent their true intentions and beliefs, and, in short, lie to us. In the last few years political language has become so imprecise that we are left with what Robert Penn Warren calls "imaginary solutions to imaginary problems of imaginary people."

Poets, on the other hand, are idealists, or Edenists—or, as someone has put it, disillusioned Edenists. They are notoriously impractical, since "poetry makes nothing happen." Like politicians, poets deal in specifics, but they do so in order to shed light on the human condition in general. That is, whereas the politician is expected to use generalities to talk about specific events, poets use specific events to discover and express larger truths. Poetry talks about the inner man in the outer world and, doing so, helps us to see what is—what might be.[20]

6. Planning is inseparable from management and both involve those elements associated with art: intuition, creativity, discernment, command of the work tools and materials, an appreciation of the interaction of form and function.

There are planners and then there are *planners*—at least two models: the Cook's-tour model, the Lewis and Clark model.

The Cook's tour defines a precise schedule on a well-defined route; it moves in orderly progression amid known landmarks. The aim is to plan to avoid contingencies; the unexpected is to be avoided; all is schedule, order, routine.

I prefer the Lewis and Clark model, with its sense of adventure as it explores new frontiers. They envisioned their goal, assembled the minimum resources, and had the nerve and the courage to take the unexpected in stride. They knew that success depended upon painstaking completion of the smallest of plans—building of the campfires, fording of the stream, delicate negotiations with the Indians. Their epic success was a triumph of small, daily successes—all within the context of a goal and clear sense of direction. The Cook's tour provides the illusion of planning in a world of imagined stability. The Lewis and Clark tour is an adventure into the unknown. Can there be any choice for us?[21]

[20] Peter Klappert, "Let Them Eat Wonderbread," *Saturday Review*, 7 October 1972, p. 48.

[21] Harold L. Enarson, "The Art of Planning, or Watching You Get It All Together," *New York Times*, 4 October 1975.

THEME TOPICS

1. Write a theme in which you contrast the first-rate with the shoddy. To make your theme concrete, you may deal with some specific facet of one of the arts, for example, architecture, music, literature, painting—taking two or more works for close examination; or you may prefer to work with some more mundane subject like compact cars, new homes for the poor, stereo sound systems, photographic prints, bicycles, omelet pans.

2. Using comparison and contrast, write a theme on one of the following pairs:

(a) City living and suburban living
(b) Having a job and working for yourself
(c) Bachelorhood and the married state
(d) Liberals and conservatives
(e) The urban college and extra-urban college
(f) Traditional furniture and modern furniture

3. Write a full-length theme defining one of the qualities listed in Exercise A (page 129). Begin in any way you see fit.

4. Write the *whole* theme suggested in Exercise C on page 130.

5. Write a full theme on one of the topics listed in Exercise D (page 130), developing your subject by means of cause and effect.

6. Write a theme on one of the following topics, using any appropriate analytical methods.

(a) Choosing a career (or hobby)
(b) The ideal roommate (or friend)
(c) Self-sufficiency for America's energy needs
(d) Study techniques
(e) The unemployables
(f) Labor-saving in the home
(g) Alternatives in college teaching methods
(h) The punishment of criminals
(i) Required vs. elective courses
(j) Tools for effective study

8 Argument and Persuasion

As a writer, you have occupied occasionally the role of confider, at other times the role of observer, guide, or instructor. Your objective, in each role, was to address the reader as a willing partner and expose to his examination such events, personal experiences, and ideas as you wished to communicate. There was no question of agreement or disagreement on the reader's side, only the question of whether you were interesting, clear, and accurate.

Now it is time to examine another kind of writing—one in which exposition still plays an important part, but which removes you from the role of neutral communicator and puts you in the role of advocate. No longer are you concerned only with sharing ideas with the reader; you want to influence or control his thoughts and actions. Writing undertaken with that purpose is known either as argument or persuasion. Although the distinction between the terms is not uniformly observed, we will use *argument* to mean the use of rational means to reach a valid and convincing conclusion, and *persuasion* to define writing that influences the reader through appeals to the emotions. The techniques of persuasion may not be valid in a logical sense, but they still have the potential to bring about the desired result. Thus an advertisement, or an editorial, or a political tract is often persuasive even when it is not convincing.

Argument: The Proposition

You can hardly begin arguing a point rationally until the subject you are arguing is clear, at least to yourself. The subject of the argument is generally referred to as the proposition or thesis. In a debate, the proposition may be stated as a resolution, "Resolved that . . ."; in other instances, the proposition is a simple declarative statement requiring support: "The proceeds of the Senior Class book sale should go to the United Fund." Sometimes the proposition is not directly stated because it is implicit in the argument, or it is withheld until later in the composition in order to give the reader a chance to arrive at the desired conclusion by himself. Whatever the proposition, however, it should be sufficiently unambiguous to permit an examination on its merits. To say that the domestic oil companies' profits are "not large enough" leaves the question, "Large enough for what?" The proposition might be more clearly stated, "The oil companies are not making enough profit to ensure increased production of domestic oil." Now it is possible to address oneself directly to the question raised.

The Issues

After the proposition is clear in your mind, the next step is to divide it into the related points, or "issues," on which the outcome of the argument depends. In his essay "In Favor of Capital Punishment" Jacques Barzun sets forth the issues as stated by the opponents of the death penalty.[1]

1. Punishment for crime is primitive and vengeful.
2. The death penalty does not deter.
3. The risk of taking life in error is appalling.
4. A civilized state must be committed to the sanctity of life.

Barzun then addresses himself to the issues. He agrees with the first two points, but maintains that the imposition of the death penalty is not so much to punish the culprit or to hold him up as an example, but to protect others. With respect to the third point, the possibility of judicial error, Barzun falls back on several cases of record. In one typical instance a man unjustly imprisoned for a year is offered a small payment in compensation by the state, but not before his wife has died, his children and his aged parents have been moved to the workhouse, and he himself is incurably insane. Barzun questions whether, in such circumstances, the punishment is any more revocable than death. The remedy, he says, is not the abolition of capital punishment, but the reform of the criminal justice system, including the jury system, the rules of evidence, and the machinery of appeal.

In approaching the final issue, the need to uphold the sanctity of life, Barzun argues that "most abolitionists belong to nations commit-

[1] Jacques Barzun, "In Favor of Capital Punishment," *American Scholar,* 31 (Spring 1962), 181–91.

ted to spend half their income on the instruments of war" and that we can expect from experience that the clergymen in the movement will bless their arms, "the sixth commandment notwithstanding."

If believers in the sanctity of life prefer to think of it as something to be observed only within the nation, Barzun asks whether they are also against the principle of self-defense against cutthroats, or of policemen firing at fleeing bank robbers, even when they miss and hit an innocent bystander instead.

Putting aside the author's acknowledged wit and incisive expression—putting aside the interest arising from what must be for many of his readers an unpopular position—the effectiveness of Barzun's argument depends on a number of rational supports. These boil down essentially to *evidence* and *reasoning*, the two substantive means on which all argument depends. Let's see what can be learned about using them effectively in your own writing.

Evidence

To argue rationally, you use what evidence you can to support your position. Evidence takes the form of facts and, to some degree, opinions. The valid use of both is subject to some important qualifications.

Facts. Factual evidence is information known to be true. It may consist of your own observations and experiences, as well as the reports of others, including a great variety of published data. These are facts:

I was graduated from the Thomas Jefferson High School. [From a student's autobiography]

John Walker of New Zealand was the first man to run the mile in less than 3 minutes, 50 seconds.

Charles Dickens is the author of *David Copperfield.*

The United States formally entered the Second World War on December 7, 1941.

Dr. Walter Reed reported in 1901 that yellow fever was transmitted by the mosquito *Aëdes aegypti.*

Facts are most convincing when they meet the following criteria.

1. They come from reliable sources. These sources include first-hand experience, reports of reliable witnesses, court records, government publications, the official proceedings of professional and scientific bodies, audited and notorized statements, and such standard reference books as dictionaries, encyclopedias, and annuals.

2. *They are clearly stated.* The statement "4,356 contributors gave up to $10,000 each to their Alma Mater last year," leaves considerable doubt both as to individual and total contributions. A clearer statement would read, "4,356 contributors gave $1,560,000 to their Alma Mater last year."

3. *They are verifiable.* The statement "A nationwide survey taken by the National Commission on Marijuana and Drug Abuse in 1972 indicated that 15 percent of the eighteen and over population and 14 percent of the twelve–seventeen age group had used marijuana at one time or another" can be verified by reference to the Commission's report. However, the statement "Marijuana smoking is immoral" is personal opinion; and although many persons may have the same belief, there is no way in which the statement can be verified. What can be verified is the attribution of such a statement. Thus "The Reverend Thomas Sykes says that marijuana smoking is immoral" is a fact if, indeed, it represents the minister's view.

4. *They are relevant.* The argument may be made that the helicopter is an ideal transport medium for inner cities because it needs little landing space. However, the fact that the American Electric Power Company used a helicopter to haul steel to build 29 miles of remote power lines is irrelevant to the argument because the instance cited does not relate to intra-urban transport.

In this day of the computer and instant information, a great deal of confidence—perhaps too much—is placed in facts. Executives are often pictured as hard-headed individuals constantly demanding, "Give me the facts." As we get into other forms of evidence and other modes of argument, we should bear in mind that facts can tell only what has already happened; they cannot tell what will happen. And, of course, convincingly predicting what *will* happen, or maintaining what *should* happen, is really at the core of all argument. Facts do help. They help us to make inferences, to draw analogies, to predict the future on the basis of past events. But they cannot do the work by themselves. They need the application of sound judgment and valid reasoning.

Opinion. An opinion is a personal belief or a judgment that can be drawn from facts, but it cannot be accepted with certainty. Two opinions:

The new library is an architectural disaster.

Stricter government control of over-the-counter drugs will result in greater safety and the saving of millions of dollars a year for the unwary consumer.

Neither of these statements can be proved. The first is a value judgment on which there could be considerable disagreement even among experts. The second is a belief stated as a prediction that may or may not turn out to be correct. Even though these statements are not facts, however, they may yet carry some weight as evidence. The first statement, for example, would be convincing to many if it came from, say, Philip Johnson or some other respected architect; the second, if it was the expression of the director of the federal government's Food and Drug Administration.

The ideal conditions for the use of opinions as evidence include the following.

1. *The opinion comes from a person qualified as an expert.* An opinion on the best preparation for a career in law can be expected to carry more weight coming from a successful practicing attorney than from a grocer. A prediction about the turn of events in Greek politics during the next six months is more credible from a *New York Times* correspondent assigned to Greece than from a student of Homer.

2. *The opinion relates to the specific subject area in which the expert practices.* A couturier, for instance, is qualified to express an opinion on fashion, but he would be far less credible if he expressed an opinion on the Federal Reserve Bank's monetary policy.

3. *The opinion comes from an unbiased source.* The opinion of a literary work can be expected to carry more conviction when it comes from a reviewer in the *Atlantic* than from the publisher's blurb. Even when the person expressing an opinion is not an expert in the usual sense, he may yet be believed if he is perceived as having no incentive to exaggerate or lie. Thus many prospective car buyers would rather accept the opinion of a neighbor who owns a particular make of car than that of a salesman for the same make.

For another example, Barzun expresses many opinions in the essay cited earlier, among them the belief that under many conditions imprisonment is worse than death. Possibly some experts would agree. On the other hand, many other experts undoubtedly would support the opposite view, and probably not the least convincing among them would be those men and women who had already served time in prison.

4. *The opinion is timely.* For instance, a 25-year-old opinion on the causes of lung cancer may not be relevant today because of more recent findings and because of changes brought about by social and environmental conditions.

Reasoning

The development of evidence is but one of the starting points from which reasoning may proceed. Reasoning itself is the process by which conclusions are drawn. Although reasoning is common in all discourse, it is so much a part of our intellectual development that we are not always aware that we are using it. We make statements like, "The small potato crop means higher prices this winter," or "April is an uncertain time for a vacation," and we hardly realize that the statements are the result of a computerlike logic that gives them their validity. Of course, not all our reasoning is so automatic. Often we do not have enough data in our heads to indicate a conclusion, and we must get the data first. Sometimes, even when we present no evidence, our conclusions are incontrovertible; at other times, with a rash of evidence, our conclusions are still open to dispute. If the process of argument thus seems capricious, perhaps it will appear less so after an examination of the several kinds of reasoning. The principal methods are inductive and deductive reasoning. Less disciplined, but widely employed, are reasoning by analogy and causal reasoning.

Inductive Reasoning

Sometimes called the "scientific method," inductive reasoning draws conclusions from supporting evidence. The starting point is a hypothesis, or supposition, which is to be proved true or untrue. If, for example, you think that there has been an "inflation" in college grades over the last ten years or so—your hypothesis—you might try to get some evidence from published sources, from college records, and from personal inquiry among senior members of the faculty. As a result of your research, you may be able to draw some conclusion about the truth of your hypothesis.

The following passage is an extract from evidence given by an executive of the Exxon Company, U.S.A., before a Congressional committee, on competition in the oil industry. The charge had been made that the larger companies were squeezing the smaller companies out of business in order to monopolize the field. Note the hypothesis at the beginning and the use of facts to disprove it. (Incidentally, you should distinguish between *inductive reasoning* and the *inductive order*, which is explained on page 26 and illustrated in Rule 31d(2).)

A frequent charge made against the structure and performance of the industry is that small, nonintegrated firms are not able to enter the industry because of certain barriers to entry created by the major oil companies. Again, for each level of activity, these charges can be disproved with facts. Small, nonintegrated and partially integrated firms have grown and prospered.

In *exploration and development*, thousands of independents are engaged in the effort to find and produce oil and gas. In 1973 (according to an *Oil & Gas Journal* survey) independents and drilling funds were involved in 78.1% of the 2,208 new field discoveries, new pay openers and extensions based on the number of wells drilled. (These data may not accurately reflect the amount of reserves discovered by independents versus majors, however.) They have demonstrated their ability to expand and compete against the majors even in the very high-risk, high-cost areas such as offshore and in Alaska. For example, in the December 1972 and June 1973 sales in the Gulf of Mexico, about 75 companies competed either singly or in combines. In the Alaska/North Slope lease sale, over 130 competitors bid and independents spent over one third of the total dollars. . . .

In *refining*, the capital requirements to enter on an efficient scale are often larger than in production, but this has not prohibited smaller firms from entering or expanding. Since 1950, about 80 refineries have been built with a total capacity of about 3 million barrels/day. About one fourth of this new capacity was built by independent refiners. . . .

In *marketing*, entry of non-major gasoline marketers has already been shown in the section on concentration ratios and in Exhibit 1. From 1968 through the first half of 1974, independent marketers have increased their share of the U.S. market from 22.1% to 29.5%. This is conclusive proof not only of entry, but of the profitability of nonmajor brand marketing. . . .[2]

The conclusions reached through inductive reasoning are not always correct, but efforts can be made to ensure against some common errors.

[2] W. T. Slick, Jr., Senior Vice President of Exxon Company, U.S.A., before the Senate Judiciary Committee on Antitrust and Monopoly, 21 January 1975, transcription issued by the Company in *Competition in the Petroleum Industry*, n.d., p. 14.

1. *The evidence should be sufficient.* It would be unreasonable, for instance, to conclude that canned peaches are in short supply just because your local market was out of them the last time you were there. Again, when sampling methods are used in research, precautions must be taken that the sample is large enough to minimize the margin of error. For example, you cannot reasonably take the result of interviews with three students in a freshman class of two hundred and then draw statistically valid conclusions applicable to the whole class.

2. *The evidence should be representative.* Let us assume that you want to learn the amount of consumer information to be found in magazine advertisements. If you pick *The New Yorker* for your study on the premise that it carries more consumer advertising than any other magazine in the country (at last count, it did!), your results will not be typical. The reason is that *The New Yorker* is a "class" magazine carrying a great deal of *prestige advertising*, a type notoriously low in information content. Magazines like *Good Housekeeping, Esquire,* and *Time* would be more representative.

3. *Negative instances should be taken into account.* If you mention only those instances that support your hypothesis, or if you fail to give enough weight to contrary information, your conclusion will have no adequate support. Some years ago a cigarette manufacturer had a research firm conduct tests to determine the brand preferences of college students. Advertisements later reported a marked preference for the manufacturer's brand in college after college. One wondered how the results could be so one-sided until he realized that the advertiser was reporting only the "successful" tests.

4. *The conclusion should not embrace more than the evidence warrants.* Often the refusal to believe an inductive argument is caused not by any distrust of the evidence, but by a failure to accept the inferences. "These facts prove that Computer A is better than Computer B" may cause the reader to question the meaning of the word "better" and wonder whether the issue is as clear as it is made to appear. A more acceptable conclusion might read, "These facts suggest that Computer A will serve our special needs for at least the next five years, with considerable savings over Computer B in installation and operating costs." Qualifying terms like *may, should,* and *probably* also play an important part in making conclusions acceptable when they might otherwise arouse some skepticism.

Deductive Reasoning

Most of our reasoning in ordinary discourse is deductive. Unlike inductive reasoning, which arrives at general conclusions from an examination of specific evidence, deductive reasoning takes the generalizations and uses them as a way of finding new knowledge. Thus specific research and experience lead inductively to the conclusion that "machines save labor." Deductive reasoning will assume that conclusion and build upon it to reach a new conclusion applicable to a specific instance—for example, "The Magnus Electric Saw saves labor." If no evidence is given to support the initial assumption, it is because the evidence was confirmed long ago and is now taken for granted.

In the following paragraph from a concurring decision of the United States Supreme Court, the accepted truth is in the italicized sentence "Only a free and unrestrained press can effectively expose deception in government." The rest of the paragraph—in fact, the whole opinion—rests on that premise, with weight given to it by the fact that it was incorporated into the First Amendment to the Constitution.

In the First Amendment the Founding Fathers gave the free press the protection it must have to fulfill its essential role in our democracy. The press was to serve the governed, not the governors. The Government's power to censor the press was abolished so that the press would remain forever free to censure the Government. The press was protected so that it could bare the secrets of government and inform the people. *Only a free and unrestrained press can effectively expose deception in government.* [Italics added.] And paramount among the responsibilities of a free press is the duty to prevent any part of the government from deceiving the people and sending them off to distant lands to die of foreign fevers and foreign shot and shell. In my view, far from deserving condemnation for their courageous reporting, the *New York Times*, the *Washington Post*, and other newspapers should be commended for serving the purpose that the Founding Fathers saw so clearly. In revealing the workings of government that led to the Vietnam War, the newspapers nobly did precisely that which the Founders hoped and trusted they would do.[3]

[3] Mr. Justice Black, Concurring, United States Supreme Court, October Term, 1970, No. 1873, *New York Times Company* vs. *United States*, and No. 1885, *United States* vs. *The Washington Post Company et al.*, June 30, 1971.

Deductions are drawn from a form of argument called a *syllogism.* In formal logic, the syllogism consists of a major premise, a minor premise, and a conclusion. The major premise is the broad initial assertion, the minor premise names a specific application, and the conclusion is the deduction drawn from the two premises. An example would go like this:

MAJOR PREMISE: All full-time students at the college are covered by health insurance.

MINOR PREMISE: Joe Smith is a full-time student.

CONCLUSION: Joe Smith is covered by health insurance.

In practice, the syllogism is invariably abbreviated, so that it takes a form like "Joe Smith must be covered by health insurance because he's a full-time student" (major premise omitted); or, simply, "Joe Smith is covered by health insurance" (major and minor premise omitted). Even though it is not formally expressed, the syllogism is a useful means of testing the validity of a deductive argument. Basically, the validity lies in the truth of the premises and the correctness of the structure of the syllogism. Without becoming unnecessarily technical, the rules of validity can be stated as follows:

1. *The premises must be true.* If, for example, one builds an argument against the government-owned Tennessee Valley Authority (TVA) power project on the premise that government ownership is inconsistent with democracy, his argument is weak because his premise is false. No doubt many examples can be found to show that government ownership is practiced in democracies. A more valid argument against government ownership of TVA might be that it competes unfairly with privately owned power companies.

2. *The major premise must include all cases.* "We have to raise our prices because our labor costs have gone up" assumes the major premise "Higher wages make higher prices necessary." But this is only sometimes true. It is possible that economies can be effected in areas other than labor that would make higher prices unnecessary.

3. *The parts of the syllogism must be correctly related; otherwise the conclusion will be invalid.* This syllogism is badly constructed:

MAJOR PREMISE: All citizens pay taxes.

MINOR PREMISE: Helen pays taxes.

CONCLUSION: Helen is a citizen.

The fact that Helen pays taxes does not make her a citizen. The faulty conclusion derives from a basic fault in the structure of the syllogism. If the parts are to be correctly linked, they should follow the pattern below:

A1 C1
MAJOR PREMISE: All citizens pay taxes.
B1 A2
MINOR PREMISE: Helen is a citizen.
B2 C2
CONCLUSION: Helen pays taxes.

Here the subject of the major premise (A1) is correctly echoed in the predicate of the minor premise (A2), the subject of the minor premise (B1) is also the subject of the conclusion (B2), and the predicate of the major premise (C1) agrees with the predicate of the conclusion (C2).

Causal Reasoning

In causal reasoning, the writer seeks to establish a connection between cause and effect. The gist of the argument that follows is that the failure of food production to keep up with uncontrolled population growth (the cause) will lead to the extinction of the human race (the effect).

Medical discoveries and widespread advances in sanitation have improved health and prolonged life spans and thus have lowered *death rates*. But *birth rates* have not gone down proportionately.

In Mexico, for example, four persons are born for one who dies. At this rate there will be 84,000,000 Mexicans in 20 years compared with 42,000,000 now. Many other countries have similar growth rates.

The *rate* of world population growth is also going up and up. It was 1.8 percent annually in 1955. If present trends continue, it will be 3.0 percent in 1985.

This means that world population will grow from 3.3 billion in 1965 to more than 5 billion in 1985.

Two simple figures highlight the extent of the population deluge. From the dawn of history until 1930, the world only reached a population of 2 billion. But in one century thereafter, population at present trends will multiply *seven* times to 14 billions. . . .

But this is not the whole story. Population in most hungry countries is growing much faster than in the opulent countries. For instance, in Latin America population will almost triple from 250 millions to about 700 millions by the end of the century. India, kept from the brink today by U.S.

wheat shipments, will add 200 million people by 1980. By contrast, in Europe the growth rate of 0.8 percent a year is expected to remain constant over the next two decades.

Food production is not keeping step with this rocketing population growth. Latin America, as an example, increased its total production of food over the last five years, but with 25 million more people, the *average individual* had 7 percent less to eat.

As the population flood inundates the world, time runs out at frightening speed. Either we grasp the sane solution of population control now or we are headed towards mass suffocation. Unless we act, man may have to "accept extinction with the dinosaur and dodo bird," historian Arnold Toynbee concludes.[4]

Although, as in the instance cited, causal reasoning may be supported by hard facts and figures, some readers may find the connection between the facts (the causal data) and the conclusion (the predicted effect) untenable. For example, it might be argued that nature has its own way of controlling large populations, or that technological developments will increase the food supply to the point where it will support much larger populations, or that the problem is not the shortage of food, but its inequitable distribution.

One common fallacy in causal reasoning is attributing an effect to one cause when the real cause may very well be something else. A student of economics writes:

Retail sales were down 5 percent last week in comparison with the same period a year ago. This proves that people are hoarding their money.

What the student failed to consider were the heavy rains during the week as well as the Department of Labor statistics showing more unemployment and smaller paychecks than a year ago.

Another fallacy is concluding that something is necessarily a cause when it merely precedes. A new driver is involved in an automobile accident. His parents jump to the conclusion that his inexperience was the cause. Actually, his inexperience was only a prior condition. The real cause, it turned out, was a malfunctioning brake. In another situation, the hiring of a new sales manager is immediately followed by a rising sales curve. Was the executive responsible for the rise? He would certainly like everyone to think so, but the "insiders" know

[4] *The Population Bomb*, a pamphlet published by the Population Policy Panel of the Hugh Moore Fund, New York, reprinted from Morris Freedman and Paul B. Davis, *Contemporary Controversy*, 2nd ed. (New York: Macmillan, 1973), pp. 232–33.

that the real cause was the introduction of a popular new line that just happened to coincide with the new appointment.

Still another fallacy in causal reasoning is confusing the cause with the effect. A paper manufacturer, for example, advertises as follows:

> We asked 100 company officers, "How many magazines, books, and newspapers have you read in the past week?" The total of their answers: magazines, 338; books, 53; newspapers, 1,490.
>
> Then we asked 100 men in the same age group whose salaries had never quite reached $7,500 a year. 229 magazines for them—and only 28 books. That's about a fourth of a book apiece. The conclusion is as clear as print. *Men who read more achieve more.*

Much as one would like to believe that heavy reading leads to advancement in business, isn't it just as probable that advancement in business leads to heavy reading? And might not the last sentence have said, "Men who achieve more read more"?

Reasoning by Analogy

Useful in other literary forms, analogy can also strengthen argument and persuasion. Through analogy, the writer draws conclusions about one instance on the basis of its similarities to another. The writer must take care, however, that the things being compared are sufficiently similar to permit valid inferences. In arguing against making the Postal Service self-supporting, one may, for example, cite the fact that other major departments of the federal government are traditionally run at a deficit. The question remains, however, whether the services performed by the Postal Service are comparable to those performed by, say, the State Department or the Department of Agriculture.

The example just given involved a *literal analogy*, that is, one in which the terms of the comparison are to be taken in their strict sense. A *figurative analogy*, on the other hand, is one in which a metaphoric, or imaginative, element is present. In the following paragraph, for instance, the author draws a conclusion about racial strife in South Africa on the basis of an Arthurian legend:

> The white man's "no" to the black man is daily more uncompromising and automatically induces an equal and opposite charge in the spirit of the black man. On both sides the eve has darkened and still is darkening. Anatole France said that human beings frequently kill one another over the

words they use, whereas if only they had understood the meaning the words were trying to convey they would have embraced. There is a higher level to that truth. I wonder if you remember the legend of the white and the black knight in the saga of the Round Table? Two knights, one in black armour and one in white, were riding through a dark and dangerous wood in search of a chivalrous errand when they met. Visors down because of probable danger they challenged one another and, without further explanation, fought. They fought until they were both wounded to death and finally lay stretched out on the grass beside each other. Then, in dying, they uncovered their heads—and saw that they were brothers.[5]

Both literal and figurative analogy require the reader to take a big jump from the instance at hand to the instance offered as a parallel, and the leap is always logically hazardous. Still, as in the example just cited, the analogy can be quite moving. To take yet another example, one might see flaws in the following analogy equating Britain's troubles with "uncollected garbage," but the metaphor makes an effective conveyance for the writer's point.

The London street where I live and work was built up in the Edwardian heyday—a church and churchyard on one side, on the other a row of low apartment houses, their red-brick façades elaborated with domes and pediments, bays and balconies, mullioned windows and ornamental ironwork. It seems at first glance the very picture of a prosperous, well-ordered community. But look a little closer. Alarming piles of garbage lie heaped along the curb; soggy debris clogs the gutter; the sidewalk wobbles with loose, broken paving blocks. Wherever the eye rests, past solidity collides with present disorder.

So it is with Britain. Yesterday's glories and today's troubles mingle in perplexing confrontation. We all know that Britain is awash in a sea of adversity—that year after year it spends more than it earns, that its industrial plant is obsolescent and its labor force unproductive, that it totters on the brink of runaway inflation, that it has dropped within living memory from being the richest of Europe's nations to a position where it will soon be running neck and neck with Italy for tenth place in the continent's pecking order. These unpleasant truths make up the uncollected garbage on the curb, but they seem so utterly discordant with what we know of British history, so out of tune with British tradition, that we avert our eyes and focus instead on the imposing edifice behind—on the mother of Parliaments, the cradle of industrial technology, the land of poets and philoso-

[5] Laurens van der Post, *The Dark Eye in Africa* (New York: William Morrow, 1955), pp. 76–77.

phers and explorers and scientists—whistling to ourselves all the while that there'll always be an England.

But the garbage continues to accumulate. . . .[6]

Emotional Appeals

A common characteristic of persuasion is the use of emotional appeals. Such appeals are based on the recognition that people have a variety of motives, needs, and desires, and that these have an immeasurable influence on their behavior. People have likes and dislikes; fears, ambitions, and prejudices; and a consuming interest in their own comforts, appetites, and well-being. The effectiveness of any appeal is naturally decided not only by its substance but by the language and tone. A susceptible audience may respond well to the writer's use of humor, sarcasm, ridicule, or name calling. Another audience may be more responsive to a matter-of-fact presentation.

In the sensational Leopold-Loeb trial of more than a half century ago, the renowned attorney Clarence Darrow pleaded in a Chicago courtroom for the lives of the two young men with good family backgrounds who were alleged to have kidnapped and brutally murdered a child. This short excerpt is an example of Darrow's use of emotional appeal to influence the court. Note, in the plea for consideration of the families of the accused, the use of the words "proud names," "bar sinister" (stigma), "unborn children," and "honorable families."

Has Your Honor a right to consider the families of these two defendents? I have been sorry, and I am sorry for the bereavement of Mr. and Mrs. Franks [parents of the dead child], for those broken ties that cannot be healed. All I can hope and wish is that some good may come from it all. But as compared with the families of Leopold and Loeb [the accused], the Franks are to be envied—and everyone knows it. . . . Have they [the family of the accused] any rights? Is there any reason, Your Honor, why their proud names and all the future generations that bear them shall have this bar sinister written across them? How many boys and girls, how many unborn children, will feel it? It is bad enough however it is. But it's not yet death on the scaffold. It's not that. And I ask Your Honor, in addition to all that I have said, to save two honorable families from a disgrace that never ends, and which could be of no avail to help any human being that lives. . . .[7]

[6] Roland Gelett, "Is Britain Dying?" *Saturday Review*, 8 February 1975, pp. 12–13.

[7] Quoted from Frank B. McMahon and Sarah B. Resnick, *The Self in Society* (Englewood Cliffs, N.J.: Prentice-Hall, 1973), pp. 89–90.

A different situation calls for a different approach, and in the following example, the author derisively introduces the reader to at least one cause of the present sad state of the American Indian. Although the appeal to prejudice has its humorous overtones, it effectively drives home the author's point.

Into each life, it is said, some rain must fall. Some people have bad horoscopes, others take tips on the stock market. McNamara created the TFX and the Edsel. Churches possess the real world. But Indians have been cursed above all other people in history. Indians have anthropologists.

Every summer when school is out a veritable stream of immigrants heads into Indian country. Indeed the Oregon Trail was never so heavily populated as are Route 66 and Highway 18 in the summer time. From every rock and cranny in the East *they* emerge, as if responding to some primeval fertility rite, and flock to the reservations.

"They" are the anthropologists. Social anthropologists, historical anthropologists, political anthropologists, economic anthropologists, all brands of the species, embark on the great summer adventure. For purposes of this discussion we shall refer only to the generic name, anthropologists. They are the most prominent members of the scholarly community that infests the land of the free, and in the summer time, the homes of the braves.

The origin of the anthropologist is a mystery hidden in the historical mists. Indians are certain that all societies of the Near East had anthropologists at one time because all those societies are now defunct.

Indians are equally certain that Columbus brought anthropologists on his ships when he came to the New World. How else could he have made so many wrong deductions about where he was?

While their historical precedent is uncertain, anthropologists can readily be identified on the reservations. Go into any crowd of people. Pick out a tall gaunt white man wearing Bermuda shorts, a World War II Army Air Force flying jacket, an Australian bush hat, tennis shoes, and packing a large knapsack incorrectly strapped on his back. He will invariably have a thin sexy wife with stringy hair, an IQ of 191, and a vocabulary in which even the prepositions have eleven syllables.[8]

Consistency of Belief

A common method of persuasion is based on a psychological theory known by various names, including "the theory of cognitive dissonance" and, more simply, "inconsistency theory." This theory is

[8] Vine Deloria, Jr., *Custer Died for Your Sins* (New York: Macmillan, 1969), pp. 78–79.

based on the observation that people tend to resist a belief that runs counter to one they already possess. The theory holds that the inconsistency in beliefs produces a disequilibrium, or mental conflict, which can be resolved only through the rejection of one of the beliefs. The advocate of a contrary belief is obviously anxious that his view prevail. A key method for achieving the desired end is to suggest that the new idea is consistent with some other belief the reader already holds.

Let us say that a large segment of the public believes that the big oil companies are at least indirectly responsible for much of the pollution of our air and waters. Let us also assume that the same public believes that the money poured into the construction of highways through the federal government's Highway Trust Fund would be better spent in developing mass transit facilities. What more imaginative way is there, then, for an oil company to help dissipate distrust than by expressing the view that some of the money now spent for highway construction should be used to develop mass transit? When a large oil company did, in fact, take such a position publicly, it probably hoped to carry the more general impression that it was concerned with the public good and could be trusted to act responsibly in its normal business operations.

Many other instances can be found in which the writer, at least temporarily, abates the reader's doubts or opposition by introducing ideas that are likely to be consistent with those he already holds. Thus, in a speech before a group of journalists, who are not always known for their sympathy toward business, the chairman of a large banking conglomerate began his case against government regulation with a statement supporting the principles of the Founding Fathers—a posture with which hardly any American would find fault. The compliment to the press in the last sentence of the following excerpt from the speech is also consistent with the view they hold of themselves.

> As we approach the bicentennial of our republic, it is useful to remember that our founding fathers faced hard times—much harder than those which are with us today. They, too, had to make some tough choices. Thomas Jefferson expressed the problem in a nutshell: "We are not to expect to be translated from despotism to liberty in a featherbed."
>
> The great principles of our government laid down by our founding fathers embody a vast distrust of centralized governmental power and an unswerving dedication to the proposition that government rests on the

consent of the governed. No sector of our society has been more vigilant than the press in keeping that proposition always before us.[9]

A somewhat more artful application of the principle of consistency is evident in an essay on Utopian thinking by Paul Goodman, the educational philosopher. Realizing that he has a reputation for being "impractical," he begins by setting forth some of his impractical ideas.

The ceremony at my boy's public school commencement is poor. We ought to commission the neighborhood writers and musicians to design it. There is talk about aiding the arts, and this is the way to advance them, for, as Goethe said, "The poetry of public occasions is the highest kind." It gives a real subject to the poet, and ennobles the occasion.

Similarly, we do not adequately use our best talents. We ought to get our best designers to improve some of the thousands of ugly small towns and make them unique places to be proud of, rather than delegate such matters to professionals in bureaucratic agencies, when we attend to them at all. A few beautiful models would be a great incentive to others.

In our educational system, too much is spent for plant and not enough for teachers. Why not try, as a pilot project, doing without the school building altogether for a few hundred kids for most of the day? Conceive of a teacher in charge of a band of ten, using the city itself as the material for the curriculum and the background for the teaching. Since we are teaching *for* life, try to get a little closer to it. My guess is that one could considerably diminish the use of present classrooms and so not have to increase their number.

After citing more than a half dozen such ideas, the author concedes the faults of the style of thinking they represent. He says that it is risky, that it confuses administrative divisions, that it throws incompatibles together, that the proposals themselves are impracticable and probably illegal. "Finally," he says,

such proposals are impractical if only because they assume that the mass of people have more sense and energy than they in fact have. In emergencies, people show remarkable fortitude and choose sensible values and agree to practical expedients because it is inevitable; but not ordinarily. . . .[10]

With the grounds for opposition to his proposals thus laid out,

[9] Remarks by Walter B. Wriston, chairman, Citicorp, before the Society of American Business Writers, Washington, D.C., 5 May 1975.

[10] Paul Goodman, *Utopian Essays and Practical Proposals* (New York: Random House, 1961), pp. 12–15.

Goodman proceeds to examine the dilemma created by the conflict between the things he believes people want and the apparent hopelessness of obtaining them; and he concludes with a number of illustrations showing how the dilemma can be solved. From this outline of Goodman's argument, one can see how it is possible for a writer to mute opposition by at least beginning on a track the reader can follow without strain on his existing beliefs.

Authority

Inconsistency theory has another application in the citing of credible sources in support of the persuader's thesis. In the banker's speech mentioned earlier, we saw the author call on Thomas Jefferson for support. Later, in a part of the speech not shown here, he cites a supportive decision by the United States Supreme Court and quotes an expert he describes as "the Pulitzer Prize historian Daniel J. Boorstin." At the very end he claims that his views accord with sound liberal doctrine as expressed by Woodrow Wilson: "The history of liberty is a history of limitations of governmental power, not the increase of it." In thus citing a number of authorities, the writer or speaker is in effect borrowing their credibility to enhance his own.

It is not to be assumed that the appeal to authority is useful only in supporting a weak pleader or a weak case. In fact, all good scholars make it a point to know the views of others in their field and often cite those views. And if the liberal footnoting required by the rules of scholarship also enhances the scholar's reputation for learning, who is to quarrel with this result?

Benjamin DeMott is himself a scholar, but in an article arguing for a reexamination of the premises of the Scholastic Aptitude Test (SAT), he draws liberally on the testimony of several other scholars, including Dr. Michael Wallach, whom he describes as "a Duke University psychologist, whose specialty for a decade has been intelligence and 'creativity' "; Dr. Herman Witkin, head of the Personality and Social Behavior research group at the Educational Testing Service, which administers the SAT; and Dr. Robert Glaser, head of the University of Pittsburgh's Learning Research Center—all of them individuals with impressive credentials.[11]

[11] Benjamin DeMott, "Beyond the SAT's: A Whole-Person Catalog That Works?" *Saturday Review*, 4 May 1974, pp. 68–70.

At one point in his article, DeMott seeks support for the argument that the present tests "are blind to the very nature of what they seek to evaluate," and that "they take no account of the variousness of the ways in which human beings learn, the extent to which learning is an act of adaptation to the environment, and the likelihood that alterations and variations in learning environments can call into being aptitudes unknown to anyone now." In a quotation from Dr. Glaser, DeMott obtains the support he needs, as we see in this continuation of the article.

Speaking to this theme at another meeting held last year, Robert Glaser, head of the University of Pittsburgh's Learning Research Center, noted: "What used to be called general animal intelligence, and tested in the old experiments as general problem-solving ability, now appears to be an aggregate of special specific abilities, each ability evolving in response to environmental demands. Animals are "intelligent" in quite different ways that can be better understood in relation to the ecological demands of their particular environments than in terms of the older notion of [an] ordering of animals according to their intelligence. . . . Gophers are better at maze problems than horses and other open-range animals. Animals show a great many different talents evolved as adaptations to their different worlds. The older work in animal behavior appears to have overemphasized abstractions like general maze brightness as a criterion behavior for study."

To this statement by Dr. Glaser, DeMott adds his own comment, at the same time drawing additional support from Dr. Witkin.

And a parallel overemphasis on abstractions is standard in human-aptitude testing. To correct it, Witkin contends, we need "comprehensive coverage of the whole cognitive domain—extending into the personality domain." That is to say, we need tests which reveal the cognitive style of persons, clarify relationships between learning methods and aptitude, and predict the kind of instructional setting or option likeliest to nourish the personal gifts in question.

Emotive Language

The suggestion carried by words has much to do with their power to persuade. Informative, or literal, language is intended to represent things as they are—clearly and accurately, with little room for interpretation. Emotive language, on the other hand, changes the literal truth to accord with the feelings of the writer and the effect he wants to create. As a weapon, however, emotive language must be used with care, for it can strike the user as well as the target. When a man speaks of his young *daughter* (literal word) as a *brat* (emotive word), we learn something about the child, but we probably also learn more about the parent than he wants us to know.

One kind of emotive language is the euphemism. This is a mild, indirect, or vague expression that serves as a substitute for an equivalent expression that might be considered offensive, blunt, or harsh. One might, for example, call a man convicted of bribing a public official a "crook"; but the accused will try to soften opinion by claiming to have "made a mistake in judgment." In wartime, an army command will say its troops "took up new positions" when in fact they "retreated." While feeling about the Vietnamese "war" was still running high, President Ford was careful to refer to it, in a press conference, as the Vietnamese "experience." To lessen the shock to the financial community of a dismal quarter-year performance, a company, rather than admitting a "default" on the dividend, announces that it has "postponed action" on the dividend, meaning that no dividend will be paid.

Another kind of emotive language consists of prejudicial words that proclaim a speaker's low esteem of a subject without qualification. Some of these are "stereotypes," class symbols used to stigmatize an individual. Thus, merely labeling a person as an "intellectual," a "liberal," a "capitalist," or a "politician" may be sufficient to create a bias against him. A related technique is to substitute for the standard class designation another word of less favorable connotation; thus a union leader is called a "union boss," the head of a government department is called a "bureaucrat," and a business manager is called a "capitalist stooge." Even more abusive names are used to demean a person's racial, religious, or ethnic background.

An opposite technique is the use of prepossessive words, those intended to create a bias in favor of a person or idea. "The Palm Garden" creates an image that "Lizzie's Tea Room" does not. "Congress of Industrial Organizations" is more dignified than "Workers' Association." Words like *American, independence, equality, intelligent, discriminating, exclusive,* and, yes, *mother,* are also generally in favorable repute, and writers and speakers often use them for persuasive purposes. Sometimes the prejudice words and prepossessive words are used together, as in the following paragraph. Note especially the prejudicial use of the words *media, doomsayers,* and *alarmist,* on the one hand, and the prepossessive use of the words *distinguished, human ingenuity,* and *free society,* on the other.

> The compulsion of the media to turn every scrap of bad news into a full-blown crisis distorts our perspective. It neglects to remind us that troubles may be news, but they are by no means new. This negative emphasis ignores the decisive role of human ingenuity in a free society. One of our distinguished historians, Barbara Tuchman, recently put it this way: "The doomsayers work by extrapolation; they take a trend and extend it, forgetting that the doom factor, sooner or later, generates a coping mechanism. . . . You cannot extrapolate any series in which the human element intrudes; history, that is the human narrative, never follows, and will always fool, the scientific curve." How right is her insight; alarmist's curves frequently are based upon downward trends. As early as the sixth chapter of Genesis some believed the world was headed downhill. The doomsayers were already looking back upon better times: "There were giants in the earth in those days."[12]

To this day, Abraham Lincoln's speeches move readers by their religious and moral force. In the closing paragraph of his Second Inaugural Address, note the invocation of God's name and the number of words with connotations of sympathy, words like *charity, right, widow, orphan,* and *peace.*

> With malice toward none; with charity for all; with firmness in the right, as God gives us to see the right, let us strive on to finish the work we are in; to bind up the nation's wounds; to care for him who shall have borne the battle, and for his widow, and his orphan—to do all which may achieve and cherish a just and lasting peace among ourselves, and with all nations.[13]

In contrast, the following paragraph reflects the attitude of a vintage author, H. L. Mencken, known at least partly for his misanthropic excesses. The paragraph consists entirely of brazen assertions—a common technique of propagandists—but these combined with the abundant use of invective had undoubted appeal to the prejudices of Mencken's many devoted readers.

> Whatever may be the good faith of the plain people in their recurrent moral rages, it must be obvious that the politicians who heat them up are

[12] Walter B. Wriston, "The Whole Oil, Chicken, and Energy Syndrome" (Address to The Economic Club of Detroit, 25 February 1974).

[13] From *Selections from the Letters, Speeches, and State Papers of Abraham Lincoln,* ed. Ida M. Tarbell (Boston: Ginn and Company, 1911), pp. 118–19.

mainly frauds. This has been visible in every war that the United States has ever seen, including even the Revolution. The more the history of the revolutionary era is studied, the more it becomes apparent that most of the current prophets were smart fellows with something to sell. Sam Adams offers an excellent example, and John Hancock is another; there were plenty more to the southward. Abolition, a moral movement quite typical of America, was largely staffed by shysters of the same sort. The example of Prohibition is too recent to need mention. Its clerical leaders were all fanatics lusting to rule or ruin, and their political accomplices were almost unanimously plain mountebanks. I was familiar with both groups during the 1910–30 period, and I can think of no exception. Bishop Cannon was a sadist not far from downright insanity, and most of the more conspicuous drys in the two houses of Congress were notoriously boozers. Once I asked William H. Anderson, then head of the Anti-Saloon League in Maryland, how it came about that perhaps a majority of his supporters in the Maryland Legislature were drunkards. He replied that they were more truthworthy—at least for his purposes—than honest drys. The latter, two times out of three, would have ideas of their own, and it would be difficult to keep them from objecting and rebelling against orders from headquarters. But the dipsomaniacs could be trusted, for all they thought of was their jobs, which the Anti-Saloon League undertook to guarantee. For the rest, they were free to pursue their villainies unimpeded.[14]

EXERCISES

A. What kinds of information might you seek in order to argue each of the following propositions? Do any of the propositions themselves need to be defined more clearly? Explain.

1. We are seeing the beginning of the decline of the cities.
2. School busing increases racial tensions.
3. The loss of farmlands to housing developers threatens our food supplies.
4. Commercialism in sports encourages cynicism about the American ideal of sportsmanship.
5. Family ties are strengthened by open attitudes toward sexual conduct.

B. Comment on the methods of reasoning used in each of the following statements. Do you find the statements convincing? Explain your answer.

[14] H. L. Mencken, *Minority Report* (New York: Knopf, 1956), No. 255, pp. 180–81.

1. ON THE FAILURE OF PREFABRICATED HOUSING:

There cannot be any true prefabrication of building components unless and until the nation's building industry agrees to adhere, rigorously, to a set of dimensional and qualitative standards. In a free society, in which manufacturers of building components are at liberty to concentrate upon clobbering the competition rather than collaborating with it, the tendency is for each manufacturer to establish standards that will be as different as possible from those of all his competitors. A manufacturer of kitchen appliances, for example, makes a point of scaling and coloring his wares so that they cannot easily be used in conjunction with those of another manufacturer. The reason, of course, is that the manufacturer wants his customers to use *only his* products. Thus it is highly unlikely that dimensional and qualitative standardization, without which true prefabrication is unthinkable, can be impressed upon today's U.S. building industry—either by persuasion or by force.[15]

2. ON THE MORAL CLAIMS OF AMERICAN MINORITIES:

I think there is a good deal of weight in the view that blacks and Hispanics (and American Indians) have a larger moral claim on American society than the white ethnic groups. At the same time, we should not exaggerate its weight. Many blacks, after all, were also free immigrants, from the West Indies and elsewhere. Most Mexican-Americans were free immigrants or the descendants of free immigrants, and all Puerto Ricans voluntarily chose to enter an English-speaking environment. And if the argument is that the black and Spanish-speaking immigrants were forced to migrate for economic reasons, so were the immigrant ancestors of the present-day European ethnic groups.

The fact is that we cannot separate ethnic and racial groups into two classes: those who have suffered, economically and culturally, in America, and therefore deserve redress, and those who have not. Perhaps at the extremes we might make such a distinction, but each group's history is so special that no such broad separation makes sense. Consider the Asian-Americans—Chinese and Japanese. They are neither European nor white; they did not come as slaves; they were not conquered; they did suffer race prejudice and, in the case of

[15] Peter Blake, "Can Technology Solve the Housing Crisis?" *Atlantic*, October 1975, p. 54.

the Japanese-Americans during World War II, confiscation of their property and even incarceration; they do well economically and their children do well in school. To which class of immigrant groups do they belong?[16]

3. ON THE IRRESPONSIBILITY OF SOCIAL SCIENTISTS:

Scientists can destroy public trust by deed as well as by word. Jane and Irving Piliavin, for instance, conducted an experiment in Philadelphia in which they had a confederate collapse in a moving subway train. They were trying to test people's inclination to help their fellow human beings. As the stooge fell, he released a trickle of "blood" from an eyedropper in his mouth. Sometimes the experimenters placed another confederate near the impending drama. He wore an intern's jacket, priest's attire or ordinary street clothes. These variations were used to see what effect they would have on the passengers' reactions. The Piliavins staged this gory melodrama about 50 times on the same subway line.

Stanley Milgram is so clever at devising his experiments that their ingenuity blinds us to their manipulative and condescending nature. He dubbed one famous deception "The Lost-Letter Technique" [see PT, June 1969]. Here researchers walked around a city dropping several hundred stamped letters. The envelopes were addressed to organizations such as "Friends of the Nazi Party" or "Friends of the Communist Party." On the basis of whether people ignored the letters, mailed them, destroyed them, opened them, or whatever, Milgram judged how the citizens felt about diverse organizations. Those who found these letters were unwitting participants in social research.

Recently, Milgram devised a "lost-child technique." He turns a nine-year-old youngster out on the street, and the lost child tries to enlist adult aid to telephone home. Milgram has staged fights between husbands and wives on the Massachusetts Turnpike, and concocted other schemes of public deception.

This type of research is not only devious, it is irresponsible. As the news spreads that bloody victims are only research stooges, that lost children are in fact part of an experiment, and that lost letters are really props to test political attitudes, the already scant propensity for one person to help another seems likely to diminish.[17]

[16] Nathan Glazer, "Ethnicity and the Schools," *Commentary*, September 1974, p. 57.

[17] Donald P. Warwick, "Deceptive Research: Scientists Ought to Stop Lying," *Psychology Today*, February 1975, p. 40.

4. ON THE NATURE OF HUMAN FULFILLMENT:

The natural direction of human ripening is from the smaller to the larger world, is toward the realization and habitation of ever-widening realms of meaning and value. Just as the young are moved from the inside out through increasingly complex stages of perception and thought demanding corresponding changes in their environment, so, too, adults are moved from inside themselves through increasingly complex stages of relation: past the limits of ego and into a human community in which the self becomes other than it was. Seen in this way, human fulfillment hinges on much more than our usual notions of private pleasure or self-actualization, for both of those in their richest forms are impossible without communion and community, an acknowledgement of liability, and a significant role in both the polis and the moral world. To be deprived of those is to be deprived of a part of the self, and to turn away from them is to betray not only the world but also the self, for it is only in the realms in which others exist that one can come to understand the ways in which the nature of each individual existence is in many ways a collective act, the result of countless other lives.

The traditional image for what I am talking about has always been the harvest: the cooperative act in which comrades in a common field gather from it what they need. One finds the image repeated in the work of Camus, Giono, Kropotkin, Lawrence, Silone, and many others, but the most vivid example I know is the scene in *Anna Karenina* in which Levin labors in a field with the peasants, losing all sense of himself in the shared rhythms of the work, the deep blowing grain, and the heat of the sun on his body. It is an image of ecstatic relation which is as much an expression of Eros as is the emblem of two lovers tangled in embrace, and it can stand for almost every aspect of our lives. Every privilege, every object, every "good" comes to us as the result of a human harvest, the shared labor of others: the language we use and the beliefs we hold and the ways we experience ourselves. Each of these involves a world of others into which we are entered every moment of our lives. . . .[18]

C. Following are integral parts from three student papers intended to demonstrate methods of argument. How persuasive do you consider each of the several statements? In what respects are they weak or strong? What suggestions for improvement can you make?

[18] Peter Marin, "The New Narcissism," *Harper's*, October 1975, pp. 55–56.

1. New York is the greatest sports city in the world. New York has a couple of baseball, football, hockey, and basketball teams. These teams accumulate a higher attendance at games during a season than any equivalent team in the country. This fact shows that New Yorkers support and appreciate their sports teams. Ask any professional athlete and he will tell you that there is something special about New York fans.

2. A bill which would allow people to deduct tuition payments from their income taxes would provide substantial assistance not only to those who must make tuition payments, but to the colleges and universities as well. Many families, especially those with more than one child, would be able to finance their children's education if they were allowed some form of tax break. If more people could afford to go to college, the colleges and universities would be able to improve the quality of education they are now providing.

It appears to me that the economy of this country would benefit from such a program as well. While tax deductions would place a small drain on the federal income tax revenues, the financial loss would certainly be made up as students completed their education and began to pay their own income taxes. Because college graduates earn substantially more money over their lifetime than do high school graduates, any money the federal government lost on income tax deductions would be made up several times over in the course of a college graduate's working life.

3. But there are other, equally valid, reasons for becoming a vegetarian. One of them is the desire to eat a more healthful diet. Perhaps this may surprise you. Maybe you are one of those people who believe that adequate protein cannot be derived from a diet devoid of meat. But actually, all the protein and vitamins one needs can easily be supplied by a vegetable diet. Even a diet that omits dairy products and consists of foods from only vegetable sources can supply the needed nutrition. By necessity, a vegetarian learns to avoid high-calorie, low-protein, processed foods and eat the natural, chemical-free foods instead. One of the health dangers of eating meat lies in the fact that it is a processed food. You have no way of knowing what chemical treatments your meat has received to make it appear fresh and palatable. Also, high levels of toxic pesticides accumulate in the tissues of the animals raised for food. In addition, the growth-inducing chemicals which these animals are sometimes fed may wind up in the meat you purchase at the supermarket.

D. Comment on the logic of the following statements.[19]

1. In Lincoln's time a doctor charged 25 cents for an office visit and 50 cents for a house call. A prescription at 10 cents was common; none ever cost more than 50 cents. Those were also the days of rickets, high infant mortality, and the deadly scourges of tuberculosis, pneumonia, typhoid fever, diphtheria, measles, scarlet fever, smallpox, meningitis, and other infections now all but conquered. Would you want to go back to those "good old days"? Would you exchange the penny prescriptions of those days with the dollar ones of today? Would you trade modern wonder drugs for old-fashioned medicines? When it comes to your health, "cheap is cheap." You can rely on your modern pharmacist.

2. In 1917, Russia took all status away from its officers. It ruined the army. No titles, salutes, or privileges. Troops followed only the orders they liked. Of course, when the Russians saw the mess this made of the army, they restored their officers' first-class status completely. Orderlies, epaulettes, and all. This interests us because status is also the reason many firms ask their men to fly first class. Not only so the man on the mission will have a place to work. But also as an investment in his frame of mind. A good mind is a fragile thing. A man simply cannot think "poor" on his way to a client and then think like a vice president when he gets there. Men do not turn on and off like this. We might add that first class is not even very expensive any more. . . .

3. Tomato addiction is a menace to the national health. Statistics show that, of all people born between 1800 and 1850 who ate tomatoes, not one is living today; all have perished. The figures show, further, that of the people born between 1860 and 1910 an overwhelming number died, and among those who are still living many show signs of physical weakness—loss of hair and teeth, poor vision, and diminishing vitality. Even more significant, statistics also show that of all juvenile delinquents arrested between 1960 and 1970, 84 percent had eaten tomatoes at one time or another. Scientific studies support these statistics. In a carefully controlled experiment at one of our most eminent universities, fish of all sizes and kinds were put into

[19] The examples in this problem are freely adapted from the following sources: (1) *Medicine at Work*, published by the Pharmaceutical Manufacturers Association, (2) advertisement of American Airlines, (3) instructional example in *Practical English*, a publication of the National Council of Teachers of English, (4) testimony before the Interstate Commerce Commission, and (5) syndicated leaflet published by the Kirkley Press, Towson, Md.

individual bowls filled with tomato juice, rather than water. Every single fish died.

4. I shudder to think what would happen to New York City if it were allowed to get into the urban transportation mess in which Los Angeles now finds itself. That city, which has operated on a policy of using highway transportation as the principal means of access to the core of the metropolitan area, now finds that the necessary roads and parking lots are devouring it. Los Angeles finds that it has been eating its own vital organs and is now frantically searching for ways and means to reverse this suicidal trend. It is finding that the cost will be tremendous but cannot be avoided if it is to survive.

The same thing could happen in New York. For example, if the 35,000 suburban riders per day on the New Haven were to use private automobiles they would require the equivalent of the entire area between Third and Eighth Avenues, from 42nd to 50th Streets, just for parking space. In addition, billions of dollars would be required for additional urban highways in the city as well as in Westchester and Fairfield counties. In my opinion, the present rail service is the best and cheapest form of transportation.

5. Time your work to fit the next man's or the next department's schedule. Did you ever look inside a watch? It keeps correct time as long as every wheel keeps moving, but if one wheel stops, the watch stops. Each team or department in a business is dependent on the completion of the work of one or more other teams, so keep your teamwork moving on schedule.

E. Comment on the emotional appeal of each of the following advertisements.

1. For people who are still individuals . . . the original Irish country hat. Each hat is handcrafted with pride by skilled artisans on the wild, western coast of Ireland. These hats are created by individuals, not production lines, and are designed to become an extension of your own personality.

Shape your Irish hat to suit yourself. The style of your hat can say a lot. That's why the Irish hat leaves the final shape up to you. Shape it any way . . . change it whenever you want. The handwoven tweed is extra thick, and fully lined in the crown. It sheds rain, protects from the wind, and can give you a comfortable shade from the sun. Colors: brown or grey. (Norm Thompson, Portland, Oregon)

2. Do you look older than your husband? When you're running a home, raising children, doing all you can to help your husband keep ahead in business and, these days, perhaps holding a job yourself, sometimes you're so preoccupied that you don't pay close attention to how you look. Then one day you realize that you look older than your husband, the one man in the world you hope most to please.

You don't like it. Most likely he doesn't either. Probably every man likes his wife to look her best, perhaps because it makes *him* feel more attractive. So if you seem to grow older-looking while your husband seems to grow more distinguished-looking as his hair gets slightly grey at the temples, it's undoubtedly time you discovered the secret of a unique beauty fluid, a secret known to younger-looking women from many parts of the world.

Beauty connoisseurs discovered this remarkable beauty fluid, known in the United States as Oil of Olay beauty lotion. . . .

3. [Photograph of David Janssen, the television actor]

If I said Excedrin has worked better than regular aspirin you might not buy it. But doctors said it did in two medical studies.

In two research studies on pain, one at a major hospital and another at an important university medical center, the doctors reported Excedrin worked significantly better than the regular aspirin tablet. So the next time you get a headache, try Excedrin, the extra-strength pain reliever. See if it doesn't work better for you.

F. How is the principle of consistency of belief demonstrated in the following advertisement run some years ago by the Investor-Owned Electric Light and Power Companies? What is the intended effect of the choice of words? Be specific.

[Photograph of an elderly gentleman, physician's bag in hand, alighting from a vintage-model sedan and approaching the picket gate of a farmhouse. Headline: The Country Doctor—Symbol of American Strength.]

The country doctor: living American symbol of a time when an independent spirit was a man's chief strength. Today there may not be as many country doctors. But the spirit they symbolize is still a part of all that is America.

That spirit lives on in the professions, businesses and industries that serve you today—enterprises built and run by free and independent people. Businesses owned by investors—people like you—who prize freedom and individuality.

Yet some other people think that our federal government—rather than individuals—should own certain businesses. Our investor-owned electric light and power companies are one of their chief targets. These are companies built, run, owned by and employing people who believe in individual effort—companies that have served you well. You, and others, have helped them grow by your support as a customer.

When you consider what our country has always stood for, can you see why anyone should want our federal government to do any job it doesn't have to do—such as owning and managing the electric light and power business? Isn't it best to leave that to individuals, like you, who believe individual effort is the quality that will always keep our nation strong?

G. Comment on the references to authorities in the following statement from *Newsweek's* cover story "Why Johnny Can't Write." For what purpose are the references made? With what point of view, if any, do you side? What do your fellow students think? What does your instructor think? How does *Newsweek* communicate what *it* thinks?

In the opinion of many language experts, another major villain is the school of "structural linguistics." Writing is far less important than speech, the structural linguists proclaim, because only about 4 percent of the world's languages have a written form; they believe that there are no real standards for any language, apart from the way it is commonly spoken. Philologist Pei traces the predominance of this school to the 1961 publication of Webster's Third International Dictionary, the first English dictionary that did not give preference to the way the language is used by its best-educated writers. Since then, he suggests, teachers in the classrooms have come increasingly under the sway of the structural-linguistic dogma: that the spoken idiom is superior to the written, and that there is no real need for students to study the rules of their language at all. "If you will scoff at language study," asks Pei, "how, save in terms of language, will you scoff?"

The pervasive influence of the structural linguists, coupled with the political activism of the past decade, has led many teachers to take the view that standard English is just a "prestige" dialect among many others, and that insistence on its predominance constitutes an act of repression by the white middle class. Last year, after a bitter dispute within its own ranks, the Conference on College Composition of the National Council of Teachers of English adopted an extraordinary policy statement embodying that philosophy. Entitled "Students' Rights to Their Own Language," the document is more a political tract than a set of educational precepts. "Linguistic snobbery was tacitly encouraged by a slavish reliance on rules," it argues, "and these attitudes had consequences far beyond the realm of language. People from different language and ethnic backgrounds were denied social privileges, legal rights and economic opportunity, and their inability to manipulate the dialect used by the privileged group was used as an excuse for this denial."

The supporters of this argument reject the notion that public education is designed to help those who do not use standard English to survive in a society that does. "We tend to exaggerate the need for standard English," insists Elisabeth McPherson, an English teacher at a St. Louis community college who helped draft the declaration. "You don't need much standard English skill for most jobs in this country." True enough. But won't students, denied the opportunity to master standard English because their teachers refuse to teach it, also lose the chance at higher-ranking jobs where standard English does prevail? McPherson, who calls herself "idealistic," replies that "the important thing is that people find themselves through their own language."

But, "prestige dialect" or not, standard English is in fact the language of American law, politics, commerce and the vast bulk of American literature—and the traditionalists argue that to deny children access to it is in itself a pernicious form of oppression. They also emphasize that the new attempt to stress the language as it is spoken rather than as it is written has significance far beyond the basics of jobs or social mobility. "Learning to write is the hardest, most important thing any child does," says Dr. Carlos Baker, chairman of the English department at Princeton University and author of a best-selling biography of Ernest Hemingway. "Learning to write is learning to think."

Baker and like-minded colleagues stress that setting down thoughts in writing forces students to examine the actual meaning of their words and the logic—or the lack of it—that leads from one statement to another. "You just don't know anything unless you can write it," says semanticist S.I. Hayakawa. "Sure, you can argue things in your head and bring them out at cocktail parties, but in order to argue anything thoroughly, you must be able to write it down on paper." The late James Knapton, a former supervisor of remedial English at Berkeley, quit the university in disgust eight years ago when officials dropped the school's essay requirement for admission. "I really worry about the great unwashed mass of students sloshing around out there," said Knapton, who before his death last summer was teaching English at a San Francisco high school. "Diagraming sentences is out, no one teaches Shakespeare any more, and there are all those kids talking and rapping with each other, not knowing how to examine what they think in one discursive sentence." [20]

H. How is the language in the following statements intended to influence the reader? Explain by reference to specific words. Do you consider the statements effective? Who might be influenced by them?

1. Excerpt from an article in *Field & Stream*, a magazine for sportsmen:

Clearcutting, an abomination practiced by the big timber interests with the enthusiastic cooperation of the U.S. Forest Service, has just taken it on the chin in a major and possibly fatal way, and it is a time for rejoicing. But it is also a time for renewed vigilance by all outdoors people, for as we have repeatedly seen, the predatory special interests are at their most dangerous when they are trapped and on the edge of defeat.

Not to put too fine a point on it, clearcutting is nothing less than the systematic rape of the national forests that belong to all of us. The literature is full of self-serving alibis for this vile practice—alibis that range all the way from pleas that clearcutting is a useful forest management tool to the claim that housing our nation's teeming millions would be impossible without it. That's baloney, of course. The only real rationale for clearcutting is that it makes more money quicker for the timber barons.

Clearcutting is a system of harvesting timber whereby huge blocks of woodland are leveled. Everything goes—mature, marketable timber, deadwood, immature trees, underbrush.[21]

2. Public statement by General Electric at the time of a strike by one of its unions:

Mr. Carey's latest "gimmick" was a counterfeit truce proposal. In effect, he would call off his law-breaking tactics at defense and

[20] "Why Johnny Can't Write," *Newsweek*, 8 December 1975, pp. 60–61, Copyright 1975 by Newsweek, Inc. All rights reserved. Reprinted by permission.

[21] Richard Starnes, "The Clearcutters Lose a Big One," *Field & Stream*, December 1975, p. 9.

essential plants in return for the Company's giving in to some extra demands.

The truce offer was another red herring. It is an attempt to get General Electric, in effect, to pay a bribe so that Mr. Carey will stop interfering with the livelihood of thousands of employees who want to work. Mr. Carey should not be so bribed by anyone in return for simply obeying the law. Nor should IUE agents be bribed by special truce deals to get them to stop violence on the picket lines.

3. Excerpt from a handbill distributed by the "NYU Workers League Club" at the time of a strike by maintenance workers:

SHUT NYU DOWN. The struggle of Local 810 (Teamsters Union) for a decent living has now entered the critical stage. Hester [the University president at the time] and the bosses sent in police and armed scabs against 810 workers and student supporters in an effort to undermine the strike. This vicious unionbuster now points the finger of violence at the students.

A court injunction has been issued by the City giving the City the right to enforce scab deliveries of fuel. These attacks are part of the plans of Nixon and the whole capitalist class to break the labor movement from Laos to Newark and force it back to the position of the 1930s. If Nixon and Hester are allowed to break the 810 strike it will be a tremendous blow against the entire workers movement. But if we stop them now, our offensive will give a tremendous lead in the growing offensive of the working class as expressed in the British General Strike and the call for similar action by the New Jersey AFL-CIO. There must now be an all-out offensive to escalate and win this struggle. . . .

SMASH NIXON'S WORLDWIDE OFFENSIVE TO SAVE THE ROTTEN CAPITALIST SYSTEM ON THE BACKS OF THE WORKING CLASS! . . .

THEME TOPICS

1. Develop through logical means a theme on one of the following topics:

(a) The case for (or against) euthanasia
(b) The dark (or bright) future of mass transportation
(c) Thought control by the media
(d) Do colleges provide a refuge from reality?
(e) The case for (or against) the survival of the small businessman

2. Write, for the opinion page of your local newspaper, a persuasive statement on one of the following topics. Take either the affirmative or the negative side of the subject.

(a) Making English composition compulsory for every first-year college student
(b) The legalization of the sale and use of marijuana
(c) Outlawing the strip mining of coal
(d) Banning offshore drilling for oil
(e) Extending free public education to the undergraduate college years
(f) Reviving compulsory military training
(g) Creating a federal department for the protection of consumers
(h) Gun control
(i) The value of jogging (or other form of physical or mental activity)
(j) "Living arrangements" as a substitute for marriage

3. Take any of the suggested topics in (2) above and write an argumentative theme in which you balance the positive and negative factors and draw a rational conclusion.

4. Write a persuasive theme espousing a cause you believe in and feel worthy of greater support than it is getting.

9
Researching and Organizing the Library Paper

College courses require the writing of many papers based on library research and other forms of investigation. The value in these papers is not only that they develop knowledge of some special subject and give practice in writing, but also that they provide experience in the complexities of finding, selecting, evaluating, and organizing ideas. These skills will serve you well after college, when your professional or business responsibilities require you to submit a report, write an article, prepare a speech, or engage in informed discussion. Even more, they will have sharpened your ability to weigh evidence, draw inferences, and make decisions—attributes highly respected and well rewarded.

As the name suggests, the library paper is based on published information; its purpose is to reveal new relationships and significances through a study of what has already been said and written. It is thus different from other research papers which attempt to develop new information first-hand through such means as observation, experiment, interviews, and questionnaires. Reports incorporating such research experiences are touched on in Chapter 13, "Memorandums and Reports."

Writing the library paper entails a number of steps, of which writing is among the last. A great deal of work and time enter into the preparation for writing. And it is the effort put into the preliminary steps that largely determines how successful the writing will be. The more diligent you are in doing the groundwork, the more easily and swiftly will you be able to compose the draft. The essential preliminaries to actual composition include the selection of a limited topic, obtaining and organizing the library material, and preparing an outline.

Selecting a Limited Topic

The topic you choose should be one that interests you. The reason is simple: Your project will require so much work and concentration that unless you have a genuine feeling for the subject, you will find the task boring and unrewarding. Possessing such an interest, however, you should thoroughly enjoy the work and add a great deal to your knowledge and insight.

Although your personal interests are a good starting point for the selection of a topic, you should also give weight to several other requirements.

1. The subject should not be so technical that your prospective readers will be unable to share your interest in it.
2. The subject should be one about which there is a published body of material accessible to you.
3. The subject should be important enough to warrant your treating it at the length required.
4. The subject should be so limited in scope that it can be treated adequately in the space and time available to you.

The last requirement in particular requires some further explanation. A great many subjects provide potentially suitable material for reports, but before any subject becomes usable, it must be reduced to practical dimensions. To write even a long paper on "The Novels of Thomas Wolfe" would require so much ground to be covered and lead to such generalities that the paper would be all but useless. A critical paper on one of Wolfe's novels would also risk lack of focus, for there are many avenues of exploration: characters, plot, style, and autobiographical aspects, to name only a few. But now we are at least dividing the field and coming somewhat closer to the limits our paper will allow. Perhaps we can come closer still by choosing an even more limited area for development: Wolfe's family as his literary prototypes; Wolfe as seen by his teaching colleagues at New York University; Wolfe's concern with death; Wolfe's verbal excesses; the organization of the train episode in *Of Time and the River;* the character of Esther Jack in *The Web and the Rock;* the pattern of the home town in *You Can't Go Home Again.*

Probably you will not know precisely what your topic will be until you have examined the material available to you. That means that some research must precede your choice of topic as well as follow it.

But where will you look and what will you look for? Say that you are considering a paper about Thomas Wolfe. A necessary prerequisite, of course, is a familiarity with his works. You also need to find out what others have written about Wolfe. This bibliographic research may, at first, seem like an insuperable task, but with some knowledge of the library's resources and a bit of luck you may find it easier than you think. For example, you may happen upon Leslie A. Fields' anthology *Thomas Wolfe: Three Decades of Criticism* (University of North Carolina, 1966), which offers—in addition to a superb collection of essays by leading Wolfe scholars—a bibliography of some twenty-one pages. With those essays and that bibliography, you should have little trouble fixing upon a specific topic for development. You will also be able to extract an excellent list of promising books and articles for investigation. From this point, the only limitation on your search is that imposed by the library's ability to supply the materials you want. Let us therefore proceed to an examination of the library's resources and the ways of using them.

Obtaining Library Material

The library's material aids to research consist principally of (1) the card catalog, (2) the reference section, and (3) the actual books and periodicals in the shelves and files.

Card Catalog. The card catalog lists all the library's books alphabetically in three ways: by author, by title, and by subject. Each card also gives the date and place of publication and the publisher's name. If several copies of a book are available, you will probably want the latest edition or the latest printing, as indicated by the date on the card. In the upper left of the card is the call number, through which you or the librarian can locate the book in the stacks. Books on reserve or in special collections are so indicated. In addition to books and pamphlets, the catalog also lists periodicals by title and indicates what bound volumes of them are available. In some instances college libraries are replacing their catalogs, or portions of them, with computer printouts of the materials in stock. The printouts are arranged in volumes that can be consulted as conveniently as the card catalog.

Libraries generally use one of two systems of classifying their books, and the system they choose is reflected in the call numbers. One system of classification is the Dewey Decimal System; the other is the Library of Congress System. In the first, the Dewey Decimal

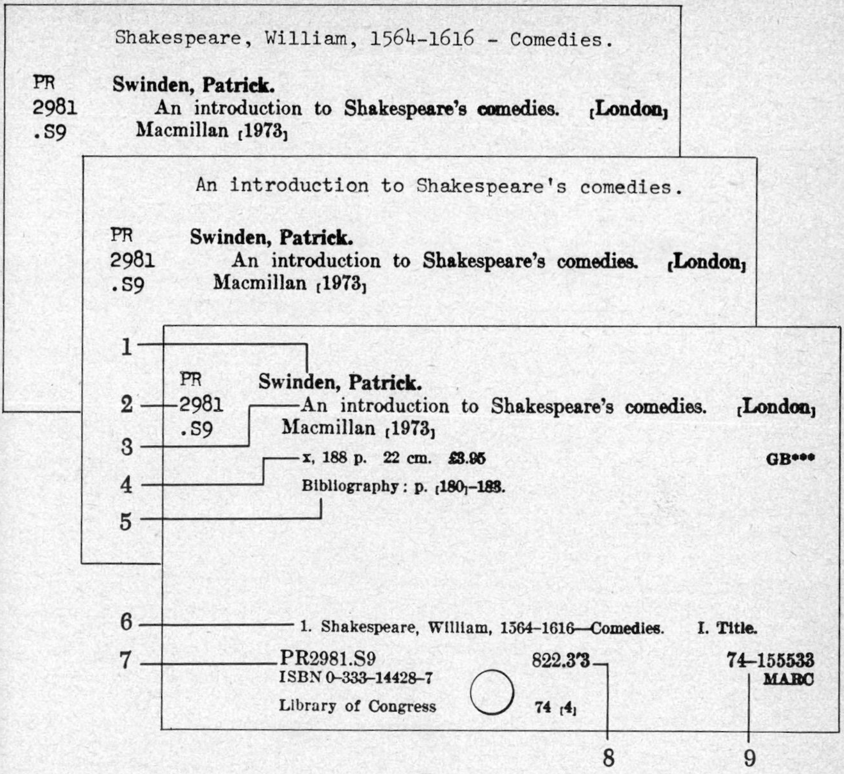

Shakespeare, William, 1564-1616 - Comedies.
PR 2981 .S9
Swinden, Patrick.
An introduction to Shakespeare's comedies. [London] Macmillan [1973]
An introduction to Shakespeare's comedies.
PR 2981 .S9
Swinden, Patrick.
An introduction to Shakespeare's comedies. [London] Macmillan [1973]
1
2
3
4
5
PR 2981 .S9
Swinden, Patrick.
An introduction to Shakespeare's comedies. [London] Macmillan [1973]
x, 188 p. 22 cm. £3.95
GB***
Bibliography: p. [180]-183.
6
1. Shakespeare, William, 1564-1616—Comedies. I. Title.
7
PR2981.S9
ISBN 0-333-14428-7
Library of Congress
822.3'3
74 [4]
74-155533
MARC
8
9

1. Author
2. Library call number
3. Title and facts of publication (place, publisher, date)
4. Number of pages in introduction and text; book size in centimeters; and price (here given in pounds because of British publication)
5. Contains bibliography on pages noted
6. Subject
7. Library of Congress classification
8. Dewey Decimal classification
9. Library of Congress card number

SUBJECT, TITLE, AND AUTHOR CARDS

System, the key to the classification is in the first three digits, which run from 000 to 999 and divide books into ten classes.

000–099 General Works
100–199 Philosophy and Related Disciplines
200–299 Religion
300–399 The Social Sciences
400–499 Language
500–599 Pure Sciences
600–699 Technology (Applied Sciences)
700–799 The Arts
800–899 Literature and Rhetoric
900–999 General Geography and History

Every three-digit number is followed by a decimal and one or more ciphers, as well as additional symbols, to differentiate a particular volume from others in the same class or subclass. Thus the call number of a book classified under this system consists of both its class number and a "book number": $\genfrac{}{}{0pt}{}{822.3}{\text{P543s}}$. The book bearing this number is *Shakespeare's Romantic Comedies: The Development of Their Form and Meaning,* edited by Peter G. Phialas. The call number 822.3 identifies the book as belonging to the category of Literature and Rhetoric; and the book number P543s identifies the author by the first initial of his last name and a code number, and the book by the first letter of its title.

The Library of Congress System uses identifying letters followed by identifying Arabic numerals. The twenty-one main classes are represented by single capital letters, but main divisions are represented by two capital letters, as shown under class P in the outline below.

A General Works, Polygraphy
B Philosophy, Religion
C History—Auxiliary Sciences
D History and Topography (except America)
E–F America
G Geography, Anthropology, Folklore, Sports
H Social Sciences
J Political Science
K Law
L Education
M Music
N Fine Arts
P Language and Literature
PN Literary History and Collections (General)
PR English Literature
Q Science
R Medicine
S Agriculture, Plant, and Animal Industry
T Technology
U Military Science
V Naval Science
Z Bibliography and Library Science

Following the initial letter (or letters), a topic under a class and division is represented by an Arabic number from 1 to 9999, and the book number by a decimal letter and number. The Library of Congress number for the Phialas title already cited is $^{\mathrm{PR2981}}_{\mathrm{.P5}}$. If you should look on the library shelves for a book so classified, it is important to know that the numbers following the decimal point are read decimally, so that .P5 stands *after* .P462.

Reference Section. The reference section of the library contains a body of standard works that must be used in the library. Some of the most valuable books here are the bibliographies, or printed book lists, and the indexes to periodicals and newspapers, which tell where you can find published articles in your subject area. The reference section also includes encyclopedias, dictionaries, atlases, directories, and guides to government publications. The following selection of useful reference books in various categories can only suggest what a specific library may offer.

SELECTED LIST OF REFERENCE BOOKS

General Works

GUIDES

Aldrich, Ella V. *Using Books and Libraries.* 5th ed., 1967.

Barton, Mary Neill, and Bell, Marion V. *Reference Books: A Brief Guide.* 7th ed., 1970.

Barzun, Jacques, and Graff, Henry F. *The Modern Researcher,* 1957.

Gates, Jean Key. *Guide to the Use of Books and Libraries.* 3rd ed. 1974.

Winchell, Constance M. *A Guide to Reference Books.* 8th ed. 1967 (with later supplements).

BIBLIOGRAPHIES

Bibliographic Index. 1938—.

Books in Print. 1948—.

Cumulative Book Index: A World List of Books in English. 1898—.

Guide to Microforms in Print. 1961—.

New York Times Index. 1913—.

Paperbound Books in Print. 1957—.

Poole's Index to Periodical Literature. 1802–1907.

Reader's Guide to Periodical Literature. 1900—.

Subject Guide to Books in Print. 1955—.
Vertical File Index. 1937—. Lists leaflets, pamphlets, etc.

BIOGRAPHICAL AIDS

Biography Index. 1947—.
Chambers's Biographical Dictionary. Rev. ed. 1969.
Current Biography. 1940—.
Dictionary of American Biography. 13 vols. 1927–1974.
Dictionary of National Biography [British]. 22 vols. 1922. Supplements carry biographies to 1960.
Encyclopedia of American Biography. Ed. John A. Garraty. 1974.
International Who's Who. 1935—.
Webster's Biographical Dictionary. 1971.
Who Was Who. 5 vols. [British]. 1897–1960.
Who Was Who in America. 4 vols. 1607–1968.
Who's Who [British]. 1949—.
Who's Who in America. 1899—.

ENCYCLOPEDIAS

Collier's Encyclopedia. 20 vols.
Encyclopedia Americana. 30 vols.
The New Columbia Encyclopedia
The New Encyclopaedia Britannica. 30 vols.

UNABRIDGED DICTIONARIES

Funk & Wagnalls New Standard Dictionary of the English Language. 1963.
Oxford English Dictionary. 12 vols. and supplement, 1888–1933. New supplement, Vol. 1 (A–C), 1972.
Random House Dictionary of the English Language. 1966.
Webster's Third New International Dictionary. 1966.

ALMANACS AND YEARBOOKS

Britannica Book of the Year. 1938—.
Europa Yearbook. 1959—.
Facts on File. 1940—.
Information Please Almanac. 1947—.
McGraw-Hill Directory and Almanac of Canada. 5th ed. 1970.
The Statesman's Year-Book. 1864—.
Statistical Abstract of the United States. 1878—.
Statistical Year Book [United Nations]. 1948—.

World Almanac and Book of Facts. 1868—.
Yearbook of the United Nations. 1946/47—.

ATLASES AND GAZETTEERS

Columbia Lipincott Gazetteer of the World. 1962.
Historical Atlas. Rev. ed. 1968.
Larousse Encyclopedia of World Geography. 1964.
National Geographic Atlas of the World. 3rd ed. 1970.
The Odyssey World Atlas. 1967.
Rand McNally Cosmopolitan World Atlas. 1971.
The Times Atlas of the World. Rev. ed. 1968.
Webster's New Geographical Dictionary. 1972.

QUOTATIONS

BARTLETT, JOHN, ed. *Familiar Quotations.* 14th ed. 1968.
EVANS, BERGEN, ed. *Dictionary of Quotations.* 1968.
The Oxford Dictionary of Quotations. 2nd ed. 1953.
STEVENSON, BURTON E., ed. *Home Book of Quotations.* 10th ed. 1967.
TRIPP, RHODA T., ed. *International Thesaurus of Quotations.* 1970.

Specialized Works

LANGUAGE AND LITERATURE

ALTICK, RICHARD D., and WRIGHT, ANDREW. *Selective Bibliography for the Study of English and American Literature.* 4th ed. 1971.
BLISS, A. J. *A Dictionary of Foreign Words and Phrases in Current English.* 1966.
BOND, DONALD F. *A Reference Guide to English Studies.* 2nd ed. 1971.
Book Review Digest. 1905—.
Cassell's Encyclopedia of World Literature. Rev. and enl. J. Buchanan Brown, 1973.
Granger's Index to Poetry. 6th ed. 1973.
HART, JAMES D. *The Oxford Companion to American Literature.* 4th ed. 1965.
HARVEY, SIR PAUL. *The Oxford Companion to English Literature.* 4th ed. 1967.
HAYAKAWA, S. I. *Modern Guide to Synonyms and Related Words.* 1969.
HORNSTEIN, LILLIAN, ed. *The Reader's Companion to World Literature.* 1956.

KLEIN, ERNEST. *Etymological Dictionary of the English Language.* 2 vols. 1966–1967.

PARTRIDGE, ERIC. *A Dictionary of Slang and Unconventional English.* 7th ed. 1970.

Webster's New Dictionary of Synonyms. 1968.

WENTWORTH, HAROLD, and FLEXNER, STUART B. *Dictionary of American Slang.* 1967.

THE ARTS

BREED, PAUL F., and SNIDERMAN, FLORENCE, eds. *Dramatic Criticism Index.* 1972.

Dramatic Index. 1909–1949.

Encyclopedia of World Art. 15 vols. 1959–1968.

FEATHER, LEONARD. *The Encyclopedia of Jazz in the Sixties.* 1966.

Grove's Dictionary of Music and Musicians. 5th ed. 9 vols. 1955. Supplement, 1961.

MURRAY, PETER, and MURRAY, LINDA. *Dictionary of Art and Artists.* 1965.

Music Index. 1949—.

MYERS, BERNARD S., ed. *McGraw-Hill Dictionary of Art.* 5 vols. 1969.

New York Times Film Reviews. 1933—.

REHRAUER, GEORGE. *Cinema Booklist.* 1972.

THOMPSON, OSCAR. *International Cyclopedia of Music and Musicians.* 9th ed. Rev. Arthur Sabin. 1964.

THE SCIENCES

Applied Science and Technology Index. 1958—.

Biological and Agricultural Index. 1916—.

Compton's Dictionary of the Natural Sciences. 1966.

Dictionary of Scientific Biography. 10 vols. 1970–1974.

Engineering Index. 1906—.

HOSELITZ, BERT F., ed. *A Reader's Guide to the Social Sciences.* Rev. ed. 1970.

Industrial Arts Index. 1913–1957. Succeeded by the *Applied Science and Technology Index* and the *Business Periodicals Index.*

JENKINS, FRANCES B. *Science Reference Sources.* 5th ed. 1969.

McGraw-Hill Encyclopedia of Science and Technology. 15 vols. 3rd ed. 1971. Annual supplements in *McGraw-Hill Yearbook of Science and Technology.*

SILLS, DAVID L., ed. *International Encyclopedia of the Social Sciences.* 17 vols. 1968.
Social Sciences and Humanities Index. 1907—.

BUSINESS AND GOVERNMENT

Business Periodicals Index. 1958—.
Catalog of United States Census Publications. 1790—.
COMANS, EDWARD T., JR. *Sources of Business Information.* Rev. ed. 1964.
Congressional Directory. 1809—.
Congressional Quarterly Almanac. 1945—.
Data Processing Yearbook. 1959—.
Economic Almanac. 1940—.
JOHNSTON, H. WEBSTER. *How to Use the Business Library, with Sources of Business Information.* 4th ed. 1972.
Monthly Catalog of United States Government Publications. 1895—.
MUNN, GLENN G. *Encyclopedia of Banking and Finance.* 7th rev. ed. 1973.
Rand McNally Commercial Atlas and Marketing Guide (revised annually).
SCHMECKBEIER, LAWRENCE F., and EASTIN, ROY B. *Government Publications and Their Use.* Rev. ed. 1969.
SLOAN, HAROLD S., and ZURCHER, ARNOLD J. *A Dictionary of Economics.* 5th ed. 1970.
SMITH, EDWARD C., and ZURCHER, ARNOLD J., eds. *Dictionary of American Politics.* 2nd ed. 1968.
U.S. Department of Commerce Publications. 1952—.

HISTORY

ADAMS, JAMES TRUSLOW, ed. *Dictionary of American History.* 2nd ed. 6 vols. 1942–1963.
The Cambridge Ancient History. 3rd ed. 12 vols. and plates. 1971.
The Cambridge Medieval History. 8 vols. 1911–1936.
The Cambridge Modern History. 14 vols. 1902–1926.
LANGER, WILLIAM L. *Encyclopedia of World History.* 5th ed. 1972.
MORRIS, RICHARD B. *Encyclopedia of American History.* 4th rev. ed. 1970.

RELIGION

CROSS, F. L., and LIVINGSTONE, E. A., eds. *The Oxford Dictionary of the Christian Church.* 2nd rev. ed. 1974.

GIBB, H. A. R., and KRAMERS, J. H., eds. *Shorter Encyclopedia of Islam.* 1953.
The New Catholic Encyclopedia. 15 vols. 1967.
ROTH, CECIL, ed. *The Standard Jewish Encyclopedia.* Rev. ed. 1962.
ZAEHNER, ROBERT C., ed. *The Concise Encyclopedia of Living Faiths.* 1959.

The Stacks. The stacks contain all of the library's collections except those works held in the reference section or on reserve for use only in the library. If the stacks are closed to students, you must obtain the books you want from the librarian by filling out a call slip for each book. If the stacks are open, however, you should find out how the books are arranged so that you may be able to locate those you want by their call numbers. Knowing where in the stacks the books in your field are kept, you will also be able to do some browsing independent of the card catalog. You should know, too, that a modern library has many reference materials in microform (microreproduction on film). Back issues of some serial publications (magazines and newspapers) may be available only on microfilm. Such materials must be read on special viewers in the library.

The Working Bibliography

Your acquaintance with the library's resources should enable you, with some digging, to compile a list of works you intend to look into for the information they can yield. This list is your working bibliography. Each work should be listed separately, in the manner shown on page 181, on a file card either 3 by 5 or 4 by 6 inches. The cards should then be filed alphabetically by author (or title, if no author is given), so that you can conveniently refer to them. Be sure to include not only the name of the author and the title of the work, but also the facts of publication (place, publisher, and date), and, in the upper right, the call number. You will need the facts of publication for the footnotes and bibliographical entries in your report. The call number will enable you to requisition the book from the librarian or locate it yourself. After you have examined the work, you may use the bottom of the card for a brief reference note about some part of the contents.

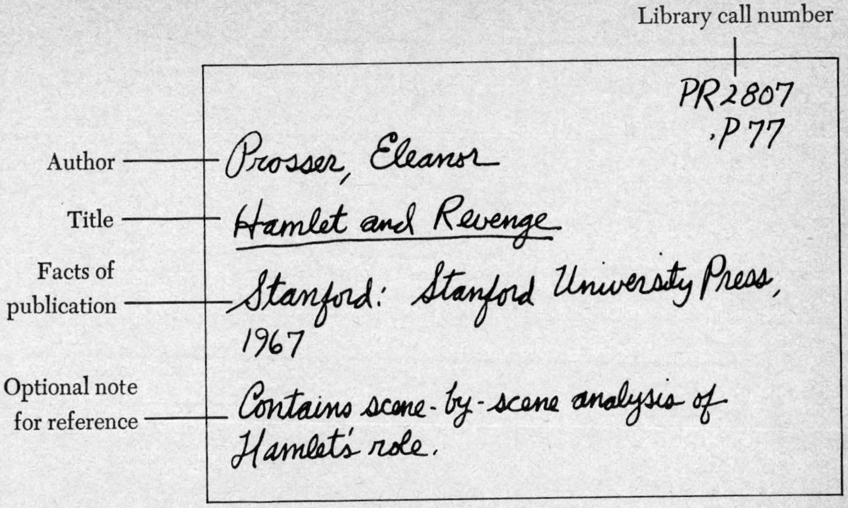

Library call number
PR2807
.P77
Author
Prosser, Eleanor
Title
Hamlet and Revenge
Facts of publication
Stanford: Stanford University Press, 1967
Optional note for reference
Contains scene-by-scene analysis of Hamlet's role.

SAMPLE BIBLIOGRAPHY CARD

Reading and Note Taking

With your working bibliography in hand, you are ready for the task of examining the actual books and articles for their value to you in developing your paper. No doubt some of the references will prove to be false leads, and you will eliminate them from your list. Others, however, will yield information that you believe will be useful. The task you face is to find such information without having to read through every book on your list. If an author has done his job well, the organization of a book should provide important clues to the data you want. Look at the table of contents, the index, and any headings and subheadings in the sections that seem promising. You may also find that the author has added chapter summaries and has within paragraphs or sections made use of topic statements and recapitulations. If the author's methods make your task easier, you should consider how you might profit from his example.

As you find useful information, take notes of it while you have the original sources in your possession. Unless these notes faithfully record the information in the source materials, your report will be inaccurate and the conclusions you come to invalid. For this reason, be prepared to read and summarize carefully. In the instance of a direct quotation, compare your own manuscript copy with the original passage before you set the original aside. You should be cautioned, however, about the overuse of direct quotation in your report, and you must be prepared to rely mainly on the paraphrasing of your source material. Under no circumstances should you offer as your own the words or ideas of the author. That is plagiarism.

Notes on your reading are best made on cards 4 by 6 inches in size or larger. Do not use the same size you used in compiling the bibliography; there is too much danger of misplacing a card. Some authors prefer to use a ruled writing tablet for their notes. In such an instance, a sheet should be treated as a card. (See the sample card below.) Your notes will be most useful to you if you observe these rules:

1. Deal with only one specific topic (or part of a topic) on a card. If you deal with more than one topic, there will be no way to collate

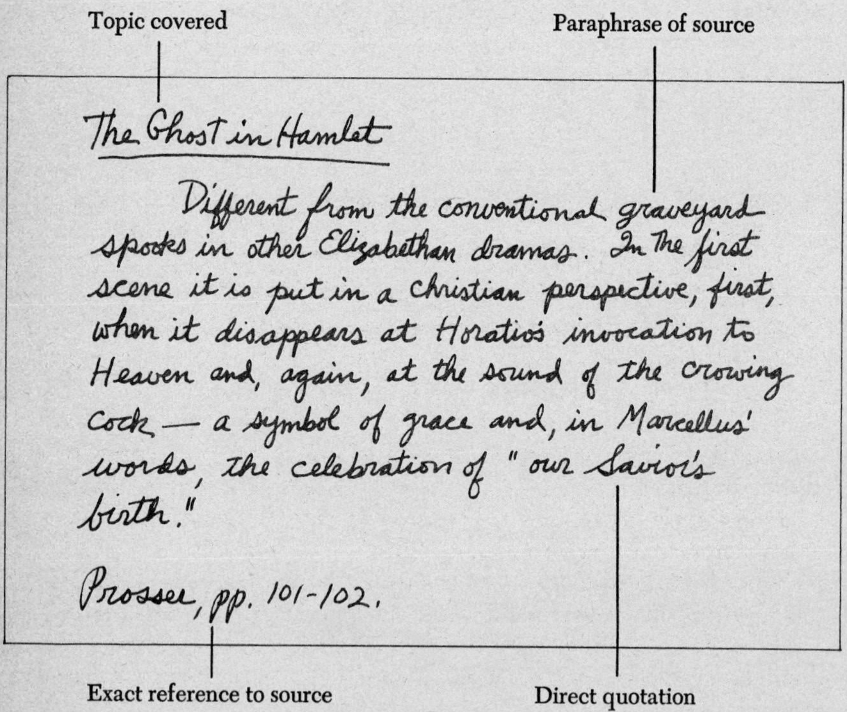
Topic covered
Paraphrase of source
The Ghost in Hamlet
Different from the conventional graveyard spooks in other Elizabethan dramas. In the first scene it is put in a Christian perspective, first, when it disappears at Horatio's invocation to Heaven and, again, at the sound of the crowing cock — a symbol of grace and, in Marcellus' words, the celebration of "our Savior's birth."
Prosser, pp. 101-102.
Exact reference to source
Direct quotation

SAMPLE NOTE CARD

the cards when you get ready to organize your material. Write on one side only and use as many cards as you need to treat a single topic. If you need more than one card for a topic, number the cards successively in the upper right.

2. If you quote directly from your source, put quotation marks around the quoted words. If you omit words in a quotation, use three spaced periods (called an ellipsis) to show the omission. (See Rule 10a(5) in the "Handbook of English.")

3. Most of your notes should be in the form of summaries of your reading. Obtain the sense of the author clearly and concisely, without using the author's own words.

4. Put at the top of the card a descriptive heading that will help you to identify the information on it and to file it with related pieces of information.

5. Show on the card the source of the material, including the page numbers. As you presumably already have a bibliography card for the source, it is enough to identify the work by the author's last name and, if you are using more than one work by the author, an abbreviated form of the title.

Evaluating the Material

Not all of the material the library affords you is of equal value, and you should apply a number of criteria in evaluating each item:

Is the material relevant? Many books and articles that may at first seem relevant to your topic will eventually prove otherwise. In your eagerness to obtain information, you should not waste your time with material that has only a peripheral relation or no relation at all to the subject of your research. Sometimes it is not easy to judge the relevance of material until you have made notes from it and tried to collate those notes with others. If you should then find that material is irrelevant, discard it. This course is painful, but the consequences will be worse if you try to force the irrelevant material into the report for the lame reason that you do not want it to be wasted.

Is the material authoritative? What is the reputation of the author? Is he writing in a field in which he is expert? What sources did he use? Where did the material appear? The better the author's credentials, and those of his sources and their publisher, the more confidence you can place in the material.

Is the material free of bias? It may be that the author has certain prejudices or leanings that give his work a one-sided character. If you are writing on environmental problems, for example, the views of the president of an oil company on the risk of spills in the oceans will no doubt be interesting and perhaps worth incorporating in your report, but you should be aware of a possible bias inherent in his statement and seek opposing views as well.

Is the material up to date? New findings are being made all the time. An old date on a book or article does not necessarily mean the material is obsolete, but you should ascertain if there have been any more recent studies of the subject.

Organizing the Material

With your note cards arranged by topic and the arrangement of the topics conforming to your preliminary conceptions of the paper, you are ready to study your material closely and decide what, in the end, the principal divisions of your report will be, what materials you will include in each division, and what order you will follow. Now make a formal outline to guide you in writing the paper. This outline will be subject to change as you write the draft of your paper and see the need for adding or eliminating material and for rearranging it to obtain a satisfying coherence.

In general, the paper should proceed from an introduction to a presentation of the relevant data and the conclusions. In addition to the customary statement of the purpose of the paper, the introduction may also—depending on the nature of the subject—state the reasons for the choice of subject, indicate the scope of coverage, sketch in some historical background, and name the methods of investigation used. In some instances, an abstract, or summary, of the paper precedes the formal introduction. The body material should include enough details and evidence to support the conclusions that follow, and there should be no conclusion unrelated to the body material. If such a conclusion is offered, either it is irrelevant or you have omitted an important body of supportive material and you should remedy the deficiency.

Methods of arranging material, and instructions for making an outline, were covered in Chapter 2, "Topic and Plan." The final outline for the report shown at the end of Chapter 10, "Writing and Documenting the Library Paper," will be found on page 201.

EXERCISES

A. Explore the library materials available on the life and work of one of the individuals listed below. Then (1) develop a topic for a research paper on the basis of your interests and the materials available; (2) compile annotated bibliography cards for five books or shorter works on the topic you have chosen; and (3) write a brief paper in which you propose the topic and suggest a possible line of development.

Susan B. Anthony	D. W. Griffith
John Jacob Astor	Alexander Hamilton
James Gordon Bennett	Herman Melville
Emily Dickinson	Delmore Schwartz
Theodore Dreiser	Frank Lloyd Wright

B. List a half-dozen recent articles, with their sources, on two of the following topics.

1. Trends in the employment of college graduates
2. Advances in federal protection of consumer interests
3. Weather forecasting
4. Safety in commercial aviation
5. Standards of English instruction in the public schools

C. Using the subject cards in your library's catalog, compile a set of a half-dozen bibliography cards consisting of the most promising material on two of the following topics.

1. Effects of the Yalta Conference (1945) on Soviet power since World War II
2. The emergence of Franz Kafka as a literary force
3. The beginnings of the feminist movement in the United States
4. The protection of endangered species
5. Afro-American influence in American music

D. Paraphrase the following paragraph, using no direct quotation.[1]

Tsar Alexander III in 1891 named his son and heir, Crown Prince Nicholas, to be head of a great governmental project aimed at linking

[1] Meribeth E. Cameron, et al., *China, Japan, and the Powers*, 2nd ed. (New York: Ronald Press, 1960), p. 349.

Russia more closely with the Far East. This was the famous Trans-Siberian Railway. Curiously enough an Englishman named Dull had first suggested the idea many years earlier. He had proposed a horse tramway which, to say the least, was somewhat impractical. At any rate, the official beginning of the Trans-Siberian soon produced widespread repercussions. The able Russian statesman, Count Sergei Witte, observed that the Sino-Japanese War of 1894–95 was a result of the building of the Trans-Siberian, a view shared by the British minister to Japan.[5]

The physical difficulties to be overcome in constructing the railway were enormous. To them was added no small amount of graft and corruption. As a consequence, the finished line was both grossly inefficient and even dangerous. A Japanese officer who traversed the road soon after its completion remarked that riding over it was "like being on board a vessel in a lively sea." The St. Petersburg correspondent of the *Etoile Belge* wrote:

> ". . . the works have been constructed in a manner which shows very little conscience. Everything, or nearly everything, will have to be done over again before the authorities can think of opening this gigantic line to regular working. In very many places the road gives way on the passage of a train a little heavier than usual or travelling at a speed of twenty miles an hour, and accidents more or less grave are continually happening. More than usual courage is demanded of anyone undertaking a journey on this railway. This construction *à la Russe* has already swallowed up hundreds of millions of roubles, or to speak more truthfully, the constructors, and not the construction, have absorbed the millions."[6]

---

[5] D. Dallin, *The Rise of Russia in Asia* (New Haven, 1949), p. 36.

[6] *The Story of Russia and the Far East, Being a Series of Papers Contributed to the Shanghai Mercury* (Shanghai, 1902), pp. 37f.

E. Paraphrase the following paragraph, quoting directly one or two brief excerpts.

At the death of a loved one, the bereaved faces significant psychological work before he can establish attachments to new objects. It is as though the individual has to settle accounts with the lost object before establishing new relationships. The psychological work proceeds in the following way: libidinal attachments to the lost object are broken upon death. The energy cannot remain free floating, so it must either attach itself to new objects or be incorporated into the individual's ego. The energy is withdrawn from the outer world and attached to the ego by the process of identifying with the lost object; the representation of the loved one is incorporated in the individual's ego, and interest in the outer world, relatively speaking, is withdrawn. The work of mourning then proceeds. This includes dealing with the ambivalences significant to most relationships with loved ones. The bereaved feels as though he has been abandoned; the hate or aggression generated by this feeling becomes focal for the hate that had already existed in the relationship. The aggression, however, cannot be readily directed outward; so it is turned inward and results in a form of depression that resembles melancholia. The representation of the object in the ego becomes the target for the reproaches meant for the lost object. Depression is amplified by the superego which directs aggression toward the ego as a form of punishment for its hostility toward the lost object. This process is evidenced in a sense of guilt during mourning. For example, the individual may feel he did not do enough for the loved one, or he was not loyal enough, or he was unworthy. This constitutes the process of grieving, or mourning the loss of a loved object. Eventually, a sense of reality and striving for gratifications in the real world takes over from the use of autistic devices. Reality is supported by the dissolution of the ambivalences that occur during mourning. New object ties then become possible.[2]

[2] Abraham Zaleznik and David Moment, *The Dynamics of Interpersonal Behavior* (New York: John Wiley, 1964), p. 245.

10
Writing and Documenting the Library Paper

If you have done the necessary research and organized your material, preferably in a formal outline, you are ready for the other steps in the production of your library paper. You must write a draft and edit it; you must provide the necessary documentation through footnotes and bibliography; and you must bring all of the elements of the report together in final, presentable form.

Drafting and Editing

The first draft is usually best written by hand on wide-ruled paper to permit interlinear corrections. With your outline before you and your note cards laid out for easy reference, study the material carefully. When you have assimilated the material and have the sequence of ideas clearly in mind, start writing. As you write, show by consecutive numbers in parentheses where references to footnotes are to be made and, on a separate sheet, write out the corresponding footnotes according to the style shown in this chapter. As an alternative to listing your footnotes separately, you may write out your footnotes immediately below the line where the footnote reference appears. The footnote can be separated from the text of your draft by horizontal lines drawn across the page above and below the footnote.

As you write the draft, you must give some attention to style and tone. Since it is the work of others you are examining, interest in your paper will come not from any revelations about yourself, or from your feelings or opinions, but from the subject you are treating and the point of view you bring to it. On the whole, strive for a restrained and objective presentation. Offer your data without embellishment and let the conclusions spring from the supporting evidence. Don't try to overwhelm the reader with footnotes; but don't, at the other extreme, leave the sources of your statements open to question. Finally, don't allow the need for scholarship to let you forget that a clear and simple style is suitable for any honest purpose.

often suggesting the influence of Manet. He would use broad tracts of color with contrasting planes, or use pale colors with juxtaposed white passages, or use pure colors in delicate hatchings.[8] During this

[8] Jacques Lassaigne, *Lautrec* (Cleveland: World Publishing, 1953), p. 25.

period his works were lifeless and lacked character, when compared with his earlier and later works.

FOOTNOTE NOTATION IN MANUSCRIPT

Before the final paper is typed, the draft must be edited. Read the whole manuscript carefully to check the order, the language, and the strength of your evidence in relation to your conclusions. Major rearrangements can be made by cutting and pasting the original copy, and material to be added can be written on separate sheets marked *A*, *B*, *C*, and so on, for insertion in correspondingly marked places in the text. Minor corrections in language can be made between the lines. Before you finish your editing, pay close attention to the beginning and end, and recast them, if necessary, to give them the emphasis their position warrants. When you are satisfied with the manuscript in its revised form, you are ready to transcribe it.

Footnotes

Footnotes are customarily used to acknowledge help received from published sources. Through the footnotes, you not only acknowledge someone else's work, as is ethically right, but you also establish the authority for statements that have their origins outside your own experience. The footnotes are also the medium for an occasional definition or explanation that might be intrusive were it included in the text.

REFERENCE FOOTNOTE

[1] Donald J. Lloyd and Harry R. Warfel, *American English in Its Cultural Setting* (New York: Knopf, 1956), pp. 63–65.

EXPLANATORY FOOTNOTE

[2] The situation is analogous to that encountered among officers in World War II. Horizontal mobility was an indicator of possible failure.

You should footnote all direct quotations as well as statements that have their origin in the works of others. Exceptions are made in the instance of familiar sayings and factual material that is generally known. The use of a footnote is indicated in the text by a number immediately following the passage to be acknowledged. The number is raised slightly above the line.

Hysterical traits, following the description presented by Wilhelm Reich,[1] include seductiveness (in the sexual sense) and liveliness and expressiveness in mode of dress, manner of speech and posture. . . .

The main outcome of adolescent development is the establishment of a basic identity.[2] Identity is the knowledge of who one is in psychological space. . . .

The corresponding footnote, which is customarily placed at the bottom of the same page, but which may be included in a list of all footnotes at the end of the paper, is prefixed by the same number. Numbers are consecutive throughout the paper.

[1] Wilhelm Reich, *Character Analysis* (New York: Noonday Press, 1949), pp. 189–193.
[2] Erik Erikson, "Identity and the Life Cycle," *Psychological Issues*, 1, No. 1 (1959), 111.

First Use. Since you may have several footnotes relating to the same work, you should use the complete footnote only the first time, and an abbreviated form in succeeding references.

FIRST USE

[1] Wilhelm Reich, *Character Analysis* (New York: Noonday Press, 1949), pp. 189–93.

SUCCEEDING USE

[5] Reich, p. 113.

The style of the first use varies somewhat, depending on the source of the material; but these general rules provide a reasonable foundation for the student. (See also the figure on page 198.)

1. Indent the first line and punctuate each footnote as a single sentence.

2. Identify the author or authors, with the given names or initials first.

3. Underline the names of books, periodicals, bulletins, and pamphlets; put quotation marks around titles of articles, chapters, and unpublished works. Separate the title from the subtitle by a colon; however, the subtitle may be omitted if the paper includes a bibliography containing the full title.

4. Put in parentheses the facts of publication (place, publisher, and copyright date). Look for this information on both sides of the title page of the work cited.

(a) If more than one city of publication is shown, use the first only. Add the abbreviation for the state if the city name alone might not be recognized.

(b) You may use an abbreviated form for the publisher's name, for example, *Macmillan,* instead of *Macmillan Publishing Co., Inc.*, provided that the form you use is readily recognized.

(c) If the edition is later than the first, so indicate, as, for example, *2nd ed., rev. ed.* Give the last copyright date, not the date of the last printing.

5. Give exact page references. Use Arabic numerals for all pages except those in the preface, which should be denoted by small Roman numerals (i, ii, iii, iv, and so on).

6. Use standard footnote abbreviations (see pages 195–96).

The sample footnotes below reflect accepted usage for a variety of reference needs. They generally conform to the footnoting style prescribed in the Modern Language Association's *MLA Style Sheet*, 2nd edition. Some specialized fields, like law and the sciences, have their own footnoting practices, which you may observe in their professional journals. In your college work, follow any preferences expressed by your instructors. Where discretion is required, conform as closely as you can to accepted usage and be as clear, concise, and consistent as you can.

SAMPLE FOOTNOTES—FIRST USE

Books and Parts of Books

ONE AUTHOR

[1] John Wain, *Samuel Johnson* (New York: Viking, 1975), p. 45.

TWO AUTHORS

[2] Neil Postman and Charles Weingartner, *Teaching as a Subversive Activity* (New York: Delacorte, 1969), pp. 33–37.

THREE AUTHORS

[3] Richard W. Budd, Robert K. Thorp, and Lewis Donohew, *Content of Communication Analysis* (New York: Macmillan, 1967), p. 41.

MORE THAN THREE AUTHORS

[4] Bruno Klopper et al., *Developments in the Rorschach Technique* (Yonkers-on-Hudson, N.Y.: World Book Co., 1956), pp. 34–38.

SECOND OR LATER EDITION

[5] S. I. Hayakawa, *Language in Thought and Action*, 3rd ed. (New York: Harcourt, 1972), pp. 21–25. [Shortened form of publisher's name]

EDITED WORK

[6] Edmund Wilson, *The Twenties: From Notes and Diaries of the Period*, ed. Leon Edel (New York: Farrar, Straus & Giroux, 1975), p. 245.

[7] Donald R. Mathews, ed., *Perspectives on Presidential Selection* (Washington, D.C.: Brookings Institution, 1973), p. iii.

TRANSLATED WORK

[8] Thomas Mann, *The Magic Mountain*, trans. H. T. Lowe-Porter (New York: Knopf, 1939), pp. 23–24.

REPRINT

[9] Arthur Quiller-Couch, *The Art of Writing* (1916; rpt, New York: Capricorn, 1961), p. 101.
[The first date is that of the original edition; the second, that of the reprint.]

VOLUME IN A SET

[10] *Europa Yearbook* (London: Europa Publications, 1965), II, 248.
[Volumes in a set are customarily indicated by Roman numerals; the page numbers following are not preceded by *p.* or *pp.*]

ARTICLE IN ENCYCLOPEDIA

[11] Tamotsu Shibutani, "Rumor," *International Encyclopedia of the Social Sciences*, 1967, XIII, 123. [Signed article]

[12] "Spartanburg," *Encyclopedia Americana,* 1973, XXV, 459. [Unsigned article]

VOLUME IN A SERIES

[13] Lawrence A. Johnson, *Employing the Hard-Core Unemployed,* American Management Association Research Studies, No. 98 (1969), pp. 210–12.

CORPORATE AUTHOR

[14] Association of the Bar of the City of New York, *Conflict of Interest and Federal Service* (Cambridge: Harvard Univ. Press, 1960), p. 59.
[The work is published under the auspices of a public or private organization; no individual author is named.]

PLAY

[15] William Inge, *A Loss of Roses* (New York: Random House, 1960), act 2, sc. 1.

[16] Ben Jonson, *Volpone,* act 1, sc. 3, lines 21–32.
[The facts of publication are omitted because the play is an old classic. The last figure is a reference to the numbered lines in the scene.]

BIBLE

[17] 1 Samuel 8:3

[18] Romans 4:13 (Revised Standard Version)
[The names of the sacred scriptures and the names of the individual books are not underlined. Chapter and verse, both represented by Arabic numbers, are separated by a colon. The King James Version is assumed unless another version is named.]

GOVERNMENT DOCUMENTS

[19] U.S. Department of Commerce, Bureau of the Census, *Pocket Data Book: USA 1975,* p. 75.

[20] U.S. Congress, Joint Economic Committee, *Report on the Variability of Private Investment,* Part II, 87th Cong., 1st Sess., p. 96.

[21] Hearings Before the Senate Judiciary Committee on H.R. 10650, 87th Cong., 2nd Sess. (1962), Part I, p. 196.

[22] *Report of the New York Joint Legislative Committee to Revise the Banking Law* (Albany, 1973), p. 22.

[23] 91st Cong., 1st Sess. (1969), S. 2231. [Senate bill]

DISSERTATION

[24] Ralph Benjamin Singer, Jr., "Confederate Atlanta," Diss. University of Georgia, 1973.

MORE THAN ONE WORK CITED IN SINGLE FOOTNOTE

[25] Stuart Chase, *The Proper Study of Mankind,* rev. ed. (1956; rpt., New York: Colophon Books, 1963), pp. xii–xiv; Desmond Morris, *The Naked Ape* (1967; rpt., New York: Dell, 1969), pp. 9–12.

CHAPTER OR ARTICLE IN COLLECTIVE WORK

[26] Joseph Conrad, "An Appreciation," in *Henry James: A Collection of Critical Essays,* ed. Leon Edel (Englewood Cliffs, N.J.: Prentice-Hall, 1963), p. 12.

Articles and Pamphlets

ARTICLE IN LEARNED JOURNAL

[27] Thomas A. Guback, "Film as International Business," *Journal of Communication,* 24 (Winter 1974), 90–101.
[Arabic numerals for the volume number of a periodical are more convenient than Roman numerals even when the publication itself uses Roman numerals. Page numbers are not preceded by the abbreviation *p.* or *pp.* if they are separated from the volume number by the issue date in parentheses.]

SIGNED MAGAZINE ARTICLE

[28] Mary Pinkham, "A Fan's Note," *Atlantic,* September 1975, p. 82.

UNSIGNED MAGAZINE ARTICLE

[29] "Approaching the Edge of Chaos," *Time,* 23 June 1975, p. 39.

UNSIGNED NEWSPAPER ARTICLE

[30] "Drug Agency Asks Rules to Clean Up Shellfish Industry," *New York Times,* 20 June 1975.
[31] *Washington Post,* 16 March 1976.
[32] Editorial, *Wall Street Journal,* 19 November 1976.

PAMPHLET

[33] Paul Meek, *Open Market Operations,* Federal Reserve Bank of New York, 1967, p. 5.
[34] *Competition in the Petroleum Industry,* Exxon Corporation, 1975, p. 8.

Later References. When additional footnote references are to be made to works already footnoted, highly abbreviated forms are used, as the following examples show.

[1] Emmet John Hughes, *The Ordeal of Power: A Political Memoir of the Eisenhower Years* (New York: Atheneum, 1963), pp. 55–57.
[2] Ibid. [Same work and page references as above]

[3] Arthur M. Schlesinger, Jr., *The Crisis of the Old Order, 1919–1933.* (Boston: Houghton Mifflin, 1956), p. 126.

[4] Ibid., p. 131. [Same work as above, but different page.]

[5] Theodore H. White, *The Making of the President 1972* (New York: Atheneum, 1973), p. 212.

[6] Theodore H. White, *The Making of the President 1968* (New York: Atheneum, 1969), pp. 94–95. [Same author as above, but different work]

[7] Hughes, pp. 146–47. [Reference to work by Hughes cited earlier]

[8] White, *1972,* p. 255. [Shortened title of book used to differentiate between the two White titles already cited]

Abbreviations. To save space, authors regularly abbreviate many of the common terms used in footnotes and textual references. Although custom has for a long time decreed that Latin abbreviations be underscored, the practice now varies to such a degree that writers may feel more secure if they do *not* underscore any Latin abbreviations.

COMMON SCHOLARLY ABBREVIATIONS

You will probably use few of the abbreviations below in your own writing, but the list will help you understand abbreviations you may come across in your research.

anon. anonymous
app. appendix
b. born
© copyright, as in © 1976
ca. (or c.) *circa,* "about." Used where the exact date is unknown, as in "ca. 1907."
ch., chs.; chap., chaps. chapter(s)
d. died, as in "d. 1826"
diss. dissertation
ed. edition, editor, edited by
e.g. *exempli gratia,* "for example." Set off by commas.
esp. especially
et al. *et alii,* "and others"; no period after *et,* which is not an abbreviation
f., ff. and the following page(s), as in "pp. 19 ff."
fig., figs. figure(s)
fn. footnote (but n. is preferred)
fol., fols. folio(s)
ibid., *ibidem,* "in the same place," that is, the reference in the immediately preceding footnote

i.e. *id est,* "that is." Set off by commas.
intro. introduction
l., ll. line(s). Because of possible confusion with the figure 1 or 11, the word is better spelled out.
loc. cit. *loco citato,* "in the place cited." Used with the author's name to refer to the same passage cited in an earlier footnote; for example, "Davis, loc. cit."
MS, MSS manuscript(s)
n. footnote
n.d. no date of publication given
no., nos. number(s)
op. cit. *opere citato,* "in the work cited," as in "Davis, op. cit., p. 86." Usually superfluous.
p., pp. page(s)
par., pars. paragraph(s)
passim here and there. Denotes scattered references, as in "pp. 35–52 passim." Takes no period because it is not an abbreviation.
pl., pls. plate(s)
pt., pts. part(s)
q.v., *quod vide,* "which see"
rev. revised by, revised edition; review, reviewed by
rpt. report, reprint
sc., scs. scene(s)
sec., secs.; sect., sects. section(s)
ser. series
sic thus. Put in square brackets following a quoted word or phrase which the reader may question because of a misspelling or other oddity. Not an abbreviation.
st., sts. stanza(s)
trans. translator, translation, translated by
viz. *videlicet,* "namely." Set off by commas.
vol., vols. volume(s)
vs. *versus,* "against"; also verse(s)

Bibliography

In addition to the footnotes, a bibliography is included at the end of all long research papers and at the end of many short ones. It is useful in bringing together in one place references to all of the works consulted in the preparation of the paper, and in supplying details or names of sources not included in the footnotes. The additional details may include such items as the subtitles of books, and the names of publishers if they have been omitted from the footnotes. Sources included in the bibliography, but not named in the footnotes, will be those the author consulted for general background and those he recommends to his readers for the same purpose. In the social sciences and some other fields, it is now customary to dispense almost entirely with footnotes and use numbered references in the text to refer to corresponding items in the bibliography.

In an early statement on "The Theory of Political Propaganda," Harold Lasswell (38, p. 627) defined propaganda as "the management of collective attitudes by the manipulation of significant symbols." . . . Students of propaganda such as Jacques Ellul (14) have come to feel that a total perspective . . . constitutes the most pervasive form of "propaganda." A study of political perspectives in nonpolitical news reporting (Gerbner, 22) seems to bear out this contention.

In your English classes, and in the humanities generally, you will be expected to follow the more conventional bibliographic style. The main differences between the footnote and the bibliographic entry are shown in the accompanying figure. The specific characteristics of bibliographies are explained below.

1. Under the heading "Bibliography" or "List of Works Consulted," the entries are listed alphabetically by author. The author's last name is shown first. Where a work has no identifiable author, the name of the work is entered alphabetically in the same list. In the instance of a corporate author, the name of the issuing agency or organization is listed in the author's position.

2. The first line of each entry is set at the margin, with succeeding lines indented about five spaces. Single or double spacing may be used, but always with double spacing between entries.

3. Where an author is represented by more than one work, an underline about an inch long may be used in place of the author's name after the first entry in his name. Several works by the same author are usually listed in the order of the date of publication rather than alphabetically by title.

4. Periods, rather than commas and parentheses, are used to set off the main divisions within an entry.

5. Page numbers are not given, except for the inclusive pages of articles in periodicals and of chapters or other parts of more extended works; but the page numbers are sometimes omitted in the instance of newspaper articles and articles in popular magazines.

FOOTNOTE

Indention and footnote number · Author—first name first · Comma · Main title · Colon · Subtitle—optional

[1]Lewis Mumford, <u>The Myth of the Machine:</u> <u>Technics and Human Development</u> (New York: Harcourt, Brace & World, 1967), p. 94.

Parenthesis · Colon · Facts of publication · Comma · Period · Parenthesis · Page number · Comma

BIBLIOGRAPHY ENTRY

Author—last name first · Full title, including subtitle · First line at margin · Period · Colon

Mumford, Lewis. <u>The Myth of the Machine:</u> <u>Technics and Human Development.</u> New York: Harcourt, Brace & World, 1967.

Indention · Period · Colon · Facts of publication · Comma · Period

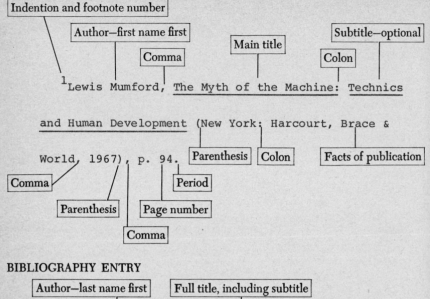

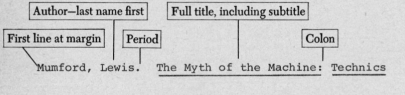

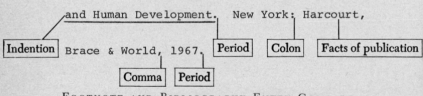

FOOTNOTE AND BIBLIOGRAPHY ENTRY COMPARED

6. A long bibliography may be divided for the reader's convenience into several parts, for example, primary and secondary sources, or books, articles, and public documents.

7. An annotated bibliography comments briefly on individual items in the list.

Rogin, Michael Paul. *Fathers and Children.* New York: Knopf, 1975. Psychological study of Andrew Jackson extending his childhood rage against his mother to his adult policies.

A SAMPLE BIBLIOGRAPHY

"Approaching the Edge of Chaos." *Time,* 23 June 1975.

Association of the Bar of the City of New York. *Conflict of Interest and Public Service.* Cambridge: Harvard Univ. Press, 1960.

DeMott, Benjamin. "Hot-Air Meeting: Golden Oldies of the Sixties." *Harper's,* July 1975, pp. 71–84.

McLuhan, Marshall. *The Gutenberg Galaxy: The Making of Typographic Man.* Toronto: Univ. of Toronto Press, 1962.

———. *Understanding Media: The Extensions of Man.* New York: McGraw-Hill, 1964.

Myers, John G. "Determinants of Private Brand Attitude." *Journal of Marketing Research,* 4 (February 1967), 73–81.

The New Encyclopaedia Britannica. 15th ed. 30 vols. Chicago, 1974.

Postman, Neil, and Weingartner, Charles. *Teaching as a Subversive Activity.* New York: Delacorte, 1969.

Spencer, Hazelton, ed. *Elizabethan Plays.* Boston: Little, Brown, 1933.

Wain, John. *Samuel Johnson.* New York: Viking, 1975.

A Sample Library Paper

On the following pages you will find a library paper, "Charles Macklin's Shylock," in a form that is widely accepted in academic work. Written by a student, the paper has these features that are especially worthy of your notice.

1. A subject of sufficiently limited scope so that it can be treated adequately in a paper of the length required.
2. The use of scholarly and evidently reliable library sources.
3. A beginning that clearly sets forth the author's purpose, and a close that establishes the significance of his findings.
4. A prose style that is factual, yet lively.
5. An attractive format, with footnotes and bibliography generally conforming to the standards of the Modern Language Association, and a long quotation properly indented and single spaced.

Richard J. Conway
English 101

CHARLES MACKLIN'S SHYLOCK

Outline

Central Idea: Charles Macklin's portrayal of Shylock marked a turning point in the stage treatment of Shakespeare's moneylender.

I. Introduction
   A. Background: Macklin's reputation
   B. Purpose of the paper
      1. To examine Macklin's handling of Shylock
      2. To note the effect of Macklin's creation on the role itself
II. Macklin's predecessor as Shylock
   A. The play: Granville's adaptation, <u>The Jew of Venice</u>
   B. The actor: Thomas Doggett, playing for low comedy
III. Macklin's premier performance of the role
   A. Interpretation
      1. Savage, fierce, ominous
      2. Revengefulness emphasized
   B. Contemporary criticism
      1. Lichtenberg's impression
      2. Impressions of other observers
IV. Effects of Macklin's interpretation
   A. Marked beginning of realistic portrayal of Shylock
   B. Made Shylock more than a farcical figure

CHARLES MACKLIN'S SHYLOCK

Although eighteenth-century London witnessed the appearance of a number of talented and spirited actors, undoubtedly one of the most interesting stage figures of this period was Charles Macklin. Macklin, whose stage career spanned some sixty years, was actively involved in virtually every aspect of theater life. As an actor, he appeared in more than fifty different roles and was instrumental in the development of a new style of acting; as a playwright, he received plaudits for his The Man of the World, one of the most popular plays of the late eighteenth century; as a figure concerned with historical accuracy on the stage, he was the recipient of much praise--and much abuse--for his handling of the costumes and setting of Macbeth. All in all, his gifts to the theater were numerous. Yet, probably Macklin's greatest accomplishment was his innovative interpretation of Shylock, the controversial usurer of Shakespeare's The Merchant of Venice. His performance in this drama not only represented a new and unique treatment of Shylock, but also raised and attempted to answer an important question: exactly how should Shakespeare's moneylender be played? The purpose of this paper is to examine Macklin's handling of Shylock and to discuss the overall effect of his creation on the role itself.

Since the importance of his performance lies, at least in part, in its radical departure from previous treatments of the character, a brief look at the Shylock which preceded Macklin's interpretation would be helpful. Although The Merchant of Venice was by no means a popular drama during the first half of the eighteenth century, one cannot presume that audiences of this period knew nothing of the play and its characters. Theater scholar Bernard Grebanier suggests that London theatergoers frequently witnessed The Jew of Venice, George Granville's adaptation of Shakespeare's comedy—an adaptation which featured Thomas Doggett, a famous low-comedy actor, in the role of Shylock.[1] Hence, when the Drury Lane Theatre announced in 1741 the revival of the long-forgotten The Merchant of Venice,[2] the anticipated production was not totally unfamiliar to audiences. In fact, it is certainly possible that the playgoers who attended the opening performance of Shakespeare's comedy—a production which presented Macklin as Shylock—were well aware of (and perhaps expecting to see) Doggett's comic creation. What they witnessed, however, was in no way similar to Doggett's Shylock.

The initial Drury Lane production of The Merchant of Venice occurred on February 14, 1741,[3] and Macklin's performance on that opening night proved to be one of the highlights of his career. Toby Lelyveld, in Shylock on the Stage, contends that the Shylock created by Macklin was fierce, ominous, and savage, and that the actor's emphasis upon the usurer's revengefulness established Shylock as some sort of demonic figure.[4] An excellent description of the forcefulness of Macklin's character is furnished by Georg Lichtenberg, a German critic who witnessed the actor's performance:

---

[1] Bernard Grebanier, The Truth About Shylock (New York: Random House, 1962), p. 313.

[2] William W. Appleton, Charles Macklin: An Actor's Life (Cambridge: Harvard University Press, 1960), pp. 43-44.

[3] Arthur H. Scouten, The London Stage, 1729-1747 (Carbondale: Southern Illinois University Press, 1960), II, 889.

[4] Toby Lelyveld, Shylock on the Stage (London: Routledge and Kegan Paul Ltd., 1961), pp. 22-23.

3

> Imagine a rather stout man with a coarse yellow face and a nose generously fashioned in all three dimensions, and a long double chin, and a mouth so carved by nature that the knife appears to have slit him right up to the ears, on the one side at least, I thought. He wears a long black gown, long wide trousers, and a red tricorne, after the fashion of Italian Jews, I suppose. The first words he utters, when he comes to the stage, are slowly and impressively spoken: "Three thousand ducats." The double "th" and the two sibilants, especially the second after the "t," which Macklin lisps as lickerishly as if he were savoring the ducats and all that they would buy, make so deep an impression in the man's favour that nothing can destroy it. Three such words uttered thus at the outset give the keynote of his whole character.[5]

Lichtenberg's impressions of Shylock's powerful presence were apparently shared by other members of the audience as well. The observations of James Boaden, in Memoirs of John Philip Kemble, are particularly revealing: "His features were rigid, his eye cold and colourless. . . . There was such an iron-visaged look, such a relentless, savage cast of manners, that the audience seemed to shrink from the character."[6] Another theater-goer, John Doran, recalls the reaction of the audience to Shylock's appearance in the trial scene: "Shylock was . . . so terribly malignant, that when he whetted his knife . . . a shudder went round the house and the profound silence following told me that he held his audience by the heart-strings."[7]

---

[5] Georg Lichtenberg, Letters from England, ed. Margaret L. Mare and W. H. Quarrell (New York: Benjamin Blom, 1969), p. 40.

[6] James Boaden, Memoirs of John Philip Kemble (London: Longman, Hurst, Rees, Orme, Brown, and Green, 1825), I, 440.

[7] John Doran, "Their Majesties' Servants," in Annals of the English Stage (New York: W. J. Widdleton, 1865, II, 293.

4

Even the scene in which Shylock laments the loss of his daughter was played with much intensity. Though Francis Gentleman notes that the character's grief was evident,[8] his villainy apparently remained unmitigated throughout the play.[9]

From these reports, one may discern that Macklin's creation was the epitome of savagery and vindictiveness. Yet these comments should not be interpreted as indicating any disapproval of his performance; for Macklin's Shylock came to be one of the most famous stage figures of the period, and between February and May, 1741, the actor appeared in this role, according to biographer William Appleton, twenty-two times[10]--an impressive figure by eighteenth-century standards. Moreover, this performance marked the beginning of a new style of acting. Allardyce Nicoll, in A History of English Drama, 1660-1900, suggests that the arrival on the stage of Macklin and David Garrick led to a more natural and realistic method of delivery. Nicoll notes that Macklin's portrayal of Shylock was one of the earliest examples of this trend,[11] and thus it becomes evident that his performance, in addition to its immense

---

[8] Francis Gentleman, The Dramatic Censor (London: Bell, 1770), p. 292.

[9] Appleton, p. 52.

[10] Ibid., p. 55.

[11] Allardyce Nicoll, A History of English Drama, 1660-1900 (Cambridge: University Press, 1925), II, 415.

popularity, contributed greatly to the development of a new school of acting.

Perhaps even more importantly, though, Macklin shed new light on Shylock himself. His successful handling of the character provided strong evidence that Shylock was more than the farcical figure portrayed by Doggett. Interestingly, this judgment has been shared by many of Macklin's successors. Though the Shylocks by such later noteworthy figures as Edwin Booth and Edmund Kean differed somewhat from Macklin's version, the character was nevertheless treated seriously. And while there still remains some debate over the precise handling of the role, there is little disagreement concerning the value of Macklin's contribution. In an artistic as well as an historical sense, then, Macklin's interpretation of Shylock represents an indelible theater landmark.

6

BIBLIOGRAPHY

Appleton, William W. Charles Macklin: An Actor's Life. Cambridge: Harvard University Press, 1960.

Avery, Emmett L., et al. The London Stage, 1660–1880. 5 pts. in 11 vols. Carbondale: Southern Illinois University Press, 1960–1968.

Boaden, James. Memoirs of John Philip Kemble. London: Longman, Hurst, Rees, Orme, Brown, and Green, 1825.

Doran, John. "Their Majesties' Servants." Annals of the English Stage. New York: W. J. Widdleton, 1865. II, 289–297.

Gentleman, Francis. The Dramatic Censor. London: Bell, 1770.

Grebanier, Bernard. The Truth About Shylock. New York: Random House, 1962.

Lelyveld, Toby. Shylock on the Stage. London: Routledge and Kegan Paul Ltd., 1961.

Lichtenberg, Georg. Letters from England. Ed. Margaret L. Mare and W. H. Quarrell. New York: Benjamin Blom, 1969.

Nicoll, Allardyce. A History of English Drama, 1660–1900. 6 vols. Cambridge: University Press, 1925.

EXERCISE

A. Put in plain language the meaning of each of the following footnotes.

[1] Hyatt H. Waggoner, *Emerson as Poet* (Princeton, N.J.: Princeton Univ. Press, 1974), p. xi.

[2] Thomas Gray, *The Correspondence of Thomas Gray*, ed. Paget Toynbee and Leonard Whibley (Oxford: The Clarendon Press, 1935), III, 1298ff.

[3] S. H. Butcher and A. Lang, trans., *The Odyssey of Homer* (New York: Macmillan, 1895), pp. 93–94.

[4] Ibid., p. 110.

[5] George V. Taylor, "The Paris Bourse on the Eve of the Revolution, 1781–1789," *American Historical Review*, 67 (July 1962), 967.

[6] Federal Reserve Bank of New York, "A Guide to Writing Reports at the Federal Reserve Bank of New York," n.d., p. 4.

[7] Waggoner, p. 79.

[8] Alexander Pope, "Rape of the Lock," Canto III, ll. 7–8.

[9] Claude Kantner and Robert West, *Phonetics* (New York: Harper & Row, 1941), pp. 126–62 passim.

[10] 2 Corinthians 10:1–6.

[11] *The Marchants Avizo* (London: Thomas Orwin, c. 1591), pp. 10–11.

[12] Carl Hovland et al., *Communication and Persuasion* (1953; rpt., New Haven: Yale, 1963), p. 31

TOPICS FOR LIBRARY PAPERS

1. Write a library paper on one of the following topics. Use at least a half-dozen different sources of information.

(a) Determining current standards of American English usage

(b) Noam Chomsky's contribution to modern linguistics

(c) Effect of violence in television on aggressive behavior of children

(d) Collective settlements (communes) in the United States today

(e) The poetry of Siegfried Sassoon

(f) The life of trade in eighteenth-century London

(g) Samuel Butler as a satirist

(h) The critical reception of Arthur Koestler's *Darkness at Noon*

(i) Calvin Coolidge to Richard Nixon—a study in the accretion of presidential power

(j) Socrates and the Socratic method"

2. In developing a library paper on one of the following topics, use a variety of printed sources, including books, reference works, and periodicals.

(a) Compare the work of two poets, two writers of short stories, two artists, two architects, or any other two individuals working in the same medium.

(b) Trace the development of some school of thought, some art form, some political policy, or some scientific or technical breakthrough.

(c) Compare the contributions of two different cultures to American life, and the degree to which the two cultures have been absorbed into the American mainstream. You may, for example, choose for your study American Negroes and Puerto Ricans, Italians and Irish, Chinese and Japanese. Try to explain the causes of their successes or failures at assimilation.

(d) Relate the biographical facts about some critically acclaimed author to the nature of the work that author has produced. Some suggestions: Charlotte Bronte, Lord Byron, F. Scott Fitzgerald, Ernest Hemingway, William James, Stendhal, Virginia Woolf.

3. After full research, write a paper on one of the topics listed in Exercise C, Chapter 9.

11 Business Letters

Letters are the most personal and probably the most versatile form of written communication in business. They answer inquiries, collect money due, adjust complaints, sell goods, promote services, and in fact handle the bulk of routine business that might otherwise be conducted face to face or by telephone. Not only business and professional people, but private individuals as well, have many occasions to write business letters. You yourself, for example, may use a letter to request a college catalog, order goods, make a complaint, or find a job. How well you write the letter helps to determine the response you get. Businessmen are thoroughly aware of the importance of letters, and many companies offer their employees training in writing them effectively. This training usually stresses not only the virtues of accuracy, clearness, and conciseness, but also the development of rapport with the reader—an important consideration in business, where good human relations are essential to success.

In keeping with their utilitarian function, business letters have a number of distinguishing characteristics: (1) their form, (2) their point of view, (3) their style, and (4) their structure.

Form

The physical arrangement of a letter follows certain accepted usages. Occasionally an individual or a business house changes the format or even omits certain parts, like "Dear Mr. Jones" or "Very truly yours." On the whole, though, changes are resisted on the theory that they call undue attention to parts of the letter that are best taken for granted. Much more concern is shown for neatness, utility, and correctness in form than for originality. If the setting is agreeably conventional—so the theory goes—then the letter can be read without distraction and its chances for success are improved.

Letterhead

HARKNESS TRUST COMPANY
800 Market Street
San Francisco, California 94105

January 22, 19—

Date

Inside address

Mr. Gelett C. Grant, Treasurer
Croesus Trust Company
505 Marquette Avenue
Minneapolis, Minnesota 55102

Salutation

Dear Mr. Grant:

We are thinking of making some revisions in our employee pension plan. Since your company has recently undergone a similar process, I wonder if you would share with us some of your experience.

On the enclosed form you will find a half-dozen questions, which I believe you will be able to answer in a few minutes. Please add any comments you wish.

If, as I suppose, your company has a printed description of the new pension plan, with its terms and conditions, will you be kind enough to put a copy in the mail along with your answer to the questionnaire.

I look forward to your response and want to assure you that if ever we can return the favor, we would be delighted to help.

Complimentary close

Sincerely yours,
Ellen R. Masters
Ellen R. Masters
Controller

Signature

Identifying initials

ERM:PE

Enclosure notation

enclosure

FORM OF A BUSINESS LETTER

The letter is usually typed on good-quality white paper, $8\frac{1}{2}$ by 11 inches in size, with the company's name and address (the "letterhead") printed at the top. A margin of white space—at least an inch at the sides and bottom—frames the letter. The body of the letter is preceded by a date, an inside address, and a salutation, and is followed by a complimentary close and signature. These parts are placed in the positions shown in the model on page 211. Except for very short letters, the lines of the body are single-spaced, with double spacing between paragraphs. Paragraph indentions are not necessary.

Some specific comments on the mechanics of the letter follow.

1. Where a printed letterhead is not used, the heading is typed in three lines, consisting of (1) the street address, (2) the city, state, and zip code, and (3) the date. No punctuation is used at the ends of the lines except for abbreviations:

1945 South Woodward Street
Detroit, Michigan 48226
November 26, 19—

2. The inside address and the envelope address are the same. Names of individuals should be preceded by their titles, for example, *Mr., Miss, Mrs., Dr., The Reverend, Colonel, Professor. Ms.* is used to designate either a married or an unmarried woman. Special forms of address for public officials, the clergy, and the like, are given in *Webster's Third New International Dictionary.*

3. The salutation (Dear____) is followed by a colon. When an organization is addressed, the proper salutation is *Ladies* or *Gentlemen,* depending on the primary composition of the group.

4. The customary complimentary close is *Very truly yours.* Other, somewhat less formal closes are *Sincerely yours* and *Sincerely.* A comma often, but not always, follows.

Point of View

A good letter shows consideration for the reader not only because good manners require it, but because good business requires it as well. In adapting to the reader's point of view, you should find the following suggestions helpful.

1. *Direct the letter to the interests of the reader.* When the letter is so written, it is said to have "the *you* attitude"; that is, it includes all the information the reader needs to make a satisfactory response and, just as important, it provides a psychological stimulus by appealing to the reader's self-interest. The presence of the pronoun *you* is not necessarily a sign that the *you* attitude is present, but the absence of the pronoun may suggest that the reader's interests have not been sufficiently considered.

Below are some additional examples showing the difference between the "*we* attitude," which concentrates undesirably on the writer's point of view, and the "*you* attitude," which concentrates on the reader's.

We Attitude	You Attitude
I need this information for a paper I am writing.	Your management record is so outstanding that I feel my paper would not be complete without a reference to it.
Our new policy will save us a great deal of money.	The new policy will help us give you prompter service.
The Excelsior model is the one we are now specializing in.	The Excelsior model is designed to give you many years of trouble-free service.
For our records, we must have your account number on all remittances.	To ensure proper credit, please put your account number on all remittances.

2. *Be courteous and tactful.* No matter what the situation, you can almost certainly win more points with courtesy than without. Words like *please, thank you,* and *I'm sorry* should be used whenever appropriate—in asking a favor, expressing appreciation, or smoothing over hurt feelings. On the other hand, expressions of suspicion and distrust should be avoided.

Brusque	Courteous
I would like a copy of your company's latest annual report.	Will you please send me a copy of your company's latest annual report.
I have your refund check for $25.	Thank you for your refund check for $25.
Attend to this matter now.	Please attend to this matter now.
You claim the stock certificate was lost.	We are sorry about the loss of the stock certificate.

Sometimes the substitution of the passive voice for the more direct active voice permits you to express tactfully an idea that would otherwise strike the reader as crude or offensive. (For differences between active and passive voice, see the "Handbook of English," Rule 30d(2).)

ACTIVE [TACTLESS]: You neglected to sign the card.
PASSIVE [TACTFUL]: The card was returned unsigned.

ACTIVE [TACTLESS]: You failed to give us your new address.
PASSIVE [TACTFUL]: We were not informed of your new address.

3. *Adopt a positive stance,* as opposed to a negative one. Let the letter tell what you can do, not what you cannot do; what your policy is, not what it is not. The language as well as the point of view should be positive. Positive words attract; negative words repel. Positive words stress the affirmative or favorable aspects of a situation; negative words stress the unfavorable aspects.

NEGATIVE

```
Dear Mr. Frantz:

You do not qualify for membership in the Byron Club be-
cause you are still a freshman and we cannot consider
your application until you reach your Junior year.
Otherwise we would be violating the club's by-laws.

I regret that your request must be denied.

                                        Very truly yours,
```

Here is the same letter recast in positive terms:

POSITIVE

```
Dear Mr. Frantz:

Your inquiry about joining the Byron Club is most wel-
come.  According to the club's by-laws, you will qualify
when you reach your Junior year.  Won't you please make
your application then?

We'll be looking forward to your active membership.

                                        Very truly yours,
```

In the instances below, note how the negative words and ideas can be either avoided or softened:

NOT: I'll try to avoid a *recurrence* of this *unfortunate delay.*
BUT: I'll try to get my papers in *more promptly* from now on.

NOT: *If I have failed to answer* any of your questions, please let me know.
BUT: *If you still have* any questions, please let me know.

NOT: I hope you *have not forgotten* my request for your service manual.
BUT: *Have you received* my request for your service manual?

Style

The character or individuality exhibited by a letter is its style. Although a great deal of lower-level correspondence is stereotyped, following ritualistic forms like "We wish to acknowledge receipt of your letter," business executives do place a high value on fresher and more personal modes of expression. The lack of originality found in routine correspondence probably has to do with the large volume and repetitive nature of the letters. Stereotyped writing in business also has its roots in the tendency of supervisors to discourage departures from phrasing that has stood the test of time and is therefore "safe." Despite the conditions that encourage conformity in expression, however, many managements have taken a close look at their companies' correspondence practices and are revising the stereotyped forms to make them sound more natural.

If the executive's letters are more original than the subordinate's—and they usually are—an important reason is that upper-echelon employees deal with situations that are less likely to be routine. Such employees are also less likely to be subject to unimaginative supervisory restraints. However, any writer wishing to develop a good letter style can benefit from the application of certain precepts.

1. *Be yourself.* A good letter sounds as if the writer were talking rather than merely mimicking the jargon unfortunately associated with "business English." Many stereotyped phrases come from the beginning and ending of letters, where the temptation to use stereotyped language is probably most acute.

Stereotyped	Natural
Subsequent to receipt of	After we receive
The said property	This property
As per your request	As you requested
Enclosed please find	You will find enclosed
We deem it advisable	We think it advisable

Note the contrast in the style of two letters:

STEREOTYPED

Dear Mrs. Pastor:

Pursuant to your communication of recent date, we are enclosing herewith the Summary of the Annual Stockholders Meeting of Excelsior Pictures Corporation. The empty envelope which you returned should have contained same.

```
As advised by you, we are changing your address on our
records to read as this letter is directed.

Regretting the inconvenience caused in this matter, we
remain

                                      Very truly yours,
```

NATURAL

```
Dear Mrs. Pastor:

Here is the Summary of the Annual Stockholders Meeting
of Excelsior Pictures Corporation.  This is the report
that should have been enclosed in the envelope you re-
ceived from us.  Please excuse the oversight.

We have changed your address as you requested.

                                      Very truly yours,
```

2. *Be personal in your language rather than impersonal or institutional.* Personal pronouns are often useful in countering the impersonalization often found in business letters. The use of the pronoun *you* in promoting the "*you* attitude" has already been mentioned. However, if they are employed not too conspicuously, the pronouns *I* and *we* are also useful. A writer uses *I* when he speaks for himself, and *we* when he speaks for the company. He may also use the *we* when he occupies a subordinate position and feels that statements made in the name of the organization carry more weight than those made in his own name. It is not unusual for a writer to use both *I* and *we* in the same letter, depending on whether he is referring to himself or to his company; for example, "*I* am sure *we* will be able to fill your order exactly as you specified."

Observe the differences between two sets of examples:

Impersonal	Personal
As requested	As you requested
It is suggested that	We suggest that
There is enclosed a memorandum	I am enclosing a memorandum
Notice has been received	We have received notice
Please address your reply to the undersigned.	Please address your reply to me.
The writer has noted	I have noted
The Grandview Corporation knows your problem.	We know your problem.

3. *Write concisely.* Business places a premium on conciseness because it believes in the adage that time is money. A concise letter is also more effective than a wordy one because it fixes attention on the important ideas and does not obscure them with either wasted words or unessential details.

In the following letter to a retailer, the last two sentences in the first paragraph are superfluous. Notice the improvement that results when they are removed.

Gentlemen:

Thank you for your order No. 53742 for the ten dozen Model 5T-537 Sonar table radios. We regret that we are out of this particular model and will not have another supply until the first of the year. ~~If we were going to fill your order, we would of course send you the advertising matter you requested, but since you will not have the goods for another six months, we think we ought to hold up the advertising, too~~.

Perhaps, in the meantime, you could select from our catalog a substitute for the model you wanted. We can supply you immediately with advertising for any model you choose. Please let us know if we can be of help.

Very truly yours,

You can save words and gain emphasis not only by carefully weighing the ideas that compose the whole letter, but also by editing the individual sentences for conciseness.

NOT: We acknowledge receipt of your letter of April 14 and in reply wish to state that the order you inquire about was mailed yesterday.

BUT: The order you inquire about in your letter of April 14 was mailed yesterday.

NOT: On June 6 I wrote you for an additional copy of Form 1027A, but to date I have not received an answer.

BUT: May I have the additional copy of Form 1027A I asked for in my letter of June 6.

Observe also the effect of omitting superfluous words.

During ~~the course of~~ our examination . . .

The matter is now ~~in the process of~~ being reviewed.

We appreciate your cooperation ~~in this matter.~~

~~For your information,~~ this certificate was canceled on . . .

~~We wish to take this opportunity to~~ thank you for . . .

Structure

The arrangement of ideas in a letter is functional; each part moves the letter farther toward its goal.

The Opening. The purpose of the opening is to attract the reader's attention and at the same time introduce the subject of your letter. You may refer to a letter received or a recent transaction, give information or ask for it, or make some other statement that concerns the reader. Dates and specific details are important especially when you write to a busy organization, for often the receiver cannot identify a transaction without such information. The openings that follow suggest a variety of possibilities. Pay particular attention to the simplicity, directness, and naturalness of the language.

I have your letter asking for payment of my account.

We are pleased to reply to your letter expressing an interest in our Morgate carpets.

Thank you for your thoughtful invitation.

Perhaps you can help me with a problem I have been experiencing with your stereo receiver No. A35, which I bought from you two months ago.

Will you please send me a copy of the study "Children in Custody," recently published by your office.

Yes, we do have a record of the transaction you inquire about in your letter of June 6.

As you requested, we are adding your name to our mailing list so that you may receive our house magazine, *The Lantern.*

We're planning a little party next week to celebrate our store's Fifth Anniversary.

The Body. The body of the letter gives the reader the details of the subject raised in the opening. In addition to providing current information, it may review pertinent facts, conditions, and policies. It may also tell why you will or will not comply with a request made by the reader. Try to explain your decision, especially if it is a negative one, in terms that will make it acceptable, as, for example, showing that your action promotes the reader's interests or that it is motivated by your desire to be fair to others.

Another point is that, in disputes, negative decisions are usually explained most effectively in an inductive arrangement, that is, with the facts or reasons given before the conclusion. By thus paving the way for the conclusion, you help to ensure its acceptance. A related procedure is to begin with uncontroversial points, or those on which there is agreement, before proceeding to those on which there is likely to be some disagreement. When, however, a conclusion favors the reader, it is generally wise to put it near the beginning of the letter. In other instances, the nature of the material may suggest the chronological order, the order of importance, or any of the other traditional arrangements of data. (See Chapter 2, "Topic and Plan.")

The contrasting letters on pages 220–221 show the effects of the selection and arrangement of material on the total impression.

The Close. In some instances, the purpose of the letter is fulfilled with the presentation of the body material, and no special close is necessary. More often, however, the letter requires a concluding statement, preferably in a separate paragraph. Its main function is to tell the reader what you want him to do or, if the purpose requires, what you are going to do for him. But whether or not some action is to be taken by either side, the close is also a good place for an expression of appreciation, assurance, or the like. Avoid overdoing the sentiment and, instead, end pleasantly but crisply. The temptation to sign off with such stereotypes as "Hoping this is satisfactory" and "We remain" should also be steadfastly resisted.

The sample endings that follow are recommended for their variety and directness.

ACTION CLOSINGS

When you have the opportunity, please let us know what you think of this proposal.

Please fill in the change-of-address form and return it to us.

I look forward to hearing from you soon.

May I drop in at your convenience and discuss this problem with you.

GOOD WILL CLOSINGS

Thank you for your interest in writing.

If there is anything more I can do, please let me know.

We appreciate very much your efforts on our behalf.

I hope this information will be helpful to you.

[After a complaint:]

You may be sure that we'll try to do better next time.

We sincerely regret the inconvenience caused you.

TWO LETTERS

1. This letter shows the effects of care with content, order, and tone:

Dear Senator Bell:	
Knowing your interest in higher education, I am writing on behalf of the Student Council of Metropolitan University about the Johnson bill, now before the State Senate.	Positive opening—Subject introduced
As you know, continual rises in tuition are making it difficult for students from middle-income families to continue their college education. The Johnson bill would provide subsidies which, though small, would permit many to remain in college who would otherwise have to drop out. A survey among our own student body shows that 10 percent would have to drop out at the end of this school year if help is not provided.	Facts and figures
We understand the many priorities that must control the allocation of State funds. We do believe, however, that our young people, especially those eager to improve themselves and the society in which they live, have a special claim to consideration. Their parents, all taxpayers and voters, share that claim.	Supportive emotional appeal
We ask you to consider this important segment of your constituency and vote "yes" for the Johnson bill.	Stimulus to action
Most respectfully,	

2. This is what the letter might sound like if needed care were not taken with content, order, and tone:

Dear Senator Bell:	
Your record on budget cutting suggests that you will vote against the Johnson bill to aid college students. This would be tragic. As student representatives of Metropolitan University, we urge you to vote for it.	Negative opening Stimulus to action misplaced

```
Our students are having difficulty staying
in college because of constant increases in
tuition.  If the Johnson bill is defeated,
the alternative for many of them will be to
quit college and go out on the streets,
where they will add to the army of the un-
employed and the antisocial elements.

We hope this letter clearly expresses our
sentiments.

                       Most respectfully,
```

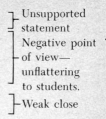

Unsupported statement

Negative point of view—unflattering to students.

Weak close

EXERCISES

A. Recast the following statements in order to improve the tone.

1. We are surprised to have your complaint in which you claim that you have not yet received your order of April 16.
2. Since your payment arrived late, we assume that you must be ignorant of our terms.
3. We will have to hold up your request for your new checkbook until you tell us whether you want the flat or the folding type.
4. Contrary to your opinion, this matter does not come within the jurisdiction of this department.
5. Your letter of December 2 alleges that one of the three packages we sent you was lost in transit.

B. Rewrite the following statements in better business-letter style.

1. If the above-stated terms are agreeable to you, kindly verify same by signing the enclosed copy of this letter and returning said copy to the undersigned.
2. Thanking you in advance for your kind assistance, I remain
3. Kindly contact the writer if the goods referred to in yours of the 19th are not received by you on or before the date requested as per this confirmation, and oblige.
4. Please be advised that we have not yet been in receipt of your reply to ours of the 14th in re our request for payment of your past-due account.
5. Replying to your letter of recent date, the booklet mentioned by you therein is now being reprinted and a copy of same will be sent to you forthwith.

C. Offer your opinion of the effectiveness of the following letters. Consider the tone, style, and arrangement. If a letter is faulty in any respect, recast it in line with your criticism.

1. Dear Mr. Avery:

We have received the flashlight which you say was damaged by the deterioration of your Neverfail batteries.

It is obvious that you did not take proper precautions to prevent corrosion. As you must know, a flashlight should not be allowed to lie idle for a long time without being checked for battery damage; and, if possible, old batteries should be removed altogether.

As you point out in your letter, Neverfail batteries are guaranteed against corrosion, so we suppose we will have to replace the batteries and the flashlight. They will be sent to you under separate cover.

Very truly yours,

2. Dear Miss Barton:

We wish to acknowledge receipt of your application for employment with this company. Since you are lacking the qualifications we seek, we do not think there would be any point in arranging an interview.

We regret that we cannot be of further assistance.

Very truly yours,

3. Dear Mr. Carey:

We have in hand your subscription to the *Monday Quarterback* under our special offer.

Please be so kind as to jot down at the bottom of the order blank the school or college you are attending and the year you expect to graduate.

This offer is for undergraduate students only.

Very truly yours,

4. Dear Mrs. Evans:

I am pleased to explain the $5 charge on your December statement.

Because of the misreading of your sales slip, your November account was charged $12 instead of $17 for the man's shirt you bought on October 19. The $5 debit on your December statement was made to reverse this error.

Of course, there should have been an explanation of the charge on the statement. Please excuse our oversight. We do appreciate your patience.

Sincerely yours,

LETTER PROBLEMS

1. You are doing some course research on monopolistic practices in the telephone industry. To get a corporate view of the subject, write to the Public Relations Department, American Telephone and Telegraph Company, 195 Broadway, New York, N.Y. 10007, asking if they could send you any company press releases or other printed material.

2. Assume that you wish either to continue your present undergraduate work at another college or to enter a graduate or professional school following completion of your present degree requirements. Write a letter to the Director of Admissions of the school of your choice. Ask for a catalog and application forms. Take the opportunity to ask any relevant questions you may have.

3. Assume that you are ready to apply to the school mentioned in Problem 2. You require several letters of recommendation. Write to a professor in your present school, asking him to write such a letter for you and to send it directly to the Director of Admissions.

4. Write a letter to your congressman or senator asking him or her to support legislation on behalf of some cause in which you are personally interested.

5. Write a letter to the editor of your local newspaper, commenting on, or taking issue with, an editorial that has appeared recently in the same paper.

6. Think of an unsatisfactory purchase you have recently made or unsatisfactory service you have recently received from a store or other place of business. Write a letter of complaint to the management.

7. For a college report, assume you are researching a subject for which information may be available from a large company. Write to the public relations department of the company for assistance. If you cannot think of a suitable research subject, look ahead to Chapter 13, Problem 5, page 251.

8. The MacAdam Department Store, 100 Main Street, your city, has today advertised in the *Daily Gazette* a sale on a Harmony AM-FM table radio at $59.50, reduced from $99. Write a letter ordering one for yourself. You are enclosing your personal check, which should include any local sales tax.

9. Assume that you have written the letter called for in Problem 8. Five weeks have gone by, and you have received neither an acknowledgment of your order, nor the radio. You have telephoned the store several times, but each time you were told by an indifferent clerk that a return call would be made to advise you of the status of the order. It may be that you were out when the return calls were made, but in any event your check has been returned by your bank, marked "paid" and you have still not heard from the store. You now decide to write a letter asking for satisfaction. Address the store manager by title (you do not know his name).

10. Take the role of the manager referred to in Problem 9. The order in question has been located. The radio was delivered by the United Parcel Service two weeks ago, but it was returned to the store because no one was at home to receive it. A notice should have been left advising the customer to call the store about another delivery date. Apparently something went wrong. Your own people were at fault for not following through. Write a letter of apology. Ask the customer to call your office directly (give telephone number and extension) to arrange for delivery.

12 Job Applications

A type of letter that almost every college student or graduate has occasion to write is the job application letter. This letter is usually accompanied by a résumé. Both should be neatly typewritten on plain white paper of good quality, size $8\frac{1}{2}$ by 11 inches.

The Résumé

Prospective employers almost invariably want a résumé because it provides, usually on a single sheet, a convenient reference to the applicant's record. The résumé is, in effect, a topical outline or summary of your qualifications for a job. Once it is composed, copies can be made and sent with a covering letter to a number of prospective employers. The objective is to obtain an interview. When, at a later date, you seek another job, the résumé can be brought up to date.

The basic requirements of a good résumé are that it be factual and very specific, that it be logically organized and neatly presented, and that the qualifications it offers satisfy the requirements of the position sought. The résumé usually bears the title "Résumé," "Personal Résumé," or "Data Sheet" at the top, and continues with a summary of your qualifications:

1. Your name, address, and telephone number.
2. Personal data: age, height and weight (optional), and any other personal information you consider relevant and advantageous to you.
3. The position desired.
4. Your education, including the names of relevant courses taken, extracurricular activities, awards, and so forth. Schools, with dates attended, should be listed in inverse chronological order (the last first). It is usually enough to mention the college or colleges attended, and to name the secondary school only if you were recently graduated from it or feel that your experience there would be of interest to the employer.

RÉSUMÉ

Jill M. Carey
56 Huguenot Place
Scarsdale, N. Y. 10583
Tel.: (914) 505-1212

Age: 20
Height: 5 ft. 5 in.
Weight: 114 lbs.

Position Desired: Summer sales work

Education

September 1976–Present, Fordham University
1972–1976, New Rochelle High School

Major Courses

English literature
Economics
Psychology

Minor Courses

Business Communication
Marketing Methods and Procedures

Work Experience

Summer 1977	Swimming counselor, Camp Honeybee, Keene, New Hampshire
Sept. 1976–June 1977	Bonwit Teller, Eastchester Store; sales and clerical work
Summer 1976	Revelation, White Plains, fashion boutique; sales

University Activities

Rush Chairwoman, Alpha Omega Chi
Dorm representative
Economics Club

Hobbies:

Tennis, Fashion, Music, Cooking

Reference

Dr. Frank C. Taylor
Professor of Marketing
Fordham University
Fordham Heights
New York, N. Y. 10458

A Sample Résumé

5. Your job experience, if any, including nonpaying or voluntary services. As with schools, list jobs in inverse chronological order, and give dates, names of organizations, and specific duties performed.

6. References: the names, titles, and addresses of several persons who will vouch for you. You need not list names of employers if you have already given their names under job experience. You may, however, give the name of a teacher or dean, a minister, or a friend of the family. References are not absolutely essential in the résumé, but you will undoubtedly be expected to provide them at the time of the job interview or before reporting for work.

A sample résumé is shown on page 226. You may use it as a guide, but you should not feel constrained to follow it too closely, especially if you find that some changes in content or order will better show off your particular qualifications or minimize some seeming deficiencies. Still, you should note in the sample several qualities worth emulating, including attractive appearance, good organization, and consistency in format and phrasing.

The Application Letter

The letter accompanying the résumé provides a personal touch that cannot be achieved with the résumé alone. Even if the letter does not have all the information in the résumé, it has all the important information and often some additional details. Perhaps the most notable advantage of the letter is that it gives you the opportunity to reveal yourself in a more original way than you can in the résumé, while at the same time you adapt the letter to the particular employer to whom you are writing. Through your use of language and the selection of details, you can impart something about your intelligence, personality, ambition, sincerity, and similar qualities. You can also appeal to the reader directly for consideration of your application and for a personal interview.

In its functions and organization, the letter of application is similar to a sales letter. It attracts favorable attention through its appearance and opening statement; it creates desire for your services through a description of your qualifications; it instills conviction through its tone and the specific details with which it backs its claims; and it stimulates action through its bid for an interview. In addition, the qualities that characterize all good business letters apply as well to the letter of application, and you will find it advantageous to review those qualities in the preceding chapter before you write.

Following are some comments on the specific parts of application letters.

HEADING

Type your address and the date in three lines at the upper right.

INSIDE ADDRESS

If possible, address the letter to the head of the personnel department or of the department in which you want to work. You may find the person's name in the company's literature or by telephoning the company. If you do not have a name, address the person by title, as, Personnel Director, or General Manager. If you are answering a help wanted advertisement, use the address in the advertisement. When a box number is given, use the following style:

X2531
New York Times
New York, N.Y. 10036

OPENING

The beginning should state your reason for writing and your most important qualification for the job you want. In some instances, your reason for wanting to work for the particular company you are addressing also makes a strong opening. Avoid clichés. Express yourself simply, directly, and naturally.

I believe that my love of children and my experience in caring for them will be a big asset to me as an aide in your summer nursery program.

As a sophomore majoring in biology, I have several free afternoons a week, during which I should like to be a laboratory assistant. Do you have an opening for an earnest, hard-working young woman willing to do any of the routine lab jobs you may assign her?

For the past two years I was a junior counselor at Camp Wah-loo in the Adirondacks. This summer I feel ready to take on the responsibilities of a full-time counselor. I am especially anxious to work at your camp because some of my friends have gone there and told me what a fine establishment you have.

Can you use an ambitious and personable young man in your Sales Department? The enclosed résumé will tell you something about my background and qualifications.

A major in mathematics, with honors, I should like to join your tutorial staff. I can give ten hours a week to the position.

BODY

Review your qualifications in detail, using somewhat the same order as in the résumé. Unless you answer a "blind" advertisement, you will know the organization to which you are writing. Use that information to adapt your letter to the reader. In a particular circumstance, for example, you may be able to say, "Your reputation for product development is well known and would, I believe, offer a fruitful outlet for my engineering training." Use the body also to give some idea of your personal qualities. You can do this without boasting if you rely on facts rather than mere claims. It is unbecoming for an applicant to say, for example, "I am a born leader and have an excellent personality," but the applicant may convey the same idea with a statement like, "As a member of the Student Council, I was chosen to lead the Blood Bank campaign, with results that the Dean described as the best in our history."

It is usually advisable not to mention salary in your letter, nor to express any reservations or give any information that may work to your disadvantage. For instance, do not begin a statement, "Although I have no practical experience," for it only underlines your doubts about yourself. The fact that you have no "practical experience" will be clear from your record. You should try to compensate by emphasizing your training, scholastic record, and personal qualifications. If you left another job because of a disagreement with the boss or because he refused to give you a raise in salary, it is better to omit the reasons from your letter. The important fact is that you want *this* job because you know you can fill it proficiently and enthusiastically.

CLOSE

End the letter by asking for an interview. Suggest a telephone call if you can be conveniently reached in that way. Use the complimentary close "Sincerely yours," typewrite your name several spaces below it, and sign your name in the space between.

May I have the opportunity to discuss this application with you in person. You may reach me by telephone at 777-4652.

If you wish to know more about my training and personal qualifications, I would be glad to see you at your office. A letter to the above address will reach me promptly.

I am sure that you will be able to tell more about my qualifications by seeing me and talking with me in person. Won't you arrange an interview soon? My telephone number is (212) 850-2220.

A sample letter intended to accompany the résumé on page 226 is shown below.

56 Huguenot Place
Scarsdale, New York 10583
April 18, 1978

Miss Joyce Benedict
Personnel Director
Bloomingdale's
Main Street
White Plains, New York 10602

Dear Miss Benedict:

Will you please consider my application for a sales position in your store this summer. I am just completing my sophomore year at Fordham University and look forward to obtaining some work experience that I am sure will be as rewarding to you as it will be to me.

In addition to taking work in English, economics, and psychology, I have been applying my basic knowledge in these subjects to such business areas as marketing and sales communications. During my senior year in high school, I had a sales position at Bonwit Teller in Eastchester, and during the previous summer I worked in a White Plains boutique. I enjoyed this experience and gained much knowledge about retailing operations at the same time.

Last summer I worked as a swimming counselor at Camp Honeybee, near Keene, New Hampshire. I have been invited to come back this summer, but I feel that I could spend my time more profitably in a job that demanded more of my academic background and natural interest in interacting with people in a business setting.

My parents have a charge account at your store, and I have shopped there often. I believe I would enjoy the experience of serving your customers in the attentive manner I know they are accustomed to.

May I have the chance to see you and have you judge my qualifications. I will look forward to hearing from you.

Sincerely yours,

Jill M. Carey

Jill M. Carey

Résumé enclosed

JOB APPLICATION PROBLEMS

1. Construct a one-page résumé which you will be able to use in applying for a job of your choice. In presenting your qualifications, use facts only.

2. Write a letter to accompany the résumé mentioned in Problem 1. Select a prospective employer that you feel you would like to work for. You may apply for a part-time, summer, or full-time job.

3. Assume that you have written the letter mentioned in Problem 2. It is now two weeks later and you have not received a reply. Write a follow-up letter, emphasizing your desire to work for the organization you have chosen.

4. Assume that you have just had an interview in response to your job application (Problem 2). The interviewer, Henry Cartelli, has told you that he is impressed with your qualifications, but that several more applicants have to be interviewed before a decision is made. That evening you decide to write a "thank you" letter to Mr. Cartelli. Use the letter to help swing the decision in your favor.

13 Memorandums and Reports

Much of the communication in business and technical fields is meant to serve the internal needs of the organization. There is a stream of written messages relating to personnel, work flow, methods, procedures, performance, and policies. Some of the messages come down from management, some are sent up from the operating departments to management, and some travel between or within departments. The long, formal messages, especially those representing considerable investigation, are usually classified as reports. Shorter messages, which might be described as internal letters, are called memorandums. Both types of messages are primarily informative; hence the qualities most valued in them are clarity, precision, conciseness, and convenience to the reader.

Memorandums

Prolific in its uses, the memorandum may give or request information, provide instructions, make or analyze a proposal, state a policy, record information for future reference, or perform any other function required for management of the enterprise. Many memorandums are technical, relating to inspections, laboratory tests, and analyses of the performance of machines and equipment. Others deal with more mundane matters like employee attendance, coffee breaks, and changes in work assignments.

The physical form of memorandums varies among organizations, but special stationery is usually provided, sometimes with the printed heading "Interoffice Memorandum," and a format that designates the space for the date, names of the addressee and sender, and the title or subject. A number of different arrangements are shown in the sample memorandums reproduced in this chapter.

More objective than a letter, the memorandum relies for its effectiveness almost entirely on its data and reasoning, and on such authority as the writer may have. Technical memorandums and policy statements coming from higher management lean to formality in language, but other memorandums may be more personal, with the writer using the first person *I* to refer to himself and first names to refer to the reader and others in the organization. Normal courtesies are also observed, as in such expressions as *please* and *thank you.* Where the subject permits, enumerations and subheadings are used to divide material, and tables and charts may be included for documentation or ease of comprehension.

Here is a short, informal memorandum concerning a production problem.

MEMORANDUM

November 6, 19—

TO: Joe Hymes

FROM: Dave Weiss

SUBJECT: Job No. 820-A

Production is having problems with the thru-bolt that holds the crossbar in place. Either the bracket is too long or the screw is too short. There doesn't seem to be enough thread to secure the nut properly. Four washers are being used as spacers. Bill Ryer was called in to help with this problem and is checking it. I'll keep you posted.

The memorandum below, designed to guide management planning, is supported by an attached table.

INTEROFFICE CORRESPONDENCE

May 24, 19—

<u>Memorandum to Mrs. Lisa Dalton, Supervisor:</u>

Our records of Red Cross Bloodmobile visits for the past two years show a drop-out rate of 33 percent among those who signed up to donate blood. The schedule attached summarizes our experience. The reasons for the disparity between the number who agree to give blood and those who actually do are shown as follows:

1. Postponement by Red Cross

2. Appointments canceled

3. No show

If the Red Cross provides equipment for processing 125 donors a day on Wednesday, June 13, and Thursday, June 14, as they propose, we should have at least 375 employees signed up for the two-day visit.

I am sure you will want to keep these figures in mind when you make your arrangements.

Dennis T. Fielding

Dennis T. Fielding

encl.

[Attachment]

Record of Bloodmobile Visits

	May 1977	May 1976
Signed up to donate	393	374
Pints donated	282	249
Postponed by Red Cross	35	51
Appointments canceled	11	14
No show	65	60

Reports

Because business and technical reports are prepared in much the same way as other research papers and share most of their characteristics, as detailed in Chapters 9 and 10, we will confine our comments here to those differences worthy of special attention.

Purpose. Like their shorter counterparts—memorandums—business and technical reports are a response to a particular need for information by administrators, technicians, professional staffs, and the like. The purpose of these reports is to assist in controlling the quality, cost, and volume of work and to aid in anticipating and treating problems of all sorts. A report, for example, might deal with the choice of a site for a new plant, the feasibility of changing hours of work, the desirability of substituting one method of production for another, or the consequences on profits of a proposed change in the tax laws. Although this chapter is concerned primarily with internal reports, other reports published in technical and professional journals deal with problems of more general significance and reach a wider audience. Some reports are purely factual; these are informational reports. Other reports go beyond the facts to an analysis of them, with conclusions and recommendations; these are analytical reports.

Research. Whereas the library report is based on reading, the business or technical report is more likely to be derived from personal observation and experience, interviews and questionnaires, and laboratory and field experiments. The standards generally accepted for research in your particular field of investigation—for example, economics, thermodynamics, sociology, marketing—should be observed; and where statistical methods are involved, the sampling and projective techniques should be valid.

Organization of Data. Like any other research report, the business or technical report—except for the purely informative kind—originates with a hypothesis that leads to an investigation and a conclusion. In many instances, however, the report places the conclusion first and then adds the supporting data. This procedure is followed when the authority of the writer is established or when, under any circumstances, the reader is likely to be more interested in the conclusion than in the evidence from which it is drawn. When it is possible that the reader will disagree with the conclusion, wisdom may dictate that the report be presented inductively, with the conclusion following the evidence.

Although every report is unique in content, close study of reports often shows certain similarities in structure. Some organizations even develop model formats for their writers. The models shown here are not intended to be adopted without change, but they suggest a number of possible arrangements. Within the several parts, sections, and paragraphs of the report, the conventional principles of literary organization apply. (See Rule 31 in the "Handbook of English.")

Some Basic Report Formats

A.

I. Introduction
II. Discussion
III. Conclusions

B.

I. Statement of the problem
II. Recommendations
III. Supporting data

C.

I. Introduction
II. Analysis of problem
III. Proposed solution
IV. Anticipated results
V. Recommendations

D.

I. Background
II. Faults of present system
III. Alternatives
IV. Recommendations
V. Conclusion

E.

I. Introduction
II. Recommendations
III. Background
IV. Present procedure
V. Proposed procedure
VI. Conclusions

F.

I. Introduction
II. Summary of conclusions and recommendations
III. Investigative data
IV. Conclusions
V. Recommendations
VI. Exhibits

Tone and Style

Ideally, the language of a formal report is objective, clear, and as plain as the subject and audience permit. A good report puts a premium on facts and presents its findings in a temperate, unbiased way. It is not a forum for prejudicial statements, opinionated remarks, or unsupported assertions. Judgments and inferences should be based on specific data and logical reasoning. The resulting style may be described as "dry," but it will not be dull if the interests of the reader are carefully considered and the ideas are well expressed. Expressions like "These facts conclusively prove," "It is absolutely essential that," and "Obviously, Dempsey is an incompetent," are the earmarks of ill-considered report prose. Better are such expressions as:

These facts suggest that . . .

More efficient production of this item requires . . .

Dempsey's performance has been criticized on more than one occasion by his immediate superior.

To achieve objectivity, try to concentrate on the objects, facts, and processes you are concerned with rather than on your personal reactions to them. You may also use the passive voice or other constructions that bypass the need for your personal intrusion.[1] For example:

PERSONAL (ACTIVE): *In my investigation I found* that the consumption of copying paper reached a high point of 245 reams during October.
OBJECTIVE (ACTIVE): *Investigation showed* that the consumption of copying paper reached a high point of 245 reams during October.
PERSONAL (ACTIVE): I propose three alternative solutions.
OBJECTIVE (PASSIVE): Three alternative solutions are proposed.

When the context requires that you refer to yourself, you may of course use the *I* or a less personal designation like *the writer, the analyst,* or *this investigator.*

When the study was half completed, *I* [or *this analyst*] received a call from Miss Flexner suggesting an interview in her office.

Word choice in the report is largely influenced by the need to adapt to the specific reader or audience you wish to reach. The use of technical language is desirable and necessary in writing to the specialist, but the language may need to be modified if the report is to be read by people in the organization who are not specialists in the subject covered or by laymen not connected with the organization at all. When technical terms are used, it is sometimes necessary to define them, as in the examples on pages 114–115. Whatever audience you aim for, language that is specific and concise is better than language that is general and wordy.

Two contrasting examples of business-report style are shown below. The first is taken from a draft on cost control. Here the wordiness and abstract language tend to hide the meaning.

The basic objective of the program is to assist management in reducing the controlling clerical costs. Broadly speaking, reduction in clerical costs is achieved through simplification of the operations performed and measurement of the work involved in daily routines. In this manner, unnecessary

[1] Except for this or some other good reason, use the active voice. See "Handbook of English," Rule 30d(2).

work is eliminated and substandard employee efficiency is highlighted together with the reasons for such inefficiency.

Since the program is designed to provide a continuing mechanism for achieving performance improvements and maintaining good levels of performance, the savings achieved will be obtained every year in the foreseeable future. In this manner, the program affords management the means of insuring continued clerical cost control and counteracts the tendency on the part of supervisors to increase staff after completion of a "one shot" staff reduction program.

Since the program has been viewed in terms of long-range planning by management, no major emphasis has been placed during installation on improving performances in areas where efficiency is below standard. After installation of the incentive system, certain supervisors immediately set about improving performance through training and regulation of work flow while others made little or no attempt to correct the conditions leading to inefficiency. The control and reporting system will provide the basis for future evaluation of the performance of supervisors with regard to proper planning and scheduling of work flow. Other benefits are development of a sound on-the-job training program and maintenance of effective levels of clerical productivity.

Note the improvement in clarity and interest when the passage is made more specific and concise. The enumeration is also helpful.

The basic aim of the program is to reduce costs by simplifying work and measuring and improving individual efficiency.

Properly administered, the system will ensure good performance and continued savings for years to come. It is designed incidentally to counteract the tendency of supervisors to increase the staff following a "one-shot" staff reduction program.

In line with our objective, efforts are being made to help supervisors in these areas:

1. Plan and schedule work flow.
2. Develop an on-the-job training program.
3. Maintain effective levels of clerical productivity.

So far the cooperation of supervisors has not been uniform. However, the program's control and reporting system provides the basis for rating them on their performance in the future.

Format

A long report sometimes takes the form of a long memorandum. In other instances, the report may be put within covers and include any or all of the following features:

1. *Title page.* This may have, in addition to the title, the name and position of the author, the name of the organization for which the report was prepared, and the date.

2. *Letter of Transmittal.* The letter, addressed to the reader, indicates the authorization for the report, its purpose and scope, and the information sources used (for example, "first-hand observation" or "interviews.") The letter is either clipped to the top cover of the report or bound into it directly following the title page.

3. *Abstract or Summary.* Technical and professional papers prepared for publication in scholarly journals often begin with an abstract, or brief summary, which appears on the first page of the text immediately below the title. Some organizational reports follow the same practice, although they are more likely to begin with a summary of only the conclusions and recommendations.

4. *Headings and Enumerations.* The use of divisional headings and the occasional listing and numbering of coordinate elements improve display and facilitate reading.

5. *Tables and Charts.* Except for simple "spot" tables, which form an integral part of the text, exhibits are usually placed on the pages

FIGURE 4

U.S. HOUSEHOLDS HAVING CARS, TV, AND TELEPHONES

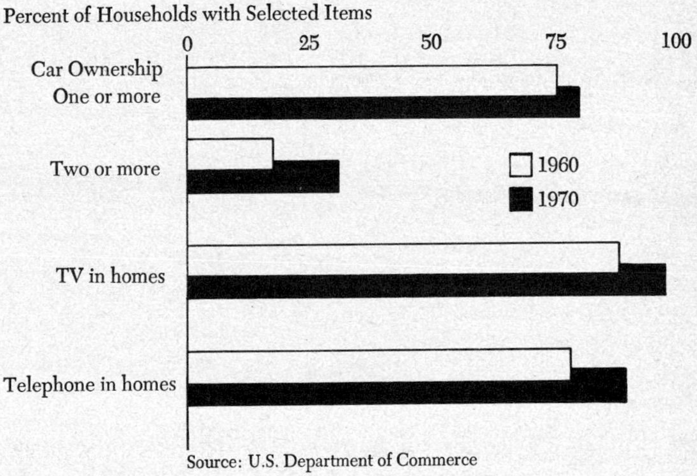

A Chart for Use in a Business Report

immediately following the text reference to them, or, as an alternative, in an appendix at the end of the report. The exhibits should be numbered and titled as in the example on page 239, and reference to each should always be made by number in the appropriate place in the text.

6. *Footnotes and Bibliography.* If more than a few reference footnotes are necessary, they are often placed consecutively after the last page of the text. If only several books and periodicals have been used in the research, references to them may be incorporated into the text or mention made in the preface. If more than a few books have been used, a bibliography should be appended.

A Sample Report

A type of report common to many organizations is shown on the following pages. Based on first-hand research, it offers you the opportunity to examine the content, language, and make-up of a fairly formal, but not over-technical treatment of a familiar business problem.

INCREASING THE NUMBER

OF QUALIFIED JOB APPLICANTS

Helene Rivera
Personnel Recruiting

Dasher and Blitzen, Inc.

February 2, 19--

February 2, 19--

Mr. Helmut Garson
Personnel Director
Dasher and Blitzen, Inc.
Chicago, Illinois

Dear Mr. Garson:

You asked me in your memorandum of January 14 to look into our experience over the past year in obtaining qualified employees and the prospects for meeting our needs in the year ahead.

The material for the accompanying report was drawn from our personnel records and from the experiences of other companies whose personnel managers I consulted. I have included my recommendation, which I believe can be instrumental in helping us find the people we need.

I shall be pleased to discuss my report with you at any time.

Sincerely,

Helene Rivera

Helene Rivera

INCREASING THE NUMBER OF QUALIFIED
JOB APPLICANTS

Background

Last year applicants qualified for Company openings were as difficult to obtain as the year before. The number of applicants rose perceptibly—about 10 percent—but the number of qualified applicants remained relatively small. The purpose of this report is to help determine what can be done to find qualified workers to fill open positions.

Recent Employment Experience
by Source of Applicants

In the past, one of the best sources for job applicants has been Company employees who have referred their friends to us. Last year we employed one in four of those applicants referred to us by our own employees, as compared to about one in ten through referral by employment agencies and one in eight from all other sources, including advertising. Although the percentage of those hired through employee referral is high, the actual number employed is relatively small, only 96 out of a total of 1,225 persons employed in 19—.

Employee Referrals

Our success with employee referrals can probably be

2

attributed to three factors. First, the employees act as an effective preliminary screen because they are familiar with our high standards for employment. Second, since their names will be used, they are apt to refer only those who are likely to be regarded as a credit to them. And third, the applicants themselves have a realistic picture of the Company and the jobs available because they have had the opportunity to talk to these employees beforehand. Recruiting workers through employee referrals has the added advantage of being inexpensive.

Agency Referrals

While we have been successful in placing a significant proportion of those applicants referred to us by our employees, our experience with referrals by employment agencies has been disappointing. On average, only 10 percent of the applicants referred to us through agencies are placed. When one considers the large number of applicants referred to us in this manner--6,300 in the past year--the time wasted by our interviewers in speaking with unqualified applicants becomes evident. This source is expensive as well as time-consuming; the average fee paid for each employee hired through an agency in 19-- was $225.

Community Practice

Because of the difficulty of getting qualified employees through other means, many companies are now paying a bonus to every employee who refers an applicant

3

who is hired. The employee is thus given an added incentive to refer qualified friends.

A survey of eleven downtown companies, three major banks, and three brokerage firms—all requiring office skills similar to those we seek—shows that twelve of the seventeen employers provide some form of bonus for employee referrals. Of the eleven downtown companies in the survey, six have a regular bonus plan. The awards range downward from $150 to small prizes such as desk sets, small electronic calculators, etc. The majority of those giving gifts, nine out of twelve, give cash or presents valued between $25 and $50. In every plan, all members of employment departments and all officers are excluded.

Problems Encountered

Only two problems were cited by the respondents. With proper restrictions on the program and better supervision, both problems can be controlled. The first problem is that of the employee who refers a friend only to collect the bonus. The friend works a short time and resigns. Among the organizations surveyed, four which give cash bonuses have a waiting period of two or three months. If the new employee has left in the meantime, no bonus is awarded. Three other companies give only part of the bonus immediately and the remainder not less than three months later. All other companies offering gifts distribute them when the new employee is hired.

4

The second problem arises from the posting of inadequate descriptions of the jobs available. If the nature of the openings is not made clear, friends are referred for whom there is no suitable opening. The resulting disappointment breeds ill will. With careful monitoring of the job announcements, this problem can undoubtedly be mitigated.

Recommendation

In view of the shortage of qualified personnel and following the practice of other companies of paying a referral bonus, the writer recommends that the Company institute the following program on a six-month trial basis:

A $50 United States Savings Bond be given an employee if the following conditions are met: (a) the employee refers an applicant; (b) the applicant is hired; and (c) the applicant is still in our employ at the end of two months.

The program, with a list of vacancies, would be advertised on bulletin boards throughout the Company, in the Company's house magazine, and in letters distributed to all employees. Care would be taken to make the job descriptions as specific as possible. Referral cards would be distributed to employees for their use. All officers of the Personnel Department would be excluded from the program.

Careful records would be kept during the trial period of six months, and evaluation would be made at the end of that period to determine whether the program should be continued.

EXERCISE

A. Comment on the style of the several report paragraphs reproduced below. What differences do you find? Consider the degree of formality, ease of reading, and appropriateness to particular audiences or purposes.

1. Data in the core memory of the Honeybee 20 computer may be in binary form as a six-bit character, or as a signed decimal number. Instructions are variable in length. Hardware interrupt is a standard feature of the central processor, which enables automatic branching between the main program and service routines. Simultaneous I/O operation with computing is possible through two read/write channels, one of which is optional.

2. Our Borehole Televiewer was patented in 1968. This instrument records the "fractures," or cracks, through which an oil well is drilled, and indicates the direction in which such fractures run. The Borehole Televiewer works even when the well is filled with oil or drilling mud, and can probe miles below the earth's surface with such precision that fractures as fine as $1/32$ of an inch can be detected. Locating fractures is a key element in the discovery and production of oil and gas.

3. For the first half of 19—, my preliminary data on cooperative advertising for the New England Division shows that seven District Offices ordered 3,956 mats[2] for bulk distribution to wholesalers. During the same period we paid $36,920 to 163 wholesalers as our share of their advertising. From the information we have, I'd be inclined to conclude that here in the East at least one half of our wholesalers are using some part of our advertising and promotion program.

4. Tabulation I also shows that there are 176.59 excess hours per month in the night file clerk position. It is therefore suggested that in addition to work from peak periods, work from the day force be assigned to the night force. Perhaps some of the pulling for vault papers, treasury bills, and/or bond maturities could be delegated to them. . . . The analyst will be glad to work with the Supervisor in determining the hours required for each of the suggested jobs and the possibilities for redistribution of the night force.

5. It is considered that the increased responsibility assumed will be balanced by the diminished ineffectual intelligence originating in

[2] These are forms from which newspaper advertisements are reproduced.

the departmental activities of the various subdivisions delegated under the new setup. Each will be responsible for its own. Pending the reissue of the organizational procedure to be adopted, it will be deemed sufficient for our purposes if uncoordinated activity be confined to those specific groups not immediately concerned and then only on such matters as are not within the scope of the above. Any retroactive action will be considered at a later date.

REPORT PROBLEMS

1. Assume that you are working for Helmut Johnson, a real estate developer. He has expressed an interest in population trends and land and water resources on a national scale. Working from the table below, write a memorandum to Mr. Johnson,

Table 1 **U.S. Population and Area From 1790**

Data 1790–1970 for census dates (Apr. 1 for 1930–70).

Year	Resident population: Number (1,000)	Resident population: Percent increase over prior year shown	Resident population: Per square mile of land area	Area (1,000 sq. mi.): Land	Area (1,000 sq. mi.): Water
1790	**3,929**	(X)	4.5	865	24
1800	**5,308**	35.1	6.1	865	24
1810	**7,240**	36.4	4.3	1,682	34
1820	**9,638**	33.1	5.5	1,749	39
1830	**12,866**	33.5	7.4	1,749	39
1840	**17,069**	32.7	9.8	1,749	39
1850	**23,192**	35.9	7.9	2,940	53
1860	**31,443**	35.6	10.6	2,970	53
1870	**39,818**	26.6	13.4	2,970	53
1880	**50,156**	26.0	16.9	2,970	53
1890	**62,948**	25.5	21.2	2,970	53
1900	**75,995**	20.7	25.6	2,970	53
1910	**91,972**	21.0	31.0	2,970	53
1920	**105,711**	14.9	35.6	2,969	53
1930	**122,775**	16.1	41.2	2,977	45
1940	**131,669**	7.2	44.2	2,977	45
1950	**151,326**	14.5	42.6	3,552	63
1960	**179,323**	18.5	50.5	3,541	74
1970	**203,185**	13.3	57.4	3,541	74

X Not applicable.

Source: U.S. Bureau of the Census.

putting into a paragraph or two the gist of the table's contents and significance. Assume that the table will accompany your memorandum.

2. At the request of Anton Pulaski, advertising manager of the Acme Postage Meter Company, you are making a case study of the results of the installation of an Acme Postage Meter at the Williams Furniture Company of Moline, Illinois. Mr. Pulaski wants to use your report for sales purposes. During interviews with several Williams executives, you jotted down the following notes. After making an outline, write a memorandum to Mr. Pulaski, incorporating your findings. Submit the outline to your instructor with your memorandum.

Meter resulted in 25-percent decrease in amount of postage used, as compared with previous year.
Previously, no check on stamps taken by employees for personal use; accounting difficult and inaccurate.
Meter does away with loose stamps.
Company mails 100 to 150 pieces daily.
1,500 to 5,000 pieces mailed regularly at end of month.
Handling of mail not previously centralized; each department handled own mail.
Present Model H installed in April, just one year ago.
Since installation, office boy handles all mail himself; means saving in time for other employees.
Machine saves at least two hours' time in getting out big end-of-month mailings which used to cause confusion and delay, upset office routine.
Postage cost before installation was $10,400 annually.
Most employees had access to stamps, but no more.
Meter makes accounting for postage easy and accurate.
Sixty employees on Lawson payroll.

3. The dean of your school is interested in determining the extent to which the new communication techniques and media are finding their way into the classroom. He has asked a number of students, including you, to report to him on the teaching aids used in four of your classes (taken now or in the recent past). Specifically, he has asked for information about

(a) Methods of presentation, for example, lecture, discussion, recitation.

(b) Use of printed materials, such as textbooks, readings, "handouts," cases.

(c) Use of computer and audio visual media: overhead projector, slides, films, tapes, records, etc.

In preparing a formal report for the dean, keep in mind that this is to be an objective survey of methods and media, not an evaluation of individual performance by any instructor. Include a tabular summary of the data, as well as your conclusions based on the evidence. You may also feel free to make any suggestions your experience suggests.

4. On the basis of your personal interest in and knowledge of the subject, and your ability to obtain the particulars, you are asked to write a formal report in which you make a technical comparison and appraisal of two or three fairly complex products, machines, methods, or processes of the same class. Address your report to some private individual or some executive who has presumably authorized the report and would therefore be interested in your findings. The report should include any appropriate exhibits and full acknowledgment of your sources of information. If your instructor directs, propose your report project in a memorandum to him, and proceed only after you have received his approval.

5. Assume that an executive in some existing organization has asked you to make an investigation of some aspect of communication or business procedure that may have considerable significance for his organization and to submit to him a written report of your findings. Your information may come from work experience, interviews, or library research. In any case, choose a topic sufficiently limited in scope so that it can be covered in depth in a report of about eight or ten pages of text (documentation and exhibits additional). See below for formal procedure and list of suggested topics. Do not proceed with Part II until Part I has been approved.

PART I. Submit, in memorandum form addressed to your instructor, a proposal for the report, stating the following:

(a) Title and business connection of the executive asking for the report.

(b) Subject of the investigation and the purpose to which the report will presumably be put.

(c) Prospective sources of information.

PART II. Submit the formal report, including a letter of transmittal, introduction, body, conclusion and/or recommendations.

SOME SUGGESTED TOPICS

(a) A study of the efficiency with which some particular part of the work is performed.

(b) An analysis of your college bulletin, with recommendations aimed at making it more helpful to students and more valuable as a showcase of the school's offerings.

(c) A formal proposal for a new course, new program, or some other improvement in the programs or facilities of your school.

(d) A study of a particular communication activity (consumer relations, employee relations, and so on) in a specific organization.

(e) The treatment of current social problems in company annual reports (for example, equal employment, ecology, health hazards, strikes, unemployment).

(f) Effects of the consumer movement in advertising strategy.

(g) The use of audio-visual techniques in company training programs.

(h) Tuition remission plans for employees in companies of your area.

(i) Methods of a particular company in dealing with adverse public opinion (for example, a public utility, an oil company).

(j) Analysis of the content of several comparable company newspapers or magazines.

Part II
A Handbook of English

GRAMMAR

1. The Grammar of Sentences
2. Sentence Fragment
3. Comma Fault
4. Agreement of Subject and Verb
5. Agreement of Pronoun and Antecedent
6. Case
7. Reference of Pronouns
8. Adjectives and Adverbs
9. Verbs

PUNCTUATION

10. End Punctuation
11. The Comma
12. The Semicolon
13. The Apostrophe
14. Quotation Marks
15. Other Marks
16. Unnecessary Punctuation

MECHANICS

17. Capitals
18. Underlining (Italics)
19. Abbreviations
20. Numbers and Amounts

SPELLING

21. Spelling

WORD USE

22. Word Use

SENTENCES

23. Sentence Sense
24. Unity
25. Order
26. "Dangling" Modifiers
27. Parallel Structure
28. Faulty Omissions
29. Point of View
30. Emphasis and Variety

PARAGRAPHS

31. Paragraphs

1 The Grammar of Sentences

gr

Grammar, from the Greek *gramma,* meaning "a letter of the alphabet," is the set of formal patterns in which words are arranged to convey larger meanings. It is also a branch of linguistics concerned with a study of those patterns, including their sounds. And it is the "etiquette" of language, differentiating between those word structures that are characteristic among literate people and those that are not. Our concern here is with the grammar of the written sentence.

A sentence is a grammatical unit of one word or a group of related words that is separated from other grammatical units, usually by a period, sometimes by a question mark or an exclamation point. A sentence is spoken of as *grammatically complete,* however, only when it has a subject and predicate (see **Rule 1b**).

I have lost my watch. Alas! [Two sentences; only the first is grammatically complete, but together they make complete sense.]

The ability to compose sentences is the most important technical qualification of the writer. It is the key to clarity, interest, and force. It also gives the writer the status that literacy invariably confers.

A change of order in the sentence may change the meaning.

The man bit the dog.
The dog bit the man.

Incorrect word order may mislead the reader.

Walking across the street, the car nearly hit the pedestrian. [The *car* walked across the street?]

Sentence structure affects emphasis.

WEAK: There are many children who are undernourished.
STRONG: Many children are undernourished.

An incorrect grammatical form suggests illiteracy.

He must have *lied* on the sidewalk for hours. [For *lain*]

1a. The Parts of Speech

The words that make up the language are classified, according to their use in a sentence, into eight parts of speech: nouns, pronouns, verbs, adjectives, adverbs, prepositions, conjunctions, and interjections.

(1) Nouns

A noun is the name of a person, place, thing, concept, or action (*doctor, river, locket, democracy, walking*). It changes its form to denote whether it is singular or plural (*method, methods*) and to show possession (*girl, girl's*). Proper nouns, that is, the names of particular persons, places, and things (*Theodore, Chicago, Xerox*) are capitalized; all other nouns—common nouns—are not capitalized unless they begin a sentence.

The presence of a noun is often indicated by the article *a, an,* or *the* which precedes it (*a boat, an apple, the country*). Many nouns are also identified by such characteristic endings as *-er, -or, -ence, -ance, -tion, -ment,* and *-ness* (*worker, tailor, presence, performance, decoration, attainment, loneliness*).

The principal uses of nouns are subject of a verb, object of a verb, and object of a preposition (See **Rules 1b** and **1c**).

The *President* will speak tomorrow in Chicago. [Subject of verb]
I accepted the *compliment.* [Object of verb]
Sue charged the purchase to her *account.* [Object of preposition]

(2) Pronouns

A pronoun is a word used to substitute for a noun or to denote persons or things understood from the context. In the sentence "When Mary arrived, *she* gave *her* name to the receptionist," the words *she* and *her* are pronoun substitutes for the noun *Mary*. The pronouns *I* and *you* are, respectively, substitutes for the person speaking and the person or persons addressed.

Pronouns may be classified as follows:

PERSONAL: I, you, he, she, it, we, they
RELATIVE: who, which, what, that. See also **Relative pronoun.**
I want a dog *that* can be trained.
DEMONSTRATIVE: this, that, these, those
That is a mackintosh apple.

INTERROGATIVE: who, which, what
What shall I say to him?
INDEFINITE: one, none, some, any, anyone, someone, somebody, nobody, each, everyone, everybody, either, neither, and so on.
REFLEXIVE: myself, yourself, himself, herself, itself, and so on
I asked *myself* the same question.
INTENSIVE: Same forms as reflexive pronouns, but used for emphasis.
You *yourself* drove the car that night.
They *themselves* are the victims.
RECIPROCAL: each other, one another
They congratulated *each other.*
Love *one another.*
NUMERICAL: one, two, three, and so on; first, second, third, . . .
Only *three* were present.
He was the *first* to claim the honor.

Many pronouns change their form to denote case (nominative, possessive, and objective) and number (singular and plural).

NOMINATIVE: I, he, she, who, and so on

POSSESSIVE: my, mine; his; her, hers, whose, . . .

OBJECTIVE: me, him, her, whom, . . .

SINGULAR: I, myself, he, she, . . .

PLURAL: we, ourselves, they, . . .

Choosing the correct form of the pronoun often causes difficulty. (See **Rule 5**, "Agreement of Pronoun and Antecedent," and **Rule 6**, "Case.")

I admired *him* as a person to *whom* [NOT: *who*] one could go for help.
She urged *me* to give the award to *whoever* [NOT: *whomever*] deserved *it* most.

(3) Verbs

A verb expresses action (*walk, take, speak*) or state of being (*is, appear, remain*). Verbs are identified by the fact that they change their form to express time (*walk, will walk, walked*) and, with some exceptions, add an *s* in the present tense to mark a singular subject in the third person (*I walk,* first person, BUT: *he walks,* third person). All verbs also have a form ending in *–ing* (*walking, taking, being, remaining*). The verb is the key word in a sentence because without it the sentence cannot be grammatically complete. Some sentences have more than one verb. (See also "Verbs," **Rule 9**.)

All of the following statements are sentences. The verbs are italicized.

Hurry!
I *am going* to college.
My paper *has been graded.*
Whoever *did* it *will pay* for his mistake.
If you *could see* her now, you *would be* very proud of her.

Verbs are classified as transitive (*v.t.*) or intransitive (*v.i.*), depending on whether or not they take an object. (See **Rule 1b(2)**.)

(4) **Adjectives**

An adjective is a word that modifies—that is, limits or describes—a noun or pronoun. Its usual place is before the noun element, although it sometimes follows (a *friendly* face, a *long* and *arduous* task, the air *dry* and *cold*). Some nouns are converted to adjectives by the addition of endings like *–ic*, *–ive*, *–ous*, *–ly*, *–ish*, and *–like* (*atomic, sportive, decorous, manly, bearish, lifelike*). Other adjectives are the articles *a, an*, and *the;* nouns that modify other nouns (the *Peale* portrait, an *oil* well); and certain verb forms called participles (a *working* man, the *tailored* look). Possessive nouns and pronouns are also adjectives when they modify other nouns or pronouns (*her* trousseau, *Karl's* theme, a *day's* work). Many adjectives add *–er* and *–est* to their base for use in comparisons (*sound, sounder, soundest*). (See also "Adjectives and Adverbs," **Rule 8**.)

This is *a lovely* day.
His long gray beard gave him *a distinguished* look.
With *a lower* hemline, *the beige party* dress could be worn again, and look *stunning*, too.

(5) **Adverbs**

An adverb is a word that modifies a verb (worked *hard*), an adjective (a *very* sour taste), or another adverb (objected *most* vehemently). An adverb may also modify a whole clause or sentence (*No,* I will not be there.) Adverbs conventionally answer the questions When? (*never, late, finally*); Where? (*there, above, west*); How? (*bravely, better, so*); Why? (*therefore, consequently*); To what degree? (*much, less, almost*); and Yes or no? (*yes, no, certainly*).

Many adverbs end in *–ly* (*highly, princely*), and many have the same form as adjectives (*bad, cheap, deep, hard*). Some of the adverbs ending in *-ly* also have a form that omits the ending ("Go *slow*" or "Go *slowly*"; "Hold *tight*" or "Hold *tightly*"). Like adjectives, many adverbs can be used in comparisons with the addition of *-er* and *-est* (*hard, harder, hardest*). (See also "Adjectives and Adverbs," **Rule 8**.)

The boy had run *away* from home.
I arose *still* sleepy, had some *barely* warm coffee, and dashed *nervously* for the train. It arrived *late.*
The car, which was built *especially* for the owner, had a *beautifully* appointed interior and a *fully* insulated roof.

(6) Prepositions

A preposition is a word that links a noun or pronoun, called the object of the preposition, to the rest of the sentence. Unlike most other parts of speech, the preposition is not inflected, that is, its form is always the same. Many prepositions are short: *by, in, at, of, on, to, for, into, with.* Longer prepositions include *after, around, before, against, through,* and such compound forms as *in spite of* and *because of.* Some words—for example, *before, after, since*—are either prepositions or conjunctions, depending on their function in the sentence. Each of the italicized phrases below consists of a preposition and its object.

She walked *with* (PREP.) *her friend* (OBJ.)/*to* (PREP.) *the edge* (OBJ.)/*of* (PREP.) *the lake* (OBJ.).
In the morning, I jog *around the park.*
With luck, I will finish the report *by Wednesday.*
He found his eye glasses, still *in good condition,/on the tile floor/of the bathroom,* where they had fallen *from the wall shelf.*

(7) Conjunctions

A conjunction is a word that joins words and groups of words. Like the preposition, it is not inflected.

The *coordinate conjunctions* (*and, but, for, or, nor, yet*) join grammatical elements of the same rank.

Gwen *and* Laura will compete in the finals. [Joins two nouns]
Whether in the city *or* in the country, Mr. Day could enjoy himself completely. [Joins two prepositional phrases]
Tennis is the sport I enjoy most, *but* I am an excellent swimmer, too. [Joins two grammatically complete statements]

A *subordinate conjunction* joins a complete statement with another statement that is grammatically dependent on it. Common subordinate conjunctions include *if, as, when, before, after, because, since,* and *although.*

They would come *if* they were given an incentive. [The word group beginning with "if" is dependent on "They would come"; it cannot stand alone as a sentence.]

The conjunctive adverbs, which include *however, nevertheless, therefore, furthermore, consequently, accordingly, besides,* and *still,* are used only to join statements that would stand independently as sentences if they were not already united in a single sentence by a semicolon.

The market was slipping very badly; *nevertheless,* the broker's newsletter struck an optimistic note.

OR

The market was slipping very badly. *Nevertheless,* the broker's newsletter struck an optimistic note.

A conjunctive adverb may also stand in some position other than the beginning of a clause. (See **Rule 30b(1)**.)

The market was slipping very badly. The broker's newsletter *nevertheless* struck an optimistic note.

(8) **Interjections**

An interjection is a grammatically independent word of exclamation or feeling (*ouch, oh, ah, alas, bravo, hurrah*). It is followed by a comma, a period, or an exclamation point.

Ah, I see.
We won. *Hurrah.*
Ooh! That's a nasty cut.

1b. Subjects and Predicates

To be grammatically complete, a sentence requires a subject and a predicate. The subject (S) is a noun or noun element about which an assertion is made. The predicate is what is said about the subject. The controlling word of the predicate is the verb (V), sometimes called the predicate verb.

These are minimally complete sentences:

Birds sing.

Daylight came.

Sometimes the subject or verb is understood rather than stated.

[You] Wait: [The subject *You* is understood.]

Who comes? John [comes]. [The verb of the second sentence—*comes*— is understood.]

(1) The Subject

The subject answers the question *Who?* or *What?* before the verb.

The *chemist* finished the analysis. [Who finished? The chemist. *Chemist* is the subject.]

In a sentence that takes the form of a question, you may find it helpful to rearrange the words in order to find the subject.

Did *you* agree to go? [*You* did agree to go.] [Who did agree? You. *You* is the subject.]

The sentence may have a *compound subject*, that is, two or more subjects of the same verb.

Trucks and *buses* were diverted to a side street.

Books, periodicals, and *pamphlets* make good research materials.

The *complete subject* is the subject and all its modifiers. In the sentences that follow, the italicized words are modifiers of the subject.

Few aspects *of contemporary life* escape him.

Some animals *hunted to excess, like the beaver and the fisher,* are coming back.

(2) The Predicate

The predicate consists of the predicate verb, the words that modify it, and its complements. The predicate verb includes the verb and its auxiliaries (*go, has gone, should have gone*). Words that modify the predicate verb are adverbs or word groups performing the function of adverbs. In the following sentences, the words in italics are modifiers of the verb.

She sat[V] *patiently under a casque-like head of marcelled hair.*

The screen play was rejected[V] *originally because it was thought to be too expensive to film.*

In most sentences a complement (C) is required to complete the meaning of the verb.

Roy[S] enjoyed[V] the *lesson*[C].

Cows[S] give[V] *milk*[C].

Complements are of several kinds, chiefly the direct object (O), indirect object (IO), and predicate noun (PN) or predicate adjective (PA).

A direct object (O) names the receiver of the action of the verb. Always a noun element, it answers the question Whom? or What? after the verb.

Roy[S] enjoyed[V] the *lesson*[O]. [Roy enjoyed what? Roy enjoyed the lesson. *Lesson* is the direct object of *enjoyed*.]

George[S] likes[V] *Jill*[O]. [George likes whom? George likes Jill. *Jill* is the direct object of *likes*.]

An indirect object (IO) is a "second object" after some verbs like *ask, tell,* or *give.* It answers the question To whom? For whom? To what? or For what?

They[S] gave[V] *Mary*[IO] a reception[O]. [They gave a reception (for) Mary. *Mary* is the indirect object.]

The teacher[S] told[V] the *class*[IO] a story[O]. [The teacher told a story (to) the class. *Class* is the indirect object

The predicate noun (PN) and predicate adjective (PA) complement linking verbs (LV), that is, any forms of the verb *to be* and of such verbs as *seem, feel, remain,* and *become.* The predicate noun invariably represents the same thing as the subject. The predicate adjective modifies or qualifies the subject.[1]

[1] The predicate noun and predicate adjective are also called *subject complements* because they relate to the subject. *Object complements* are those nouns or adjectives that complete the meaning of the object. (They named the baby *Carol;* Color it *red.*)

S LV PN Mr. Thompson is the *secretary.*	[*Secretary,* a predicate noun, follows the linking verb *is* and stands for the same thing as the subject.]
S LV PA They remained *hopeful.*	[*Hopeful,* a predicate adjective, follows the linking verb *remained* and modifies the subject.]

1c. Phrases and Clauses

Groups of related words in a sentence are either phrases or clauses.

(1) Phrases

A phrase is a group of related words without a subject and predicate verb. For purposes of grammatical analysis, four types of phrases are recognized: prepositional phrases, infinitive phrases, participial phrases, and gerund phrases.[2]

A *prepositional phrase* begins with a preposition and is followed by a noun—the object of the preposition—and its modifiers.

PREPOSITIONAL PHRASES:

I will see you *after the meeting.*
The tree *by the road* provided magnificent shade.
Her choice *of wallpaper* was an inspiration.

Infinitive, participial, and gerund phrases are, collectively, verbal phrases. Individually, they take their names from the kind of verbal with which they begin: infinitive, participle, or gerund. A verbal is a form derived from a verb, but functioning as another part of speech.

An *infinitive* is recognized by the sign of the infinitive *to* before the verb form. It is used as a noun, an adjective, or an adverb.

To err is human. [Noun, subject of the verb *is*]
We stopped *to quench* our thirst. [Adverb modifying the verb *stopped*]
He gave me the letter *to read.* [Adjective modifying the noun *letter*]

[2] Loosely, a phrase is *any* group of related words without a subject and verb. Thus a noun phrase would consist of a noun and its modifiers (*the complicated plot, a loosely knit fabric*), and a verb phrase would consist of a verb and its auxiliaries or modifiers (*have been going, talked slowly and deliberately*). In the last example, *slowly and deliberately* is an adverbial phrase. Prepositions consisting of more than one word are also phrases: *in place of, contrary to, because of.*

A *participle* is a verb form used as an adjective, that is, as modifier of a noun or noun element. Participles have present-, past-, and perfect-tense forms. The present participle ends in *–ing* (*knowing, saying, continuing*). The past participle usually ends in *–ed, –en, –n,* or *–t* (*walked, taken, grown, caught*). The perfect participle employs the auxiliary verb *having* with the past participle (*having walked, having taken,* and so on).

We saw her *standing* in the doorway. [Modifies *her*]
Taken by surprise, the burglar gave up. [Modifies *burglar*]
Having waited for hours, she finally went home. [Modifies *she*]

A *gerund* is a verb form ending in *–ing,* like the present participle, but it is used only as a noun—as subject or complement of a verb, or as object of a preposition.

Swimming is good exercise. [Subject of verb *is*]
A gourmand enjoys *eating.* [Object of verb *enjoys*]
I got tired of *waiting* [Object of the preposition *of*]

A verbal phrase performs the same function or functions in the sentence as the verbal from which it takes its name. It includes the verbal—the infinitive, participle, or gerund—and any modifying words. Like a verb, a verbal may also take a complement. For example, in the sentence, "I decided *to take a walk,*" *walk* is the object of the infinitive *to take* and completes the verbal phrase. (See also "Split Infinitive," **Rule 25b(2)**, and "'Dangling' Modifiers," **Rule 26**.)

INFINITIVE PHRASES:

He is not a man *to put off important decisions.*
I will try *to fill you in on what happened.*
To arrive at a party a day late can be terribly embarrassing.

PARTICIPIAL PHRASES:

Knowing her preference for drama, I took her to see the Ibsen play.
Carroll spent the morning at the office, *dictating and signing letters.*
Juan, *thoroughly alarmed by the turn of events,* decided to talk with his father.

GERUND PHRASES:

Walking five miles a day is a good prescription for longevity.
William regretted *having acted in such a childish way.*
Some individuals get ahead by *stepping over the prostrate bodies of their rivals.*

(2) Clauses

A clause is a group of related words having a subject and a predicate. When such a group of words can stand alone as a sentence, it is a *main* or *independent clause.* When it cannot stand alone as a sentence, it is a *subordinate* or *dependent clause.* A subordinate clause must be linked to a main clause in order to form a grammatically complete sentence. A sentence may consist of two or more main clauses; and as long as it has at least one main clause, it may also have one or more subordinate clauses. (See also "Sentence Fragment," **Rule 2**, and "Comma Fault," **Rule 3**.)

I shouted.	[Main clause (a sentence)]
Because I wanted to be heard.	[Subordinate clause (not a sentence)]
I shouted because I wanted to be heard.	[Main clause and subordinate clause (a sentence)]

Main Clauses

Main clauses are joined by coordinate conjunctions or conjunctive adverbs, or simply by a semicolon.

Henry called off the figures, *and* I checked them.
You have met all the academic requirements for graduation; *accordingly*, you will get your diploma.
The mortgage market is improved; an increase in housing starts should occur soon.

Subordinate Clauses

Subordinate clauses are introduced by relative pronouns, (*who, which, that*) or subordinate conjunctions (*if, as, while*), and perform the functions of nouns, adjectives, or adverbs.

NOUN CLAUSES:

That he should have left us was a cause of bitter disappointment. [Subject of verb *was*]
He knew *that he would be vindicated.* [Object of verb *knew*]
The department in *which she worked* was eliminated. [Object of preposition *in*]

ADJECTIVE CLAUSES:

Anyone *who wishes to attend the concert* need only leave a note for Mr. Dawson. [Modifies the pronoun *Anyone*]
The couch, *which stood against the far wall,* was covered in faded blue velvet. [Modifies the noun *couch*]

ADVERBIAL CLAUSES:

If he wished to discuss the matter, he should have seen me during my visit. [Modifies the verb *should have seen*]

The guests arrived earlier *than we expected*. [Modifies the adverb *earlier*]

1d. Sentences

A sentence is a unit of thought consisting of one or more words. It begins with a capitalized word and ends with a period, a question mark, or an exclamation point.

I'll see you tomorrow.
Have you finished your report?
Stop! Thief! [Two sentences]

(1) Grammatically complete sentences are classified structurally as simple, compound, and complex.

A *simple sentence* consists of a single main clause.

Television is a major source of entertainment.
The house at the beach has the taste of salt and sunshine.
At midnight, people of every age were still milling about in the street.

A *compound sentence* consists of two or more main clauses.

Henry gave me his suitcase,/and I stowed it in the trunk.
They went to the beach to swim,/but the heavy surf kept them on shore.
I did not know what I was going to do;/I certainly had no conscious plan.

Each clause in the pairs above has its own subject and verb. A sentence with two or more verbs is still a simple sentence, however, if the verbs have the same subject.

Joe *walked up* to the counterman *and asked* for a ham sandwich. [Simple sentence]

A *complex sentence* consists of at least one main clause and one or more subordinate clauses. The term *compound-complex sentence* is often applied to a complex sentence having two or more main clauses.

When I entered the street,/I saw a police car blocking the next crossing. [One subordinate clause and one main clause]

We wondered/where Miss Page had gone/and whether she would ever be back. [One main clause and two subordinate clauses]

Donald saw the performance,/and he was ecstatic/as he described it to Anne the next day. [Two main clauses and one subordinate clause]

(2) Sentences are also classified as declarative, interrogatory, imperative, and exclamatory, according to the type of statement they make.

A *declarative sentence* makes an ordinary statement or assertion. Most sentences are declarative.

We had fond recollections of the time we spent in Maine.
The mention of his orphaned state seemed to heighten the interest of strangers.

An *interrogative sentence* asks a question.

What shall I tell Miss Bolton?
Why didn't you tell me you had made no arrangements for dinner?

An *imperative sentence* gives a command.

Redeem the coupon at your local supermarket.
To preserve books, keep them away from heat and moisture.

An *exclamatory sentence* makes a statement with great emphasis or strong feeling.

What a beautiful serve!
Ouch! That hurts! [Two sentences]
No! No! No! [Three sentences]

1e. Glossary of Grammatical Terms

Use the following list in conjunction with the cross references in boldface type. If a term you want is not listed here, consult the index.

Absolute phrase. A word group performing a parenthetic function and having no connecting word to link it to the rest of the sentence.

A motion having been made, the meeting was adjourned.
No one, *sad to say,* would take the responsibility.

See also **Rule 26c**.

Active voice. A verb whose subject represents the performer of the action of the verb is said to be in the *active voice.*

The judges *gave* the winners their trophies. [The subject *judges* names the performer of the action of the verb *gave.*]
The treasurer *had signed* the check.

See also **Passive voice** and **Rule 30d**(2).

Adjective. A word that modifies a noun or pronoun. Except when it follows a linking verb, it usually precedes the word it modifies. The articles *a, an,* and *the* are adjectives.

a colorful display, *dainty* pastries, *hot* rolls, *those* apples, *some* mustard, *most* students, *a few* friends, *ten* times, *American* soldiers, *childhood* memories, *my* grades, *their* problem, *William's* promise
The melon is *ripe.* [Modifies *melon*].

See also **Rules 1a**(4) and **8**.

Adjective clause. See **Rule 1c**(2).

Adjective phrase. See **Phrase**.

Adverb. A word that modifies a verb, an adjective, or another adverb; it may also modify a whole clause or sentence.

walked *slowly,* start *soon, so* interesting, a *wholly* satisfactory solution, *very happily* married, arrived *there too early*
Surely, he is not without friends. [Sentence modifier]

See also **Rules 1a**(5) and **8**.

Adverbial clause. A subordinate clause with the characteristics of an adverb; shows time, place, degree, manner, condition, concession.

When the army rebelled, the king was forced to abdicate.
Tom would be a good driver *if only he would keep his eye on the road.*
The dog looked at me so wistfully *that I wanted to take him along.*

See also **Rule 1c**(2).

Adverbial phrase. See **Phrase.**

Antecedent. The word or word group to which a pronoun refers.

A *person* who cannot be trusted makes a poor friend. [Antecedent of *who*]

Grogan and Herbers said they would help. [Antecedent of *they*]

See also **Rules 5** and **7**.

Appositive. A noun or other substantive following a noun or pronoun which it explains or identifies.

Alfred, my *roommate,* asked if he could come along.
The church, a beautiful Romanesque *structure,* was declared a landmark.

See also **Rules 6c** and **11d(2)**.

Article. The definite article *the* and the indefinite articles *a* and *an* are adjectives. They signal the fact that a noun follows: *the* examination, *a* treat, *an* agreement.

Auxiliary verb. A word (or words) that, with a verb, forms a verb phrase.

will be talking, *should have* gone, *had* believed, *was* wrecked, *am* appalled

Case. The inflectional form of a noun or pronoun that shows its relation to the rest of the sentence. The three cases are *nominative, objective,* and *possessive.* Their main functions are as follows.

NOMINATIVE CASE

Subject of verb	The *conductor* raised his baton. *I* [NOT: *Me*] ran all the way. The *camera* was a Minolta.
Predicate noun	It was *I* [NOT: *me*] who complained loudest.

OBJECTIVE CASE

Direct object of verb	The Times praised the *performance.* *We called them* [NOT: *they*] yesterday.
Indirect object of verb	She bought *him* [NOT: *he*] a wool scarf.
Object of preposition	I'll be with *them* [NOT: *they*] in a moment.
Subject of infinitive	We asked *her* [NOT: *she*] to come with us.

POSSESSIVE CASE

Possession	*Karen's* face showed *her* delight.
Subject of gerund	I disapproved of *his* [NOT: *him*] leaving so abruptly.

See also **Rule 6**.

Clause. A group of words having a subject and a predicate. A *main* (or *independent*) *clause* can stand alone as a sentence; A *subordinate* (or *dependent*) *clause* cannot.

SUBORDINATE CLAUSE — MAIN CLAUSE

Although he was displeased, he concealed his feelings.

See also **Rule 1c(2)**.

Collective noun. A noun that, in its singular form, stands for a group of persons or things.

army, company, committee, family, team, herd, remainder

See also **Rule 4e**.

Colloquial. Informal usage, characteristic of ordinary speech and of writing that imitates such speech.
See **Rule 22b**.

Common noun. See **Noun**.

Complement. A word or word group that completes the meaning of the verb. See **Object**, **Predicate noun**, and **Predicate adjective**; also **Rule 1b(2)**.

Complex sentence. A sentence consisting of at least one main clause and one subordinate clause.

When the fog lifted, the highway was again opened to traffic.
Tell me if you think you will be going.

Compound predicate. Two or more predicates having the same subject.

The defendant *was convicted of bribery* and *sentenced to jail*.

Compound sentence. A sentence having two or more main clauses.

The house was finished in August, but it remained vacant until January.

Compound subject. Two or more subjects having the same predicate.

The turntable and *the tape deck* were part of the same sound system.

See also **Rules 4b** and **4c**.

Conjunction. A word that joins together other words, phrases, or clauses. *Coordinate conjunctions* link any grammatical elements of equal rank. *Subordinate conjunctions* link main clauses with subordinate clauses.

COORDINATE:

every man, woman, *and* child [Joins nouns]
in class *or* at home [Joins prepositional phrases]
if the weather is good *and* there is snow on the ground [Joins subordinate clauses]
He accepted the penalty gracefully, *for* he knew he was at fault. [Joins coordinate clauses]

SUBORDINATE:

I will come *when* I am told. [Links main clause with subordinate clause]

See also **Rule 1a(7)**.

Conjunctive adverb. An adverb that links main clauses. Conjunctive adverbs include *therefore, however, accordingly, nevertheless, furthermore, besides, consequently, so, then.* See also **Rules 1a(7)** and **3b**.

Coordinate. Refers to related elements having the same grammatical rank, for example, two nouns, two prepositional phrases, two main clauses. See **Conjunction**

Coordinate conjunction. See **Conjunction.**

Correlative conjunctions. Coordinate conjunctions that are used in pairs: *not only . . . but also; neither . . . nor; either . . . or; both . . . and; whether . . . or.*

Dependent clause. See **Clause.**

Direct address. Refers to words by which persons or things are addressed directly.

Tom, will you please open the door.
River, stay away from my door.

See also **Rule 11d(2)**.

Direct object. See **Object**.

Direct quotation. The exact rendition of words written or spoken. The quoted words are enclosed in quotation marks.

"I'll meet you at the airport," she promised.

See also **Rule 14**.

Ellipsis. The use of periods (...) or other marks (***) to show the omission of words in quoted material. See **Rule 10a(5)**.

Elliptical clause. Usually a clause of comparison in which one or more words needed to complete the comparison are understood rather than stated.

I can work as hard *as you* [can]. [The last word is omitted but understood.]

See also **Rules 6f** and **26b.**

Exclamation. An expression of strong feeling, usually followed by an exclamation point.

Oh! You're here!

See also **Rule 10c**.

Expletive. The word *it* or *there* in such constructions as "*it* is" and "*there* are." Sometimes called the "anticipatory subject," the expletive is merely a substitute for the real subject, which follows the verb.

It is a pity to go. [The real subject is *pity*.]
There are few places as beautiful. [The real subject is *places*.]

See also **Rules 4f** and **30b(1)**.

Gerund. See **Verbal.**

Idiom. An expression peculiar to a language; in good usage even though it cannot always be explained by logic or grammar.

a run of bad luck   looked up to his father
a cut above the ordinary

See also **Rule 22c.**

Imperative sentence. A sentence that gives a command.

Don't wait until it's too late.

See also **Mood** and **Rule 1d.**

Indefinite pronoun. See **Pronoun.**

Independent clause. See **Clause.**

Indirect discourse. See **Indirect quotation.**

Indirect object. See **Object.**

Indirect quotation. Another's words, paraphrased or summarized, rather than quoted exactly. No quotation marks are used. Also called "indirect discourse."

He said that he would be there. [If a direct quotation were used, the sentence would read: He said, "I'll be there."]

See also **Rule 16d.**

Infinitive. See **Verbal.**

Inflection. Refers to changes in the form of words to show grammatical relationships. For example, nouns and pronouns are inflected to show number and case (*I, my, me; we, our, us; father, fathers, father's*); verbs to show tense and number (*go, went; is having, were having*); and adjectives and adverbs to show degrees of comparison (*lively, livelier, liveliest*).

Intensive. A word used to emphasize the meaning of another word, like *too* (an adverb) in "*too* much," and *myself* (a pronoun) in "I *myself* will go."

Interjection. An exclamatory word: *alas, heavens, indeed.* See also **Exclamation**.

Intransitive verb. A verb that does not take an object.

The sun *rose* at 6:42 A.M.
She *seemed* irreconcilable.

See also **Transitive verb**.

Irregular verb. A verb that does not add *-ed* to form the past tense and past participle.

REGULAR VERB:	walk	walked	(have) walked
IRREGULAR VERBS:	break	broke	(have) broken
	do	did	(have) done
	go	went	(have) gone

See also **Rule 9**.

Linking verb. A verb followed by a predicate noun or a predicate adjective. Such verbs include *is, look, seem, become, appear, feel, taste.*

She is my *sister.* [Predicate noun]
The orange tastes *sour.* [Predicate adjective]

See also **Rule 1b(2)**.

Main clause. See **Clause**.

Modifier. A word, phrase, or clause that describes or limits another sentence element and has a subordinate relationship to it. All modifiers perform either an adjective or adverb function.

Mood (*also* **mode**). A form of the verb through which the writer or speaker expresses the way he regards a statement. The moods are *indicative, subjunctive,* and *imperative.*

INDICATIVE	States a fact or asks a question.	You *will go* with me. *Will* you *go* with me?

SUBJUNCTIVE	Expresses a wish or condition	I wish you *were going.* If you *should go* . . .
IMPERATIVE	Expresses a command or request	*Go* alone if you can.

See also **Rule 9c**.

Nominative case. See **Case**.

Number. An attribute of nouns, pronouns, and verbs through which they denote singular or plural.

I, we; room, rooms; (he) has, (they) have

See also **Rules 4** and **5**.

Nonrestrictive modifier. A modifying phrase or clause not essential to the sense of the sentence; it is set off by commas.

The wind, *gusting to fifty miles an hour,* tore at the awnings and trees.
Selma, *who had arrived early,* was the first to leave.

See also **Restrictive** modifier and **Rule 11d(1)**.

Noun. The name of a person, place, thing, or abstract quality; it changes its form to show number and possession (*driver, drivers; driver's, drivers'*).

Nouns are either *common* or *proper. Proper nouns,* which begin with a capital letter, are the names of particular members of a class. All other nouns are classified as *common nouns.*

PROPER: George, Sam Levy, the Ohio River, Des Moines
COMMON: boy, woman, marigold, steel, house, river, city

Among common nouns, the following classes are recognized:

CONCRETE: chair, typewriter, sky, pitcher
ABSTRACT: truth, happiness, kindness, daring
COLLECTIVE: group, class, committee, herd, flock

Principally, nouns perform the following grammatical functions: subject of verb, object of verb, object of preposition, indirect object, predicate noun, appositive, direct address. All these terms are defined in this Glossary. See also **Rules 1a(1)** and **17a**.

Object. A noun or noun equivalent that is affected by a preceding verb, verbal, or preposition. Sometimes, for emphasis, an object precedes a subject and verb to form an "inverted sentence." A direct object answers the question Whom or What? after the verb. An indirect object answers the question To whom or To what? or For whom or For what?

DIRECT OBJECT

He paced the *floor.* [Object of *paced*]
The threatening *gesture* he saw clearly. [Object of *saw*]

INDIRECT OBJECT

Give *me* the large size. [Answers the question *To whom?*]

OBJECT OF VERBAL

I was very happy to see *him.* [Object of the infinitive *to see*]
Knowing *her* was a privilege. [Object of the gerund *Knowing*]

OBJECT OF PREPOSITION

To *whom* shall I give the message? [Object of *To*]
He put the notebook on the *bureau.* [Object of *on*]
In *winning* the election, she gained new confidence in herself. [Gerund (verbal noun), object of *In*]

See also **Rules 1b(2), 6b, 6c,** and **6e.**

Objective case. See **Case.**

Object complement. A noun or adjective that completes the meaning of the object.
See also **Rule 1b(2), footnote.**

Participial phrase. See **Phrase.**

Participle. See **Verbal.**

Parts of speech. The eight classes of words as determined by their use in the sentence: nouns, pronouns, adjectives, verbs, adverbs, prepositions, conjunctions, interjections.

Passive voice. A verb whose subject names the receiver of the action of the verb is said to be in the *passive voice.* It invariably consists of a form of the verb *to be* as an auxiliary, and the past participle of the base verb.

The winners *were presented* with their trophies.

The check *had been signed* by the treasurer.

See also **Active voice**.

Person. An attribute of pronouns that makes it possible to distinguish between the speaker (first person), the individual addressed (second person), and the person or thing spoken about (third person).

FIRST PERSON: *I* bought, *we* shall see
SECOND PERSON: *you* can see, *you* are right
THIRD PERSON: *he* walks, *she* tells, *it* works, the *sun* rises

See also **Rule 29a**.

Personal pronoun. See **Pronoun**.

Phrase. A group of related words having no subject and predicate and performing the function of a single part of speech.

NOUN PHRASE: *A suitable gift* was presented.
VERB PHRASE: He *had been attending* classes regularly.
PREPOSITIONAL PHRASE: Sherry belonged *to the Psychology Club.* [Adverb function]
A pall *of smoke* covered the area. [Adjective function]
PARTICIPIAL PHRASE: *Knowing his interest in botany,* I showed him the plant specimen. [Adjective function]
GERUND PHRASE: *Visiting my Aunt Mabel* was always a delight. [Noun function]
INFINITIVE PHRASE: They ran *to catch the train.* [Adverb function]
The best way *to see America* is *to take a bus.* [Adjective and noun functions, respectively]

See also **Rule 1c(1)**.

Predicate. The sentence element that says something about the subject. The simple predicate consists of the verb alone; the complete predicate consists of the verb and its modifiers and complements.

SIMPLE PREDICATE

The candidate grudgingly conceded defeat.

COMPLETE PREDICATE

See also **Rule 1b(2)**.

Predicate adjective. An adjective following a linking verb and modifying the subject.

The day was *hot*.

See also **Rule 1b(2)**.

Predicate noun. A noun following a linking verb and standing for the same thing as the subject.

Lincoln became *president* in 1861.

See also **Rules 1b(2) and 4g**.

Predicate pronoun. A pronoun serving the same function as a predicate noun.

Predicate verb. Same as simple predicate. See **Predicate**.

Preposition. A word that links a noun or noun equivalent (the object of the preposition) with some other part of the sentence. Common prepositions include *in, at, by, for, to, before, after, behind, around.*

I walked *to* the post office. [Links the noun *post office* with the verb *walked*]

See also **Rule 1a(6)**.

Prepositional phrase. A phrase beginning with a preposition, for example, "to the post office," in the immediately preceding example.

Principal parts. The forms of a verb from which the various tenses are derived. The principal parts are the *base form* or *infinitive* (talk), *past tense* (talked), and *past participle* (talked).

See also **Irregular verb** and **Rule 9**.

Pronoun. A word used in place of a noun or of a person or thing understood in the context. Pronouns are classified principally as *personal* (*I, you, he, she, they*), *indefinite* (*one, each, either, nobody*), *demonstrative* (*this, that, these, those*), and *relative* (*who, which, that*).

See also **Rule 1a(2)**.

Proper adjective. An adjective, capitalized, derived from a proper noun.

Machiavellian [from *Machiavelli*]
Swedish [from *Sweden*]

Proper noun. See **Noun.**

Regular verb. See **Irregular verb.**

Relative pronoun. A pronoun (*who, which, what, that*) introducing a subordinate clause.

SUBORDINATE CLAUSE
Anyone *who* wants to come will be welcome.

See also **Rule 1a(2).**

Restrictive modifier. An identifying phrase or clause essential to the sense of the sentence.

The boy *playing with Ted* is my brother. [Phrase]
An engine *that sputters* needs a mechanic's attention. [Clause]

See also **Nonrestrictive modifier** and **Rule 11d(1).**

Sentence. A unit of thought beginning with a capital letter and ending with a period, a question mark, or an exclamation point.

Will I come? Yes. [Two sentences]

To be grammatically complete, a sentence needs a subject—expressed or understood—and a predicate.

SUBJECT PREDICATE
The chairman closed the meeting.

PREDICATE
Wait for me at the dock. [The subject *You* is understood.]

For types of sentences, see **Simple sentence, Compound sentence,** and **Complex sentence.** See also **Rule 1d.**

Simple predicate. The predicate verb. See **Predicate.**

Simple sentence. A sentence consisting of one main clause.

The book proved easy to read.

Simple subject. See **Subject.**

Strong verb. Same as **Irregular verb.**

Subject. A noun or noun equivalent about which something is said. It answers the question Who? or What? before the predicate.

The *gift* arrived early. [What arrived early? The gift. *Gift* is the subject.]

The subject with its modifiers is the *complete subject.*
The subject without its modifiers is the *simple subject.*

The verdant mountain looming above the bay afforded a favorite view for photographers. [*Mountain* is the simple subject; the whole italicized phrase is the complete subject.]

See also **Rule 1b(1).**

Subject complement. A complement that relates to the subject: the predicate noun or predicate adjective.

See also **Complement** and **Rule 1b(2).**

Subjunctive mood. See **Mood.**

Subordinate clause. See **Clause.**

Substantive. A noun or a noun equivalent—a pronoun, a gerund, a noun clause.

NOUN GERUND
Davidson enjoyed walking .

PRONOUN NOUN CLAUSE
She implied that she would come.

Syntax. The grammatical relationship of words and word groups in sentences.

Tense. The form of a verb that indicates time and time relationships.

The tenses are the present (I *go*), the past (I *went*), the future (I *shall go*), the present perfect (I *have gone*), the past perfect (I *had gone*), and the future perfect (I *shall have gone*).

See also **Rule 9b**.

Transitive verb. A verb that requires an object to complete its meaning.

He *received* the visitor in his study. [Transitive verb because its meaning is completed by an object, *visitor*]

See also **Intransitive verb**.

Verb. A word used to form the predicate of a clause or sentence (*have, was, tried, will send*). A verb may also consist of a verb-adverb combination (*team up, play down, put forward*).

I *have* the map.
They *will return* when they *are* ready.

See also **Rule 9**.

Verb phrase. See **Phrase**.

Verbal. A verb form used as a noun, adjective, or adverb. The verbals are *gerunds, participles,* and *infinitives.*

GERUND: A verbal noun ending in *-ing* (*walking, taking, writing*).

Lending a hand is an American tradition. [Subject of the verb *is*]
He was a master at *keeping* a secret. [Object of the preposition *at*]

PARTICIPLE: A verbal adjective usually ending in *-ing, -ed, -en,* or *-t* (*walking, walked, taken, lent*).

Trudging wearily, we came to an old farmhouse. [Modifies *we*]
The burglars, *surprised,* fled through the rear door. [Modifies *burglars*]

INFINITIVE: A verb form usually (but not always) preceded by *to* and used as a noun, adjective, or adverb.

To anticipate the future is a sign of intelligence. [Noun, subject of verb *is*]
I like having money *to spend.* [Adjective; modifies *money*]
They all went *to see* the game. [Adverb; modifies the verb *went*]
Let him ∧ go. [The sign of the infinitive, *to,* is understood.]

See also **Rules 1c(1)** and **26a.**

Voice. A verb form showing the relation between the subject and the action expressed by the verb.

See **Active voice** and **Passive voice.**

EXERCISES

A. Identify the parts of speech of every numbered word in the paragraph below:

Visitors[1] to[2] China[3] in recent[4] years[5] consistently[6] report[7] that[8] the population[9] appears[10] to be healthy[11] and[12] adequately[13] nourished.[14] In[15] the[16] light[17] of China's[18] reputation[19] as[20] a country[21] where[22] hunger[23] has been[24] no[25] stranger[26] for[27] centuries[28] and catastrophic[29] regional[30] famines[31] used[32] to be almost[33] annual[34] events,[35] many[36] Western[37] agriculturists[38] have reacted[39] to[40] these[41] reports[42] with[43] skepticism.[44] Last[45] year[46] I[47] served[48] as chairman[49] of a group[50] of twelve[51] visitors[52] from[53] the United States,[54] including some[55] of our[56] foremost[57] agricultural[58] scientists,[59] who[60] were[61] able[62] to judge for[63] themselves[64] how[65] matters[66] stood.[67] We[68] traveled[69] in China[70] for 28[71] days[72] in[73] August[74] and[75] September.[3]

B. Use each of the following words in a sentence, giving the word the function indicated in parentheses.

1. white (noun)
2. for (conjunction)
3. to (preposition)
4. replace (verb)
5. measure (noun)

[3] Sterling Wortman, "Agriculture in China," *Scientific American*, June 1975, p.13.

6. personally (adverb)
7. rise (noun)
8. puzzling (adjective)
9. meeting (noun)
10. wider (adverb)
11. right-wing (adjective)
12. never (adverb)
13. sickened (adjective)
14. bellowing (noun)
15. summer (adverb)
16. hard (adjective)
17. when (conjunction)
18. hurrah (noun)
19. heavens (interjection)
20. as (conjunction)

C. Copy the following sentences, underlining the subjects, verbs, and complements and identifying them with the symbols used in **Rule 1b**.

EXAMPLE:

PA LV S S V O
Happy is the man who has found his work.

1. Was he aware of the commotion he was causing?
2. The small size of the book gave it a distinct advantage.
3. When I buy a stereo radio and phonograph, I will want a tape deck to go with it.
4. Mrs. Perkins had gone South every winter since 1965.
5. Money he has; taste he will acquire.
6. Timmie seems small for his age.
7. In the event of a fire, the elevators will descend immediately to the first floor and discharge all passengers.
8. Cohen's novel is a literary feat.
9. The building program is continuing, but unless patrons donate additional funds, the work will stop by mid-January.
10. Plants thrive only when they have been given proper care.

D. From the following statements[4] select

10 prepositional phrases
2 participial phrases
2 infinitive phrases

[4] Freely adapted from John Gregory Dunne, "So You Want to Write a Movie," *Atlantic*, July 1974, pp. 39–40.

1 gerund phrase
5 subordinate clauses

Write the statement number in parentheses after each phrase or clause you name.

1. The producer was not ecstatic when he read the script.
2. I asked how much change in the script would be needed.
3. The producer had made a good deal for the house, renting it for only $1,250 for the entire week.
4. Shooting over our budget was hardly an innovation.
5. I sat through three consecutive showings of *Seven Days in May* to count the number of sequences that made up a well-crafted picture.
6. "You're hot now," she said, "but in six months the bloom will be off the rose."
7. The producer liked to scream at us. He screamed that we were amateurs.
8. The heroine is a living lie; she never loved her husband.
9. The young reporter, sickened by these revelations, declares his love for her.
10. The heroine says that she will publicly avow her love for the young reporter.

E. Identify the subordinate clauses in Exercise D as noun, adjective, or adverbial.

F. Identify the sentences in Exercise D as simple, compound, or complex.

G. Write a statement of about 150 to 200 words describing an experience at school, at home, or elsewhere. Vary the sentence types so that the statement includes not only declarative sentences, but at least one of each of the other types—interrogative, imperative, and exclamatory.

2 Sentence Fragment *frag*

Do not mistake a sentence fragment for a complete sentence. A fragment is a grammatically incomplete statement—a nonsentence. The italicized parts of the statements below are fragments.

Both ends of the room are miniature musicians' galleries. *Each with cello and open music stand.*
I opened the door and there he was. *Tall, smiling, impeccably dressed.*
For a while the profession was in the doldrums. *Because no new talent was being developed.*

2a. Methods of Correction

To correct a sentence fragment, either join it to the main clause or make it into a complete sentence, with its own subject and predicate.

At both ends of the room are miniature musicians' galleries, *each with cello and open music stand.*
At both ends of the room are miniature musicians' galleries. *Each contains a cello and an open music stand.*
I opened the door and there he was—*tall, smiling, impeccably dressed.*
For a while the profession was in the doldrums *because no new talent was being developed.*

2b. Stylistic Use

Sentence fragments are sometimes intentionally used as a stylistic device, especially to create a mood in descriptive writing. They are frequently found in advertising copy.

Snow. Snow in London. Millie with the early cup of tea. "There's been a terrible fall in the night, Sir."—KATHERINE MANSFIELD

Beating the traffic and the high cost of gas. Riding out of town with the wind in your face and the sun at your back. Following rugged new trails to exciting new places. Doing and seeing those things you've never done and seen before. Those are some of the good things that happen on a Honda.

2c. Words Understood

Some seeming fragments are actually whole statements for which the missing words are understood. Such statements constitute grammatically complete sentences. Exclamatory statements, with or without understood words, may also stand as complete sentences.

[You] *Please stop in for a moment.* [Subject understood]
"Will you come in?" "*Of course* [I will]." [Subject and verb understood]
Heavens! He nearly smashed into the bridge. [Exclamation]

EXERCISE

A. Identify the following sentences as fragmentary (F) or grammatically complete (C). In the instances of fragmentary sentences, make the corrections required or explain why no correction is necessary.

1. Although the tourist industry remains the focal point in Greater Miami's economy. Other industries contribute as well.
2. Stories of sunshine and orange blossoms, and trainloads of visitors—these are no surprises in Miami lore.
3. The maintenance of the ball park has become increasingly costly. While at the same time attendance figures have dropped sharply.
4. Dawn. Down the long quivering line of the shore, the sky goes battleship gray. Then a splash of soft rose. The Leonardo da Vinci approaches, its upper decks ablaze with lights.
5. Jai-alai means "merry festival" in Basque. First played in the United States at the St. Louis World's Fair in 1904.
6. Take the case of four churches which sat, like gas stations, on each of four corners of a city.
7. Good! Now we won't have to go to that silly party.
8. In attempting to convert the old loft buildings to other uses, the owners got little encouragement from the city. Tax incentives, for instance.
9. At a chemical plant, accidents will happen regularly. Unless, of course, every employee is constantly alert.
10. At last the guide appears. Disheveled, breathless, waving wildly to attract the attention of the bus driver.

3 Comma Fault *cf*

Avoid running two sentences into one.

This rule is violated when a comma is used to separate two main clauses not joined by a conjunction (comma splice) or when no punctuation at all is used between the clauses (fused sentence).

COMMA SPLICE: It was nearly five o'clock when we arrived, | we were met at the door by Mrs. Madison.

FUSED SENTENCE: It was nearly five o'clock when we arrived | we were met at the door by Mrs. Madison.

3a. Methods of Correction

Use one of the following methods to correct the error:

(1) Separate the main clauses by a period. This is the simplest method and usually the most effective.

It was nearly five o'clock when we arrived. We were met at the door by Mrs. Madison.

(2) Link the main clauses with a semicolon.

It was nearly five o'clock when we arrived; we were met at the door by Mrs. Madison.

(3) Link the main clauses with a comma and a coordinate conjunction.

It was nearly five o'clock when we arrived, and we were met at the door by Mrs. Madison.

NOTE: Unless the clauses connected by *and* are closely related in thought, there is the risk of disunity in the sentence. See **Rule 24a**

3b. With Conjunctive Adverbs

When the second of two main clauses begins with a conjunctive adverb, the correct punctuation between the clauses is a semicolon or period. (See **Rule 12b.**)

NOT: He did not care for most shellfish, however, he had an insatiable craving for softshell crabs in season.
BUT: He did not care for most shellfish; however, he had . . .
OR: He did not care for most shellfish. However, he had . . . [OR: He had, however, an insatiable . . .]

3c. Some Exceptions

Commas are acceptably used to separate very short unconnected main clauses, main clauses in a series, and main clauses that are antithetical. (But see **Rule 12c.**)

I *can* do it, I *will* do it.
The estate is a mile from town, it covers three acres, and it has a marvelous wooded area.
It was not a house, it was a mansion.
You will come, won't you?

EXERCISE

A. Find and correct the comma faults in the following statements. Suggest alternative treatments of the errors where possible. Some sentences are correct.

1. Harry made it perfectly clear, he was not born yesterday.
2. She is loyal to her husband, but she is not his apologist.
3. None of his books are dull, however, I find his latest novel disappointing.
4. Jill majors in chemistry, Carrie thinks she will specialize in music education, Liz just hasn't made up her mind.
5. The agency had a number of employees on "special assignment," their real assignments were to be chauffeurs, personal servants, and office boys to the director.
6. His scorn for the hifalutin', and his gift for ridiculing it, makes fine theater, the crowd loves to hear about those pointy-headed

intellectuals, the college elite, who can't even park their bicycles straight.

7. Because of the configuration of the hills, our winds come almost always from the east and southeast.

8. There are no sycamore trees on the block, not even little ones pushing up in neglected corners.

9. Mr. Denny says we are captives to the politicians, he ignores the fact that we have the right to vote, that we can throw the rascals out any time we want to.

10. It's been five years since I was in a high-school gym class, but I'll never forget the day someone stole my tennis shoes from the locker room, my punishment was five laps around the track—barefoot.

4 Agreement of Subject and Verb

SV

A verb should agree in number with its subject.

A singular subject should take a singular verb. A plural subject should take a plural verb.

The day was full of surprises.
Two rooms were to be set aside.

This rule is so simple and so well known that few college writers should have trouble with it. Questions do arise, however, when sentences do not follow the normal subject-verb order, when subjects and verbs do not follow closely, and when there is some question about whether a subject is singular or plural.

4a. Intervening Words

Do not be influenced by words that come between the subject and the verb.

The last shipment of English sweaters *was* [NOT: *were*] sold out in a day.
One of the files *belongs* [NOT: *belong*] to Mr. Grayson.
The six packages of cellophane tape *were* [NOT: *was*] eventually found in the cellar.

Parenthetic phrases beginning with such expressions as *as well as*, *together with*, and *including* do not influence the number of the subject.

Bert, with his brothers and sisters, *was* [NOT: *were*] soon eagerly at play.
Boston, like other large cities, *has* [NOT: *have*] a serious mass transit problem.
The big oak, as well as some of the less sturdy trees, *was* [NOT: *were*] affected by the blight.

4b. Subjects Joined by *And*

Singular subjects connected by *and* usually take a plural verb. An exception is made (1) when the singular subjects stand for the same thing, and (2) when the singular subjects are introduced by *each* or *every.*

Our analysis of the situation *and our recommendation* for dealing with it *were* well received.
A *skilled typist and receptionist is* needed in this position. [The typist and receptionist are a single individual.]
Every student and staff member was [NOT: *were*] solicited for a contribution.
Each morning and evening presents [NOT: *present*] another problem for the commuter.

4c. Subjects Joined by *Or, Nor*

When two subjects are joined by *or* or *nor,* the verb agrees in number with the nearer one. If the result is awkward, recast the sentence.

Neither Tom nor his classmates have yet *responded.*
Neither they nor he has yet *responded.*
Neither *Hazel nor I was* [NOT: *were*] aware of the situation.
AWKWARD: *Either they or I am* responsible for the error.
BETTER: *Either I or they are* responsible for the error.
OR: *Either they are* responsible for the error *or I am.*

4d. *Each, Every*

A singular subject preceded by *each* or *every* takes a singular verb. (See also **Rule 4b**.)

Each person is obligated to share in the cost.
Every flight was grounded by the storm.

(1) Certain indefinite pronouns used as subjects are regularly followed by singular verbs. The pronouns include *each, either, neither, anyone, anybody, anything, someone, somebody, something, everybody, everything, no one, nobody,* and *nothing.*

Each was eligible for the prize.
Everyone takes pride in our accomplishment.
Either of the models *is* acceptable.
Fortunately, *no one was* hurt.

(2) Although *no one* is always singular, *none* is treated as singular or plural, depending on the sense of the sentence.

Of all the students in the class, *none is* more responsive than Lauren. [Only one person is indicated.]
None of the faculty *live* on campus. [More than one is indicated.]

(3) Other subjects that take singular or plural verbs, depending on the sense, are those that relate to parts of the whole: *all, any, some, part, half, two-thirds,* and so forth.

He lost everything in the fire. *All is* lost.
All of the workers *have agreed* to stay on the job.
Half of the pie *was* eaten.
Fully *half* our friends now *live* in the suburbs.

4e. Collective Noun as Subject

A noun representing a group of similar persons or things—for example, *group, jury, committee, staff, faculty, team, herd*—takes a singular verb when the reference is to the group as a unit; it takes a plural verb when the reference is to the individual members of the group.

The committee has issued a report on its investigation.
The committee are divided on a course of action.
The faculty has voted for the change in curriculum.
The faculty were not all present at the meeting.

(1) *The number* takes a singular verb, but *a number* takes a plural verb.

The number of supporters *is* small.
A number of us *are determined* to stay.

(2) Numbers expressing fixed quantities follow the same rule as collective nouns.

A hundred pages is enough.
A hundred participants were scattered over the field.

4f. Subject Following Verb

When the subject follows the verb, be sure they agree in number.

There *is one more point* to be discussed.
There *are several points* to be discussed.
In the cookie jar *were the missing letters.* [*Jar* is not the subject of the verb, but the object of the preposition *in.*]

The anticipatory subject *it* is always followed by the singular *is* or *was* even though the real subject following is plural.

It is many years since I have visited the West Coast.
It was four books, not three, that I returned.

4g. Predicate Noun

The number of the verb is not affected by the number of a predicate noun following it.

A *full program is* four courses. [The verb agrees with the subject *program,* not with the predicate noun *courses.*]
BUT: *Four courses are* a full program. [The subject is *courses.*]

4h. Nouns Ending in *-s*

Some nouns ending in *-s* regularly take singular verbs. They include *news, measles, mathematics, physics,* and *semantics.* The nouns *scissors, trousers, tidings, riches,* and *means* usually take plural verbs. Some nouns ending in *-ics—acrobatics, tactics, athletics, economics, acoustics*—take singular or plural verbs, depending on the sense.

The *news has been* unbelievably good.
Measles is contagious.
The scissors are mine.
His *riches were* more of a handicap than an advantage.
Tactics is an important branch of military science.
His *tactics are* questionable.
Acrobatics is not my forte.
His acrobatics were thrilling.
Economics is important to everyone. [The science]
The economics of the transaction *are* clearly unsound. [The financial considerations]

4i. Relative Pronoun as Subject

When a relative pronoun is a subject, its verb is singular or plural, depending on the number of the pronoun's antecedent.

I admire a *student* WHO *works* for his tuition.
Students WHO *work* for their tuition are to be admired.
His is one of the few engineering *firms* THAT *have bid* on the project. [The antecedent of *that* is *firms* (plural), not *one*.]

Following a relative pronoun, the verb must also agree in person with the antecedent of the pronoun.

It is *I* WHO *am* [NOT: *is* or *are*] to blame.

EXERCISE

A. Check every verb in the following sentences to see if it agrees with its subject in number, and correct any errors. Some sentences require no change.

1. From these facts have emerged the conviction that even the ordinary person, given the opportunity and training, have a good chance to achieve success in this difficult field.
2. Every man and woman among them are potential users of this low-calorie dressing.
3. The row of new cars that filled the lot were already showing signs of rust. One of the station wagons were missing the two front tires.
4. Whether they go or not are a matter for them to decide.
5. The threat of winds and high tides are usually sufficient to deter even the staunchest boat enthusiasts.
6. The President and Commander-in-Chief is usually present at the ceremonies honoring the Unknown Soldier.
7. None of the respondents have indicated acceptance of the invitation.
8. When a child is delinquent, it is often the parents who is to be blamed.
9. Patience and eagerness to help is essential for the work of the guidance counselor.
10. If Brad, together with his father and mother and brothers and sisters, decide to come for the weekend, I will positively scream.

11. The acoustics of the new Philharmonic Hall was disappointing, to say the least.

12. When I looked around, I saw that the swarm of bees were heading in my direction.

13. Fifteen dollars seem like too much to spend on an ordinary shirt.

14. There is more than money involved; there is also the considerations of loyalty and peace of mind.

15. Two texts and a supplementary reader, an anthology of nineteenth-century English poetry, is used in the course.

5 *pron*
Agreement of Pronoun and Antecedent

A pronoun should agree in number, gender, and person with its antecedent (the noun the pronoun stands for).

Gwen asked for the return of *her* notes.
If your *brother* comes, you must try to please *him.*
The *hikers* lost *their* way.
My *father and I* did *our* best to save the lawn.

5a. Mistaken Antecedent

When a sentence contains several nouns, be sure the pronoun agrees with its real antecedent.

If you want a *list* of the jobs to be done on those houses, I will give *it* [NOT: *them*] to you.

5b. Antecedents Construed as Singular

A singular pronoun is generally needed to agree with an antecedent construed as singular. Such antecedents include the words *man, woman, person, one, any, each, every, many a, anyone, everyone, no one, nobody, kind, sort, either,* and *neither.*

It is now up to the modern *woman* to exercise *her* [NOT: *their*] rights.
No one can have *his* [NOT: *their*] cake and eat it, too.
Neither of the culprits can be held responsible for *his* [NOT: *their*] actions.
Many a tree climber has broken *her* arm.

NOTE: Good sense and the need to avoid awkwardness may dictate the use of a plural pronoun even when the antecedent is singular.

Every guest wanted the home-baked pie; *they* [NOT: *he*] just had to share it.

5c. Antecedents Joined by *Or* or *Nor*

When the antecedents of a pronoun are joined by *or* or *nor*, the pronoun usually agrees with the nearer one. If any awkwardness or distortion of meaning results from the application of this rule, common sense should prevail.

Neither the president nor the *treasurer* turned in *his* ballot.
Neither Johnson nor his *customers* expressed *their* dissatisfaction with the arrangement.

Either they or *I am* going to run this organization.
CONFUSING: *Neither Dorothy nor Tom* would tell *his* story.
AWKWARD: *Neither Dorothy nor Tom* would tell *her or his* story.
IMPROVED: *Neither Dorothy nor Tom* would tell *their* story. [Plural pronoun used]

5d. Collective Noun as Antecedent

A collective noun is referred to by either a singular or a plural pronoun, depending on whether the collective noun refers to the group as a unit or to the members of the group individually.

The *team* did *its* best.
The *team* went *their* separate ways after the game.

It is inconsistent to treat the collective noun as singular and plural in the same context.

INCONSISTENT: The regiment *is* [singular] now displaying *their* [plural] colors.
CONSISTENT: The regiment *is* [singular] now displaying *its* [singular] colors.

5e. Antecedent of Indeterminate Gender

When a noun antecedent can be taken as masculine or feminine, the pronoun reference *he or she* is usually awkward. Try, instead, to settle on a single gender or reconstruct the sentence to avoid the problem.

AWKWARD: If a *commuter* objects to the proposed fare increase, *he or she* should register a complaint.
BETTER: A *commuter who* objects to the proposed fare increase should register a complaint.

EXERCISE

A. Provide the correct pronoun for each of the blank spaces below. If the context leaves any doubt as to the right pronoun, explain why.

1. He never sold an article of clothing to anyone if he thought it looked bad on ______.
2. When a city grows large, many of ______ residents tend to lose ______ civic pride.
3. No one liked the idea of giving up ______ place in the line.
4. Either of the two girls would have been glad to contribute ______ services at the church bazaar.
5. The coach put the squad through ______ paces for several hours each day before the game.
6. Every man and woman in the room committed ______ time and energies to the cause.
7. I loved the sound of the horns, but I could not believe ______ came from the band I knew.
8. None of the union's leaders had reason to believe that ______ demands would be met.
9. When Helen and Polly agreed to accompany Sara to Jim's debut, none of us could have known how successful ______ would be or how much pleasure was in store for ______.
10. No record of these events would be worth saving if ______ did not promise to be useful in the future.

6 Case

ca

Use the correct case forms of nouns and pronouns.

The three case forms—nominative, objective, and possessive—show the grammatical function of nouns and pronouns. Thus nominative (or subjective) case forms are used for subjects, objective case forms are used for objects, and possessive case forms are used to denote possession. The nominative and objective case forms of nouns and of the indefinite pronouns (*someone, everyone, anybody,* and so on) are the same; only in the possessive case does the form change through the addition of an apostrophe and, with few exceptions, an *s*. (The possessive case forms of nouns are discussed in **Rule 13a**.)

NOMINATIVE: Smith, child, bookkeeper, someone
OBJECTIVE (NO CHANGE): Smith, child, bookkeeper, someone
POSSESSIVE: Smith's, child's, bookkeeper's, someone's

Eight common pronouns form their possessives without apostrophes, and six of the same pronouns have distinctive forms in all three cases.

NOMINATIVE:	I	he	she	we	they	who	you	it
OBJECTIVE:	me	him	her	us	them	whom	you	it
POSSESSIVE:	my	his	her	our	their	whose	your	its
	mine		hers	ours	theirs		yours	

6a. Subject, Predicate Noun

Use the nominative case forms for the subjects of verbs and for predicate nouns or pronouns.

They approved the plan. [Subject of *approved*]
I do not know *who* will take the responsibility. [Subject of *will take*]
Who shall I say called? [Subject of *called:* "I shall say *who* called."]
Give the book to *whoever* needs it most. [Subject of *needs.* The object of the preposition *to* is the noun clause "whoever needs it most."]

The two representatives will be *Jim and I.* [Predicate noun and pronoun following the linking verb *will be*]

NOTE: Informal usage would sanction "Jim and me" in the last example. *It's me,* another departure from the rule, is also well established in informal English.

6b. Objects

Use the objective case for the direct object and indirect object of a verb, and the object of a preposition.

They asked *Jim as well as me* for our home addresses. [Direct objects of *asked*]
Eric does not care *whom* he hurts. [Direct object of *hurts*]
Please give *them and us* the benefit of your advice. [Indirect objects of *give.* The direct object is *benefit.*]
To *whom* shall I send my request? [Object of preposition]

In informal usage, *who* is used instead of *whom* as an object at the beginning of a sentence.

GENERAL: *Whom* he goes with does not concern me. [Object of preposition *with*]
INFORMAL: *Who* he goes with does not concern me.

6c. Appositive Element

A pronoun in apposition with a noun or other pronoun takes the same case as the word with which it is in apposition.

Two campers—*Ronald and I*—were chosen to help with the boats. [*Ronald and I* are in apposition with the subject *campers.*]
The host met us—*Jodi and me*—at the door. [*Jodi and me* are in apposition with the object *us.*]

When an appositive follows a pronoun, be sure the pronoun is in the correct case.

We classmates [NOT: *Us classmates*] should keep in touch with each other.

6d. Modifier of Gerund

The modifier of a gerund is usually in the possessive case.

I objected to *his* going without me.
Your telling of the story was delightful.
Myra Grant's playing showed great sensitivity.

Do not confuse the gerund (verbal noun) with the present participle (verbal adjective).

Myra Grant playing Chopin is an experience no one should miss. [Here *playing* is a participle modifying *Myra Grant.*]

6e. With Infinitive

Use the objective case for the subject of an infinitive and for an object or predicate noun (or pronoun) following the infinitive.

I wanted *him* to come with me. [Subject of *to come*. The object of the verb *wanted* is the whole phrase that follows, *him to come with me.*]
It turned out to be *her*. [Predicate pronoun following *to be*]

6f. In Comparisons

In elliptical (uncompleted) clauses of comparison beginning with *than* or *as*, the pronoun is either nominative or objective, depending on whether it is the subject or object of the understood verb.

She is as good a scholar as *I* [am]. [Subject of understood verb]
I would much rather she had written him than [had written] *me*. [Object of understood verb]

EXERCISE

A. Examine the case of each noun and pronoun and correct the errors. Give the reason for every change you make and for every one you do not.

1. Who would you say was responsible for the error?
2. I do not like the idea of him wearing my clothes when he is perfectly capable of having a whole wardrobe of his own.
3. Waiting in the lobby for Neil were Luke, Tim, and me. When we spied a figure in a mink coat coming toward us, we could hardly know that it would turn out to be him.

4. Your grades are excellent, but our's will need improvement if we are going to be included among those whose names will adorn the honor roll.

5. It's you and we they depend on; let us try not to disappoint them.

6. Between you and I, there's some skulduggery in the scullery.

7. If he would only say to us—you and I—that he is sorry.

8. I wish I were her; she says she wants to be me. Us two girls are the daffiest people!

9. The other couple, like we, expressed their gratitude to the hostess, she with the orchid pinned to her gown.

10. Flint, who I could always depend on, went back on his word. All of us now, including you and I, have reason to be disappointed in him.

7 *ref*
Reference of Pronouns

The antecedent of a pronoun should be unmistakably clear.

Pronouns—words like *he, she, it, they, this*—are substitutes for other words. When a pronoun is used, the reader must know what word or other expression it refers to. When too many words separate antecedent from pronoun, when there is some question as to *which* word the pronoun refers to, or when the pronoun refers to some vague idea rather than a specific unit of meaning, confusion sets in.

7a. Ambiguous Reference

Do not use a pronoun in such a way that it may refer to more than one possible antecedent. Either substitute a noun for the pronoun or recast the sentence to avoid error.

AMBIGUOUS: Philip told Donald that *he* had misjudged the situation. [*Who* had misjudged the situation?]
IMPROVED: Philip told Donald that *Donald* had misjudged the situation.
OR: Philip acknowledged to Donald that *he* had misjudged the situation. [Here the reference to Philip is clear.]

AMBIGUOUS: Mr. Damon said that although Mr. Whyte was pleasant, *he* remained unconvinced of *his* sincerity. [*Who* remained unconvinced of *whose* sincerity?]
IMPROVED: Mr. Damon said that Mr. Whyte was pleasant, but not convincing in his sincerity.

7b. Indefinite Antecedent

Avoid using pronouns so loosely that their reference is either lost to the reader or nonexistent.

(1) The pronouns *it, which, that,* and *this* are sometimes used to refer to the general idea of a preceding clause. You should avoid this construction, however, if it leads to awkwardness or vagueness.

VAGUE REFERENCE: The vegetables are kept in refrigerated cases, *which* eliminates spoilage.
IMPROVED: Keeping the vegetables in refrigerated cases eliminates spoilage.

VAGUE REFERENCE: They do not permit earrings to be returned because *it* is against the sanitary code.
IMPROVED: The sanitary code does not permit them to accept the return of earrings.

ACCEPTABLE: They evicted the rightful tenants and took away their possessions. *This* was unconscionable. [The reference to the idea in the first sentence is clear.]

In some instances you may be able to improve on a pronoun that refers vaguely to the idea of a preceding clause by substituting a noun or noun phrase for the pronoun.

VAGUE REFERENCE: Josie proposed that we go to the beach, *which* I accepted readily.
IMPROVED: Josie proposed that we go to the beach, a *suggestion* I accepted readily. [Summarizing noun]

VAGUE REFERENCE: Helen has done well in college despite her unpromising start. *This* should help her when she looks for a job.
IMPROVED: Helen has done well in college despite her unpromising start. *Her record* should help her when she looks for a job. [Summarizing noun phrase]

(2) Except in informal writing, do not use the pronouns *you* or *they* in an indefinite sense.

INDEFINITE: In New York, *they* call that kind of sandwich a "hero."
IMPROVED: In New York, that kind of sandwich is called a "hero."

INDEFINITE: In many homes, *you* say grace before meals.
IMPROVED: In many homes, grace is said before meals.

(3) Avoid having a pronoun refer to an antecedent that is inferred rather than expressed.

INDEFINITE: The company offered to renegotiate the contract, but the workers refused *it.*
IMPROVED: The company offered to renegotiate the contract, but the workers refused *the offer.*

(4) Avoid having a pronoun refer to an antecedent that performs a

subordinate function in the sentence or is so far removed that the relationship is unclear.

ANTECEDENT IN SUBORDINATE ROLE: Whatever *democracy's* imperfections, *it* is the only system that makes possible change without violence. [The antecedent of *it* is *democracy's,* an adjective.]

IMPROVED: Whatever *its* imperfections, *democracy* is the only system that makes possible change without violence. [The pronoun *its* now refers to the subject of the sentence, *democracy.*]

REMOTE ANTECEDENT: *Corruption* in government is almost impossible to control, and probably more so in a democracy than in more authoritarian societies, but one should not think *it* is inevitable. [By the time the reader gets to the pronoun, he has forgotten the antecedent.]

IMPROVED: . . . but one should not think *corruption* is inevitable. [For the pronoun so far removed from its antecedent, a noun is substituted.]

EXERCISE

A. Change a word, or recast the sentence where necessary, to clarify the reference of pronouns in the following statements. Explain the error and the effect of your correction in each instance.

1. No matter where you live, it isn't perfect.
2. Frye asked that his attorney return the letter to him because he thought it was incriminating.
3. We stood in line for breakfast, but by the time we reached the counter, they had no food left.
4. The muscles in my arm were knotting into spasms. I started to wonder if it could hold the pole upright much longer.
5. Three national parks are within hitching distance, which is a must for students without cars.
6. The sun was already blazing, and I judged from its intensity that it would be another scorching day.
7. I begged the dry cleaner to have my jacket ready by five o'clock, which he did.
8. When I came to register, I found they had misplaced my application and my high school records.
9. My father is a professor at the school, which qualifies me for tuition remission.
10. There stood a huge vat with a strange odor coming from it. I learned that it was acetone, a solvent for paint.

11. We enclose the original and a copy of a letter which will serve to confirm our agreement. The original of this letter should be signed by a parent or guardian and returned to us.

12. The public library is closed on Mondays, which is very inconvenient for those working people who have the day off.

13. She has already missed the first four class sessions; this worries her.

14. In my town transportation is very poor. In fact, they have no trains or buses.

15. Do not take the life out of your woolen sweaters by washing them. Let us do it in a scientific way.

8 Adjectives and Adverbs

ad

Distinguish the adjective from the adverb, and use the correct form of each.

Adjectives regularly modify nouns or pronouns; adverbs modify verbs, adjectives, or other adverbs, and sometimes whole clauses or sentences.

ADJECTIVES: *Many good* men shy from *public* office.
ADVERBS: *Happily*, the snow plow *soon* cleared the *almost* impassable street.

Some adjectives and adverbs have the same form (*slow, late, well*); and both adjectives and adverbs have several forms that show degrees of comparison. Some of these forms are irregular, that is, they do not follow the normal pattern. If you have any doubt about the form of an adjective or adverb, consult your dictionary.

	Positive	Comparative	Superlative
ADJECTIVES	sure	surer	surest
		more sure	most sure
		less sure	least sure
Irregular:	good	better	best
ADVERBS	often	oftener	oftenest
		more often	most often
		less often	least often
Irregular:	far	farther	farthest
		further	furthest

A great many adverbs are formed by the addition of *-ly* to adjectives and participles (*surely, nearly, winningly, admittedly*). Some adverbs have two forms—with the *-ly* ending, and without it ("Walk *slow*"; "Walk *slowly*")—though the shorter form is more likely to be found in informal English.

To identify adverbs fairly easily, look for words that answer the question How? (*wildly, badly*); When? (*lately, then, finally*); Where? (*there, outside*); How much? (*too, rarely, almost*); or With what degree of certainty? (*yes, not, surely, possibly*).

8a. Misuse of Adjective for Adverb

Do not use an adjective when the grammar of the sentence requires an adverb.

MODIFIER OF ADJECTIVE

NOT: Jim has a *real* fine voice.
BUT: Jim has a *really* fine voice

MODIFIER OF VERB

NOT: She works very *diligent.*
BUT: She works very *diligently.*

MODIFIER OF ADVERB

NOT: He drove *awful* close to the edge of the cliff.
BUT: He drove *awfully* close to the edge of the cliff.

8b. Correct Form in Comparison

Use the comparative form of the adjective or adverb when comparing two units; the superlative when comparing three or more units.

TWO UNITS: Of the two men, Henry is the *more* [NOT: *most*] experienced.

THREE OR MORE UNITS: With a choice of road, rail, air, and water transportation, shipping by water is the *least expensive* [NOT: *less expensive*] method.

BUT: Shipping by water is far less expensive than shipping by rail, road, or air. [The comparative is used because only two units are involved: shipping by water and shipping by other means.]

8c. Adjective After Linking Verb

After a linking verb—for example, *look, feel, prove, remain, see, taste, smell, sound*—use an adjective, not an adverb, to describe the subject.

Joseph looks *handsome* in his new sweater.
I felt *terrible* about the error.
Their new recording sounds *excellent.*
The customer is *firm* in his objection.

8d. Absolute Adjective

Avoid using the comparative or superlative form of an adjective that is already absolute in its meaning.

NOT: If we could make a *more perfect* product, we would.
BUT: If we could make a *perfect* product, we would.
OR: If we could make a *better* product, we would.

NOT: Davies has a *most unique* talent.
BUT: Davies has a *unique* talent.
OR: Davies has a *most unusual* talent.

EXERCISE

A. For each adjective or adverb misused in the following sentences, supply the correct word and explain the error.

1. He looked suspicious to the manager, who quick took up a position behind the cash register.
2. Of the two friends, Jim was always the smartest.
3. We were so close to each other in childhood that I felt near like a brother to him.
4. With six deaths reported, it was the most fatal fire in the town's history.
5. I felt real glad about Marie's good fortune.
6. The store had to be closed temporary because of the owner's illness.
7. Whether Joan or Carol is chosen, they are the more promising of all the young talent I have seen.
8. Baby Robert was at his most worst in the presence of strangers, but he had a pleasing pretty smile for those he knew.
9. The sewing machine operates more quiet now that it has been oiled.
10. The cheese blends especially good with cream to produce a most delicious sauce.

9 Verbs

v

Use the correct form of the verb.

Verbs are needed to make grammatically complete sentences and clauses.

Night *came.*
Mr. Gray *sold* his house.
When I *went* to the window, I *saw* the taxi.

All verbs have at least three inflectional forms, most have four, and some have five or more.

set, sets, setting
walk, walks, walked, walking
rise, rises, rose, risen, rising
be, am, is, are, was, were, been, being

Verbs like *walk*, which have a form ending in *–ed*, are "regular"; other verbs are "irregular." The dictionary gives the principal parts of all irregular verbs, and of those regular verbs with peculiarities of spelling in any of their forms. The principal parts consist usually of the base word (also the infinitive), the past tense, the past participle, and the present participle. All verbs are characterized by an *–s* ending in the third person present and by the addition of *–ing* to form the present participle. Verbs are also formed with such auxiliaries as *be, do, have, can, may, will, would, could, might, must,* and *should* (*will be helped, can go, must tell, should ask*).

An important characteristic of verbs is tense, or the capacity to make distinctions in time through changes in the verb forms. Grammatically, verbs have six tenses: present, past, future; present perfect, past perfect, and future perfect. As we shall see, these tenses do not always coincide with the actual time the verbs denote. For ease of comparison, all of the tenses are treated below with special reference to the verb *ask*. A conjugation of the verb *ask*, including the passive voice forms is shown on pages 312–13. For an explanation of the passive voice, see **Rule 30d(2)**

PRESENT TENSE

ask, asks (simple present)

I *ask* a favor. [Action is present]
Next Wednesday, I *do not ask,* I demand. [Future action]
He *asks* frequently about his mother. [Continued action]
Roosevelt *asks* for a declaration of war. [Historical present]

am asking, is asking, are asking (progressive present)

I *am asking* you to come.
They *are asking* for their change.

do ask, does ask (emphatic present)

I *do ask* for what is mine.
Fido *does* ask for his supper.

The present progressive and emphatic forms are also used in forming questions and negative statements.

Am I asking for too much?
Do I ask for too much?
I am not asking for much.
I do not ask for much.

PAST TENSE

asked (simple past)

I *asked* a favor.
They *asked* about their mother.
Roosevelt *asked* for a declaration of war.

was asking, were asking (progressive past)

I *was asking* a favor.
They *were asking* about their mother.

did ask (emphatic past)

I *did ask* a favor.
They *did ask* about their mother.

The past progressive and emphatic forms are also used in forming questions and negative statements.

Was I asking for too much?
Did I ask for too much?
I was not asking for much.
I did not ask for much.

FUTURE TENSE

shall ask, will ask (simple future)

Next Wednesday, I *shall see* my counselor.
He *will not ask* for a raise.

shall be asking, will be asking (progressive future)

Next Wednesday, I *shall be asking* for a raise.
He *will not be asking* for a favor.

[For the distinction between *shall* and *will*, see **Rule 9d**.]

PRESENT PERFECT TENSE

have asked, has asked

I *have asked* for a raise. [Action before present time]

PAST PERFECT TENSE

had asked

By last Wednesday, I *had* already *asked* for a raise. [Action before past time.]

FUTURE PERFECT TENSE

shall have asked, will have asked

By Wednesday, I *shall have asked* for a raise. [Action before future time]

The present perfect, past perfect, and future perfect tenses also have progressive forms: *have been asking, has been asking; shall have been asking, will have been asking.*

CONJUGATION OF THE VERB *ASK*

(For additional forms, see **Rule 9**)

PRINCIPAL PARTS: ask (present infinitive)
asked (past tense)
asked (past participle)
asking (present participle)

INDICATIVE MOOD

ACTIVE VOICE		PASSIVE VOICE	
SINGULAR	PLURAL	SINGULAR	PLURAL
		Present Tense	
I ask	we ask	I am asked	we are asked
you ask	you ask	you are asked	you are asked
he asks	they ask	he is asked	he is asked
		Past Tense	
I asked	we asked	I was asked	we were asked
you asked	you asked	you were asked	you were asked
he asked	they asked	he was asked	they were asked
		Future Tense	
I shall (will) ask	we shall (will) ask	I shall (will) be asked	we shall (will) be asked
you will ask	you will ask	you will be asked	you will be asked
he will ask	they will ask	he will be asked	they will be asked
		Present Perfect Tense	
I have asked	we have asked	I have been asked	we have been asked
you have asked	you have asked	you have been asked	you have been asked
he has asked	they have asked	he has been asked	they have been asked
		Past Perfect Tense	
I had asked	we had asked	I had been asked	we had been asked
you had asked	you had asked	you had been asked	you had been asked
he had asked	they had asked	he had been asked	they had been asked
		Future Perfect Tense	
I shall (will) have asked	we shall (will) have asked	I shall (will) have been asked	We shall (will) have been asked
you will have asked	you will have asked	you will have been asked	you will have been asked
he will have asked	he will have asked	he will have been asked	they will have been asked

IMPERATIVE FORMS: ask, be asked
INFINITIVES: to ask, to have asked, to be asked, to have been asked
GERUNDS: asking, having asked, being asked, having been asked
PARTICIPLES: asking, asked, having asked, being asked, having been asked

9a. Correct Forms

Be sure to use the correct principal parts of verbs.

NOT: He *laid* beside the lake, entranced by its beauty. [Past tense of *lay*, "to put down"]
BUT: He lay beside the lake, entranced by its beauty. [Past tense of *lie*, "to recline"]

NOT: I would have *swam* to the island, if I could.
BUT: I would have *swum* to the island, if I could.
ALSO CORRECT: I *swam* to the island.

NOT: The horse *drug* him by his feet.
BUT: The horse *dragged* him by his feet.

9b. Time Relationships

Let the tenses show the proper relationship in time.

(1) See that there is a logical relation between the tenses of verbs in both main and subordinate clauses.

He *talked* as he *drove*. [Past tense in both the main and the subordinate clause shows actions occurring at the same time.]
I *have known* about her illness, but I *have not spoken* about it. [Present perfect tense in both main clauses shows actions occurring at the same time.]
Sims *had arranged* for the flowers before he *received* her letter. [The past perfect tense in the main clause shows time before that of the past tense verb in the subordinate clause.]

(2) Use the present infinitive and present participle to denote action occurring at the same time as that of the verb they relate to; use the perfect infinitive and perfect participle to denote action occurring before the time of the verb.

I wanted *to shout*. [Present infinitive expresses same time as verb.]
He was said *to have lived* very frugally. [Perfect infinitive expresses time before that of verb.]
Living frugally, he has all he needs. [Present participle expresses same time as verb.]
Having lived very frugally, he died a rich man. [Perfect participle expresses time before that of verb.]

9c. Subjunctive

Use the subjunctive mood where good usage requires it. (See also "Mood," **Rule 1e**.)

The subjunctive of the verb *to be* is limited to *be* in all forms of the present tense (I *be,* you *be,* he *be,* and so on) and *were* in all forms of the past tense (I *were,* you *were,* he *were*). The subjunctive of other verbs is confined to the third person singular (he *ask,* NOT he *asks*).

Use the subjunctive mood as follows:

(1) In a "that" clause expressing a suggestion, request, command, order, motion, or resolution

I suggest that the penalty *be rescinded.*
I request that he *go* now.
She moved that the amendment *be adopted.*
Resolved, that the cafeteria *remain* open until 10 P.M.

(2) In a wish, or an "if" statement contrary to fact

I wish I *were* in Paris.
If she *were* in Paris, she could practice her French.
BUT: If I *was* rude, I am sorry. [No subjunctive because the condition may be true.]

In informal usage, this rule is often not observed.

GENERAL: I wish he *were* more considerate.
INFORMAL: I wish he *was* more considerate.

(3) In certain idiomatic expressions

Suffice it to say
Be that as it may
Heaven *help* us

9d. *Shall, Will; Should, Would*

Use *shall* and *will,* and *should* and *would* according to modern preferences.

Many of the distinctions formerly made in these word pairs are no longer observed, and most writers are content to use the words they are most comfortable with, provided that the meaning is accurately communicated.

(*1*) **Shall *and* will.** *Will* is generally used in all persons to express simple future time. In questions, *shall* is used in the first person and *will* in the second and third persons. In orders, rules, laws, and resolutions, *shall* is traditionally used in the second and third persons.

I *will arrive* at 9 P.M. [Simple future]
They *will not regret* their generosity. [Simple future]
Shall I tell him you called? [Question, first person]
Will Donna agree to the plan? [Question, third person]
No funds *shall be disbursed* without the approval of the treasurer. [Law or rule]

In formal usage, simple future time is expressed by *shall* in the first person (I *shall*, we *shall*), and *will* in the second and third persons (you *will*, she *will*, they *will*). The order is reversed in the emphatic future, where the speaker's or writer's determination is denoted by the use of *will* in the first person (I *will*, we *will*), and *shall* in the second and third persons (you *shall*, he *shall*, they *shall*).

FORMAL: I *shall* go. [Simple future]
I *will* go. [Determination]
You *shall* go; I insist. [Determination]
They *will leave* when they are ready. [Simple future]
They *shall* not *pass*. [Determination]

(2) **Should *and* would.** *Should* is customarily used to express an obligation, a condition or an expectation.

They *should* [*ought to*] *pay* their fair share of the cost. [Obligation]
If he *should* falter, will you help? [Condition]
She *should arrive* on the 7:15 from Montauk. [Expectation]

Would is used as an auxiliary in all persons to express a polite request, but formal usage sometimes favors the use of *should* in the first person.

She would appreciate your meeting her at the station.
Would you please telephone me.
I would like to pay my own way.
OR (FORMAL): *I should like to* pay my own way.

Would is used to express a habitual action or a wish.

I *would telephone* the agency every day.
Would that Ray had taken his father's advice!

EXERCISE

A. Check the forms and tenses of the verbs in the sentences below and make any changes you consider desirable or necessary. Suggest alternative usages where you can. Be prepared to justify the verb usages you do not alter.

1. On September 1, Professor Camp will be with the university for twenty-five years.
2. If Jim was as interested in math as he is in girls, he might still be in school.
3. Now that I have began to think about the decision, I am disturbed by its implications.
4. The girls laid the children's presents in a circle around the tree, which I thought might be a little bigger.
5. The paper-wrapped package set in the rain for at least two hours before it was moved under the shed.
6. He will never cross my threshold; that I promise you.
7. I am hoping that you shall come to my party.
8. Bill asked that he be considered for the position, but deep down he rather wished that he was not selected.
9. When Gloria lived closer, I would visit her every week. Usually I brang flowers.
10. They thought I would want to have taken advantage of the offer before it expired.

10 End Punctuation ./?/!

End a sentence with a period, a question mark, or an exclamation point.

The end of a statement requiring a period is usually marked by a downward vocal slide. The end of a statement requiring a question mark or an exclamation point is usually marked by an upward vocal slide.

The book is hugely entertaining.
Shall I call you tomorrow?
Give up? I should say not!

10a. Period •

Use a period at the end of a declarative statement, an indirect question, or a mild exclamation. Use a period, also, after an abbreviation, where custom requires, and use a series of three spaced periods (an ellipsis) to show an omission in quoted material.

(1) Use a period after a declarative statement.

Advertising is not usually subtle.
I have just finished the assignment.
Humboldt's Gift was written by Saul Bellow.

(2) Use a period after an indirect question.

He asked me where I was working. [The direct question would be part of the statement, He asked, "Where are you working?"]
I wondered what was on the program.
My host wanted to know if I had transportation home.

(3) Use a period after a mild exclamation or command, and after a question regarded as a polite request.

Heavens. What a night. [COMPARE: Heavens! What a night!]
Enjoy yourself.
Will you please call for me.

(4) Follow current practice in putting periods after abbreviations. In some instances, the use of such periods is optional. In other instances, especially when an abbreviation spells a pronounceable word, the periods are regularly omitted.

PERIOD REQUIRED

A.M. P.M. Mr. Mrs. St. Ave. A.D. B.C.

NO PERIOD

WCBS IBM ASCAP NATO AFL-CIO
HOLC (Home Owners Loan Corporation)
USDA (U.S. Department of Agriculture)

PERIOD OPTIONAL

r.p.m. or rpm A.T.&T. or AT&T T.V.A. or TVA

Do not use a period after a shortened word or contraction.

ad [for advertisement]
tab [for tabulator]
cont'd [BUT: contd.]
Sam or Sam'l [BUT: Jos.]

(5) Use three spaced periods (called an ellipsis) to denote an omission in quoted material. Add a fourth period if the omission occurs at the end of a sentence requiring a period.

Even if the worker joins the union in fear . . . he is doing something not only emotional, but also rational. He wants to live with the people in his department in peace. . . .—T.V. PURCELL

NOTE: Some authors, including advertising writers, occasionally use three spaced periods not to signify omissions, but to achieve emphasis or establish a mood. The practice is generally not recommended in college compositions, where it smacks of affectation and where other punctuation will serve as well, if not better.

Amazing isn't it, how many people want the family copy . . . or the office copy . . . or the last copy on the newsstand . . . just when you do!—TIME

10b. Question Mark ?

Use a question mark at the end of a direct question, but not at the end of an indirect question.

When may I expect your call?
Did Marcus really expect to avoid the consequences?
Have you completed your paper?
You have completed your paper? [Question phrased like a declarative sentence]
BUT: I asked whether he had completed his paper. [Indirect question; period at end]

(1) A question mark is used after a direct question within a declarative statement.

I wanted to know, How did he do it? And where? And when? [For use of capitals, see **Rule 17d**.]
What does he mean? is a question I cannot answer.
COMPARE WITH: What he means is a question I cannot answer.

(2) A question mark, usually within parentheses, is used to express doubt about a preceding figure or other datum, but it is better not used as an expression of sarcasm.

CORRECT: About Plotinus (205?–270 A.D.), the Egyptian-born Roman philosopher, it is a pity that more is not known.
CORRECT: The place of publication was given as New York, N.J.(?).
NOT FAVORED: His eagerness (?) to perform the favor touched me deeply. [Sarcasm]

10c. Exclamation Point !

Use an exclamation point after an interjection or other statement expressing strong feeling.

Help!
Indeed I will!
Well! So that was the scheme!
How incredible! How perfectly delightful!

After a mild interjection, use a comma or period rather than an exclamation point and, in general, use the exclamation point sparingly.

Oh, I see.
Indeed, we will come to visit you.
Well, I'd like to reserve my decision.
Yes. I do believe I will come.
What a day. We don't get many so sunny and warm.

EXERCISES

A. Punctuate the following sentences with periods, question marks, and exclamation points where needed. Capitalize the first word of each new sentence.

1. What was important was that Dove held strongly to the essence of nature even while he freed himself from fidelity to it his pictures are now at the Whitney
2. He said that Washington, DC, was the most beautiful city in the world what drivel had he ever seen Paris "have you" he asked "yes, several times," I replied
3. He used to work as an announcer for NBC, but he got tired of the routine I asked him what was tiring about it "Would you believe getting up at 3 AM" I said I would
4. What a character he eats snails for breakfast and asks for the dessert menu before he will order dinner one evening he wanted a huge lobster and insisted that the waiter bring it live to the table before it was boiled it nearly ate him don't you believe me
5. "He appeared in the stage presentation of *Will Rogers, USA*" "is he the same actor who played Abraham Lincoln in the movie" "indeed I like especially the way he delivered the Gettysburg Address what dignity"
6. Murderer what else would you call an unscrupulous seller of pets who will let his animals develop fatal illnesses through lack of care fortunately, a new law requires that no pet merchant can now sell a pet without giving the purchaser a health certificate signed by a licensed veterinarian will the law help I certainly hope so

B. Supply the following examples from your reading, or compose them yourself.

1. An indirect question
2. A direct question
3. Five abbreviations requiring periods
4. Five abbreviations not requiring periods
5. A quoted passage with an ellipsis occurring in the middle
6. The use of spaced periods to establish mood or emphasis
7. The use of a question mark to express doubt
8. The use of a question within a declarative statement
9. Three exclamatory sentences
10. A declarative statement containing a mild interjection

11 The Comma

,

Use a comma wherever the sense requires.

The need for a comma is usually evidenced by a pause in the reading of a sentence and a change in intonation. A more reliable guide, however, is the sentence structure, which provides the writer with specific clues to comma placement.

11a. Between Main Clauses

Place a comma between main clauses joined by one of the coordinate conjunctions: *and, but, yet, for,* or *nor.*

The pen felt strange in my hand, and its scratch on paper sounded offensively loud.—ROBERT GRAVES
The summer is hot in Spain, but it is hottest in Andalusia.
He left behind most of the religious concepts that were so important to his mother, yet in his heart he valued her abiding faith.
Help him, for he cannot help himself.
Spanish moss is not a moss at all, nor is there anything Spanish about it.

NOTE: When the main clauses are short, the comma before the coordinate conjunction is often omitted.

He was short and he was fat.
I will return the book or I will pay for it.
BUT: They had no power, for they were poor. [Comma used to prevent misreading]

11b. After an Introductory Element

Place a comma after an introductory subordinate clause; after a long introductory phrase, especially if it contains part of a verb; and after an introductory word or short phrase not closely connected to the rest of the sentence.

When he finally arrived at the party, he was drenched. [Subordinate clause]

If you think you were marked unfairly, you should speak to the instructor. [Subordinate clause]

Faced with the prospect of a cold winter, the O'Neills gathered up a reserve supply of dry forest timber. [Participial phrase]

By making their reservation early, they were assured of getting the accommodations they wanted. [Prepositional phrase containing a gerund]

By the beginning of the twenty-first century, it may be possible to increase the harvest of ocean fish fourfold.—ROGER REVELLE [Long prepositional phrase]

After all, the record had to be broken sometime. [Short connecting phrase]

Yes, I will telephone you when I arrive. [Mild interjection]

11c. Between Elements in Series

Use commas to set off the elements in a series.

The series may consist of words, phrases, or clauses. In literary usage (though not in newspaper writing), a comma is usually placed before the *or* or *and* connecting the last members of the series.

I noticed numerous fractures of the shaft, of the os calcis, of the pelvic girdle.—DONALD BARTHELME [Prepositional phrases]

The Okefenokee is a mysterious realm of stately cypresses, peat quagmires, and dim waterways. [Noun phrases]

To get under way, you simply hooked the third finger of the right hand around a lever on the steering column, pulled down hard, and shoved your left foot forcibly against the low-speed pedal.—E. B. WHITE [Verb phrases]

We were prosperous, we got what we wanted, and we had a relatively stable economy without totalitarian rule. [Independent clauses]

Coordinate adjectives (adjectives modifying the same noun or noun phrase) are separated by commas. Such adjectives are identifiable by the fact that they can be connected by *and* without injury to the sense. Adjectives in series that cannot be connected by *and* are not coordinate and should not be separated by commas.

The builder specialized in *split-level, semi-detached, fundamentally identical* homes. [Commas separating coordinate adjectives]

He thought he would like to work for a *conservative Wall Street investment* house. [Adjectives not coordinate—no commas]

11d. To Set Off Parenthetic Elements

Use commas to set off a parenthetic sentence element, or "interrupter." Such an expression serves to explain, describe, amplify, or connect. Place a comma after, before, or before and after the parenthetic element, depending on whether the element comes at the beginning, at the end, or in some other position within the sentence.

COMMA AFTER: *In time,* he will get to know us better.

COMMA BEFORE: No one has a better grasp of the subject than Gwen Rath, *a longtime friend of mine.*

COMMA BEFORE AND AFTER: He will, *I know,* pay his share of the expenses.

(1) Use commas to set off a *nonrestrictive* phrase or clause. A nonrestrictive phrase or clause is one that is not essential and therefore can be omitted without damage to the sense of the sentence. It usually has an adjective function, but the noun it modifies is already independently identified. A *restrictive* phrase or clause, on the other hand, has an important identifying function and may not be omitted without damage to the sense of the sentence; such a modifier is not set off by commas.

The huge generator, *which had never failed before,* was now quiet. [Nonrestrictive clause—can be omitted without damage to the sense of the sentence.]

He gave the notes to Joseph, *who quickly copied and returned them.* [Nonrestrictive clause]

He took off his coat, *intending to find some dry clothes upstairs.* [Nonrestrictive phrase]

We do not drown ourselves, *like Narcissus,* in the pool that reflects us; we try to stop it up instead.—OCTAVIO PAZ [Nonrestrictive phrase]

A student *wishing to be excused from gym* has to present a doctor's note. [Restrictive phrase—cannot be omitted without damage to the sense of the sentence.]

Who and *which* may introduce either restrictive or nonrestrictive clauses, but *that* introduces only restrictive clauses.

A child *who misbehaves* may be seeking attention. [Restrictive]

A child, *who is not yet fully formed physically or mentally,* must not be asked to do what is beyond a child's capacity. [Nonrestrictive]

The rug, *which costs a thousand dollars today,* was selling for half as much three years ago. [Nonrestrictive]

A rug *that costs a thousand dollars today* was selling for half as much three years ago. [Restrictive]

Sometimes a phrase or clause may be punctuated as restrictive or nonrestrictive, depending on the sense intended. Note the lowered pitch as well as the pause as you read the nonrestrictive clause in the first sentence below.

NONRESTRICTIVE: The policeman, *standing outside the front door,* greeted the visiting dignitary. [This sentence suggests that the policeman has been mentioned earlier.]

RESTRICTIVE: The policeman *standing outside the front door* greeted the visiting dignitary. [In this sentence the policeman is apparently mentioned for the first time.]

(2) Use commas to set off sentence elements in apposition, contrast, or direct address. This rule includes the use of commas to set off titles and the elements that make up dates and addresses.

The Everglades kite, *a bird native to southern Florida,* eats only apple snails. [Appositive phrase]

Mr. Daly is the brother, *not the son,* of the sculptor. [Contrasting phrase]

Friends, I have a surprise for you. [Word in direct address]

Please send the letter to Miss Jean Belding, *Vice President, International Oil Company, 600 Fifth Avenue, New York,* N.Y. [Elements in an address]

Payment will become due on *April 1, 1985,* at the office of the company's treasurer. [Date]

EXCEPTION: Appositive expressions that are restrictive [see **Rule 11d(1)** above] are not set off by commas.

My friend *Cary* is playing right field. [*Cary* is a necessary identifying element.]

Joe *the cobbler* is known for his fine-quality work.

11e. To Prevent Misreading

Use a comma whenever necessary to prevent misreading.

To begin with, the figures were more optimistic than the situation warranted. [NOT: *To begin with the figures . . .*]

Inside, her anxiety increased.

I don't recommend any mutual *fund, any more* than I recommend individual stocks.

EXERCISE

A. Place commas wherever they are required in the following sentences.

1. As a result of a complex of formative influences the college student often suffers from an extreme imbalance in emotional and intellectual growth.
2. If I described a passage on a Greek steamer you would not believe me nor would anyone else who has not experienced it.
3. True the process of extracting oil is a complicated one but it has so far not produced any problems that could not without sufficient capital be solved.
4. London is millions of small chimneys millions of Victorian doorways and millions of windows and walls.
5. We were walking just the two of us in our usual silence to and from church.
6. The set of curly-maple furniture which was deep seasoned-yellow like satin stood in a dark corner of the shop.
7. When my aunt died only the youngest member of her family was left her sole brother my uncle Tom.
8. It was just radical students frustrated in their efforts to help the Russian peasant that helped Lenin gain his political power.
9. If I were a hothead I might be tempted to whip him; if a humanitarian to strangle him and earn the gratitude of the wretches under his heel.
10. I was seeing Times Square New York now for the first time.
11. My taste does not run to small cars; however I rather like this small stripped-down 4-cylinder General Motors toy.
12. I stopped at only one cup of tea for two would have strained her capacity as a hostess.
13. Abetted by a delectable French cast Dunlop has made Scapino as Italian as *scallopine alla francese* as British as a good plum pudding and as international as ice cream.
14. Certainly the author Henry Fields is entitled to his characters but I find Maria too unpleasant to add anything to the evening's entertainment.
15. On December 15 1985 he will be twenty-one mature enough to acquire his handsome inheritance and I think smart enough to know what to do with it.

12 The Semicolon

;

Use the semicolon (1) to separate main clauses not joined by a conjunction, (2) to separate main clauses joined by a conjunctive adverb, and (3) to separate coordinate sentence elements that are internally punctuated by commas.

In the first two uses, the semicolon may be regarded as a desirable alternative to the period when the main clauses are closely related in thought.

MAIN CLAUSE ; MAIN CLAUSE.

MAIN CLAUSE . MAIN CLAUSE.

12a. Between Main Clauses

Use a semicolon between main clauses not joined by a conjunction.

A personal grudge does not necessarily imply faulty political judgment; it merely spurs a man to action. —ROBERT GRAVES

Many of the students found jobs for the summer; others went to summer school.

12b. Before Conjunctive Adverb

Use a semicolon to separate main clauses joined by a conjunctive adverb: *therefore, however, furthermore, nevertheless, accordingly, thus, so,* and so on.

MAIN CLAUSE ; *therefore* MAIN CLAUSE.

The conjunctive adverb at the beginning of the clause is followed by a comma in some instances, but not in others. The test is whether there is a pause after the adverb.

He wanted very much to join the club; *however,* he was not sure he could afford the dues.

The inner-directed man was not supposed to have fun; *indeed,* it was proper for him to be gloomy and even grim.—David Riesman

The customer did not return the sales slip with the goods; *therefore* the store maintained she was not entitled to a refund. [A comma after *therefore* would create an awkward pause.]

ALSO: The customer did not return the sales slip with the goods; the store *therefore* maintained she was not entitled to a refund.

12c. Between Elements Containing Commas

Use a semicolon to separate any coordinate sentence elements internally punctuated by commas, when confusion might otherwise result.

Art is creative for the sake of realization, not for amusement; for transfiguration, not for the sake of play.—Max Beckmann

Some persons ascribe their attachment to nature to the beauty of the land, sky, and water; others to the freedom from care, the silence, and the tranquillity which nature affords; and still others to the healthy pursuits they can engage in outdoors.

EXERCISE

A. In the passages below, some of the commas are deliberately misused for semicolons. Find the commas and substitute semicolons for them.

1. Two wardens marched on either side of the prisoner, with their rifles at the slope, two other marched close against him, gripping him by arm and shoulder, as though at once pushing and supporting him.—George Orwell

2. The opposite number to the silent picketer would be the silent poet, which is a contradiction in terms, yet there are these days nonsingers of (perhaps) great talent who shrug off the temptation to song with the muttered comment, "Creativity is out."—Leslie Fiedler

3. His instinct is to plant, his next instinctive move is to put a fence around what he has planted, even if it is only made of a few stones and only three inches high.—V.S. Pritchett

4. Stern farmers have drawn my attention to the NO FISHING signs, from cars passing me on the highways have come wild howls of derision, sleepy dogs, though mindful of the worst bum, have perked up and come at me, snarling, tiny tots have pointed me out to their puzzled mammas, broadminded vacationists have asked me whether I was catching bugs for bait, and one morning on a wasteland, lit by tall yuccas in bloom, near Santa Fe, a big black mare followed me for more than a mile.—VLADIMIR NABOKOV

5. Among individuals, Mayor Leon Denny, who was supposed to "know the buck," ex-Mayor David Wills, who is alleged to have given the city away, and former Governor Sanford Taylor, who combined the grandiose with the inane, have attracted the most enthusiastic notice.

6. There are people who, notwithstanding reverses, are congenitally cheerful, who, with no apparent preparation, can turn their hands to almost anything, who manage quite happily, though sometimes dumbly, to do contradictory things.

7. Although every precaution was taken to pack the goods carefully, they suffered considerable damage, with resulting loss to the shipper, and unfortunately this incident is only one of a series of similar occurrences.

8. Some weeks not a screed [by H. L. Mencken] would go into the mailbox without some complaint, such as, "I have a sore mouth, can't smoke, it is 90 degrees, and at least twenty pests are in town," or, "My liver is swelled to a thickness of seven inches, and there are spiders in my urine."—WILLIAM MANCHESTER

9. I have a hard time remembering whether the great man said, "Happy families are all alike, each unhappy family is unhappy in its own way," or the reverse.—EDWARD HOAGLAND

10. In January 1950 only 3.2 million Americans owned television sets, however, a decade later the figure was 50 million and in January 1952, for the first time, according to Nielsen, more television sets than radios were being turned on between 9 P.M. and midnight.

13 The Apostrophe

’

Use the apostrophe to mark possessives and contractions, and to signify the plural of letters, numbers, and signs.

13a. Possessive

Use the apostrophe to form the possessive of nouns and indefinite pronouns. The possessive denotes ownership or some other relationship that can be expressed by an “of” phrase.

the *child’s* hair [the hair of the child]
the *teller’s* duties [the duties of the teller]
season’s greetings [greetings of the season]
anyone’s guess [the guess of anyone]

(1) Add the apostrophe and *-s* to a singular or plural noun that does not already end in *-s*.

a *boy’s* coat	a *month’s* pay
a *man’s* duty	*Jane’s* boots
a *woman’s* career	a *teacher’s* classes
the *company’s* policy	*men’s* wear
no one’s fault	*women’s* rights
a *day’s* work	*children’s* schooling

(2) Add only the apostrophe to a plural noun ending in *-s*.

boys’ coats	*teachers’* associations
tellers’ windows	*accountants’* responsibilities

(3) Add the apostrophe and *-s* to a singular noun of one syllable ending in *-s* (or an *s* sound). If a singular noun ending in *-s* has more than one syllable, use the apostrophe alone or the apostrophe and *-s*, depending on ease of pronunciation.

the *boss's* daughter
the *lass's* kilt
Mr. *Jones's* prerogative
The *Times's* assets
Davis's election
Paris's attractions
Los Angeles' population [NOT: *Los Angeles's*]
Jesus' teachings [Two sibilant (*s*) sounds before the apostrophe]
for *conscience'* sake [Two sibilant sounds (*sh* and *s*) before the apostrophe]

(4) In forming the possessive of a compound noun, add the possessive ending to only the last word to show collective possession, but add the possessive ending to each noun to show possession on the part of each.

General Electric's employee pension plan
my *brother-in-law's* house
Lord & Taylor's jewelry department
Joe Darcy and Bill Martin's boat [COMPARE WITH: *Joe Darcy's and Bill Martin's* boats.]

13b. Misuse with Personal Pronouns

Do not use the apostrophe to form the possessive case of *who*, or of any of the personal pronouns. The following forms are correct:

whose, its, hers, yours, ours, theirs [No apostrophes]

Note that *it's* is the contraction of *it is* and *who's* is the contraction of *who is* or *who has*.

It's none of their business.
Who's going to be responsible for the damage?
Who's got the ignition key?

13c. Contractions

Use an apostrophe in contractions as a substitute for the omitted words, letters, or digits.

can't (can not)	e'er (ever)
I'll (I will)	o'clock (of the clock)
you're (you are)	Class of '80 (1980)
'tis (it is)	back in '48 (1948)

The apostrophe is similarly used to show omitted sounds in representations of speech.

mornin', ma'am
time o' day
books 'n' things

13d. Formation of Certain Plurals

An apostrophe and *-s* are usually added to form the plural of letters of the alphabet, figures, signs, and words stated as words. (See also **Rule 18c** governing the use of underlining in these instances.)

knows his *p's* and *q's*
cross the *t's*
asked the teller for *5's* and *10's* [BUT: asked the teller for *fives* and *tens*]
&'s that looked like *8's*
no *if's, and's,* or *but's*
He uses too many *I's.*

The apostrophe, but not the *-s*, is often omitted in journalistic and technical writing when there is no danger that the expression will be misunderstood.

the Treasury *6s* [OR: *6's*]
the *1980s* [OR: *1980's*]
always got *As* and *Bs* [OR: *A's* and *B's*]
NOT: Dotted his *is* [Confusing]
BUT: Dotted his *i's*

13e. In Coined Verbs

Use the apostrophe to form certain coined verbs. Avoid such verbs, however, in formal usage.

x'd out the error
O.K.'ing the copy [OR: *okaying* the copy]
M.C.'d the show

EXERCISES

A. Put apostrophes or apostrophes and *-s*'s where they belong in the following sentences. If a noun or a pronoun has the wrong form, change it.

1. Bess smile is grim, but Debbies is soft and appealing.

2. The 1985 bonds pay 8 percent, but the 2000s are up in the 9s and 10s. Their a good investment in the opinion of my friends, the Bradburys.

3. Your handwriting is usually legible, but I cant tell the *ms* from the *ns*

4. The Deerfields were up and around by 7 o clock, and soon I could hear Gregs voice calling, "Come n get it; come n get it," as he summoned his family to breakfast.

5. The cobra flattens its neck into a hoodlike form when its disturbed.

6. Theirs is a common reaction to too much wealth, but whose going to say he wouldnt do the same?

7. He was a drug addict who O.D.d; that could be his obituary. But was he societys victim?

8. Moses legacy to the world is still ours to cherish and observe.

9. If all of Harrys efforts go into talk instead of study, what business is it of yours? Goodness knows, hes no teachers pet.

10. Anyones eligible for any of the clubs offices if hes paid his membership dues.

B. Show by use of an apostrophe or otherwise the possessive form of each of the following terms. Do not change the number.

1. Johns Hopkins Hospital
2. deans (plural)
3. Davies (singular)
4. parents (plural)
5. Harvey Bliss
6. ladies (plural)
7. seamen (plural)
8. Casey
9. the Joneses (plural)
10. classmates (plural)

C. Show with the use of apostrophes the contraction or the shortened (or poetic) form of the words below. Do not use abbreviations.

1. cannot
2. association
3. secretary
4. we will
5. they have
6. they are
7. over
8. who are
9. beneath
10. will not

14 Quotation Marks

“/”

Use quotation marks to enclose words quoted directly, words used in a special sense, and certain literary titles.

Double quotation marks (“/”) are used regularly to enclose words quoted directly from a written or spoken source. Single quotation marks (‘/’) are used to enclose a quotation within a quotation. Should the second quotation incorporate a third quotation, the last is enclosed again by double quotation marks. Words not quoted directly should not be included within quotation marks.

“Open wide,” said the dentist.

“And then,” related Dorothy, “the pilot was on the loudspeaker announcing, ‘The tower has signalled “all clear.” We'll be landing in a few minutes.’ ”

14a. Direct Quotations

Use quotation marks to enclose direct quotations—words taken without change from any written or spoken source.

“Killing is one form of our wandering sadness,” wrote Rilke.

“They live from hand to mouth,” wrote Hazlitt about actors. “They plunge from want to luxury. They have no means of making money breed.”

My friend complained, “How am I going to get to the concert if you don't lend me your car?”

Apply this rule also to any reconstruction of a direct quotation.

The problem of space conception is everywhere under discussion. Scholars ask themselves, for example, “What things have changed and what have remained unchanged in human nature throughout the course of human history? What is it that separates us from other periods? What is it that, after having been suppressed and driven into the unconscious for long periods of time, is now reappearing in the imagination of contemporary artists?” —S. GIEDION

Do not use quotation marks to enclose an indirect quotation. However, quotation marks may be used to enclose one or more of the words to show that they are exactly as used by the source.

Mr. Simpson said that he would meet me at his office. [If Mr. Simpson were quoted directly, the sentence would read: Mr. Simpson said, "I will meet you at my office."]

One of the classic complaints of welfare workers against their destitute clients is that they're "spendthrift."—HARRIET VAN HORNE

The refusal to exercise controls, Skinner continues, may be "a lethal cultural mutation."—NOAM CHOMSKY

(*1*) ***Dialogue.*** Paragraph separately each unit of dialogue. The unit may include such interpolations as "he said" and other expository matter related to the quotation.

Henry put on his joking tone. "There's fights tonight. How'd you like to go to the fights?"

"Oh, no," she said breathlessly. "No, I wouldn't like fights."

"Just fooling, Elisa. We'll go to a movie. Let's see. It's two now. I'm going to take Scotty and bring down those steers from the hill. It'll take us maybe two hours. We'll go in town about five and have dinner at the Cominos Hotel. Like that?"

"Of course I'll like it. It's good to eat away from home."

"All right, then. I'll go get up a couple of horses."—JOHN STEINBECK[1]

(2) ***Long Quotation.*** An unbroken quotation (*not* dialogue) is preferably set close—single spaced—and indented five spaces on both sides, in addition to any indention for paragraphing. No quotation marks are used unless they are part of the quotation.

Writing on the morality of Americans, Alexis de Tocqueville observed:

> In England, as in all other countries of Europe, public malice is constantly attacking the frailties of women. Philosophers and statesmen are heard to deplore that morals are not sufficiently strict, and the literary productions of the country constantly lead one to suppose so. In America all books, novels not excepted, suppose women to be chaste, and no one thinks of relating affairs of gallantry.[2]

When quotation marks are used for quoted copy of more than a single paragraph, the marks are placed at the beginning of each

[1] From "The Chrysanthemums," in Steinbeck's *The Long Valley* (New York: Viking, 1937, 1965), p. 411.

[2] *Democracy in America,* (New York: Knopf, 1945), II, 215–16.

paragraph and at the end of only the last paragraph. The spacing and margins remain the same as those of the rest of the manuscript.

The closing argument in the case of *Tennessee* v. *Wash Jones* included these words by Joe W. Henry, Jr., the defense attorney:

"Time was when pigs, horses, and cattle were tried and executed for murder. It was the law of the state.

"In 1474 a rooster was tried for the heinous and unnatural crime of laying an egg and sentenced, together with the egg, to be burned at the stake. It was the law of the state.

"There is a recorded case in England of a nine-year-old girl being hanged for stealing two pennies worth of salt. It was the law of the state.

"I am sickened every time I hear a prosecutor apologetically asking for the death penalty and offering the pitiful excuse, 'It's the law of the state!' "[3]

(3) ***Poetry.*** Quoted poetry should be indented and set off in lines exactly as written, without quotation marks except for those in the verse.

The nostalgia common to Longfellow's poetry is not in fashion today. Typical, perhaps, of his sentimentality are these lines from "My Lost Youth":

> Often I think of the beautiful town,
>   That is seated by the sea;
> Often in thought I go up and down
> The pleasant streets of that dear old town,
>   And my youth comes back to me.
>   And a verse of a Lapland song
>   Is haunting my memory still:
>   "A boy's will is the wind's will,
> And the thoughts of youth are long, long thoughts."

When only a line or two of quoted poetry are to be used, they may be incorporated into the text. In such an instance, the copied material is enclosed in quotation marks and a diagonal is used to show the separation of lines. The punctuation of the original and the initial capitals are retained.

The situation seemed to call for the lines of Browning: "The lie was dead/And damned, and truth stood up instead."

[3] American Bar Association *Journal*, 46 (January 1960), 52.

14b. Words in Special Sense

Use quotation marks to enclose words used facetiously or in a special sense.

They have just been sued by their "friendly" competitor.
With another such "windfall," they'll be bankrupt.
"Man or beast" means "man or sub-man," which means "good or bad."
—ALLEN WHEELIS

A "universe" of sand, marbles, or other free-flowing material can readily be measured by sampling. When units are not free flowing, they are said to be "clustered," and the sample must then be composed of similar clusters.—STUART CHASE

14c. Titles of Shorter Works

Use quotation marks to enclose the titles of articles in periodicals or books, the names of chapters or selections of books, and the titles of monographs, and other short literary works. (The titles of newspapers, pamphlets, periodicals, and books are usually underlined, without quotation marks. See **Rule 18a**.)

E. B. White's article, "Farewell, My Lovely," first appeared in *The New Yorker.*

Methods of handling controversy are discussed in Chapter 15, "Influencing Opinion Change."

At the end of the book you will find a poem by W. H. Auden, "Victor, a Ballad."

In preparation for our class, we were asked to read Willa Cather's short story, "The Sculptor's Funeral."

14d. With Other Punctuation

Follow accepted practice in using quotation marks with other marks of punctuation.

(1) When a dialogue indicator like "he said," is used with a quotation:

(a) Use a comma to set off the indicator when it precedes or follows the quotation.

Then he asked, "What can I do for you?"
"You have my word," he said.

(b) Use commas to set off the indicator when it interrupts a quotation that calls for a comma or no punctuation at all at the break.

"In any event," she said, "we will all have much work to do."
"I will pay you," he wrote, "as soon as I have the money."

(c) Use a semicolon after the indicator when the quotation calls for a semicolon at the break.

"The tank seems full," said the attendant; "however, I'll see if I can pump another gallon in."

(d) Use a period after the indicator when the break in the quotation represents the division between two sentences.

"How much do you want?" he shouted. "We've already offered more than we should."

(2) At the end of a direct quotation, a comma or period is conventionally placed inside the quotation mark, a semicolon or colon outside the quotation mark, and an exclamation point or question mark either inside or outside the quotation mark, depending on whether the mark belongs to the quotation alone or to the whole statement.

"I will meet you at the airport," he wrote.
The notice read, "Past due. Please remit."
His door is marked "Private"; that's a word we respect around here.
Here are your "orders": Go south, bask in the sun, and don't come back until you miss the sight of dirty, slushy snow.
He has a habit of yelling "Ouch!" before he's hurt.
You must not toss around packages marked "Fragile"!
The clerk asked, "When did you receive notice of delivery?"
Shall I write "I suggest" or "I request"?

(3) No other punctuation is used with quotation marks when the quotation is closely integrated into the text.

Her "ooh's" and "ah's" were embarrassing.
Keats wrote "Endymion" when he was twenty-three.
Credible means "worthy of belief."

EXERCISES

A. Use single or double quotation marks in the passages below, as the text requires or the bracketed instructions indicate. Where a quotation mark is used with other punctuation, arrange the marks in proper order.

1. There are only two persons in the country, Mark Twain says on October 28, who have not communicated their views on the Byron questions to the newspaper, and they are the citizens of Cape Cod who went off mackerel fishing six weeks ago and haven't returned. Then he tells of a [quote] lazy lad, who did not go to church until the congregation was coming out [unquote]. The lad: Is it all done? No, was the reply, it's all said, but I think it will be some time before it's all done. In a third item, Twain [quote] whispers [unquote] that a gentleman was recently [quote] blackballed in an English club because his wife was in the habit of dropping her h's [unquote]. And, in a final paragraph, he comments, Nobby hat, nobby coat, nobby pants, nobby tie and nobby cane, make a man now-a-days.[4]

2. Our first lecture was in a university building. On the table in our room were glossy reprints of articles from *Scientific American* and the *Wall Street Journal* telling us how TM would fix us up. . . . Our instructor was a cleancut junior called Buzz. . . .

What we would do, if we wanted to sign up, was to come to two lectures, and then be initiated on the weekend, and then one more lecture and one more weekend—that's all there was.

Previously, we had three states of consciousness, Buzz said. Waking, sleeping, and dreaming. This is the fourth state, cosmic and all-inclusive. The mind is evolutionary, a blessing of the Creator, approaching the Infinite One—Buzz giggled a bit, and the audience got restless—but there's nothing to believe in TM. You don't have to believe in anything. And nothing to give up.

Is this the same as yoga? somebody wanted to know.

No, all you do in TM is sit still, Buzz said. Yoga will give you a charley horse. Zen monks meditate for twenty-five years and get the same result TM will give you in two weeks. It's different from concentration, and from contemplation.[5]

[4] Adapted from Henry Duskis, ed., *The Forgotten Writings of Mark Twain* (New York: Citadel Press, 1963), p. 117.

[5] Adam Smith, "The Meditation Game," *Atlantic*, October 1975, p. 35.

3. Wallace's thesis, The Physiological Effects of Transcendental Meditation, went off to the prestigious journal *Science*. . . .

Benson [Wallace's co-author] had been in the Public Health Service in Puerto Rico, working on blood pressure. Why did the Puerto Ricans have fewer cardiac ailments than the mainlanders?

I give up. Why? I said.

Because of their attitude, Benson said. *Manana.* We need some of that if everybody doesn't want to keep dying so young, a different attitude.

. . . Wallace and Benson combined on a couple of experiments, and now the results went out with the prestige of a Harvard Medical School by-line. Mental states can markedly alter physiologic function, wrote Benson and Wallace. They called the meditation state a wakeful, hypometabolic physiologic state, a phrase that went ringing through the journals. Wakeful because the subjects were awake and you would think they would have to be asleep to get those numbers; hypometabolic, well, remember *hypo* is under, Greek, and *hyper* is over, excess.[6]

4. [James] Buckley's *Principia* as outlined to me included: [Direct quotation follows to end.]

To preserve a society where an individual has maximum control over his own destiny within a framework that holds the society together.

There are no problems to which you cannot apply the experience of 25,000 years of Western society. There is a reservoir of wisdom, of understanding human behavior and motivation—as an example, when you have an option, it is wiser to choose a nongovernmental option over a governmental option.

My philosophical touchstone—I think it comes from Plato or Aquinas—is the rule of subsidiary; no government should be exercised at a higher level than the lowest competent authority.[7]

5. In a conversation with Dr. Bok in her home in Cambridge, I asked when, in her estimation, the developing fetus becomes [quote] a person [unquote]. Bok . . . shook her head quickly. I think that's a wrong question to ask, she said. People have become mesmerized by that question, and it's really a question that has no answer. Because we are, after all, talking about something that is biologically [quote] human [unquote] not only after fertilization, but before—the ovum

[6] Ibid., p. 37.

[7] Richard Reeves, "Isn't It Time We Had a Senator?" *New York* Magazine, 25 February 1974, p. 38.

cell and the sperm cells are certainly both living and human even before they meet.

But if we are talking about [quote] personhood, [unquote] then I believe it's impossible to speak of the fertilized egg, early in gestation, as [quote] a man, [unquote] she continued, although I realize that some others do. . . .[8]

B. Write the sentences described below:

1. A sentence containing a broken quotation.
2. A declarative sentence ending with a quoted question.
3. An exclamatory sentence ending with a quoted question
4. A question containing a declarative quotation.
5. A declarative sentence beginning with a short quoted exclamation.
6. A sentence containing a word used in a special sense.
7. A sentence containing a quotation within a quotation.
8. A sentence containing an indirect quotation.
9. A sentence containing the title of an article in a periodical.
10. A sentence that runs in two short lines of quoted poetry.

[8] Maggie Scarf, "The Fetus as Guinea Pig," *The New York Times Magazine,* 19 October 1975, p. 94.

15 Other Marks

:/—/( )/[ ]

The colon, the dash, parentheses, and brackets have special uses that you should observe in the interests of clarity and emphasis.

15a. The Colon :

Use a colon to direct attention to the following statement and to form certain numerical symbols.

Do not confuse the colon (:) with the semicolon (;). The colon introduces and anticipates what follows; the semicolon separates, as in this sentence.

The first word following a colon is usually capitalized if it begins a sentence.

(1) Use the colon after a formal introduction to a list, an appositive expression, or a quotation. Even when the introduction does not include such words as "the following" or "as follows," the sense is usually implied in these usages.

To renew your car registration, submit the following: application, renewal stub, proof of insurance, and check for $20.

For the rent I paid I was assured of two things: a room and a view of a brick wall through the window.

Henry Dalton echoed a common view: "I came to Denver because I wanted to make a change in my life."

CAUTION: Do not use a colon unnecessarily.

NOT: For his first class he brought: a pencil, a protractor, a ruler, and graph paper. [The first part of the sentence is not a formal introduction and should not be followed by a colon.]

BUT: For his first class he brought a pencil, a protractor, a ruler, and graph paper.

OR: For his first class he brought these supplies: a pencil, a protractor, a ruler, and graph paper. [Here the colon is correct because it is preceded by a formal introduction.]

(2) Use a colon between two main clauses when the second clause explains or amplifies the first.

Sea squids are exceptionally versatile: They change color, for instance, like a chameleon.—LEO ROSTEN

One thing is clear: The challenge to the dollar represented by gold is not going to be beaten off.—C. GORDON TETHER

Leave the fire-ashes: what survives is gold.—ROBERT BROWNING

(3) Use a colon between a title and a subtitle, after a salutation, in Biblical references, and in expressions of time.

Herbert L. Mathews' *Revolution in Cuba: An Essay in Understanding* [Book title]

Dear Miss Chen: [Salutation]

Gourmets: Feast on passion fruit in the Arawak Dining Room [Salutation]

Isaiah 8:19 [Separates numbers of chapter and verse]

meeting at 8:45 P.M. [Numerical expression of time in hour and minutes]

ran the mile in 4:3.5 [Colon and decimal: 4 minutes, $3\frac{1}{2}$ seconds]

blast was registered at 3:12:26 A.M., EST [Two colons: 12 minutes and 26 seconds after 3 o'clock]

15b. The Dash —

Use the dash to indicate an abrupt change in thought, to set off a parenthetic or appositive expression, or to emphasize a following word or phrase. (See box, page 344.)

The dash is formed on the typewriter by two hyphens, with no space before or after.

(1) Use a dash (or dashes) to indicate a sharp break or an interruption in thought or mode of expression.

What I was going to say was—but why revive an old feud?

Why—why, Eliza! What have you done to your hair?

What would you do if—there's that *if* again.

I would not—could not—agree to such a plan.

On our most recent visit to the museum—I can't remember the date—we made it a point to see the Dürer engravings.

(2) For emphasis or clarity, use dashes instead of commas to set off a parenthetic or appositive phrase, or a summary statement.

Thus it is impossible for her to have a personal, private life, for if she were to be herself—if she were to be mistress of her own wishes, passions, whims—she would be unfaithful to herself.—OCTAVIO PAZ

PUNCTUATING PARENTHETIC ELEMENTS

Of the several marks used to punctuate parenthetic elements, commas produce a minimal separation; parentheses produce a wider separation; and dashes, the widest and most emphatic. Both parentheses and dashes should be used sparingly and with discretion.

Note These Alternatives[*]

In exercising their new aesthetic function, more felt than clearly articulated, artists must continually challenge their methods and materials.

In exercising their new aesthetic function (more felt than clearly articulated) artists must continually challenge their methods and materials.

In exercising their new aesthetic function—more felt than clearly articulated—artists must continually challenge their methods and materials.

[*] Susan Sontag, author of the essay "One Culture and the New Responsibility," from which this sentence has been adapted, used parentheses.

He is still changing, still sure of himself, and perhaps—just perhaps—still on the right track.

This country also needs deep-water terminals to handle—with greater safety and efficiency than existing facilities—increasing amounts of imported crude and heavy fuel oil.—EXXON

Both processes look promising, and one of them—flue desulferization—is ready to be demonstrated commercially.

The symbol of Project Y was the letter *Y* framed in a circle—an inverted peace sign.

He was bloody, wet, begrimed, unkempt—a human wreck.

New products, new markets, new jobs—these were the promises of the scientific revolution.

(3) Especially in persuasive writing—advertising copy, for example—the dash is used to emphasize a following word or phrase.

The job must be done—and done right!

Mail the order card—now!

Join our Museum family as a Family Member and get your free "Family of Man" book—and innumerable other benefits, too.—THE MUSEUM OF MODERN ART

15c. Parentheses ( )

Use parentheses to enclose explanatory terms or remarks, editorial references, and letters or numbers used to identify the elements in a series.

Debussy persuaded other composers that there were serious (as distinct from merely exotic) alternatives to the Western European tradition.

The next step (collating the answers to the questionnaire) will have to be undertaken in my absence.

The "and" in the company's name is represented by an ampersand (&).

The "greatest scientist" in our poll turned out to be the partnership of Watson and Crick. (Each has gone on to do other, independent research.)—SATURDAY REVIEW

Magnetic ink character recognition (MICR) is part of all check processing.

Newspaper advertising falls into three categories: (1) general, (2) retail, and (3) classified.

During the same period the cost of living rose 12 percent (Exhibit B).

OTHER PUNCTUATION WITH PARENTHESES. When parentheses are used within a sentence, any other punctuation the sentence requires at the break is placed after the closing parenthesis.

NOT: ______, (______) ______.

BUT: ______ (______), ______.

Knowing your fastidiousness (in food, I mean), I wonder why you chose the Burger Joint for your party.

I sympathize with you (I really do); however, I am not about to risk my own reputation to save yours.

A question mark, an exclamation point, or a quotation mark is placed inside the closing parenthesis if the sense requires.

It was Mamma (who else?) who stayed up and waited for Nora to come home.

His new book (what a bore!) will no doubt be well received by his friends.

The last section ("Deferred Tuition") has not yet been proofread.

When a statement in parentheses follows a sentence, the end punctuation required by the statement should be placed inside the closing parenthesis.

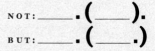

NOT: ______. (______).

BUT: ______. (______.)

It was 6 A.M. and still dark. (I hate these early risings.)
He was very thin. (Was he dieting?)

CAPITALS WITH PARENTHESES. When parentheses are outside a sentence, capitalize the first word. When parentheses are inside a sentence, do not capitalize the first word unless it is a proper noun or the start of a formal quotation.

Sale merchandise is not returnable. (No exceptions.)
William finally completed the assignment (it took five hours).
The date (April 15—income tax day) was terribly inconvenient.
We did not find his excuse ("We always did it that way") worthy of consideration. [Formal quotation—capital *W*]
The type size ("excelsior" is the printer's name for it) is much too small to be readable. [Informal quotation—small *e*]

15d. Brackets [ ]

Use brackets to enclose your own emendation, interpolation, explanation, or question in quoted material.

Brackets are formed on the typewriter by use of the diagonal and underline keys /thus/.

Take the word of the report: "Only one of the ten biggest coal companies [North American Coal] is independently owned and managed."
"Part II applies these [principles] to the everyday realities of city life."

The letter said, "Examined in this contec [context?], the decision appeared sound."
OR: The letter said, "Examined in this contec [sic], the decision appeared sound." [*Sic*, meaning "thus," is used to show that the apparent error was in the original document.]

EXERCISES

A. Provide colons and dashes where appropriate. If a choice is to be made, justify your choice.

1. The allusion that [Nathaniel] West did intend his name, changed from Weinstein, was part of the allusion is to the historical movement of Americans toward the Pacific, the last western frontier. But California lacks the one essential feature of the frontier somewhere to move on to and the myth easily turns to disappointment as the seemingly endless space is used up.—MICHAEL WOOD

2. Ralph Drew long remembered Perry's reply "Ralph, we were never friends. You were my lawyer."

3. One more vignette Will and I are to meet for our monthly lunch at a good restaurant around the corner from my office. . . .

4. One suspects that he's an opportunist and not a very good one at that whose good fortune it was to fall in with a crafty Wall Street crowd.

5. The *Permamatic* can handle all the things you usually pick up at the start of your trip and all the things you pick up along the way.—LARK LUGGAGE (*advertisement*)

6. He has chosen to discount the philosophers' and environmentalists' warning that the manic technology which makes life intolerable for the many will in somewhat less than the long run make life impossible for all.—CHARLES DE LACY

7. When I travel I take only a few essentials a toothbrush, a raincoat, and plenty of Kaopectate.

8. Who does not recall the famous incident at Sybil Seretsky's, when her goldfish sang "I got rhythm" a favorite tune of her recently deceased nephew.—WOODY ALLEN

9. At the time I was reading *Mobile Homes The Low-Cost Housing Hoax.*

10. "But but how could he be so gauche?"

B. Provide parentheses or brackets where appropriate. Suggest alternative punctuation, if you wish.

1. After the operation he said he felt as if he were an amputee. This condition sometimes called negative phantom-limb is common when the leg is enclosed in a plaster cast.

2. I take issue with the notion that meditation or yoga, for that matter is to be utilized for personal gain or even relaxation.

3. Ernie in what must be his middle seventies he never talks of age walks at an amble into the restaurant, shakes hands with the headwaiter, and orders what he calls a "martin."

4. The essay, "A Message to Boonville, begins, "When concorb corncob? pipes went up from a nickel to six cents, smoking traditions tottered."

5. There have been periods in our history when certain people appeared to rise above conventional self-interest the Constitutional Period 1787–1791 may have been such a period.

16 Unnecessary Punctuation

X

Do not overpunctuate.

16a. Commas

Do not use commas that are not needed for the sense of the sentence. Unnecessary commas interrupt the flow of thought and lead to confusion. (See also "The Comma," **Rule 11**.)

(1) Do not put an unnecessary comma between a subject and its verb, a verb and its object, or an adjective and a following noun.

X A great deal of negotiation between the parties to the dispute(,) finally resulted in a settlement. [Comma separating subject and verb]

X In time we developed fully(,) the core of our argument. [Comma separating verb and its object]

X Fuller loudly protested(,) that he had not been consulted. [Comma separating verb from its object (a noun clause)]

X It was a hard, long(,) road to travel. [Comma between adjective and following noun.]

EXCEPTION: For improved clarity, a comma is sometimes placed before a verb when many modifying words come between the verb and the subject.

Thousands of books on subjects ranging from algebra to zoology, on levels from primers to professional treatises, and in editions running from a few hundred copies to a few million[,] are published each year. [The comma before the verb *are published* helps the reader retain the sense of the whole sentence.]

(2) Do not use commas to set off a restrictive phrase or clause. (See also **Rule 11d(1)**.)

X The man(,) who had first told them of the treasure(,) now denied the story.

X Any student, wanting to enter the program, must apply to the Dean.

(3) Do not use commas to set off a mildly parenthetic element. (See also **Rule 11d**.)

X You will, therefore, report for your first drill on Monday.
X So, there was actually nothing to gain from our resistance.
X I will, indeed, be pleased to attend the inauguration.

(4) Do not use a comma after a coordinate conjunction followed by the last member of a series, or between two words or phrases joined by a coordinate conjunction.

X Among his obvious talents were a prodigious memory, a faultless knowledge of his subject, and, a flair for publicity.
X The guests included a senator, and a former judge.
X The wind usually came up in the early morning, and again in the late afternoon.

(5) Do not use a comma before the first word or after the last word of a series.

X Such foods as, ham, cheese, and shellfish, were strictly off his diet.
X Please send me, a dozen No. 2 pencils, a ream of white typewriter paper, and a bottle of erasing fluid.

16b. Parentheses

Do not use parentheses to enclose a simple parenthetic element that may or may not require commas. (See also "Parentheses," **Rule 15c**.)

X The letters tell of Steinbeck's service (during World War II) as a correspondent in North Africa and Italy. [No punctuation required]
X NOT: The drama (it seemed) had originally been presented as a comedy.
BUT: The drama, it seemed, had originally been presented as a comedy.

16c. Colon

Do not use a colon except after a formal introduction. (See "The Colon," **Rule 15a**.)

X Performances are given on(:) Thursday, Friday, and Saturday evenings.
X At eighteen he emerged as(:) a virtuoso violinist.

16d. Quotation Marks

Do not put quotation marks around the title at the head of a theme, nor around nicknames, slang words, or trite expressions. Do not use quotation marks to enclose an indirect quotation. (See also "Quotation Marks," **Rule 14**.)

X (")My Journey to India(") [Title above theme]
X We often made fun of (")Lumpy,(") but he never understood why.
X The guard told us to (")scram.(")
X While she (")bent my ear,(") I was thinking of ways to escape.
X Gary said (")it was all right; we'd get together another time.(")

NOTE: Removing the quotation marks from slang and trite expressions is not usually as good a solution to the writer's problem as the use of standard English and fresh expressions.

EXERCISE

A. In the sentences below, which punctuation marks do you consider superfluous? What justification can you offer for the other marks, or what substitutions might you make?

1. Cantwell was a loyalist, a man who discharged decisions, faithfully, whether he agreed with them or not.
2. In the fall of 1975, in his ninety-first year, my great-grandfather, a man of humor, as well as wisdom, decided it was time he left his room, for a few days, to come into the family den, and take a look at modern television.
3. When Gail shouted after us that, "the stairway out of the house was slippery," we were already on our "backsides"; lucky, though, our heavy coats (which we had worn only reluctantly) saved us from injury.
4. Occasionally, the woodcutting doesn't go well: a tree chosen for cutting, because it is no longer a sturdy member of its company, falls with a hollow thump, and shatters, revealing a rotted interior.
5. What I saw when I opened the door was: an overturned chair, a chest, with every drawer pulled open, and a television stand, without the television.

6. "Wimpie" figured that anyone, who wears a shirt and tie, and straight pants, must be an "intellect."

7. It is arduous, dangerous, work, and so frustrating, that I sometimes wanted to shriek.

8. In a sense, my father was a gentleman (of the old school); he removed his hat in elevators, gave his seat to ladies in buses, and always walked on the curb side, when he was with a female companion.

9. However, you examine the illustration, you see that, the subject, to say the least, is "banal," and that the printer did a lot of "corner cutting" to achieve an effect, that he later justified on the ground that it was, "art for the masses."

10. Their reputation was based on: good quality, baked goods, and, for over twenty years, a refusal to use any shortening (except butter).

17 Capitals

cap

Capitalize words whenever good usage requires. Do not capitalize words unnecessarily.

A word requiring a capital is shown capitalized in the dictionary entry of the word. Very often, however, a word that is not ordinarily capitalized will be capitalized in a particular context or for a particular reason. The words *evening* and *bulletin*, for example, are not regularly capitalized, but they are capitalized in a proper name: the *Philadelphia Evening Bulletin.*

17a. Proper Names

Capitalize proper names and their derivatives.

(1) Proper names include the distinctive names of persons and places; public-service, business, and governmental organizations and administrative bodies; racial, religious, and political groups and the characteristic name assigned to their members; months, days, and historical periods and events; and words relating to the Deity or the Bible.

George Davies
Martha Washington
Chicago, Illinois
San Antonio, Texas
the Western Hemisphere
England, Poland, Morocco
Long Island, the Greater Antilles
Wilshire Boulevard, Fifth Avenue
Newsweek, *Good Housekeeping*
the *San Francisco Examiner*
Allied Chemical Corporation
the Ford Foundation, the United Fund
Memorial Hospital, the Mayo Clinic
the Government of Chile
Internal Revenue Service
Department of the Interior
the Senate, the House of Representatives
the Foreign Relations Committee
the Catholic religion, a Catholic
the Negro race, a Negro
the Democratic Party, a Democrat
January, February
Monday, Tuesday

The Renaissance
the First World War
the Great Depression
the Savior, the Holy Ghost
the Holy Scriptures, Ecclesiastes

(2) Capitalize words derived from proper names.

Asiatic treasures
the Italian language
Cuban, African, European
a Princetonian
Orwellian (after George Orwell)

This rule does not apply to some derivatives which have acquired a generic meaning. Thus Shantung is the name of the Chinese city, but *shantung*, the name of the fabric, is usually not capitalized. Other derivatives of proper names that are not capitalized include:

china (porcelainware)
plaster of paris
roman candle
pasteurize (after Louis Pasteur)
morocco (leather)

(3) Capitalize abbreviations of proper names.

U.S. (United States)
Cal., N.Y., Va. (California, New York, Virginia)
IBM (International Business Machines Corporation)
NATO (North Atlantic Treaty Organization)

Practice varies with regard to the use of periods between the units of an abbreviation. (See **Rule 10a(4)**.)

(4) Capitalize such terms as East, West, and Northwest when they refer to geographical divisions, but not when they denote direction.

lived in the East [BUT: traveled east]
states in the Northwest [BUT: sought a northwest passage]
problems of the Southeast [BUT: a southeasterly breeze]

(5) Capitalize a name that describes a following numeral.

Catalog No. 4325-B
Economics 21
Room 429
Rule 15a
Chapter XII

The words *page* and *line* are not so capitalized. (See also "Common Scholarly Abbreviations," pages 195–96.)

page 234, line 5

(6) Capitalize the pronoun *I*. (The interjection *O* is the only other single-letter word that is consistently capitalized.)

17b. Title Before Name

Capitalize a title preceding a proper name.

Chairman O'Brien
Sergeant Casper
Congressman Bingham

A title following a name or used alone is not usually capitalized except to form a part of a letter address or to signify special distinction or deference.

John O'Brien, chairman of board
Dennis Casper, a sergeant in the Air Force
Jonathan Bingham, the congressman from the 22nd District
Mr. Samuel Brown, Vice President [in letter address]
a letter for Mr. Brown, the vice president of the company [in text]
within the jurisdiction of Mr. Morton, the Secretary of Commerce [capitals for title of special distinction]
went to Dr. Clark, the Dean of Students, to inquire [capitals to show respect]
the President [of the United States]
the Chief Justice

NOTE: Whether or not to capitalize certain titles to show special distinction or respect often depends on the writer's position and point of view. Thus a particular individual may be written about as Chairman of the Board by his own executives, but as chairman of the board by a newspaper reporter.

17c. Literary Titles

In a literary title, capitalize the important words. These include the first and last words and, usually, all the other words except articles, and prepositions and conjunctions of more than four letters.

How to Do Things with Words
Men Without Women
What I Have Lived For
A Practical Style Guide for Authors and Editors

Exceptions to this rule may be made for reasons of appearance, emphasis, or consistency.

State Parks *In* and *Near* New York City [Short prepositions capitalized]
Explorations in Communication: *An* Anthology [Article following colon capitalized]

17d. Initial Words

Capitalize the first word of every sentence, as well as the first word of a direct quotation (but not of a quoted fragment), and of a direct question following a declarative statement in the same sentence.

He said, "Insanity is not to be accepted as an excusing condition for criminal acts." [Capital at beginning of sentence and of direct quotation]
He said that insanity should not be "an excusing condition" for crime. [Quoted fragment—no capital]
The question his action poses is, When does clemency become favoritism?

In poetry, the first word of every line is conventionally capitalized, but in quoting poetry, be guided by the style of the poet.

Then let us at these mimic antics jest,
Whose deepest projects and egregious gests
Are but dull morals of a game at chests.
—JOHN DONNE

Here everything is white and clean
as driftwood. Pain is localized
and suffering, strictly routine,
goes on behind a modest screen.
—GEORGE GARRETT[1]

17e. Abstract Qualities

Words standing for some abstract quality or concept are sometimes capitalized in literary usage.

Homer tells us also that Sisyphus had put Death in chains.
—ALBERT CAMUS

Why have we passions, and a dream of Truth?—SOCRATES

[1] From "In the Hospital," in *The Reverend Ghost: Poems by George Garrett*, 1956, 1957 by George Garrett. Reprinted by permission of Charles Scribner's Sons.

Man as thinker performs an Administrative Function in society. Man as doer performs a Brute Power Function.—ELDRIDGE CLEAVER

EXERCISE

A. Supply capitals where necessary.

1. what's the procedure for overtaking? you don't yell, "track!" instead, you call, "on your left!" (or "on your right!"). this tells where you're passing.

2. bower, during world war II, took part in the then secret loran project, which provided an electronic navigational aid to convoys through the hostile north atlantic.

3. one of the national gas company's most successful programs was developed under the direction of the michigan public service commission in january 1973 when dennis sutter, the company's director of energy conservation, proposed a new method of financing home insulation through the home owners loan corporation (holc).

4. the polish armed forces are the only troops of the warsaw pact with chaplains. a small catholic party holds seats in the polish parliament. . . . the man in the middle is the primate of poland, stefan cardinal wyszinski who is ambivalent about normalizing church-state relations because he believes the church is renewed by oppression. the communists seem to believe it, too.—ANTHONY ASTRACHAN

5. some of the titles reviewed in a single edition of the *new york times book review* were *power shift: the rise of the southern rim and its challenge to the eastern establishment, we almost lost detroit, write if you get work: the best of bob and ray,* and *whales to see the.* the last is not a typographical error; the book was written by glendon and kathryn swarthout and is reviewed by betsy byars, a newberry award winning author.

6. john gardner, the creator of common cause, hoped that his "citizen's lobby" would restore "responsiveness and accountability" in government. today, says george f. will, "the very idea of an elite is suspect."

7. the secretary of state stoutly denied knowledge of a cia plot to kill the chilean president.

8. father of all! in ev'ry age,
   in ev'ry clime adored,
by saint, by savage, and by sage
   jehovah, jove, or lord!

—ALEXANDER POPE

9. once our assumption of omnipotence was challenged in vietnam, in the emergence of the third world, and through a variety of other cultural and political forces, the establishment's confidence began to go.

10. i was told that sergeant murphy lives at 345 worthington street nw, washington, d.c., and that his father, a colonel, lived at no. 550 on the same street.

11. how thou art fallen from heaven, o lucifer, son of the morning!—isaiah 14:12.

12. my mathematics course is listed in the catalog on page 34, but for a description of linear programming a32.0001, i had to consult a handbill in the registrar's office, room 428, hall of mathematical sciences.

13. the purpose of hudson's last voyage, under private english auspices, was to locate the northwest passage.

14. during the era of good feelings—the term used to describe monroe's two terms in office—many intra-cabinet controversies erupted and there was rising opposition to the congressional caucus as a means of choosing the presidential candidate.

15. i suppose you could call the blue-blood mr. lounsbery anti-feminist. he's the gentleman who said, "what killed society is men marrying terrible women."

18 Underlining (Italics)

ital

Underline word elements that are normally italicized in printing. Such elements include titles of published works, foreign words, words used as words, and words requiring special emphasis.

18a. Names of Books, Periodicals, Etc.

Underline (for italics) the names of books, periodicals, newspapers, pamphlets, plays, motion pictures, and works of graphic and plastic art. Also underline the distinctive names of ships, planes, or trains.

Fitzgerald's The Great Gatsby
O'Neill's Mourning Becomes Electra
Fellini's La Dolce Vita
Rodin's The Kiss
subscriptions to Harper's and the New York Times
the sinking of the Lusitania
the old Twentieth Century Limited
H.M.S. Hornet
United's Mainliner to Chicago

(1) The initial article *The* in the name of a newspaper or periodical is often not italicized (or capitalized), and when the name of a newspaper includes the name of the city, the city name is sometimes not italicized. Whatever style is adopted, it should be used consistently.

appeared in The New York Times, OR: the New York Times,
OR: the New York Times
reads The Saturday Review, OR: the Saturday Review

In some newspapers, names that are normally italicized are put in quotation marks, or are neither italicized nor put in quotation marks. These departures from customary practice are rarely found in writing for other media.

(2) Quotation marks are correctly used for the titles of chapters in a book and of articles in a periodical, and of short poems (those not published as a book). See **Rule 14c**

(3) Names of the Bible and its parts are neither italicized nor put in quotation marks.

the Bible, the Holy Scriptures
the New Testament
the Psalms, Proverbs, the First Book of Samuel

18b. Foreign Words and Phrases

Underline (for italics) a foreign word or phrase not yet assimilated into English.

When in doubt, consult the dictionary. Non-Anglicized words and phrases are denoted by the use of italics, a double dagger or parallel bars before the entry, or some other method, depending on the dictionary.

the *sine qua non* of the whole plan (essential condition)
delivered the *coup de grâce* (final blow)
the *Weltschmerz* he carried with him (sentimental sorrow)
BUT: a chic gown [*chic* has been assimilated into English]

18c. Words, Letters, Numbers

Underline (for italics) words, letters of the alphabet, and numbers referred to as such.

Quotation marks are sometimes used for the same purpose. In a formal definition, it is common to underline the word defined and enclose the definition in quotation marks.

The word *embarrass* was misspelled.
The *p* looks like a *q*.
The *7* on my typewriter is broken. [OR: The "7" on my typewriter is broken.]
Disinterested means "impartial," whereas *uninterested* means "not interested."

18d. For Emphasis

Use underlining (italics) for emphasis, but only when the tone desired could not otherwise be achieved.

(1) The overuse of underlining is distracting to the reader and thus results in a reduction of emphasis. Some writers of advertising deliberately violate this principle in the competition for the reader's attention. Writers whose work must stand on its own merits have no such excuse. For other ways of obtaining emphasis, see **Rule 30**.

Here is the extraordinary charm of the old Greek situation—that it is so interesting.—MATTHEW ARNOLD

It's not that I was forced to go to the concert. I wanted to go.

OVERUSE: With your gift you will receive details of a plan that can help you achieve the financial security you want for your family.

(2) When words quoted from a printed source are underlined (for italics), the question arises whether the emphasis is that of the source or that of the person who quotes it. The question is customarily resolved by a qualification on the order of "The emphasis is Wilson's," or "The italics are mine," or "Italics added."

The new vision of man is encompassed partly in British physicist-philosopher Sir James Jeans's statement, "Today there is a wide measure of agreement, which on the physical side of science approaches almost to unanimity, that the stream of science is heading toward a non-mechanical reality; the universe begins to look more like a great thought than like a great machine." [Emphasis added.]

EXERCISE

A. Underline any words for which convention or emphasis requires italics.

1. I think my first reading in Latin was Julius Caesar's The Gallic Wars.
2. The sinking of the Titanic was probably the last major sea disaster caused by an iceberg.
3. The Washington Post is, in many ways, the equal of the New York Times in its foreign coverage.
4. "The World of John Hammond" received many plaudits when the program was first aired on Public Television; the sound film of Billie Holiday singing St. Louis Blues was certainly a high point.
5. Even among intellectual humanists, every woman has a Doppelgänger—every other woman.—CYNTHIA OZICK
6. Maybe you did mistake the book. Maybe you only thought the review was that of John Fowles' The French Lieutenant's Woman.

7. The antonym of different is similar; just don't make the mistake of spelling similar "similiar."

8. In Romans 8:31 we read, "If God be for us, who can be against us." The Bible is replete with such appeals to our faith.

9. John Hersey's Hiroshima first appeared in The New Yorker; it filled the magazine.

10. The Christian Science Monitor does not often make a typographical error, but if you see immaculate spelled with one m, you can be sure that it's not the form your Webster's prescribes.

19 **ab**
Abbreviations

With the exceptions noted in the rules below, do not use abbreviations in ordinary composition.

When abbreviations are used, the form should follow current practice. For the correct form of an abbreviation, consult your dictionary; the abbreviations are listed alphabetically in the main vocabulary. For the use of periods with abbreviations, see **Rule 10a**(4)

Except to save space in letter addresses, and in footnotes, tabulations, and similar uses, write out the following:

(1) Names of continents, countries, states, and cities.

a native of South America [NOT: S.A.]
a United States citizen [NOT: U.S.]
the lakes of Minnesota [NOT: Minn.]
the New York City Ballet Company [NOT: N.Y.C.]

(2) Names of months and days of the week.

born on August 13, 1962 [NOT: Aug.]
an appointment on Tuesday [NOT: Tues.]

(3) First names.

William [NOT: Wm.]
Charles [NOT: Chas.]
Robert [NOT: Robt.]

First names should never be abbreviated or shortened unless the form is one preferred by the individual named. However, initials alone are often acceptable. Note also that names like Deb, Meg, Ed, Will, and Rob are shortened forms, used in familiar address, and are not followed by a period.

ACCEPTABLE:

Mr. P. F. Granger [In a letter address]
R. L. Stevenson [In a footnote]

Chas. Addams [The cartoonist]
Dear Rob [Letter salutation]

(4) Names of college subjects. (For professorial and other titles, see **Rule 19a.**)

algebra [NOT: alg.] biology [NOT: biol.]
management [NOT: mgt.] physics [NOT: phys.]

Shortened forms, those that can be pronounced as words, are used in informal writing. They are not punctuated by periods.

phys ed [for physical education]
comp sci [for computer science]
math, psych, lit, stat

(5) Words like *street, avenue, road, volume, chapter, page, number, manufacturer, apartment, Christmas.* Do not abbreviate words like *and* (&), *company* (co.) and *brothers* (bros.) unless they are a characteristic part of an official title.

a walk on Fifth *Avenue* [NOT: *Ave.*]
the reference on *page* 14 [NOT: *p.* 14]
Haskins *and* Sells [BUT: Lord *&* Taylor]
Duke Power *Company* [BUT: First Manhattan *Co.*]

19a. Titles and Degrees

Abbreviate the titles *Mr., Mrs., Ms.* (for *Miss* or *Mrs.*), *Messrs., Dr.,* and *St.* (for Saint) when they are followed by a proper name. (*Miss*—short for *Mistress*—takes no period.) Do not use the abbreviations if they are not followed by a proper name.

Mr. Deering, *Ms.* Fowler, *Messrs.* Clark and Fox, *St.* Joan

NOT: I went to see the *Dr.* about my sore throat.
BUT: I went to see the *doctor* about my sore throat.
OR: I went to see *Dr. Smith* about my sore throat.

(1) The titles *Honorable, Reverend,* and such other titles of office as *Senator, Professor,* and *Colonel,* should be abbreviated only when they are followed by the first name or initials as well as the surname. Even then the titles should be spelled out when special formality is desired.

	Hon. Edward W. Brooke	NOT:	Sen. Jackson
OR:	Honorable Edward W. Brooke	BUT:	Senator Jackson
	Rev. Amos McIntyre	OR:	Sen. Henry A. Jackson
OR:	The Reverend Amos McIntyre	OR:	Senator Henry A. Jackson
OR:	Reverend McIntyre	NOT:	Prof. Thayer
NOT:	Rev. McIntyre	BUT:	Professor Thayer

(2) Following a name, always abbreviate the titles *Jr.* and *Sr.*, as well as academic degrees such as *M.D.*, *Ph.D.*, *M.A.*, and *R.N.* (registered nurse). The title *Esq.* is usually abbreviated.

Thomas R. Bryan, Jr.	Marian Brooke, Ph.D.
Norton Hammer, M.D.	Henry T. Farmer, Esq.

19b. Government Agencies

The names of government agencies are regularly abbreviated (FBI, IRS, FCC, FDA), as are the names of some of the better known private organizations with long names (AT&T, ITT, IBM, NAM). First references to such organizations, however, are best spelled out in order to establish unmistakably the meaning of the abbreviation.

Mr. Graham had an appointment with the *Internal Revenue Service* for 11 o'clock Tuesday morning. When he arrived at the *IRS* offices . . .

19c. With Numerals

The abbreviations B.C., A.D., A.M., P.M., and those of other terms of measure are used correctly only with numerals.

564 A.D.   21 B.C.   2 P.M.   No. 12   50 ft.

BUT NOT: twenty-one B.C.
two P.M.
No. twelve
fifty ft.

NOTE: In literary composition, terms of measure are often spelled out even when numerals are used.

The length of the carrier was *1,320 feet.*

19d. In Footnotes, Tables, Etc.

Some abbreviations for both Latin and English expressions are common in footnotes, tables, and other reference materials. See "Common Scholarly Abbreviations," pages 195–96.

EXERCISE

A. Which of the abbreviated words in the following passages would be better spelled out?

1. Col. Denby took a leave from his post at Camp Ord, Calif., and went to Eng. in 1943 to serve on Gen'l Eisenhower's staff.

2. I am now taking a course in mgt. Prof. Eames tells me that N.Y.C. still offers some pretty good job opportunities, and he was nice enough to give me a letter of introduction to the head of the Personnel Dept. at G.M.

3. When the FDA banned the pesticide, the mfr. took the case to the U.S. District Court, which gave him until Dec. 1, 1979 to remove the DDT from the formula.

4. I borrowed the book from the public library on Fri., Aug. 23, but I didn't discover that p. 26 was missing until the Wed. following.

5. Dover St. was being repaired, so I took E. 14th St. instead and got to Al's apt. about 3:15 P.M.

6. The lot measured 75 by 100 ft. and was situated next to the office of the Pacific Telephone Co.

7. I remember distinctly that it was the last Sun. in Sept. when I visited our local Cong. Church and heard Rev. Martin Thayer deliver the sermon billed as "How High Is Your Spiritual I.Q.?"

8. The visitor from Quebec, Can. spoke both French and Eng. He wanted to see a B'way show and visit Rockefeller Ctr.

9. Each capsule contained 5 mg. of the prescribed medication and was to be taken at 8 A.M. and 6 P.M. daily.

10. The Great Pyramid of Cheops, built about 2630 B.C. at Giza, now part of the U.A.R., is 481 ft. high and 755 sq. ft. at the base.

20 *nu*
Numbers and Amounts

Numbers that can be written in one or two words are usually spelled out; other numbers are usually represented by figures.

Usage in the representation of numbers varies considerably. It is determined largely by practical considerations, such as ease of reading, the demands of consistency, and the degree of formality desired. Where a choice is permitted, figures are likely to be preferred in journalistic writing and business usage, whereas words are likely to be preferred in literary usage.

The room held twenty-five students.
They are open 365 days a year.
I have already visited seventeen states.
The pact was signed by 135 countries.
Soon the company will celebrate its one-hundredth anniversary.
The manager tells me it's the 998th showing of the picture.
He used to make fifty dollars a day.
Her salary before taxes is $285 a week.

LETTER: on July 27, 1978
FORMAL INVITATION: on the twenty-seventh of July, nineteen hundred and seventy-eight

20a. Use of Figures

Figures are correct in the following usages.

(1) Statistics

Between 1966 and 1972 tuition for resident students in the major public universities rose from an average of $311 to an average of $517, a 66 percent increase. In the same period nonresident tuition rose nearly 80 percent, from an average of $734 to an average of $1,319.—ROBERT F. CARBONE

During the first five years of development, the company participated in the discovery of 64 producing gas wells and 23 oil wells out of a total 187 wells drilled.

(2) Dates

on January 1
started on September 12, 1977
the 3rd of March [OR: the third of March]
BUT: I'll see you on the third. [NOT: 3rd]

(3) Addresses

120 West 72nd Street
4250 Broadway
108-20 71st Drive

Words are often preferred for numbered street names in short addresses.

620 Fifth Avenue [NOT: 620 5th Avenue]
Ten East Fourth Street [OR: 10 East 4th Street]

(4) Numerical Divisions of a Book or Play

page 42	Act 2, Scene 3
Chapter 5	Isaiah 5:1
Part IV	line 4

(5) Decimals, Percentages, and Measurements

a standard deviation of .56
interest at 6.5 percent
a 2″ by 4″ stud
a 12-inch ruler

(6) Expressions of Time with A.M. and P.M.

a meeting at 3 P.M.
the 7:15 A.M. express from Danbury
BUT: will arrive at two o'clock

20b. Hyphenated Numbers; Commas

A hyphen is usually used to separate the members of compound numbers up to ninety-nine.

forty-eight
one hundred and sixty-two

A hyphen is also placed between the numerator and the denominator of fractions written as words unless either one is already hyphened.

three-eighths
seven-tenths
twenty-one hundredths

However, usage is leaning to including the hyphen in fractions used as adjectives, and omitting the hyphen in fractions used as nouns.

a one-half share [adjective]
lost one half of his assets [noun]

Except in serial numbers, telephone numbers, street numbers, room numbers, dates, and the like, commas are used to punctuate figures of more than four or five digits.

an account totaling $1,245. [ALSO: . . . totaling $1245.]
a population of 56,000
a total of 3,550,000 words

BUT: Check No. 2334	the year 1980
4755 Ravenwood Boulevard	call 442-8795
Room 3534	Docket 76823-B

20c. Round Numbers

Round numbers are usually spelled out; in the instance of round numbers over a million, they may, for the convenience of the reader, be expressed in words and figures.

a hundred million people
worth a thousand dollars
76 million television sets
assets of $3.2 billion
worth ten dollars [BUT: paid $10.32]

20d. Sentence Beginning

Do not begin a sentence with a figure. Either spell out the figure or, to avoid awkwardness, recast the sentence so that the figure comes later.

NOT: *352* employees were added to the payroll last year.
BUT: *Three hundred and fifty-two* employees were added to the payroll last year.
OR [BETTER]: Last year 352 employees were added to the payroll.

20e. Numbers in Series

Be consistent in the way you represent numbers that are parallel or in series.

INCONSISTENT: Some of the vases cost *$10;* others, as much as *a hundred dollars.*
CONSISTENT: Some of the vases cost *ten dollars;* others, as much as *a hundred dollars.*

INCONSISTENT: The price rose from *$7.90* in March, to *$8.45* in April, to *$11* in May.
CONSISTENT: . . . to *$11.00* in May.

Except in a series, avoid placing two figures in succession. Either write out one of them or change the sentence order.

NOT: *100 10-cent* stamps
BUT: *100 ten-cent* stamps
OR: *one hundred 10-cent* stamps
NOT: When she reached the age of *21, $20,000* from her aunt's estate was to be hers.
BUT: When she reached the age of *21,* she was to receive *$20,000* from her aunt's estate.
CORRECT: bills in *$5, $10, $20, and $50* denominations

20f. Ordinal Numbers

Except in some dates and street addresses (**Rule 20a**), ordinal numbers (those ending in *st, nd, rd,* and *th*) are preferably spelled out.

my *first choice* [NOT: my *1st choice*]
the *fiftieth state*
the *sixteenth day* of the contest

In an enumeration, *first, second, third,* . . . are now preferred to *firstly, secondly, thirdly,* . . .

Several reasons for the change were given:

First, students would have a greater choice of elective subjects during their freshman and sophomore years.

Second, the line between junior- and senior-year subjects would be all but abolished.

20g. Cents

Spell out a single amount of ten cents or less. In writing other single amounts of less than a dollar, you may use words alone or the figure and the word *cents,* not the dollar sign and decimal point. Do not use the cents sign (¢) in literary composition.

eight cents
thirty-nine cents
39 cents [NOT: $.39 or 39¢]

20h. Words *and* Figures

Except in legal documents, do not write an amount in both words and figures.

NOT: He charged *thirty (30) cents.*
BUT: He charged *thirty cents.*
OR: He charged *30 cents.*

LEGAL USAGE: promise to pay the sum of *one thousand, five hundred and fifty-two dollars ($1,552)*

EXERCISE

A. Make any changes you think desirable in the expression of numbers below:

1. In 1792, almost 200 years ago, a group of 24 stock brokers signed the Buttonwood Agreement, thus founding the nation's oldest stock exchange.
2. Citizens should apply for their Social Security benefits 2 or 3 months before they reach the age of 65. A delay can result in loss of income, for back payments can be made for no more than 12 months.
3. Horace Greeley was born in 1811 and died in 1872, the same year he ran for the Presidency. If elected, he would have been the 19th President of the United States. He was one of 3 or 4 of America's most influential journalists.

4. 50,000 fans paid admission of $10 to $50 to see the rock group called "The Why." The first 10 rows cost even more.

5. The waist sizes advertised are 28–42. If you buy 2 pairs of the trousers for $70, you save five dollars on the single-unit price of $37.50.

6. Since the 6th of August was a religious holiday, the town was practically closed except for 3 or 4 food shops and the $\frac{1}{2}$ dozen motels. We were told that August 25 was to be another holiday.

7. The space between the chest and the wall was only $1\frac{3}{8}$ inches, so you can imagine the difficulty of getting out the 2 10-cent pencils I had dropped there. It was hardly worth the trouble, except that 1 of the pencils had a No. 1 lead, which I liked to use for crossword puzzles.

8. China, with its population of 750,000,000, leads India by 200,000,000 and the Soviet Union by 500,000,000. These are 1968 figures, but one could probably figure a 1.0 to 1.5 percent annual increase since then.

9. Earning $187.50 a week seems like a lot for such a menial job until you find yourself contributing every 5th week's salary just for income taxes. Spending $12 a week for transportation, $25 for lunches and incidentals, and nine dollars for health and hospital insurance cuts even deeper into the total.

10. The book is small, with perhaps 100 pages or 30,000 words. All 11 chapters except Chapter 1 are less than 10 pages each. That contrasts with the Michener book, which runs to 1,153 pages.

21 Spelling

sp

Follow dictionary usage in the spelling of every word.

Misspelling a word is not the worst error a writer can make, but it is certainly one of the most unforgivable, for spelling is one of the few aspects of English usage for which there is a ready and undisputed authority—the dictionary.

An occasional misspelling may cause no more than temporary embarrassment. Consistent misspelling, on the other hand, may seriously prejudice the writer's claim to literacy. When the reader is a teacher, the dean of admissions of a graduate school, or a prospective employer, the consequences may be far out of proportion to the "crime." For that reason, if no other, the student who has difficulty with spelling should make every effort to remedy the condition. But there are other reasons as well. One is that the uncertain speller avoids opportunities to write when writing would be helpful to him either as an emotional outlet or as a means of getting ahead in school or at work. Another reason is that when writing cannot be avoided, the writer unable to spell a word necessary to the sense he has in mind is very likely to settle for some alternative and less satisfactory term.

If there is any comfort in the fact, spelling was not always as formalized as it is today. It was only after the development of printing, and the mass reproduction and dissemination of the written language that uniformity in spelling took hold. Standardization of spelling, however, has not resulted in simplicity, for the influence of regional dialects and a heavy influx of foreign words have brought into the English vocabulary a great many words with shapes that bear no resemblance to their pronunciation. The problem is complicated by an alphabet that does not seem to have enough vowels and consonants to take care of all the sounds the voice can produce.

21a. Suggestions for Improvement

Take specific action to eliminate or reduce spelling errors.

About the conditions that created English spelling you can do nothing, but you need not feel helpless to deal with your own spelling errors. To be sure, no perfect remedy exists; still, you can bolster your self-confidence and reduce the incidence of misspelled words materially by heeding the following suggestions:

(1) Consult the dictionary whenever you are in doubt about the spelling of a word. Keep the dictionary close by when you write, and overcome any reluctance to use it. If you do not wish to interrupt your train of thought to look up a word, draw a rectangle around the word and put a check in the margin as a reminder to look up the word when you review your draft.

(2) In a handy notebook keep a list of every word you misspell. Even a poor speller will not consistently misspell more than a relatively few words. If you can jot down those words, correctly spelled, whenever the misspellings are called to your attention, and study the list intensively and frequently, you will have an excellent base for improvement.

(3) Relate the spelling of a word to its pronunciation. Not all words are spelled the way they sound, but if words are mispronounced, the chance of error in spelling them increases considerably. Thus if *irRELevant* is pronounced *irREVelant*, or *míschieVOUS* is pronounced *mischíeVIOUS*, and *hinDRANCE* is pronounced *hinDERANCE*, the spelling is likely to be affected accordingly.

(4) Examine the form of a word carefully for clues to its spelling. Thus, *government* is an extension of the word *govern* and should not be spelled *gover-ment.* Similarly, *eighth* is formed by the addition of an *h* to *eight* and should not be spelled *eigt-h; equipment* is formed by the addition of *ment* to *equip* and should not be spelled *equipt-ment;* and *unnecessary* consists of the prefix *un–* before the word *necessary* and should not be spelled *un-ecessary.*

Some words, of course, are not spelled the way they look—for example, *villAIn, faSCinate, rHYthm,* and *marrIAge.* Close examination of such words and their peculiar construction will help you to fix their spelling in mind. Writing out each word several times will reinforce the learning process.

(5) Learn to distinguish between words that sound alike, and even

look alike, but have different meanings and different spellings; for example, *advise* and *advice, loose* and *lose, principal* and *principle, stationery* and *stationary.*

(6) If you have trouble with a word, spell it aloud as you write it, then spell aloud what you have written. Sometimes a student will spell a word aloud one way and spell it another way on paper. The exercise suggested will help to coordinate the manual process with the mental process—an absolute necessity for correct spelling.

(7) Learn the basic rules of spelling. English spelling is not notable for its adherence to rules, but the few that are available can tell you such things as when to follow the order *ei* or *ie* (rec*ei*ve, bel*ie*ve), when to change or not to change a *y* to an *i* in forming a plural (bab*ies,* attorn*eys*), and when to drop or retain a final *e* before adding a suffix (mov*able,* lik*eness*). Thus the rules provide a useful key to the spelling of hundreds of common words. The basic spelling rules are outlined in **Rule 21b**

(8) Proofread your work carefully. After a composition has been written, it should be given a final reading—in addition to any proofreading for other purposes—for errors in spelling. In this reading, you should concentrate only on the orthography; scan each word carefully for letters omitted or unnecessary letters added, for the transposition of letters and for other careless errors in typography and spelling. Give special attention to unusual words, to those with which you have had trouble in the past, and those about which you are even slightly uncertain. Look up those words in the dictionary before you continue proofreading. And don't despair if your inability to spell a word makes it difficult to find the word in the dictionary. True, there are some words whose first letters are not obvious—*psychology, wrench*—but most spelling problems involve the middle or end of a word.

21b. Basic Spelling Rules

Learning a few basic spelling rules can help you avoid many common problems.

(*1*) ***Rule of Addition.*** When you add a prefix or suffix to a root, or combine two words, with the result that two identical letters come together, be sure to retain both letters.

com miserate	with holding	ideal ly
mis spelling	barren ness	book keeper

EXCEPTION: eighteen [NOT: eightteen]

(2) **IE, EI.** In words spelled *ie* or *ei*, pronounced *ee*, regularly place the *i* before the *e*, except after *c*, when the order is *ei*. You may find it helpful to keep the word *Alice* in mind—*i* after *l*, but *e* after *c*.

IE		EI	
achieve	field	ceiling	deceive
belief	series	conceive	receipt

BUT: [*ei* pronounced *ay*]: eight, weight
SOME EXCEPTIONS: neither, species, leisure, seize

(3) ***Silent* E.** A silent *e* at the end of a word is usually dropped if a following suffix begins with a vowel, and retained if the suffix begins with a consonant.

advise + able = advisable
continue + ous = continuous
like + ing = liking
use + age = usage

BUT: advise + ment = advisement
coarse + ly = coarsely
hope + ful = hopeful
like + ness = likeness

SOME EXCEPTIONS: truly, toeing, enforceable, courageous, eyeing, mileage

(4) ***Final Consonant.*** Before adding a suffix, double the final consonant of a word ending in a single consonant following a single vowel if (1) the word has only one syllable or is accented on the last syllable, and (2) the suffix begins with a vowel. Do not double the consonant before a suffix beginning with a consonant.

bar + ing = barring
allot + ed = allotted
occur + ed = occurred

BUT: moor + ing = mooring [The final consonant is preceded by a double vowel.]

benefit + ed = benefited [The accent is not on the last syllable.]

defer + ment = deferment [The suffix begins with a consonant.]

Also note the effect of a shift in accent:

prefer + ed = preférred [Accent on last syllable; consonant doubled]

prefer + ence = préference [Accent on first syllable; consonant not doubled]

(5) ***Final*** **Y.** The final *y* preceded by a consonant is usually changed to *ie* before *s*, to *i* before any other suffix except one beginning with *i*; a final *y* preceded by a vowel is usually retained. See also **Rule 21c(1)**

Y preceded by consonant
penny + s = pennies
marry + s = marries [BUT: marrying]
empty + ness = emptiness
lively + hood = livelihood

Y preceded by vowel

allay + ed = allayed	gray + ish = grayish
employ + able = employable	survey + or = surveyor

SOME EXCEPTIONS: dryly, wryly; gaily, said, paid

21c. Plural Nouns

The plural of nouns is regularly formed by the addition of *s* to the singular and the addition of *es* when the plural creates an extra syllable.

boys	hats	tables	erasers
sashes	taxes	masses	passes

SOME SPECIAL CASES:

(1) When a noun ends with *y* preceded by a consonant, change the *y* to *i* and add *es*. When the final *y* is preceded by a vowel, retain the *y* and add *s*.

parties	dailies	attorneys	keys
countries	luxuries	displays	days

(2) The plural of nouns ending in *o* or *f* varies.

halo, halos	proof, proofs
hero, heroes	loaf, loaves

Other irregular plurals include words like *children*, *geese*, and *series*. The last has the same form in the singular and plural.

(3) In a compound noun, the plural form is given to the significant word in the group (mother*s*-in-law, assistant treasurer*s*, passer*s*-by). If two words are equally significant, both are given the plural form (coat*s*-of-arm*s*, *men*servant*s*, secretar*ies*-treasurer*s*). The special cases

(*cupfuls*, not *cupsful*) are so numerous, however, that the safest course is consulting the dictionary.

(4) The plural of letters, figures, signs, abbreviations, and words used as words is usually formed by the addition of an apostrophe and *s*. (See also **Rules 13d and 18c**.)

f's	2's	&'s	etc.'s	too's
r's	5's	$'s	ibid.'s	two's

(5) Some words of foreign origin have both an Anglicized and a foreign plural (curricul*ums*, curricul*a*), and some have only a foreign plural (phenomen*a*, alumn*ae*). Where a choice is offered, the foreign plural may be preferred in technical or scholarly usage. Consult your dictionary for guidance.

21d. Hyphenated Words

The hyphen is used to join two or more words or parts of words that make up a single expression. It is also used to divide a word at the end of a line.

Except in the division of a word at the end of a line, usage with respect to hyphenating words varies to a marked degree. Considerations of clarity, consistency, and uniformity rank high with editors who set the house style for their authors to follow.

(*1*) ***Certain Compound Nouns.*** The trend is to eliminate hyphens from nouns consisting of more than one word, either by separating the words or joining them without a hyphen.

chapter house   father figure   supermarket   layout

However, there are still many compound words requiring hyphens.

the secretary-treasurer	AFL-CIO
a free-for-all	mother-in-law
a trade-in	lady-in-waiting
the right-of-way	the nineteen-seventies

(2) ***Compound Adjectives.*** The hyphen is often used between the members of a compound adjective preceding a noun.

a three-minute egg	off-street parking
up-to-the-minute methods	a fourth-grade pupil
a well-known actor	a 320-page book

a Republican-Conservative candidate

BUT: high school students   motion picture theater
long distance calls   safe deposit box

When the compound adjective follows the noun, the hyphen is usually omitted.

parking off street   an actor well known
BUT: His methods were up-to-the-minute. [Hyphens retained]

When the first word of the compound preceding a noun is an adverb ending in *-ly*, no hyphen is used except in a part of the compound that is regularly hyphenated anyway.

an eagerly awaited announcement
a generously offered gift
an unusually warm reception
BUT: a terribly old-fashioned home

(3) ***Compound Numbers.*** Hyphenate compound numbers under one hundred. (See also **Rule 20b.**)

twenty-two
fifty-nine
one hundred and seventy-one

(4) ***To Aid Word Recognition.*** A word is hyphenated to prevent confusion with another word or to prevent misreading.

re-cover (cover again)   BUT: recover (regain)
co-op [NOT: coop]
pro-urban [NOT: prourban]

(5) ***With Certain Prefixes.*** A hyphen usually follows the prefixes *all–*, *ex–*(meaning "former"), *quasi–*, and *self–*.
all-knowing   ex-president   quasi-judicial   self-administered

A hyphen is used also when a capital letter follows a prefix and when the prefix consists of a single capital letter.

pre-Revolutionary   T-square
pro-British   L-shaped
mid-Atlantic   U-turn

(6) ***Suspension Hyphen.*** When two or more hyphenated adjectives have a common base, put a hyphen after each suspended part of the compound.

one-, two-, and three-year-olds
8-, 12-, and 16-ounce bottles
odd- and even-lot trades

(7) ***Word Division.*** Use the hyphen at the end of a line when division of a word is necessary. Keep to a minimum words carried over from one line to another. When division of a word is necessary, the division is made between the main parts or syllables—usually after a prefix, before a suffix, between a double consonant, or at any point where the word regularly requires a hyphen. If you are in doubt as to where a word may be divided, look up the word in the dictionary, which shows syllable division by a dot or other symbol.

A few cautions:

Do not try to divide a word of one syllable.

INCORRECT: prom-|pt walk-|ed four-|th sho-|uld

Do not divide a word so that one letter stands alone.

INCORRECT: e-|lude a-|natomy blear-|y phobi-|a
CORRECT: elude [No division] anat-|omy
bleary [No division] pho-|bia

If a word is already hyphenated, divide it only at the hyphen.

CORRECT: self-|service [NOT: self-ser-|vice]

Do not divide a word in such a way that misreading would result.

BAD:	reap-|pear	vehi-|cle	intravene-|ous	ope-|ra
IMPROVED:	re-|appear	ve-|hicle	intra-|venous	opera [No division]

21e. Words Commonly Confused

Do not confuse the word you want with another that looks or sounds like it.

beside	continual	effect	principal
besides	continuous	affect	principle

These and some other pairs like them are included in **Rule 22i**, "Troublesome Usages." Whenever you are confused by look-alike or sound-alike words, let your dictionary help you make the right decision.

EXERCISES

A. Write out the words formed from the following parts:

1. mis shapen
2. dis approve
3. abridge ment
4. due ly
5. un natural
6. co respond
7. dis service
8. develop ment
9. prefer ing
10. silly ness
11. artistic ly
12. courage ous
13. pleasure able
14. awe ful
15. whole ly
16. mis hap
17. occur ence
18. quiz ing
19. refer ence
20. lay ed (put down)

B. Insert *ie* or *ei* in the blank spaces:

1. h rarchy
2. counterf t
3. effic nt
4. fr nd
5. surf t
6. s ve
7. handkerch f
8. w ght
9. s ge
10. th f

C. Form the plural of the following words and signs:

1. party
2. sergeant-at-arms
3. ax
4. tea
5. proof
6. madame
7. five
8. bravo
9. 8
10. assistant vice president
11. hoof
12. solo
13. parenthesis
14. folly
15. tomato
16. talisman
17. etc.
18. f
19. alumnus
20. parvenu

D. Use hyphens where necessary in the following terms. If words or their parts should be joined without hyphens, so signify. Some of the expressions are correct as they stand.

1. a warmed over bun
2. a continuously whirring sound
3. had his come uppance
4. the five and ten cent store
5. a South American country

6. pre Shakespearean drama
7. a heavenly body
8. three hundred and sixty five days a year
9. a pseudo intellectual argument
10. 16, 17, and 18 year olds
11. a well made but over priced garment
12. was extraordinarily well behaved
13. a one sided discussion
14. a more than able judge
15. his anti Republican stance
16. a well meaning parent
17. a Duncan Phyfe chair
18. retro active benefits
19. our poet in residence
20. tell tale fingerprints

E. Use each of the following words in a sentence. Do not confuse them with others that look or sound like them.

1. formally
2. gibe
3. you're
4. incredulous
5. confidant
6. exorcise
7. torturous
8. militate
9. practicable
10. presentiment
11. lead (*not* the metal)
12. perspective
13. canvass
14. immigrate
15. dyeing
16. ingenuous
17. precedents
18. deserts (*not* sandy wastes)
19. all ready
20. descent

F. Find the misspelled words in the following list, and respell them correctly.

1. supercede
2. salable
3. benefitted
4. referral
5. grammer
6. minerology
7. dissipate
8. advertize
9. embarassment
10. intersede
11. genealogy
12. frolicing
13. annullment
14. controlling
15. undoubtably
16. stagy
17. maintainance
18. sacreligious
19. admissable
20. confectionery
21. connoisseur
22. oscilate
23. iridescent
24. persistence
25. hypocrasy
26. peaceable
27. stupefying
28. descendent
29. jewelery
30. eighth
31. counterfeit
32. liquefy
33. inocculate

34. ecstacy
35. privilege
36. concurrance
37. superviser
38. inviegle
39. proceedure
40. definately
41. arguement
42. counseling
43. harass
44. indefensable
45. seperate
46. academicly
47. criticize
48. roughly
49. revelant
50. fantasy

22 Word Use

W

Choose words that convey both the exact meaning and the suggestion intended. Use no more words than are necessary.

22a. Using the Dictionary

Use the dictionary to check on the meaning and usage of words and to help you select the words best suited to your purpose.

(1) **Choosing a Dictionary.**

Dictionaries vary in size, authority, and usefulness. A small "pocket" dictionary may be satisfactory for quick reference in class, but it cannot meet your needs for steady and thorough use. Experience suggests that the best portable dictionary for college, home, or office is a standard desk dictionary containing a vocabulary of about 150,000 words, and all the special features mentioned in **Rule 22a(2)** below. In addition, it should have been published or revised within the past several years under the name of a reputable publisher and editor. You should also be satisfied that the book is sturdily constructed for long and frequent use and that it can be read without eye strain. Such features as an attractive dust cover or gilt-edged pages should carry no influence. Do, however, compare tables of contents as well as individual word entries in a number of dictionaries before you make a choice. If a particular dictionary is required by the instructor, your problem of selection is satisfactorily solved. If you have a choice, all of the following are among a number of dictionaries that can be recommended for college and later use. Note the names carefully, for some titles—especially those with the name *Webster* in them—are hard to distinguish.

American Heritage Dictionary of the English Language
Funk & Wagnalls Standard College Dictionary
Random House College Dictionary
Webster's New Collegiate Dictionary
Webster's New World Dictionary

Catchword — **percept**

provender

Vocabulary entry — Etymology — Syllabication dots — Pronunciation — Loan phrase — Variant plural pronounced — Diagram and caption — Definition — Variant principal parts — Grammatical information — Variant spelling — Homograph number (separates words spelled identically but of different derivation) — Syntactic information — Example sentence

per·cept (pûr′sept), *n.* **1.** the mental result or product of perceiving, as distinguished from the act of perceiving. **2.** that which is perceived; the object of perception. [< L *percept(um)* something perceived, n. use of neut. of *perceptus,* ptp. of *percipere* to PERCEIVE]

per·cep·ti·ble (pər sep′tə bəl), *adj.* capable of being perceived; recognizable; appreciable. [< LL *perceptibil(is)*] —**per·cep′ti·bil′i·ty, per·cep′ti·ble·ness,** *n.* —**per·cep′ti·bly,** *adv.* —**Syn.** discernible, apparent.

per di·em (pər dē′əm, dī′əm), **1.** by the day. **2.** a daily allowance, usually for living expenses while traveling in connection with one's work. [< L]

per·i·car·di·um (per′ə kär′dē əm), *n., pl.* **-di·a** (-dē ə). *Anat.* the membranous sac enclosing the heart. [< NL < Gk *perikárdion,* n. use of neut. of *perikárdios* heart-surrounding. See PERI-, CARDI-, -OUS] —**per′i·car′di·al,** *adj.*

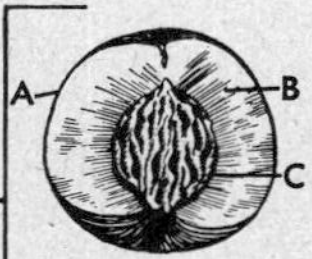

ABC, Pericarp of fruit of peach; A, Epicarp; B, Mesocarp; C, Endocarp

per·i·carp (per′ə kärp′), *n.* **1.** *Bot.* the walls of a ripened ovary or fruit, sometimes consisting of three layers, the epicarp, mesocarp, and endocarp. **2.** a membranous envelope around the cystocarp of red algae. **3.** a seed vessel. [< NL *pericarp(ium)* < Gk *perikárpion* pod] —**per′i·car′pi·al, per′i·car′pic,** *adj.* —**per′i·car·poi′dal,** *adj.*

per·il (per′əl), *n., v.,* **-iled, -il·ing** or (*esp. Brit.*) **-illed, -il·ling.** —*n.* **1.** exposure to injury, loss, or destruction; risk; jeopardy; danger. —*v.t.* **2.** to expose to danger; imperil; risk. [ME < OF < L *perīcul(um)* trial, test, danger] —**Syn. 1.** See **danger.**

per·i·o·don·tics (per′ē ə don′tiks), *n.* (*construed as sing.*) the branch of dentistry dealing with the study and treatment of diseases of the bone, connective tissue, and gum surrounding and supporting a tooth. Also, **per·i·o·don·tia** (per′ē ə don′shə, -shē ə). [< NL; see PERI-, -ODONT, -IUM, -ICS] —**per′i·o·don′tic,** *adj.*

perk[1] (pûrk), *v.i.* **1.** to act, or carry oneself, in a jaunty manner. **2.** to become lively or vigorous, as after depression or sickness (usually fol. by *up*): *She began to perk up during dinner.* **3.** to put oneself forward briskly or presumptuously. —*v.t.* **4.** to raise smartly or briskly (often fol. by *up* or *out*): *to perk one's head up.* **5.** to dress smartly; make trim or jaunty (sometimes fol. by *up* or *out*): *to perk up a suit with a new blouse.* —*adj.* **6.** perky; jaunty. [ME *perke(n)*; ? akin to PEER²] —**perk′ing·ly,** *adv.* —**perk′ish,** *adj.*

perk² (pûrk), *v.i., v.t. Informal.* to percolate: *Is the coffee*

Alternate pronunciation — Capitalization style — Synonym list — Geographical entry (location, population and date, foreign name) — Verb inflected forms (past tense and past participle; present participle) — Cross reference to multiple-word entry — Usage label — Cross reference to one-word entry — Idiomatic phrase — Adjective inflected forms (comparative, superlative) — Example phrase — Mythological entry — Abbreviation

pil·grim (pil′grim, -grəm), *n.* **1.** a person who journeys, esp. a long distance, to some sacred place as an act of devotion. **2.** a traveler or wanderer. **3.** (*cap.*) one of the Pilgrim Fathers. [early ME *pilegrim, pelegrim;* c. OFris *pilegrim,* MLG *pelegrīm,* OHG *piligrim,* Icel *pīlagrīmr,* all < ML *pelegrīnus,* dissimilated var. of L *peregrīnus* alien < *peregrē* abroad = *per-* PER- + *-egr-* (comb. form of *ager* field; see ACRE) + *-e* adv. suffix] —**Syn. 2.** wayfarer, sojourner.

Pil·sen (pil′zən), *n.* a city in Bohemia, in W Czechoslovakia. 141,736 (1963). Czech, **Plzeň.**

pin (pin), *n., v.,* **pinned, pin·ning.** —*n.* **1.** a short, slender piece of metal with a point at one end and a head at the other, for fastening things together. **2.** a small, slender, often pointed piece of wood, metal, etc., used to fasten, support, or attach things. **3.** any of various forms of fasteners, ornaments, or badges consisting essentially or partly of a pointed or penetrating wire or shaft (often used in combination): *a fraternity pin; a tiepin.* **4.** a short metal rod, as a linchpin, driven through the holes of adjacent parts, as a hub and an axle, to keep them together. **5.** a short cylindrical rod or tube, as a wristpin or crankpin, joining two parts so as to permit them to move in one plane relative to each other. **6.** the part of a cylindrical key stem that enters a lock. **7.** a clothespin. **8.** a hairpin. **9.** See **rolling pin. 10.** a peg, nail, or stud marking the center of a target. **11.** *Bowling.* one of the rounded wooden clubs set up as the target in tenpins, duckpins, etc. **12.** *Golf.* the flagstaff that identifies a hole. **13.** Usually, **pins.** *Informal.* the legs. **14.** *Music.* peg (def. 2). **15.** *Wrestling.* a fall. **16.** *Naut.* See **belaying pin. 17.** a very small amount; a trifle. —*v.t.* **18.** to fasten or attach with or as with a pin or pins. **19.** to hold fast in a spot or position. **20.** to give one's fraternity pin to (a girl) as a pledge of one's fondness or attachment. **21.** *Wrestling.* to obtain a fall over one's opponent. **22. pin down, a.** to bind or hold to a course of action, a promise, etc. **b.** to define with clarity and precision: *to pin down a vague intuition.* **23. pin something on someone,** *Slang.* to blame someone for something on the basis of real or manufactured evidence. [ME *pinne,* OE *pinn* peg; c. D *pin,* G *Pinne,* Icel *pinni;* ? akin to MIr *benn* (for *bend), now *beann* peak, steeple, gable, etc.]

pin·y (pī′nē), *adj.,* **pin·i·er, pin·i·est. 1.** abounding in, covered with, or consisting of pine trees. **2.** pertaining to or suggestive of pine trees: *a piny fragrance.* Also, **piney.**

Pi·rith·o·üs (pī rith′ō əs), *n. Class. Myth.* a prince of the Lapithae and friend of Theseus, in whose company he attempted to abduct Persephone from Hades.

requiring little or no ironing after washing.

per men·sem (pᴇʀ men′sem; *Eng.* pər men′səm), *Latin.* by the month.

Per·sia (pûr′zhə, -shə), *n.* **1.** Also called **Per′sian Em′pire.** an ancient empire located in W and SW Asia: at its height it extended from Egypt and the Aegean to India; conquered by Alexander the Great 334–331 B.C. **2.** former official name (until 1935) of **Iran.** [< L, var. of *Persis* < Gk < OPers *Pārsa*]

per·spi·ca·cious (pûr′spə kā′shəs), *adj.* **1.** having keen mental perception; discerning. **2.** *Archaic.* having keen sight. [PERSPICACI(TY) + -OUS] —**per′spi·ca′cious·ly,** *adv.* —**per′spi·ca′cious·ness,** *n.* —**Syn. 1.** perceptive, acute, penetrating. —**Ant. 1.** dull, stupid.

Peru′vian rhat′any. See under **rhatany** (def. 1).

Ph, *Chem.* phenyl.

phase-out (fāz′out′), *n.* the act or an instance of phasing out: *A phase-out of obsolete production methods is essential.*

phase′ rule′, *Physical Chem.* a law that the number of degrees of freedom in a system in equilibrium is equal to two plus the number of components less the number of phases. Thus, a system of ice, melted ice, and water vapor, being one component and three phases, has no degrees of freedom. Cf. **variance** (def. 4).

-phasia, a learned borrowing from Greek, used in the formation of compound words to refer to speech disorders: *aphasia.* Also, **-phasy.** [< Gk, comb. form akin to *phánai* to speak]

Ph.D., See **Doctor of Philosophy.** [< L *Philosophiae Doctor*]

Ring-necked pheasant, *Phasianus colchicus* (Length to 3 ft.)

pheas·ant (fez′ənt), *n.* **1.** any of numerous large, usually long-tailed, gallinaceous birds of the family *Phasianidae,* of the Old World. **2.** *Southern U.S.* the ruffed grouse. **3.** any of various other birds that resemble or suggest a pheasant. [ME *fesaunt* < AF, OF *fesan* < L *phāsiān(us)* < Gk *phāsiānós* (*órnis*) (bird) of the Phasis River]

phe·no·bar·bi·tal (fē′nō bär′bi tal′, -tôl′, -nə-), *n.* *Pharm.* a white powder, $C_{12}H_{12}N_2O_3$, available also as the sodium salt (**phenobar′bital so′dium**) for greater solubility: used as a sedative, a hypnotic, and as an antispasmodic in epilepsy. Also called **phenylethylmalonylurea.**

of action or procedure. **2.** a design or scheme of arrangement: *an elaborate plan for seating guests.* **3.** a project or definite purpose: *plans for the future.* **4.** a drawing made to scale to represent the top view or a horizontal section of a structure or a machine. **5.** a map or diagram: *a plan of the dock area.* **6.** (in perspective drawing) one of several planes in front of a represented object, and perpendicular to the line between the object and the eye. —*v.t.* **7.** to arrange or project a plan or scheme for (any work, enterprise, or proceeding): *to plan a new recreation center; to plan one's vacation.* **8.** to draw or make a plan of, as a building. —*v.i.* **9.** to make a plan: *to plan for one's retirement.* [< F: plane, plan, groundwork, scheme < L *plān(us)* level; *planum* level ground. See PLANE[1], PLAIN[1]]

—**Syn. 1.** plot, formula, system. PLAN, PROJECT, DESIGN, SCHEME imply a formulated method of doing something. PLAN refers to any method of thinking out acts and purposes beforehand: *What are your plans for today?* A PROJECT is a proposed or tentative plan, often elaborate or extensive: *an irrigation project.* DESIGN suggests art, dexterity, or craft (sometimes evil and selfish) in the elaboration or execution of a plan, and often tends to emphasize the purpose in view: *a disturbance brought about by design.* A SCHEME is apt to be either a speculative, possibly impractical, plan, or a selfish or dishonest one: *a scheme to swindle someone.* **4.** draft, diagram, chart. **7.** design, devise.

—**Usage.** Many teachers object to the phrase PLAN ON (followed by a gerund) considering it poor style for PLAN TO (followed by an infinitive): *I had planned to go to the movies tonight* (not *I had planned on going to the movies tonight*).

pop′ art′, a style in the fine arts characterized chiefly by forms and images derived from comic strips and advertising posters. —**pop′ art′ist.**

Pow·ys (pō′is), *n.* **John Cowper,** 1872–1963, and his brother, **Theodore Francis,** 1875–1953, English authors.

Pro·ven·çale (prō′vən säl′, prov′ən-; *Fr.* PRO VAN SAL′), *adj.* *Cookery.* (*sometimes l.c.*) prepared with garlic or garlic and tomato. [< F; fem. of PROVENÇAL]

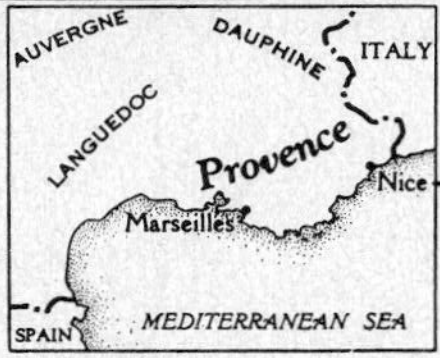

Pro·vence (PRô väns′; *Eng.* prə väns′), *n.* a region in SE France, bordering on the Mediterranean: formerly a province; famous for medieval poetry and courtly traditions.

prov·en·der (prov′ən dər), *n.* **1.** dry food for livestock or other domestic animals. **2.** food; provisions. [ME *provendre* < OF, var. of *provende* prebend, provender < ML *prōbenda,* b. *praebenda* PREBEND and *providēre* to look out for, PROVIDE] —**Syn. 1.** See **feed**.

act, āble, dâre, ärt; ebb, ēqual; if, īce; hot, ōver, ôrder; oil; bo͝ok; o͞oze; out; up, ûrge; ə = *a* as in *alone;* chief; sing; shoe; thin; that; zh as in *measure;* ə as in *button* (but′ən), *fire* (fīər). See the full key inside the front cover.

Explanatory labels, left margin: Italicized entry; Language label; Historical entry; Archaic label; Antonym list; Cross reference to hidden entry; Symbol; Hyphenated entry; Subject label; Comparison; Combining form; Illustration and caption (taxonomic name and size); Regional label; Chemical formula; Hidden entry; Variant form; Pronunciation key

Explanatory labels, right margin: Consecutive definition numbers; Etymological cross reference to foreign word; Synonym study; Example in synonym study; Usage study; Example in usage study; Stressed multiple-word entry; Run-on entry; Biographical entry (dates, nationality, profession); Foreign pronunciation; Lower-case style; Spot map; Etymological cross reference to dictionary entry; Cross reference to synonym study

A synthetic sample page, with explanatory notes. (From the *Student Guide of the Random House College Dictionary,* Revised Edition, copyright 1968 by Random House, Inc. Reprinted by permission.)

If you need more information about a word than your desk dictionary provides, consult one of the unabridged dictionaries in your college library (see list on page 176). These dictionaries are especially useful in providing word histories and examples of usage.

(2) Finding the Information You Need.

A guide to the use of the dictionary precedes the main vocabulary. Careful study of the guide will be repaid many times over as you continue to use the dictionary. In the meantime, you will do well to examine the annotated dictionary page reproduced here on pages 384–85. Below is an explanation of the principal kinds of information the dictionary offers.

SPELLING. The listing of the word—the vocabulary entry—shows the spelling of the word and the division into syllables. When a word can be correctly spelled in more than one way, the alternative spellings are also given. A variant spelling that follows the vocabulary entry with only a comma between (*pawner, pawnor*) has equal standing with the first spelling, but the first spelling has preference over a variant preceded by *Also* and is less favored than a variant preceded by the notation *Var. of.* A notation may also show that a particular spelling is favored by some specific group; for example, *harbour* is the British spelling of the American *harbor.* The syllable divisions are shown by a dot or similar mark (cor•re•late). Should you divide a word at the end of a line, you must divide it between syllables (cor-relate OR: corre-late).

PRONUNCIATION. The pronunciation of a word, including alternative pronunciations, is shown by the phonetic respelling of the word immediately after the vocabulary entry. Heavy and light stress marks (ʹ ʹ) show the primary and secondary accents, and a key at the bottom of the page provides a brief guide to pronunciation. An extensive treatment of the pronunciation key is contained in the dictionary's introductory notes.

GRAMMATICAL INFORMATION. Your dictionary should indicate the parts of speech of the words listed and tell whether verbs are transitive (*v.t.*) or intransitive (*v.i.*). When the base word is used as more than one part of speech—for example, *convert* (verb) and *convert* (noun)—the two uses follow each other under the same entry. An undefined derivative word of another part of speech—as *accidentally* (adverb) from *accidental* (adjective)—may be added to the main entry or treated separately.

Inflectional forms, including the plural of nouns and the principal parts of verbs, are usually given only when the forms are irregular. (The *American Heritage Dictionary* lists the inflectional forms of all verbs.) Thus the plurals of *meter* (*meters*) and *pearl* (*pearls*) are not given, but the plurals of *cony* (*conies*) and *wife* (*wives*) are. Similarly, the principal parts of the verb *talk* (*talked, talking*) are not given, but the verb *take* is shown to have an irregular past tense (*took*), past participle (*taken*), and present participle (*taking*).

DEFINITIONS. Depending on the dictionary, word definitions are given in either historical order or the order of frequency of use, although sometimes the two coincide. Some words have as many as twenty, thirty, or more definitions. You must look through the definitions to find the meaning you want. Many of the definitions are followed by examples of use, and often idiomatic phrases are included. Thus after *break*, the *Random House Dictionary* adds the phrase "break in," and the illustration, "to break in a pair of shoes." In many instances, synonyms (abbreviated *Syn.*) and antonyms (*Ant.*) are also listed and differentiated.

LABELS. Italicized labels or notations give a variety of useful information. The *usage label* provides guidance with respect to the customary way in which a word is employed. Common usage labels include *Slang, Colloq., Informal, Dial.* (for *dialect*), *Obs.* (for *obsolete*), and *Archaic*. (See "Varieties of Usage," **Rule 22b**.) The *geographical label* tells where the word is employed or a particular meaning given to it, as, for example, *U.S., Brit., Australian, Canadian.* The *subject label* indicates the particular field in which the word or meaning occurs, as *Physics, Chemistry, Math., Physio., Tennis.*

DERIVATION. A good desk dictionary will show in brackets the linguistic origin or development of a word. The *etymology*, as this information is called, may follow either the grammatical label, as in *Webster's New Collegiate Dictionary*, or the definitions, as in the *American Heritage Dictionary*.

22b. Varieties of Usage

Distinguish carefully among the varieties of usage, and select words best suited to your subject, audience, and purpose. (See also "Appropriateness," **Rule 22f**.)

Words can be classified as *standard* or *nonstandard.*[1] (See chart.)

(*1*) ***Standard English.*** Usages classified as standard are characteristic of the speech and writing of educated persons. Standard usage has several degrees of dignity, which sometimes impinge on each other, but which are still subject to differentiation. These are informal English, general English, and formal English.

Informal English, sometimes called colloquial English, is the language of ordinary conversation and of some writing, as in personal letters, diaries, and familiar essays. To a limited degree, it may include slang, trade terms, and the language of a particular place or ethnic group.

General English is the common language of the great body of literate writers and public speakers. It is found in works of fiction and

STANDARD ENGLISH

Informal	General	Formal
hustle →	hurry →	expedite
foot (as in "foot a bill") →	pay →	discharge (as in "discharge a debt")
cussed →	cursed →	anathematized
blast (as in "blast the media") →	denounce →	excoriate
frosh →	freshman →	neophyte

Other Formal Terms: epistle (letter); hypertension (high blood pressure); *idée fixe* (French, a fixed idea); hereinafter (later in this document); nevermore

NONSTANDARD ENGLISH

Slang	Dialect	Illiteracies
rooked (cheated)	reckon (suppose)	suicided
slammer (jail)	bub (boy)	irregardless
snatch (a kidnapping)	spicket (faucet)	disremember
take a powder	gebought (bought)	drownded
screwball	buttery (pantry)	disokay

EXAMPLES OF THE VARIETIES OF ENGLISH USAGE

[1] The classification that follows is adapted from Porter G. Perrin's *Writer's Guide and Index to English.*

nonfiction, in newspaper stories and magazine articles, and in discussion and polite conversation. This is also the most useful all-round language for college themes.

Formal English is generally restricted to special audiences and to those occasions when a high note of dignity is to be struck. It is found in government proclamations, ceremonial speeches, scholarly dissertations, critical essays, some poetry and fiction; also legal documents, resolutions, and scientific and technical papers.

(2) ***Nonstandard English.*** Used in both speech and writing (especially dialogue), nonstandard English consists of those words and idioms that are not ordinarily part of the public expression of educated persons, even though instances of such use will be found. Nonstandard English consists principally of dialectal terms (regional or ethnic), slang, illiteracies, and obscenities.

In addition to the varieties of current English mentioned, the language also includes terms that are obsolete (no longer used) and archaic (antiquated, but occasionally still used). The latter include such words as *hath* (*has*), *anon* (*soon*), *mayhap* (*perhaps*), and *y-clept* (*named*).

22c. Idiomatic Usage

Use the correct idiom. Broadly defined, an idiom is an expression peculiar to a particular language or culture. In English, for example, a traveler will ask, "Will I have the time to visit the museums?" To ask that question in French, the traveler would have to say, "Est-ce que j'aurai le temps de visiter les musées?" which, literally translated, means, "Is it that I shall have the time to visit the museums?" An idiom, in a more particular sense, is a seemingly odd expression that cannot be explained by reference to its constituent elements, but is, as a unit, an integral part of accepted usage. Examples of such expressions are "stood him in good stead," "did it on her own," and "took off after."

Idiomatic expressions are listed and defined in the dictionary following the entry for the base word. Thus, under *foot,* the *Random House Dictionary* lists and defines the idioms, "fall *or* land on one's feet," "feet first," "get off on the right *or* wrong foot," "on foot," "put one's best foot forward," "put one's foot down," "foot up" (to total or add up), "put one's foot in one's mouth," and "put one's foot into it."

The last two usages are labeled "Informal." Some of the others are also labeled "Informal" in the *American Heritage Dictionary.*

Prepositions play an important part in idiomatic expressions. Note for example, these differences in usage.

IDIOM	EXAMPLE
agree on	We could not *agree on* this point.
agree to	We *agree to* their offer.
agree with	They *agreed with* the decision.
consist in	His value to us *consists in* his skill in negotiating.
consist of	The office staff *consists of* only five employees
free from	She remains *free from* criticism.
free of	The road is now *free of* obstructions.
free to	Admission is *free to* all.
jump at	They *jumped at* our offer.
jump to	Do not *jump to* conclusions.
superior of	He is the *superior of* the two boxers.
superior to	He is *superior to* his opponent.

22d. Illiteracies

Except in dialogue or similar justifiable instances, avoid nonstandard words and misuses and corruptions of standard words. (See also "Troublesome Usages," **Rule 22i**.)

The customer was so *flustrated* in selecting a proper gift that she left the store without buying anything. [CORRECT: *flustered* or *frustrated*]

Braddock was chosen to *administrate* the new division. [CORRECT: *administer*]

When he got back from his summer vacation, Frank was sporting a *luxurious* beard. [CORRECT: *luxuriant*]

In his desire for privacy, a genuine *confliction* arose between him and his parents. [CORRECT: *conflict*]

I *suspicioned* that the "bargain" television was really a discontinued model. [CORRECT: *suspected*]

22e. Exact Words

Choose words that express precisely what you mean. Avoid words that are inexact, vague, or ambiguous.

(1) Careful writers make distinctions between words that may be close in meaning, but have certain—sometimes subtle—distinctions in meaning or usage. A *tornado,* for example, is not the same as a *hurricane; collusion* is not the same as *connivance; oral* is not the same as *verbal.*

The body was found *prone,* with the eyes staring at the ceiling. [The word desired is *recumbent* or *supine.*]

In 1908 his family *immigrated* from Ireland to Brooklyn, New York. [The word desired is *emigrated.*]

Anyone who speaks so scandalously of another person should be sued for *libel.* [The word desired is *slander.*]

(2) Vague words are those that are indefinite in meaning. Lacking specific reference, they fail to communicate accurately or convincingly. Such words are also called general or abstract. As the examples show, the use of specific words means the inclusion of details important to the reader's understanding.

VAGUE: The company is now constructing a new *unit.*
SPECIFIC: The company is now constructing a new *warehouse.*

VAGUE: Tim is a *relative* who is *now* in *college.*
SPECIFIC: *Last September* my *cousin* Tim entered *Colby College as a freshman.*

VAGUE: *Pet fishes* can be *harmed* by *polluted water.*
SPECIFIC: Small amounts of natural substances, such as their own waste, can be harmful to pet fishes. Ammonia is their major excretion, but fish culturists have found that trout kept in water with as little as six parts per billion of ammonia showed abnormal gills. Even fishes like goldfish or guppies should not be exposed to concentrations of one part of ammonia in ten million parts of water. This is the equivalent of one drop of ammonia in a 150-gallon tank. [Part of a student paper]

(3) Ambiguous words are those that can be interpreted in more than one way, with resulting confusion.

AMBIGUOUS: The drop in my grades was *hard to digest.* [Does *hard to digest* mean "hard to account for," "hard to believe," or "hard to accept"?]

AMBIGUOUS: Dan's plight *should be of no concern* to you. [Does *should be of no concern* mean "should be of no interest" or "should cause no worry"?]

22f. Appropriateness

Choose words appropriate to the reader, the subject, and the tone you wish to establish.

(1) Choose words for their *connotation.* The connotation of a word is the suggestion it carries in addition to its literal meaning. Many words with the same literal meaning have different suggestive meanings. The word *restaurant,* for example, can be interpreted fairly literally as an eating place. The word also suggests the presence of tables and service. A number of synonyms for *restaurant,* however, carry different and sometimes more pronounced connotations. Consider the intimacy suggested by the words *cafe, bistro,* and *boîte;* the dignity and privacy of *dining hall* and *dining room;* the practicality of *cafeteria, coffee shop, luncheonette,* and *lunch counter;* the conviviality of *saloon* and *bar;* and the coarseness of *hamburger joint* and *greasy spoon.* The synonyms of other words, too, carry various connotations. A person makes a *mistake.* Shall we call it a *blooper* (slang), a *blunder,* a *transgression,* an *error,* a *faux pas,* a *gaffe,* a *lapse,* a *slip,* an *inaccuracy,* an *oversight,* a *misunderstanding?* The particular choice will depend on our interpretation of the fault and our attitude toward the offender.

(2) When a word or phrase has a negative connotation, be sure that the unfavorable suggestion is intended.

NEGATIVE: My parents used to take us on many picnics and *joy rides.* [*Joy rides* suggests rowdy behavior.]
IMPROVED: My parents used to take us on many picnics and *pleasure trips.*

NEGATIVE: I *got out of* Crofts High School last spring and entered the University of Michigan in the fall. [*Got out of* suggests release from an unpleasant situation.]
POSITIVE: I *was graduated from* Crofts High School last spring. . . .

(3) Avoid using a word that creates an unintended humorous effect.

INAPPROPRIATE: The Police Department's Morals Squad now *embraces* five women detectives.
BETTER: . . . now *includes* five women detectives.

INAPPROPRIATE: Military planes *fall* into two categories: sonic and supersonic.
BETTER: Military planes *can be classified* as sonic and supersonic.

(4) Avoid mixing two or more varieties of diction with resulting incongruity. This rule does not prohibit the occasional, intentional mixing of usages for purposes of humor, sarcasm, or other stylistic effect.

INCONGRUOUS: The courtroom was still as the black-robed judge looked solemnly at the prisoner and, in a voice that showed no emotion, sentenced him to thirty years in *the joint.* [General English and slang]
BETTER: . . . sentenced him to thirty years in *prison.*

INCONGRUOUS: The chairman roundly berated the members of the building committee for their dilatory tactics and urged them to *knuckle down to business.* [General and informal English]
BETTER: . . . and urged them to *speed up their deliberations.*

EFFECTIVE MIXING: Perfect love, I suppose, means that a married man and woman never contradict one another, and that they both of them always feel the same thing at the same moment, and kiss one another on the strength of it. What blarney! It means, I suppose, that they are absolutely intimate: this precious intimacy that lovers insist on. They tell each other *everything:* and if she puts on her chiffon knickers, he ties the strings for her: and if he blows his nose, she holds the hanky.

Pfui! Is anything so loathsome as intimacy, especially the married sort, or the sort that "lovers" indulge in! [General English and slang]—D. H. LAWRENCE[2]

EFFECTIVE MIXING: Mr. Nussbaum remembered the blunder of the movie men, who wasted vast sums bellowing, "Movies Are Your Best Entertainment." Their billboards, banners, radio commercials, and newspaper pages were hastily canceled when someone pointed out that the initials of the slogan spelled MAYBE. But even when reborn as "Motion Pictures Are Your Best Entertainment," the campaign flopped. [General and informal English]—KEITH MONROE[3]

22g. Fresh, Vivid Words

Prefer words that are fresh and vivid to those that are stale and colorless.

(1) Stale words will be found in phrases that are classified as trite or stereotyped. Although the phrases were fresh at one time—many

[2] From "Love Was Once a Little Boy," in *The Later D. H. Lawrence,* ed. William York Tindall (New York: Knopf, 1959), p. 214.

[3] "They Made the Cigar Respectable," *Harper's* Magazine, February 1955, p. 39.

have their origins in the Bible and Shakespeare—they have been worn down, through overuse, to such a degree that they have lost their original meaning and power to excite interest.

STALE: *As luck would have it,* the test was postponed.
IMPROVED: *Luckily,* the test was postponed.

STALE: If he doesn't have the fracture set, he *could be in a bad way.*
IMPROVED: If he doesn't have the fracture set, he *could be permanently crippled.*

Some other examples of stale expressions:

by leaps and bounds
on the ball
head and shoulders above
rules the roost
easier said than done
seems like only yesterday
few and far between

(2) Vivid words are those that produce concrete images. One could say, for example, that "steel is a very strong metal," but note the added color and force in the statement,

Only the strength of steel has the rugged stamina to stand under the brutal slam of bucket teeth into rock, to support the hoist and sweep of tremendous loads, to gouge great trees out of their sockets.—REPUBLIC STEEL

And here is the description of a dust storm as reported by *Time* magazine:

Stagnant air hung heavy and ominous over the parched plains last week. Then a cold front hit, and the year's worst duster began to blow. Winds up to 70 m.p.h. whipped across 120,000 square miles of the Southwest dust bowl, and the earth boiled into black clouds 20,000 feet high in the sky. The dust was so thick that dawn came invisibly; when rain began to fall, tiny mud balls pelted the town of Guymon, Okla. Schools closed, stores shut down and thousands of farm families listened tensely at their radios as their lands and their livelihoods slipped away.[4]

(3) The drive for concreteness should lead to the occasional use of *figurative language.* This is a literary device employing for the most part symbolic or imaginative, rather than literal, terms. In the exam-

[4] "Big Duster," *Time,* 11 April 1955, p. 26.

ple quoted immediately above, the word *boiled* is figurative in the sense that it describes the earth with a term normally reserved for liquids.

Figurative language takes a number of forms, called *figures of speech.* The most common are the simile and the metaphor. Both involve comparisons of two unlike things, but the simile employs an expression on the order of *like* or *as,* while the metaphor does not. One might create a simile, for example, by saying, "The thermostat is like the brain of the heating plant." If the *like* is removed—"The thermostat is the brain of the heating plant"—the result is a metaphor. The metaphor is the more emphatic figure of speech because the comparison is unqualified.

These further examples of similes and metaphors—the term *metaphor* is often applied to both—will demonstrate the force and freshness they can contribute to any composition.

Talking to Phyllis seemed harder than chewing gum with my braces on.

Writing is like making love—it is astonishing how far pure instinct (if it really is pure) will carry you.—PAUL ENGLE.

Luce and His Empire is one of those dinosaur biographies, more bulk than brains, we fact-obsessed Americans go in for.—DWIGHT MACDONALD

Judy [Garland] was deeply in the middle-American grain, a small-town girl who had been led to believe . . . that the bluebird of happiness was to be found in her own backyard. Unfortunately, the backyard was an irrecoverable Eden, and the bluebird on closer inspection proved to be a raven. —PHILIP FRENCH

The fiery breath of this oxyacetylene flame helps to weld everything from ships to fenders. It slices through thick slabs of metal as if it were cheese and carves jigsaw shapes out of stacks of steel sheets.—UNION CARBIDE CORPORATION

NOTE: Avoid the "mixed" figure of speech, one that incongruously combines two or more different metaphors.

No stone was left unturned to reverse the firestorm of criticism.

As a black horse in the race for the governorship, he surprised everyone when he won by a landslide.

She was not prepared for the mountain of work that greeted her on her arrival.

It was a tempest in a teapot, designed to throw sand in the eyes of the public.

22h. Conciseness

Use only as many words as a statement requires to express your meaning accurately and completely. (See also **Rule 23c**.)

(1) Eliminate repetitious or otherwise unnecessary words.

In time the problem was ~~entirely~~ eliminated.
The whole summer's wages came to ~~the sum of~~ $280.
They did not have any record of the transaction ~~in their file~~.
When he was leaving, I thanked him for his interest ~~in the matter~~.
The experience was ~~of a~~ most disagreeable ~~nature~~.
At ~~the~~ present ~~time~~ Julia is looking for a job.
I would like to specialize in ~~the field of~~ power plant construction.

(2) Recast phrases, sentences, and longer units to eliminate wordiness and make your writing crisper and more interesting.

WORDY: My plane landed in Amsterdam in order that those passengers who wanted to continue to Milan could make a connecting flight to that city.

CONCISE: My plane landed in Amsterdam so that passengers to Milan could make the connecting flight.

WORDY: In case of an accident on the subway, overcrowding on the trains can lead to mass panic, which is of course extremely dangerous in closed-in places like a subway.

CONCISE: In a subway accident, overcrowding can lead to panic.

WORDY: It is wonderful when you know someone who has accomplished something that inspires someone else to follow in his footsteps. I have an uncle who is a neurosurgeon. In him I have found the inspiration for my goal in life. He is one of the greatest influences on me in my desire to become involved in the profession of medicine.

CONCISE: My uncle is a neurosurgeon. He is so good in his profession, such a source of inspiration to me, that I, too, want to make medicine my career.

22i. Troublesome Usages

Note carefully the usages of the words and expressions in the following list. Avoid usages that are inconsistent with your meaning and the level of diction you wish to observe.

a, an. Use *a* before words beginning with a consonant sound, *an* before words beginning with a vowel sound.

a helper	*a* useful tool	*a* onetime friend	*a* yellow bugle
	a campsite	*a* bookcase	
an heir	*an* umbrella	*an* extra dimension	*an* only child

accept, except. *Accept,* a verb, means "to receive with consent." *Except,* as a preposition means "with the exclusion of." As a verb meaning "to leave out, exclude," it is rarely used.

Mr. Fenton *accepted* the honor. [Verb]
All *except* Mrs. Humphrey were required to attend. [Preposition]
Only Mrs. Humphrey *was excepted* from the attendance requirement. [Verb]

ad, add. Do not confuse *ad,* the shortened form of *advertisement* with the verb *add,* "to make a sum." *Ad* is used only in informal English; it is not followed by a period.

The *ad* will appear on Thursday.
If you *add* two and three, you get five.

advice, advise. *Advice* is used only as a noun, *advise* only as a verb.

He took our *advice.*
We *advise* your client to drop the suit.

affect, effect. The verb *affect* means "to influence." As a verb, *effect* means "to bring about"; as a noun, it means "result."

The soggy weather *affected* his rheumatism.
It is hard to *effect* a change in people's habits.
The *effect* of the decision was to raise prices.

aggravate. *Aggravate* means "to make worse or intensify." In informal English, it is used in the sense of "to irritate or annoy."

GENERAL: The drought *aggravated* the plight of the wheat farmers.
INFORMAL: Tim's constant chattering *aggravated* the teacher.

ain't. Nonstandard for *amn't, isn't,* or *aren't, ain't* is generally avoided in the writing of educated persons except, consciously, for humorous or facetious effect, as in "It *ain't* hay!"

almost all, most all. See *most all, almost all.*

already, all ready. *Already* means "by this time." *All ready* (two words) means "entirely ready."

By Tuesday the work had *already* been completed.
On Tuesday the carpenters were *all ready* to start work.

alright. This form is not generally acceptable in standard English. Write *all right* (two words).

altogether, all together. *Altogether* means "completely, entirely"; *all together* means "in a group."

Jordan was *altogether* agreeable to the plan.
Let's sing *all together.*

among, between. *Among* is used when reference is made to more than two persons or things. *Between* is used when reference is made to two persons or things, or when—in a composite group—reference is made to the individual entities.

We divided the cake *among* our six guests.
Fred and Susan divided the work *between* them.
A seven-layer cake has butter cream *between* the layers.

amount, number. *Amount* refers to things in bulk; *number,* to a quantity of units.

The *amount* of wheat harvested was down from last year.
The *number* of working men and women increased last year.

and also. Redundant. Use one word or the other.

and etc. The *etc.* stands for *et cetera,* "and other things." The *and* before *etc.* is therefore redundant. *Etc.,* without the *and,* is often well used in business and technical writing, but try to avoid it in ordinary composition.

any place. Informally used as an adverb. *Anywhere* is better in general usage.

INFORMAL: They'll go *any place* you say.
GENERAL: They'll go *anywhere* you say.
BUT (ALSO GENERAL): They'll go to *any place* you say. [Used as a noun]

anyways, anywheres. These words are dialect. Use *anyway* or *anywhere.*

apt, liable, likely. All are used informally to express probability, but careful writers make distinctions in their use: *Apt* means "suitable, tending to, or quick to learn"; *liable* means "openness to risk or disadvantage"; *likely* means "fairly certain."

The phrase is *apt.* She is an *apt* pupil.
His successes are *apt* to go to his head.
A parent is *liable* for the debts of minor children.
The proceeding is *likely* to be drawn out.

as. *As* is used dialectically, often in the phrase *as how,* in the sense of "that" or "whether." In other instances, *as* is used ambiguously for "while," "when," or "because." (See also *like, as, as if.*)

DIALECT: I cannot see *as how* I can agree.
STANDARD: I cannot see *how* I can agree.

DIALECT: I do not know *as* I can come.
STANDARD: I do not know *whether* I can come.

DIALECT: I am not sure *as* I can do that.
STANDARD: I am not sure *whether* I can do that.

AMBIGUOUS: *As* the market fell sharply, he rushed to sell his stocks. [Does *As* mean "when" or "because"?]
CLEAR: *When* the market fell sharply, he rushed to sell his stocks.
CLEAR: *Because* the market fell sharply, he rushed to sell his stocks.

beside, besides. Both *beside* and *besides* are used in the sense of "except." *Beside* also means "by the side of," and *besides* means "in addition to" or "too".

Who *besides* [OR: *beside*] you will be present?
Please sit *beside* me.
Besides this inducement, we can offer you others.
Dalton had personality; *besides,* he was rich.

between, among. See *among, between.*

can, may. In general usage, *can* denotes ability and *may* denotes permission. In informal usage, *can* is used in both senses.

INFORMAL: *Can* I get you a drink? [Permission]
GENERAL: *May* I get you a drink? [Permission]
GENERAL: I am sure I *can* complete the report in time for the meeting. [Ability]

cannot help but, can't help but. Both are acceptable in general usage, but many purists still favor the more formal *cannot but.*

FORMAL: I *cannot but* regret his decision.
GENERAL: I *cannot help but* [OR: *can't help but*] regret his decision.
OR: I *can't help* regretting his decision.

can't hardly. This is a double negative. Use *can hardly.*

NONSTANDARD: He *can't hardly* stand on his feet.
STANDARD: He *can hardly* stand on his feet.

complected. Nonstandard for *complexioned.*

He was dark *complexioned.* [NOT: *complected*]

continual, continuous. *Continual* means "continuing in rapid succession." *Continuous* means "without interruption."

His *continual* interruptions annoyed the speaker.
The *continuous* whine of the motor was nerve-wracking.

could of. Nonstandard for "could have" or "could've." Also avoid *should of* and *would* of.

What *could have* [OR: *could've*] happened?

data. This is the plural of the Latin *datum,* but it is acceptably used as a singular noun.

The *data are* inconclusive.
OR: The *data is* inconclusive.

deal. Used informally and loosely in the sense of "a transaction." General usage requires a more specific word.

INFORMAL: The buyer gave me a good *deal* on my used Ford.
GENERAL: The buyer gave me a good *price* for my used Ford.

differ from, differ with. *Differ from* relates to unlikeness; *differ with* relates to disagreement or dispute.

The new rules *differ from* the old in some important respects.
I *differ with* her on the effects of the new legislation.

different from, different than. *Different from* is an accepted idiom in general usage, but the less formal *different than* often makes a smoother sentence when a clause follows the expression.

GENERAL: His version of the accident is *different from* mine.
INFORMAL: His version of the accident is *different than* mine.

GENERAL: The lamp was *different from* anything I'd seen before.
INFORMAL: The lamp was *different than* anything I'd seen before.

GENERAL (BUT AWKWARD): The group apparently staged the play in a very *different* manner *from* that which the author intended.
IMPROVED: The group apparently staged the play in a very *different* manner *than* the author intended.

don't. This is a contraction of *do not* and should not be used for *does not* or *doesn't.*

NONSTANDARD: He *don't* understand.
STANDARD: He *doesn't* understand.
STANDARD: They *don't* understand.

effect, affect. See *affect, effect.*

enthuse. Now finds acceptance in the sense of "to be enthusiastic" or "to stir enthusiasm" in others. However, it is frowned on in formal usage and often avoided in general usage as well.

ACCEPTABLE: The audience did not seem terribly *enthused* about the play.
OFTEN PREFERRED: The audience did not seem terribly *enthusiastic* about the play.

equally as good. A redundant version of *equally good.*

WORDY: I like the blue one, but the red one is *equally as good.*
CONCISE: I like the blue one, but the red is *equally good.*
OR: . . . but the red is *just as good.*

etc. See *and etc.*

except, accept. See *accept, except.*

expect. Informal for "suppose." In general usage it means "to look forward to."

INFORMAL: I *expect* that the terms are the best we can obtain.
GENERAL: I *suppose* that the terms are the best we can obtain.
GENERAL: I *expect* to see you in the fall.

farther, further. Many careful writers and speakers use *farther* to denote distance, and *further* to denote degree. Nevertheless, the use of *further* to express either distance or degree is common in general English.

ACCEPTABLE: They could have traveled *further* if their car had not broken down. [Distance]
OFTEN PREFERRED: They could have traveled *farther*. . . .
NO QUESTION: He said he would look *further* into the matter. [Degree]

faze. Not to be confused with *phase*, meaning "aspect," *faze* means "to disturb or disconcert." The word is now in general usage.

The prospect of failure does not *faze* him.
Research is an important *phase* of reporting.

fewer, less. In general English, *fewer* refers to number, and *less* to degree. In informal English, *less* is used in both senses.

GENERAL: The new plant will require *fewer* workers.
INFORMAL: The new plant will require *less* workers.
GENERAL: I got *less* credit for my work than I deserved.

fix. Used informally both as a noun for "predicament," and as a verb for "to repair."

INFORMAL: He found himself in a terrible *fix*.
GENERAL: He found himself in a terrible *predicament*.

INFORMAL: The mechanic said he could *fix* the transmission.
GENERAL: The mechanic said he could *repair* the transmission.

former, first. *Former* indicates the first of two, and *first* the initial member of a group consisting of any number. (See also *latter, last.*)

We received bids from Allied Power and Consolidated Electric, but we gave the order to the *former* [OR: *first*].
We received bids from Allied Power, Consolidated Electric, and Benson Utilities, and we gave the order to the *first.* [NOT: *former*]

funny. Informal in the sense of "odd" or "unusual." In general English, the word is used in the sense of "amusing."

INFORMAL: He kept hearing a *funny* sound under the floorboard.
GENERAL: He kept hearing an *odd* sound under the floorboard.
GENERAL: I don't find the new comedians very *funny.*

further, farther. See *farther, further.*

good. Used exclusively as an adjective in general English, but also, in informal English, as an adverb.

GENERAL: Martin draws *good* landscapes.
GENERAL: Martin draws *well.*
INFORMAL: Martin draws *good.*

got, gotten. Both words are accepted in general usage as past participles of the verb *get.*

We *have got* used to the idea of economic growth.
ALSO: We *have gotten* used to the idea of economic growth.

had better, had best. These are accepted idioms. But *better,* in place of *had better,* is used only informally.

GENERAL: I *had better* leave before I lose my temper.
GENERAL: We *had best* leave the work to professionals.
INFORMAL: I *better* go.

hadn't ought. A nonstandard form of *oughtn't, ought not,* or *shouldn't have.*

NONSTANDARD: He *hadn't ought* to have done it.
STANDARD: He *shouldn't have* done it.

hardly never. A double negative; nonstandard for *hardly ever.*

hopefully. Not generally accepted in the sense of "in a hopeful manner."

INFORMAL: *Hopefully*, the rain will end by tonight.
GENERAL: *I hope* the rain will end by tonight.

if, whether. Both words are used in general English to introduce noun clauses, but *whether* is considered somewhat more formal. There is also some preference for *whether* when it is accompanied by an *or* construction.

They wondered *whether* [OR: *if*] Dr. Clarke was going to come.
I doubt *whether* [OR: *if*] it will rain.

Smith inquired *whether* the goods had been sent, or had even been ordered. [Preferred over *if*]
BUT: Smith inquired *whether* [NOT: *whether or not*] the goods had been sent.

imply, infer. Many writers and speakers believe the distinction between these two words should be preserved. *Imply* means "to suggest indirectly"; *infer* means "to conclude from evidence." Thus *I imply*, but *a reader or listener infers*.

The speaker *implied* that he would support the measure.
The audience *inferred* that the speaker would support the measure.

In informal usage, *infer* is often used in the sense of *imply*.

INFORMAL: I *inferred* that I would take my trade elsewhere.

in regards to. The correct expression is *in regard to* or *about*, as "Did you receive my inquiry *about* your rates?"

irregardless. Nonstandard for *regardless*.

NONSTANDARD: I will go *irregardless* of what you say.
STANDARD: I will go *regardless* of what you say.

is when, is where. In a definition, the verb *to be* cannot be followed by a *where* or *when* clause without awkward results.

NOT: A bargain *is when* you get good quality as well as low price.
BUT: You get a bargain only when you get good quality as well as low price.

NOT: A cooperative apartment *is where* the tenant shares in the ownership of the property.
BUT: A cooperative apartment *is one* that gives the tenant a share in the ownership of the property.

kind, sort. The singular of these nouns is modified by the singular *this* or *that* in general usage; the plural, by *these* or *those.*

GENERAL: *This sort* of reply is insulting.
GENERAL: I like *this kind* of pastry. [Singular]
GENERAL: I like *these kinds* of pastries. [Plural]
INFORMAL: I like *these kind* of pastries.

kind of a, sort of a. In general usage, omit the *a.*

INFORMAL: It's an odd *kind of a* day.
GENERAL: It's an odd *kind of* day.

latter, last. In general usage, *latter* indicates the second of two, and *last* the last of three or more. In informal English, *latter* is used for *last.* (See also *former, first.*)

GENERAL: We received bids from Allied Power and Consolidated Electric, but we gave the order to the *latter.*
GENERAL: We received bids from Allied Power, Consolidated Electric, and Benson Utilities, and we gave the order to the *last.* [NOT: *latter*]
INFORMAL: We received bids from Allied Power, Consolidated Electric, and Benson Utilities, and we gave the order to the *latter.*

lay, lie. *Lay* is a transitive verb meaning "to put down"; *lie* is an intransitive verb meaning "to recline." The two are often confused. In speech, especially, the use of *lay* for *lie* is common.

PRESENT	PAST	PAST PARTICIPLE
lay	laid	laid
lie	lay	lain

LAY: *Lay* your fears aside.
Mr. Tompkins *laid* the ill child on the couch.
I have *laid* the carton on the floor.
LIE: His remains *lie* next to those of his wife.
He *lay* down by the brook.
Many nights have I *lain* in bed worrying about my next meal.
INFORMAL: He *lays* in bed until ten every morning.
INFORMAL: She didn't move; she just *laid* there.

leave, let. *Leave* means "to allow to remain"; *let* means "to allow." Idiomatic usage, however, condones the expression "*Leave* him alone."

GENERAL: *Leave* the chair where it is.
GENERAL: *Let* him go if he wishes.

less, fewer. See *fewer, less.*

liable, likely, apt. See *apt, liable, likely*

like, as, as if. In informal English, *like* is used as a preposition or as a conjunction; in general English *like* is used only as a preposition and *as* and *as if* as conjunctions.

INFORMAL: You don't see policemen patrolling the streets, *like* they used to. [Conjunction]
GENERAL: You don't see policemen patrolling the streets, *as* they used to. [Conjunction]

GENERAL: The report is bound *like* a book. [Preposition]

INFORMAL: It looks *like* your prediction was right. [Conjunction]
GENERAL: It looks *as if* your prediction was right. [Conjunction]

lot, lots of. Informal usages for *many, much, a large number, a great deal.*

INFORMAL: He has a *lot of* friends.
GENERAL: He has *many* friends.

INFORMAL: We wished him *lots of* luck.
GENERAL: We wished him *much* luck.

mad. Means "insane" in general usage; "angry," in informal usage.

GENERAL: He was *mad* to try to escape.
INFORMAL: Don't go away *mad.*
GENERAL: Don't go away *angry.*

may. See *can, may.*

might of. Nonstandard for "might have" or "might've."

She *might have* [OR: might've; NOT: might of] done better as a biologist.

most all, almost all. *Most all, most everyone, most anybody,* are informal usages. In general English, use *almost* for *most* whenever the sense permits.

INFORMAL: *Most all* he knows comes from books.
GENERAL: *Almost all* he knows comes from books.

INFORMAL: *Most everyone* agreed that the decision was wrong.
GENERAL: *Almost everyone* agreed that the decision was wrong.

nowheres. Nonstandard for *nowhere.*

His guess was *nowhere* [NOT: *nowheres*] near the mark.

number, amount. See *amount, number.*

off of. The *of* is omitted in standard English.

He nearly fell *off* [NOT: *off of*] his chair.

party. Synonymous with *person* in telephone and legal usage, but otherwise it is so used only in informal English.

STANDARD: Your *party* is on the line.
STANDARD: The *party* of the first part . . .
INFORMAL: The *party* he was with turned out to be Mr. Edmund.
GENERAL: The *person* he was with turned out to be Mr. Edmund.

per. Not in standard use, except in Latin phrases and business expressions.

NONSTANDARD: They repaired your clock *as per your request.*
STANDARD: They repaired your clock *as you requested.*

FORMAL: The interest is six percent *per annum.*
STANDARD: The interest is six percent *a year.*

STANDARD: She is a *per* diem member of the staff. [Means "paid by the day, not salaried"]

percent, percentage. *Percent* means "per hundred"; *percentage* means "rate per hundred," or "a share or portion." *Percent* is sometimes spelled as two words: *per cent.*

Wages increased 12 *percent* last year.
Interest on the notes is 8 *percent.*
The landlord takes a *percentage* [NOT: *percent*] of the gross receipts.

plenty. Not to be used in the sense of "very" in general English.

INFORMAL: She was *plenty* embarrassed.
GENERAL: She was *very* [OR: *quite*] embarrassed.

practical, practicable. *Practical* means "useful, not theoretical," or "experienced through practice." *Practicable* means "feasible, capable of being put into practice"; the word applies only to untried proposals.

A *practical* solution to the problem soon presented itself.
We need a *practical* man or woman for the job.
The plan seemed entirely *practicable.*

principal, principle. As an adjective, *principal* means "chief, most important"; as a noun it means "chief sum" or "chief person." *Principle* is a noun only and means "doctrine or fundamental truth."

The *principal* reason for the loss was bad management. [Adjective]
The *principal* in the account is $500. [Noun]
The school board elected a new *principal.* [Noun]
The *principle* of free speech is embodied in the Constitution. [Noun]

prof. Except in informal expression, use *professor.*

INFORMAL: The *prof* gave out the assignment yesterday.
GENERAL: The *professor* gave out the assignment yesterday.

quite. In general usage, *quite* means "entirely, wholly." It is somewhat less acceptable, but still in general usage, in the sense of "somewhat," "to a considerable extent," and "very." The expression *quite a,* referring either to an indefinable quality or an extraordinary one, is informal.

GENERAL: He was *quite right* in his judgment of the situation.
GENERAL: The house was *quite large.*
INFORMAL: The class had *quite a few* students.
INFORMAL: She was *quite a lady.*

raise, rise. Do not confuse the two verbs. The first takes an object; the second does not.

RAISE: Tom will *raise* the window. [Takes an object]

The Browns *raised* tomatoes in their backyard.
The Board *has raised* a question about his fitness for office.

RISE: I *rise* at six. [Takes no object]
The audience *rose* when the principal entered.
Prices have *risen* sharply in the last year.

real. This word is used only as an adjective in general English and is not to be substituted for *very* or *really*.

GENERAL: The ring is set with a *real* diamond.
INFORMAL: He seemed *real* pleasant.
GENERAL: He seemed *really* [OR: *very*] pleasant.

reason is because. A redundant expression. In general English, say the *reason is* (OR: *was*) *that*, or, if awkwardness results, recast the sentence.

INFORMAL: The *reason* he sold the car *was because* he needed the money.
GENERAL: The *reason* he sold the car *was that* he needed the money.
OR: He sold the car *because* he needed the money.

reckon. Nonstandard for "to think or suppose," but standard in other uses.

NONSTANDARD: I *reckon* I won't be going to the meeting.
STANDARD: I don't *think* I'll be going to the meeting.

Reckon is standard in the following uses:

The host did not *reckon on* my coming. [*count on*]
He is a man to *reckon with*. [*come to terms with*]
The banker *reckoned* the interest from the first of October. [*computed*]

same. Used as a noun substitute in legal documents, but should otherwise be used only as an adjective.

STILTED: We have your order and thank you for *same*.
BETTER: Thank you for your order. [Sentence revised; *same* eliminated]
ADJECTIVE USE (GENERAL): We'll make up the *same* order as last time.
I'll meet you in the *same* place tomorrow.

seldom ever, seldom or ever. The standard expressions are *seldom*, *seldom if ever*, and *hardly ever*.

sort. See *kind, sort.*

sort of a. See *kind of a, sort of a.*

sure. Informal for *surely, certainly,* or *indeed,* but in good general usage as an adjective meaning "certain."

INFORMAL: That's *sure* generous of you.
GENERAL: That's *certainly* generous of you.
GENERAL: He was *sure* he would be vindicated.

than, then. *Than* is a conjunction introducing the second member of a comparison; *then* is an adverb denoting time.

The movie was better *than* I had expected.
First we'll have dinner; *then* we'll see a movie.

that there, this here; those there, these here. Nonstandard and redundant. Omit the *here.*

This television [NOT: *This here*] has the clearest picture.

their, they're. Do not confuse the contraction of *they are,* (*they're*) with the plural possessive of *they* (*their*).

They're more sophisticated than I thought.
They accepted *their* rebuke gracefully.

try and. Informal for *try to.*

INFORMAL: The clerk will *try and* correct the error.
GENERAL: The clerk will *try to* correct the error.

type of. In standard English, do not omit the *of* in such expressions as "*type of* hammer." (See also *kind of a, sort of a.*)

INFORMAL: The store does not carry that *type* shirt.
GENERAL: The store does not carry that *type of* shirt.

wait on. Dialectal for *wait for.*

DIALECT: I'll *wait on* you at Irv's house.
STANDARD: I'll *wait for* you at Irv's house.

where. Informal when used for *that.* (See also *is when, is where.*)

INFORMAL: I see *where* the Giants won again.
GENERAL: I see *that* the Giants won again.

whether, if. See *if, whether.*

while. Avoid using *while* loosely for *but, and,* or *although.* It is best used in references to time.

QUESTIONABLE: *While* I like most foods, I find Mexican cooking too highly spiced.
IMPROVED: *Although* I like most foods, I find Mexican cooking too highly spiced.
OR: I like most foods, *but* I find Mexican cooking too highly spiced.
GOOD: *While* my parents were in Europe, they had the house painted.

would of. Nonstandard for *would have* or *would've.* (See also *could of* and *might of.*)

I *would have* [NOT: *would of*] liked to come.

EXERCISES

A. Provide the following information from your own dictionary. Write "Not given" if the information is not shown. State at the top of your paper the full name of your dictionary, the publisher, and the last copyright date.

1. What is *Dumfries?*
2. What are two informal meanings of *dump* (v.t.)?
3. What is the meaning of *period* in music?
4. Is *happenstance* a word in general usage?
5. From the definition or illustration in the dictionary, can you show by means of a freehand drawing what *crenelation* means?
6. What are the principal parts of *miscue?*
7. Give three meanings of the transitive verb *miss,* and quote from the dictionary a sentence illustrating each of those meanings.
8. Under what circumstances would you use the word *foredone,* if you use it at all?
9. What is the meaning of *character* in computer technology?
10. Give eight synonyms for the verb *change.*
11. How is *deus ex machina* pronounced? What does it mean?
12. What does *de trop* mean? Would you underscore it in writing?

13. What is *OBulg.?*

14. How does the general meaning of the word *occlude* differ from its meaning in dentistry?

15. What is the derivation of the word *harmony?*

16. How do the following words differ in meaning: *symmetry, balance, proportion, harmony.*

17. What usage label would you assign to the word *like* in such a sentence as, "There was this fellow with his hair all curly *like*"?

18. Under what circumstances might one write *materialise?*

19. When is *matter of fact* hyphenated?

20. What is the preferred pronunciation of *maturation?*

21. Why is a *taxi dancer* so called?

22. Name five idioms that include the word *look.*

23. How would you classify the usage of *count on* in the sentence, "You can *count on* me"?

24. Which spelling is favored: *advisor* or *adviser?*

25. Is *develope* an acceptable alternative spelling of *develop?*

B. List five terms with different connotations roughly synonymous with each of the words below.

1. walk (v.)
2. angry (adj.)
3. smart ["not dumb"] (adj.)
4. shop (n.)
5. house (n.)

C. What do the etymologies of the words in each of the following groups have in common?

1. fuselage, cabaret, automobile, personnel, hangar
2. linoleum, dictaphone, escalator, nylon, realtor
3. loganberry, nicotine, shrapnel, half nelson, guppy
4. worsted, milliner, sardine, billingsgate, mackinaw
5. apron, adder, umpire, nickname, newt

D. Look up the italicized usages in your dictionary; then report what you learn about their acceptance. Are there any instances in which you find the dictionary not helpful? Any in which you find yourself in disagreement with the dictionary?

1. The *admittance* of guilt by the innocent is a psychological phenomenon.

2. Anthony Burgess has just *authored* a new novel.

3. *Hopefully* the weather will improve by the weekend.
4. The manager did a satisfactory job performance-*wise.*
5. When he came late, his *alibi* was that the train broke down.
6. The *graffito* on the building walls is appalling.
7. On the boat trip, Jim was *nauseous* and had to lie down.
8. The general said he would soon *finalize* the plans for the training exercise.
9. After the way I acted, I couldn't blame Helen for being *mad* at me.
10. The *kidnap* cost the victim's family over a hundred thousand dollars.

E. Substitute exact words for those that are vague or unsuited to the sense.

1. I like the course mainly because of its total basis on nature.
2. The Italians' sense of history is one reason why so many pieces of Roman architecture are still standing.
3. The future of a team is one of the most important aspects coaches and managers must look upon.
4. Chicago has libraries, museums, theaters, and a downtown shopping district. These things are not offered by a small town.
5. In the weeks that followed, the situation within the camp began to falter seriously.
6. The pagans were given to worshiping statues.
7. The money that would be spent to control the traffic-free zone would be exorbitant, and often the task would just cause congestion elsewhere.
8. With a finished script and a tentative budget, the would-be producer is now ready to accrue funds for the picture.
9. Instead of doting on my failures, I genuinely wanted to engage in some constructive activities.
10. If the transit workers receive the demands they have made, the fare will most likely go up.

F. Put more concisely the thoughts in the following sentences.

1. In a recent game, rooky Eddy Green of the Kansas City Chiefs tackled a larger opponent through the use of a head-on collision.
2. I'll never forget my trip to Jamaica as long as I live.
3. The dean said Tom's record was in the process of being reviewed.

4. The tenants refused to pay the rent until the vermin were entirely eliminated.

5. My friend's house is in close proximity to the beach.

6. A device is to be installed for the purpose of sealing the envelopes as they are stamped.

7. I will briefly list the functions of the President's Council of Economic Advisers in a very basic way.

8. My experience with Mr. Doherty has been of a very favorable nature.

9. They said that, according to their files, they do not have any record of my application.

10. Another broad facet of influence upon our economy is the area of interest rates.

G. Rewrite the following statements in more specific and vivid language. Take only one sentence for each statement.

EXAMPLE

The audience greeted her noisily.

When she got up to speak, a peculiar rustling sound flew up from the audience as the women lifted their programs to the light, like hundreds of wings. [Adapted from CYNTHIA OZICK's "We Are the Crazy Lady."]

1. Traffic down Main Street was especially heavy.
2. The plane trip was uneventful.
3. New Year's Eve can be very lonely.
4. Lights shone in the downtown office windows.
5. The music in the discotheque was, to say the least, loud.

H. Comment on the effectiveness of the language in the following passages, especially with respect to vividness and appropriate word choice. Call attention to the use of metaphor wherever you find it.

1. The Hughes flat was one floor up a bedraggled staircase, past a pram in the hall and a bicycle. It was so small that everything seemed sideways on. You inserted yourself into a hallway so narrow and jammed that you could scarcely take off your coat.—A. ALVAREZ

2. A marvy year for Marshall McLuhan, take it all in all; Tom Wolfe compared him with Darwin, Freud, and Einstein; Susan Sontag said in public she thought he was swell.—BENJAMIN DEMOTT

3. It is at precisely this point, adolescence, when the rush of energies, that sea-sex gravitation, the thrust of the ego up through layers of childhood, makes itself felt, that the person is more like an infant, is swept once more by energies that are tidal, unfamiliar, and unyielding.—PETER MARIN

4. Of course the festival of rain cannot be stopped, even in the city. The woman from the delicatessen scampers along the sidewalk with a newspaper over her head. The streets, suddenly washed, became transparent and alive, and the noise of the traffic becomes a plashing of fountains.—THOMAS MERTON

5. The ocean is becoming rough; the waves come in slowly, tugging strength from far back. The moment before they somersault, the moment when they arch their backs so beautifully, showing white veins in the green and black, that moment is intolerable. They finally crack, dashing fiercely upon the sand, actually driving, full force downward against it, bouncing upward and forward, and at last petering out into a small stream of bubbles which slides up the beach and then is recalled.—DELMORE SCHWARTZ

6. The Londoner believes in nature and greenery, loves to walk under trees or lie in the parks with his arms round his girl to the scandal of the puritanic foreigners, who see miles of park treated as a public bedroom and think the cult of nature carried too far.—V. S. PRITCHETT

7. As to our promo on the album, the point with Patti [Smith] is: As much as we put out, she'll put out for us, and that's a great feeling, you really have to have it. That means we can take her out to a city like Philly and do a little day of radio-and-press combined tour, and when they meet her, they'll like her. Any time you have a little hook other than the little piece of vinyl, it really helps.—MICHAEL J. KLENFER [Adapted from a reported telephone conversation]

8. These perfectly straight cities bear no trace of organization. Many of them have the rudimentary structure of a polypary. Los Angeles, in particular, is rather like a big earthworm that might be chopped into twenty pieces without being killed.—JEAN PAUL SARTRE

9. If Miss [Janis] Joplin had made some sort of investment in reclaiming herself, we might have a moment or two in which to dam up some sympathy for her—but the bottle or the pill was always in her mouth, or the needle in her arm. Very few people want to see anybody die, but the drug zeitgeist has overdrawn its account. Some of us are tired of being asked to see Greek tragedy in what is simply infantilism. Our own psychic economies cannot afford the unlimited

extension of credit demanded of us by the philosophical panhandlers of the age.—ANATOLE BROYARD

10. We are going to look at our problems quite differently than we do now. There will be a coordinated comprehensive continuation of development of the child in appreciation of the subconsciously coordinate design of humans not forcing them into a prolonged focus, yet accomplishing with automated tools and instruments far greater probing than was accomplished by the utter specialist while conserving the comprehensive comprehension of the significance to society of the increasing flow of discovered data.—R. BUCKMINSTER FULLER

23 Sentence Sense

ss

See that the idea of the sentence comes through to the reader clearly and coherently.

23a. Clarity

Compose sentences so that they say precisely what you mean—no less, no more.

(1) Some sentences are vague, that is, too general for the thought to be completely realized. Thus one might be inclined to write,

A feature of the room was the radio

and let it go at that. A writer more concerned about communicating the idea accurately might say,

The den's one adornment was a ten-tube home-assembled battery radio set with a loudspeaker in the shape of a Mexican sombrero.

Also at fault are ambiguous statements, those that can be interpreted in more than one way. A bank that has changed its name tells customers:

Please continue to use your old checks until exhausted.

A customer with a sense of humor replies, "I've used one old check and I'm already completely exhausted." The facetious response could not have been made if the bank's message had read:

Please continue to use your old checks until the supply is exhausted.

In still other sentences the meaning is so obscure that the reader gets no meaning at all. How, for example, would you interpret:

I hoped there would be no untoward incident that would prevent a recurrence of this kind in the future.

Could the writer have meant:

I hoped that things would run more smoothly in the future.

(2) Just as there is no single fault that makes for lack of clarity, so there is no single cure If you can identify the error, however, the remedy may suggest itself. Vague sentences lack specific details and concrete language. Ambiguous sentences are often attributable to poor punctuation, misuse of a word, omission of a word, or incorrect word order. Obscure sentences may be the result of some small carelessness, but very likely they need a rethinking of what you want to say and a complete recasting of the statement. Since the most common errors contributing to lack of clarity are described elsewhere in this "Handbook of English," you may find the following index helpful:

Faulty reference of pronoun	**Rule 7**
Misreading	**Rule 11e**
Inexact word	**Rule 22e**
Confused sentence structure	**Rule 23b**
Misplaced sentence element	**Rule 25**
Dangling modifier	**Rule 26**
Faulty omission	**Rule 28**

23b. Confused Structure; Faulty Logic

Avoid sentences that join incompatible phrases or clauses, or make statements that are logically untenable. (For mixed figures of speech, see **Rule** 22g(3) note.)

CONFUSED: When I saw I had the power to show the children they had a place in society made me feel wanted.

IMPROVED: When I saw I had the power to show the children they had a place in society, I felt wanted.

CONFUSED: I was brought up with the idea that being Italian was just about the greatest nationality.

IMPROVED: I was brought up with the idea that Italian was just about the greatest nationality.

ILLOGICAL: Veterinarian schools have high standards because there are only seventeen of them in the United States. [The number of schools has nothing to do with their standards.]

ILLOGICAL: As anyone can tell from my accent, I was born in Lausanne, Switzerland, and was brought to this country when I was twelve years old. [One could not reasonably be expected to tell from the accent in what city the writer was born, nor that he was brought to this country at the age of twelve.]

IMPROVED: My accent is the mark of my national origin. I was born in Lausanne. . . .

23c. Awkwardness; Excessive Predication

Avoid using a subordinate clause when a single word or phrase would help produce a simpler, clearer sentence. Some phrases may likewise be reduced to simple one- or two-word modifiers. Awkwardness in any form may be corrected by recasting the sentence.

AWKWARD: Tachina is a sesame paste *which is very spicy.* [Clause]
IMPROVED: Tachina is a *very spicy* sesame paste. [Phrase]

AWKWARD: He said he would draft a plan *which was appropriate to his client's needs.* [Clause]
IMPROVED: He said he would draft a plan *appropriate to his client's needs.* [Phrase]

AWKWARD: *It is apparent/that it is quite feasible* to prepare the reports on the computer. [Two clauses]
IMPROVED: *It seems quite feasible* to prepare the reports on the computer. [One clause]

AWKWARD: Their South African mines are believed to be very *desirable from a profit standpoint.* [Redundant phrase.]
IMPROVED: The South African mines are believed to be very *profitable.* [Single word]

AWKWARD: I have found the students, as far as I can detect, to be warm and responsive to any questions about their courses in an everyday conversation. [Confusing arrangement; wordy]
IMPROVED: In my conversations with them, I have found students to be responsive to any questions about their courses. [Better arrangement; concise]

EXERCISES

A. Rewrite the following statements so that they say more clearly what you think was intended.

1. Two short rest periods were provided each day so that the tired employees could be eliminated.

2. My estate shall be divided equally between my brother and my wife's three sisters.

3. Otto Lindstrom. Piano and accordian instruction. All other instruments taught by experts. Telephone 090-0100.

4. The Senator was not controversial mainly because he raised the Communist issue and blamed the loss of China on the liberals.

5. I know the jeweler to be completely reliable, and I am sure you can deal with him in confidence.

B. Recast each of the following sentences in more specific terms. Invent any reasonable details, using more than one sentence if you wish.

1. Ours was a small but nice hotel situated on the water.

2. The garden was full of flowers.

3. Although the stockroom work was hard, I enjoyed the several breaks we got each day.

4. The first scene of the movie was set in an ordinary city street.

5. Any day's newspaper provides a microcosm of life.

C. Recast the following statements so that the thoughts are expressed more clearly and coherently.

1. City life has been described from a fantastic living experience to a rat race.

2. To think that there were no differences in the various places in the world would be a disaster.

3. My interest in law came not so much as an original chosen field as it did from many mistreatments at the hands of people who practiced it.

4. The management's point of view is taken from an economic background.

5. As a city resident for many years, I have seen good neighborhoods turned into a dumping ground for garbage and criminal assaults on citizens.

D. Simplify the following sentences by reducing the predication.

1. Anyone who is bright and has at least a twelfth-grade education can perform the work which is required.

2. One feature which this lathe possesses and which makes it very desirable is that it is easy to operate.

3. Cigarettes may cause your eyes to water and become red because the smoke is so irritating.

4. The result of the bill would be a more orderly procedure for handling citizen's grievances, which is always a prime concern of government.

5. The urban university student gets a chance to meet a cross-section of many different ethnic groups, which helps him to understand their problems and their customs.

24 Unity

un

Preserve the unity of the sentence.

A sentence should preferably have but one main idea, and all its parts should be closely related. Unrelated matter or an excess of detail should be avoided.

24a. Separating Unrelated Ideas

When a sentence has two or more ideas that are not closely related, put the ideas in separate sentences.

NOT: The company makes furniture,/and I worked in the shipping room for four weeks last summer.

BUT: The company makes furniture. I worked in the shipping room for four weeks last summer.

NOT: The ranger's name was Bill,/and he told us that the rangers had raised the bear as a cub.

BUT: The ranger's name was Bill. He told us that the rangers had raised the bear as a cub.

24b. Subordination

Adjust sentence structure to distinguish main from subordinate ideas, to limit the use of *and,* and to avoid short, choppy sentences.

(1) To avoid giving coordinate status to ideas unequal in importance, subordinate the minor elements. Conjunctions like *because, although,* and *which* are usually more accurate than *and* in showing the relative importance of ideas. Parenthetic elements and modifying phrases may also be used for ideas of subordinate rank.

COORDINATION: The company does an import and export business,/and Elwood Crane is the treasurer.

SUBORDINATION: The company, *of which Elwood Crane is the treasurer,* does an import and export business.

OR (EMPHASIS SHIFTED): Elwood Crane is the treasurer of the company, *which does an import and export business.*

ALSO (TWO SENTENCES): The company does an import and export business. Elwood Crane is the treasurer.

COØRDINATION: I was the only one up at the time,/and I fidgeted around my room/and finally decided to work on my term report.

SUBORDINATION: *Since I was the only one up at the time,* I fidgeted around my room *until I decided to work on my term report.*

COORDINATION: My uncle is a salesman by profession/and took charge of the church bazaar.

SUBORDINATION: My uncle, *a salesman by profession,* took charge of the church bazaar.

COORDINATION: The World Trade Center consists of two 100-story towers,/and they dominate the skyline of lower Manhattan.

SUBORDINATION: The two 100-story towers of the World Trade Center dominate the skyline of lower Manhattan.

(2) **When several short, choppy sentences occur in sequence, consolidate their details to reduce the number of sentences and establish better connection.**

CHOPPY: The brain is composed of three major levels of tissues. The tissues of these layers are all different. The outermost layer is the cortex. The intermediate layer is the subcortex. The innermost layer is the medulla. This is also the lowest layer.

IMPROVED: The brain is composed of three major levels of tissues, all different. The outermost layer is the cortex, the intermediate is the subcortex, and the innermost and lowest layer is the medulla.

24c. Overdetail

Do not overload a sentence with more details than the reader can conveniently grasp at one time.

To correct the fault, you can apply one or both of these remedies: (1) eliminate small or irrelevant details; (2) create an additional sentence or more to accommodate the details. (See also "Conciseness," **Rule 22h.**)

OVERDETAILED: It may sound like an exaggeration on my part, but I love to observe the greatness of that part of the world which man has left untouched, like the green pastures, trees that in the autumn take on such beautiful colors, the grandeur of the lakes and rivers that provide us with drinking water and transportation, or even the sky upon which the sun by day or the stars at night may be seen, and, in other words, all of the things that make the country my favorite place.

DETAILS REDUCED: I love the country, especially that part untouched by man: green pastures, the gold and green of trees in autumn, the grandeur of our lakes and rivers. I love a clear sky, lit by the sun in the day and the stars at night.

OVERDETAILED: My boss walked into the room and handed out everyone's check, in addition to which we each received a Christmas turkey, and for some reason I got one of the larger ones, which weighed about eighteen or twenty pounds.

DETAILS SEPARATED: My boss walked into the room and handed out everyone's check. In addition, each of us received a Christmas turkey. Mine was one of the larger ones, weighing eighteen or twenty pounds.

EXERCISES

A. Recast the following sentences to give them the unity they now lack. Do not omit any essential details.

1. I am taking French, and Professor Raumier has the most engaging Gallic wit I have ever encountered.
2. Ezra Pound was dissatisfied with America and a reputed Fascist who wrote flaming poetry which attracted young students to Paris.
3. Terry was an earnest student and made the varsity swimming team.
4. Mr. Rogers had an account at our Main Street store for five years and he moved to Seattle last June.
5. I am going to be eighteen in August and my parents promised me that I could drive with Jeff across the country in my own car.

B. Combine into a single unified and coherent sentence the elements in each of the following groups. Do not omit any of the details.

1. LSD can cause prolonged psychotic episodes and suicides. Catastrophic reactions occur infrequently. They cannot, however, be ruled out. The drug has some redeeming features. Its reputation as a highly dangerous drug is unjustified.
2. White had what seemed to his contemporaries superhuman energy. His lifetime spanned less than 53 years. Much of that time was devoted to party-giving and party-going. He also engaged in

travel and amorous dalliance. It is wonderful that he accomplished as much as he did. It is wonderful that he reached so high a level of competence. He even rose, on occasion, to the level of genius.

3. I cherished his letters to me. They were even more frequent than our talks. He loved correspondence. He always preferred the written word to the telephone.

4. Sometimes a tree looks peckish. It is no longer a sturdy member of its company. It is chosen for cutting. It falls with a distinctively hollow thump. It is far gone in corruption. It is worth no more work.

5. Down the hall is the Captain's bedroom. He and Henna slept upon this prow-shaped bed. They were to conceive over thirty-seven children. Thirty-four of them were to perish in infancy. They died as the result of swamp fox, wrist blight, and the sting of the barfly.

C. Select from the following statements whatever ideas you consider pertinent and organize them into a narrative of several paragraphs. You may also combine several related ideas into single sentences where practicable.[1]

1. John Yates is a restless young man.
2. He possesses a master's degree in business administration from Harvard.
3. He is a crack tennis player.
4. He had become disenchanted with his job.
5. He got the job through an employment agency.
6. He felt the job was leading to a dead end.
7. He gave his boss appropriate notice that he was leaving.
8. He wanted to find a post with wider horizons.
9. He wrote letters and used the phone and shoe leather.
10. The first lead came within three weeks.
11. The Postal Service is still terribly slow.
12. The Internal Revenue Service offered him a job.
13. The job was conditional on a routine reference check.
14. It is the sort of check you might undergo if you were opening a charge account.
15. There was no news for a week.
16. Yates became anxious.
17. He telephoned.
18. The personnel manager was out at the time.
19. He called again later the same day.

[1] Adapted from Lawrence Stessin, "What Your Ex-Boss Can't Tell Your Next Boss," *New York Times*, 7 December 1975.

20. He used a pay phone.

21. The personnel man was cool.

22. He said, "Your ex-boss said you were something of a character."

23. Yates asked him to repeat that.

24. The personnel man said that his ex-boss thought he was a "character."

25. Yates had no idea he had left his former employer under a cloud.

26. He had occasionally helped his employer with his income taxes.

27. He decided to file a suit in court against his former employer to clear his good name.

25 Order

ord

Put related parts of a sentence close together.

The separation of related sentence elements may cause awkwardness or, worse, confusion and misunderstanding. On the other hand, the order of sentence elements can be regulated to aid coherence and add variety and interest. (See also "Sentence Patterns," **Rule 30d**.)

25a. Position of Subject and Predicate

Avoid unnecessary separation of subject and predicate; bring them as close together as possible.

BAD SEPARATION: *Comments* on the conditions that resulted in the loss of their principal source of bauxite and the consequent necessity of shutting down their Pittsburgh plant *were included in the company's July 1 report.*

IMPROVED: *The company's July 1 report included comments* on the conditions that resulted . . .

BAD SEPARATION: *The recommendation* to engage the services of a caterer, with the cost to be divided between the school's administration and the club treasury, *originated with Bob Murphy.*

IMPROVED: *Bob Murphy originated the recommendation* to engage . . .

25b. Misplaced Modifiers

Avoid separating modifiers from the words they modify.

(1) Put words, phrases, and clauses as close as possible to the words they modify. Many adverbs are preferably placed *before* the words they modify.

MISPLACED ADVERB: I had wasted *already* a whole semester.

IMPROVED: I had *already* wasted a whole semester.

MISPLACED ADVERB: Every detergent is *not* safe for washing delicate woolens.

IMPROVED: *Not* every detergent is safe for washing delicate woolens.

MISPLACED PHRASE: Suddenly the proprietor grabbed a knife used for cutting steaks *from under the counter.*

IMPROVED: Suddenly, *from under counter,* the proprietor grabbed a knife used for cutting steaks.

MISPLACED PHRASE: I received a reply from Dean Hale's secretary, *dated April 18.*

IMPROVED: I received a reply *dated April 18* from Dean Hale's secretary.

MISPLACED CLAUSE: He had a cabin in the Lakes region *that he liked to call his second home.*

IMPROVED: In the Lakes region he had a cabin *that he liked to call his second home.*

(2) Do not separate the parts of a verb or "split" an infinitive if awkwardness results.

AWKWARD: He *had* often when he was in the mood *walked* through the woods to the lake.

IMPROVED: When he was in the mood, he *had* often *walked* through the woods to the lake.

AWKWARD: He asked me *to* promptly *call* him if I thought he could be of help. [Infinitive "split"]

IMPROVED: He asked me *to call* him promptly if I thought he could be of help.

ADMISSIBLE INFINITIVE SPLIT: If you want *to* really *appreciate* his painting, you must study it. [It would be awkward *not* to split the infinitive: "If you want really *to appreciate* . . ." An alternative is to leave out the word *really.*]

(3) Avoid the "squinting" modifier, that is, a word or phrase so placed that it could be taken to relate to either of two sentence elements.

SQUINTING: They sell at retail *only* in Chicago.

CLEAR: They sell *only* at retail in Chicago. [Relates to "at retail"]

OR: They sell at retail in Chicago *only.* [Relates to "Chicago"]

(4) Some phrases modify a whole sentence or clause rather than a particular word. Such phrases are best placed at the beginning of the sentence or clause.

MISPLACED SENTENCE-MODIFIER: I could work near my home, *fortunately*, and avoid the daily trip to the city.

IMPROVED: *Fortunately*, I could work near my home and avoid the daily trip to the city.

MISPLACED CLAUSE-MODIFIER: Jim said that he would see Joan at the Horse Show *in any event*.

IMPROVED: Jim said that, *in any event*, he would see Joan at the Horse Show.

EXERCISE

A. Rearrange the parts of the following sentences so that the sense becomes immediately clear. In instances of ambiguity, choose the meaning you believe the writer intended.

1. If possible, I would enjoy having lunch with you next week.
2. Many newspapers use the services of a news agency to which they pay a modest rate they could not otherwise afford for stories.
3. The major part of what people saw on their screens at a time when the cinema had its strongest hold over the widest audience came from America.
4. I am always refreshed when I come home on weekends by the rustling leaves and the quiet streets.
5. The degree of satisfaction employees gain from operating policies, employee benefits, and working conditions, as well as from our direct concern for their individual rights and privileges is closely related to job performance.
6. I plan to eventually practice law.
7. The most successful movies of the time were adventure stories that did not feature women, such as *The Sting* and *Papillon*.
8. In the construction of the building the contractor was able to effect savings in labor costs of $16,000.
9. He admitted when the fuss was over he would return and sign the contract.
10. The treasurer has passed on your request for credit to me.

26 *dng*
"Dangling" Modifiers

Avoid "dangling" modifiers.

A dangling modifier is one that seems to relate to some word, expressed or unexpressed, other than the word it should.

DANGLER: *Reaching the middle of the street,* the traffic light turned red.

In this sentence, the impression is given that the traffic light reached the middle of the street, a meaning obviously not intended. The error is that the initial phrase, "Reaching the middle of the street," does not logically relate to the subject, "the traffic light," which it modifies.

Dangling phrases can be corrected in three ways:

(1) Leave the dangling phrase alone, but change the rest of the sentence, so that the dangler has a word it can logically relate to.

CORRECT: *Reaching the middle of the street, I* saw the traffic light turn red. [Now the initial phrase modifies a logical subject, *I*.]

(2) Change the dangling modifier into a clause having its own subject and predicate.

CORRECT: *As I reached the middle of the street,* the traffic light turned red.

(3) Recast the sentence entirely.

CORRECT: The red traffic light caught me in the middle of the street.

Modifiers particularly apt to dangle are participial, gerund, and infinitive phrases and elliptical clauses. Danglers usually, but not always, occur at the beginning of a sentence.

26a. Dangling Verbal Phrases

Avoid dangling participial, gerund, and infinitive phrases.

(1) Dangling Participial Phrase

DANGLING: *Having succeeded in identifying the problem, the next step* is to find the possible solutions.
CORRECTED: *Having succeeded in identifying the problem, you* must next find the possible solutions.

DANGLING: I often wander about, *giving me the feeling of peace.*
CORRECTED: Wandering about, as I often do, gives me the feeling of peace.

(2) Dangling Gerund Phrase

DANGLING: After *living in the city awhile, nothing* surprises or offends you.
CORRECTED: After *you have lived in the city awhile,* nothing surprises or offends you.

DANGLING: The need for education does not end after *leaving college.*
CORRECTED: The need for education does not end after *you leave college.*

DANGLING: On *entering the room, it* impresses you with its spaciousness.
CORRECTED: On *entering the room, you* are impressed by its spaciousness.
OR: *When you enter the room,* you are impressed by its spaciousness.
OR: The room is impressive in its spaciousness.

(3) Dangling Infinitive Phrase

DANGLING: *To detect fires, a house* should have a heat-sensitive alarm system.
CORRECTED: A house should have a heat-sensitive alarm *system to detect fires.*

DANGLING: The preliminaries must be won *to qualify for the final match.*
CORRECTED: *You* [OR: *The contestant*] must win the preliminaries *to qualify for the final match.*

26b. Dangling Elliptical Clause

An elliptical, or grammatically abbreviated, clause will dangle if its implied subject is not the same as the subject of the main clause.

DANGLING: *While driving, a tremendous sense of freedom* overtakes me. [The implied subject of "While driving" (elliptical for "While *I am* driving") is not the same as the subject of the main clause.]
CORRECTED: *While driving, I* am overtaken by a tremendous sense of freedom.
OR (BETTER): Driving gives me a tremendous sense of freedom.

DANGLING: *If properly styled, no dressing* is required to keep the hair in place.
CORRECTED: *If properly styled, the hair* requires no dressing to keep it in place.

DANGLING: Vacation travel is cheap and easy *when working for an airline.*
CORRECTED: Vacation travel is cheap and easy *when you work for an airline.*

26c. Exceptions

Usage permits two kinds of phrases that might otherwise be interpreted as dangling. These are the absolute participial phrase (a participial phrase with its own subject), and an idiomatic phrase that relates to the whole sentence.

The last diner having left, the proprietor pulled down the blind and closed for the night. [Absolute phrase]
The little girl walked along the water's edge, *her drenched poodle clutched tight to her chest.* [Absolute phrase]
To tell the truth, no one could have acted the role better. [Idiomatic infinitive phrase]
Strictly speaking, Sara should have taken the prerequisite course first. [Idiomatic participial phrase]

EXERCISE

A. Wherever necessary, recast the following sentences so that the dangling elements are effectively eliminated without any change in the sense intended. If a sentence requires no alteration, leave it alone.

1. Having succeeded in defining the problem, their next step was to focus on the problem of solving it.
2. By moving up the starting time, the operation could be completed by October 1.
3. A pickpocket stole my wallet while pushing my way through the crowd.
4. "We'll be landing soon"—it's good to hear these words from the pilot, knowing that in a matter of minutes one will step into another world.

5. My experience as a strikebreaker started quite innocently by applying for a job at the White Department Store.

6. Based on these findings, I recommend that we support the Student Council in their drive to keep the library open until midnight.

7. To meet the complaints of students, additional snack machines were placed in the lounge.

8. No one having reported the incident, the Dean was naturally unable to take any action.

9. By rearranging the present layout, it could provide more laboratory space.

10. While not opposing the change, certain procedural details must be worked out.

27 Parallel Structure //str

Put parallel ideas in parallel structure.

Parallel structure is the repetition of a grammatical pattern in order to achieve a balance between ideas of the same rank. The parallel grammatical units may be nouns, adjectives, prepositional phrases, infinitives, clauses, or any other sentence elements. They usually appear in a series connected by *and* or some other coordinating conjunction, and may involve some repetition of words as well as of structure. The parallelism not only emphasizes the connection between the parallel ideas, but also prevents awkwardness caused by shifts in sentence structure.

NOT PARALLEL (AWKWARD): *He saw* the house, and *he was impressed* with it, *after which he bought* it.

PARALLEL: *He saw* the house, *he liked* it, and *he bought* it.

27a. Treating Coordinate Elements

Correct violations of parallel structure by changing words and phrases to make them coordinate in structure with other elements of the same sequence.

NOT PARALLEL: The High School of the Air gives the student confined at home the opportunity
of seeing an actual class in progress and [Prepositional phrase]
to participate by mail. [Infinitive phrase]

PARALLEL: The High School of the Air gives the student confined at home the opportunity
|| *to see an actual class in progress* and [Infinitive phrase]
|| *to participate by mail.* [Infinitive phrase]

NOT PARALLEL: *The senior year was hard academically,* [Main clause]
while also being a lot of fun. [Phrase]

PARALLEL: *The senior year was hard academically*, but [Main clause]
it was also a lot of fun. [Main clause]

OR: The senior year was
a hard one academically, but also [Noun phrase]
a lot of fun. [Noun phrase]

NOT PARALLEL: I have already learned
the formulas for designing boxes with the least amount of material [Noun followed by prepositional phrase]
ways to compute the height of the Empire State Building, and [Noun followed by infinitive phrase]
how to measure the time it would take for a person to hit the ground after falling off the Statue of Liberty. [Adverb followed by infinitive phrase]

PARALLEL: I have already learned the formulas for
designing boxes . . . , [Gerund]
computing the height . . . , and [Gerund]
measuring the time. . . . [Gerund]

27b. Correlatives

When you use correlative conjunctions (not only . . . but also; both . . . and; either . . . or), be sure that the elements that follow them are parallel in thought and structure.

NOT PARALLEL: I was torn *both* by the desire to go
and to stay home.

PARALLEL: I was torn by *both* the desire to go
and the desire to stay home.

NOT PARALLEL: Roy *neither* enjoyed driving on packed highways,
nor breathing the contaminated air.

PARALLEL: Roy enjoyed *neither* driving on packed highways,
nor breathing the contaminated air.

27c. Repetition of Article, Preposition, Etc.

Repeat an article, preposition, or other word, when necessary, to establish clearly the connection between the parallel sentence elements.

CONFUSING: The Council voted funds *for the purchase of the park site and legal expenses.*

BETTER: The Council voted funds *for the purchase* of the park site and *for legal expenses.*

AMBIGUOUS: I spoke to *the owner and manager.* [Are the owner and manager the same person?]
CLEAR: I spoke to *the owner* and *the manager.* [The owner and manager are different persons.]

AMBIGUOUS: It will be necessary for *you to have your mother sign* the affidavit *and return* it to Mr. Clark. [Who is to return the affidavit?]
CLEAR: It will be necessary for *you to have your mother sign* the affidavit *and to return* it to Mr. Clark. [In this version, it is indicated that *you* are to return the affidavit.]

27d. "And Which," "And Who"

Do not begin a clause "and which" or "and who" unless you are connecting it to a preceding "which" or "who" clause. To correct the error, either eliminate the "and" or reconstruct the sentence to provide proper linkage.

MISTAKEN PARALLELISM: Steve Gray was a young man with a whimsical sense of humor *and who always made a pleasant companion.*
BETTER: Steve Gray was a young man with a whimsical sense of humor, *who always made a pleasant companion.*

MISTAKEN PARALLELISM: She is sure to succeed as a singer, with her warm personality, splendid voice, *and which she has spent many years training.*
BETTER: She is sure to succeed as a singer, with her warm personality and pleasant voice, *which she has spent many years training.* [The two parallel adjective phrases are joined by *and,* and the *which* clause, without the *and,* is made subordinate to *voice.*]
OR: Her voice, *which she has cultivated for many years and which she combines with a warm personality,* assures her eventual success as a singer. [The two *which* clauses are parallel and can therefore be joined by *and.*]

27e. Parallelism Misused

Do not put into parallel structure ideas that are not coordinate or compatible in thought.

PARALLELISM MISUSED: As a child, I was taught by *my mother, my grandparents,* and *a healthy curiosity* about everything around me. ["Curiosity" is not coordinate in thought with "mother" and "grandparents," and should not be in the same series.]

BETTER: As a child, I was taught by my mother and my grandparents. I was also helped by a natural curiosity about everything around me. [The last idea is put in an independent statement.]

PARALLELISM MISUSED: We had no criminal class, no crooks as you know them in the big city, no cranks, no anarchists, *no elaborate structure of the law.* [The italicized phrase is not coordinate in thought with the other elements in the series and should not be included in the parallelism.]

BETTER: We had no criminal class, no crooks as you know them in the big city, no cranks, no anarchists—so we did not require an elaborate structure of law.—JOYCE CARY [A second main clause is used to show the effect of the conditions mentioned in the parallel series preceding the dash.]

EXERCISES

A. All of the following sentences have faults in parallel structure or faults that parallel structure can correct. Recast the sentences for consistency of phrasing or compatibility of thought.

1. I had to cancel my trip when my father was stricken with appendicitis, necessitating an operation.
2. Knowing what the teacher wants is better than to guess.
3. I was told either to see the Dean or his secretary.
4. There is a Chinese folk saying that the best of all possible worlds is Chinese cooking, marrying a Japanese wife, and a home in America.
5. For several decades conservationists have been interested in recycling garbage, sewage, and to reclaim trash, as the Chinese have been doing for about five thousand years.
6. Members of the "privacy lobby" are warning that the child-support program could turn into a nightmare, force disclosure of irrelevant information buried in government files, lead to violations of the confidentiality between husband and wife, and encouraging local officials to poke into the records for their own purposes.
7. In general, the American author was perceived abroad as an essayist, versifier, storyteller, and who was also a narrative historian.
8. The huge antennas were not only required for long-range radar, but also trans-horizon communications, telemetry tracking, and to provide other early-warning alert applications.

9. In those dark days, ersatz bread and potatoes were the staple foods, when they were available.

10. What I wanted to know was a way to figure the velocity of a projectile and how does the rate differ at high and low altitudes.

B. Some elements in the following sentences seem to be parallel in structure when they are not. Correct the mistaken parallelism wherever it occurs.

1. English is a required course in every primary, secondary, and most higher schools.

2. Jean bought a blouse, skirt, shoes, and only tried on an expensive fur coat.

3. I liked walking my dog along the beach, sniffing at the waves washing ashore, chasing the seagulls, and puffing with the excitement of it all.

4. The choice open to him was either to take a job after school or cutting down on his expenses.

5. The main objectives of a candidate are, first, to secure the nomination and, second, win the election.

6. Bromley was either very clever or he had some lucky breaks.

7. Juan excelled not in Spanish, as his parents had expected, but economics.

8. Irma was just naturally attracted to men of means or who were adept in the art of flattery.

9. He knew what the stakes were and the consequences of failure.

10. I enjoyed the day in the country, the chance to breathe some fresh air, and do some deep thinking.

28 Faulty Omissions ‸

Do not leave out words essential to the meaning or grammatical completeness of the sentence.

Words are sometimes left out through sheer carelessness; such errors will be found if the manuscript is painstakingly read before it is submitted. But words are also left out when the writer is too casual in expression or otherwise fails to pay enough attention to sense, logic, or grammar. These omissions can be detected and remedied only through analysis of the structure of the sentence.

28a. Words Needed for Clarity

Do not omit an article, adjective, or other word necessary to prevent misreading or otherwise to convey the desired sense. (See also Rule 27c.)

UNCLEAR: Mr. Rhodes asked his wife and‸mother to accompany him.
CLEAR: Mr. Rhodes asked his wife and *his* [OR: *her*] mother to accompany him.

UNCLEAR: He knew‸the boy from up the street was a friend of his son. [Possible misreading]
BETTER: He knew *that* the boy from up the street was a friend of his son.

UNCLEAR: I failed to realize the lack of campus life and‸student cohesion at the university.
BETTER: I failed to realize the lack of campus life and *of* student cohesion at the university.

28b. Incomplete Comparison

Do not leave out words needed to complete a comparison or to complete the sense of an intensive adverb.

(1) Omission in Comparison

FAULTY: Compton is *one of the best*^, *if not the best, tackle* I have seen. [The plural *tackles* is needed to complete the first part of the comparison.]

BETTER: Compton is one of the best tackles, if not the best tackle, I have seen.

FAULTY: I liked the play *as much*^, *if not more than,* Dorothy. [*As much* must be completed by *as,* not *than.*]

BETTER: I like the play *as much as Dorothy, if not more.* [The words "than Dorothy" are understood at the end of the sentence; such an omission, called an *ellipsis,* is grammatically correct.]

FAULTY: The *Washington Posts's* reputation for quality rivals^the *New York Times.* [Here *reputation* is illogically compared with *New York Times.* What should be compared is the "reputation" of one paper with the "reputation" of the other.]

BETTER: The *Washington Post's* reputation for quality rivals *that* of the *New York Times.*

(2) Omission After Intensive Adverb

FAULTY: The concert was *so exciting*^.

BETTER: The concert was *so exciting that the audience was moved to cheers.*

FAULTY: Minkoff was *such a good pianist*^.

BETTER: Minkoff was *such a good pianist that he almost overcame the handicap of his arthritic hand.*

NOTE: Use of the intensive adverb without a completing phrase or clause is often acceptable in informal speech and writing. In other usage the need to complete an intensive adverb can be avoided simply by not using the intensive word; for example, "The concert was *exciting,*" not "*so* exciting."

28c. Idiomatic Preposition

Do not omit the preposition in an idiomatic phrase requiring it.

FAULTY: We recognized her *interest*^and *talent for graphic expression.* [The word *interest* needs its own preposition.]

BETTER: We recognized her *interest in* and *talent for graphic expression.*

OR: We recognized her *interest in graphic expression* and her *talent for it.*

FAULTY: The new rules *add*^not *detract from* the game.

BETTER: The new rules *add to,* not *detract from,* the game.

FAULTY: Of all the places I have gone^, my favorite is Nova Scotia.
BETTER: Of all the places I have gone *to,* my favorite is Nova Scotia.

FAULTY: ^June I will get my diploma.
BETTER: *In* June I will get my diploma.

NOTE: In informal usage, expressions like "I will see you Wednesday," instead of "I will see you *on* Wednesday," are acceptable.

28d. Verb or Part of a Verb

Do not leave out a verb or part of a verb necessary for the grammar of the sentence.

FAULTY: One *tree was* oak and the *others*^maple.
BETTER: One *tree was* oak and the *others were* maple. [The sentence has a singular and a plural subject, requiring a singular and a plural verb respectively.]

FAULTY: Dougherty never *has*^and never *will be elected* to office.
BETTER: Dougherty never *has been* and never *will be elected* to office.

FAULTY: The *tables were ordered* on January 12, and the *shipment*^ *received* on February 2.
BETTER: The *tables were ordered* on January 12, and the *shipment was received* on February 12.

EXERCISE

A. Supply the missing words in the following sentences, or remedy the omissions by rephrasing.

1. Of all the places I have been, I think I like my home town best.
2. I believe the customer is not telling the entire truth.
3. Orlon is one of the softest, if not the softest, synthetic fiber available.
4. One bedroom was painted light blue and the others decorated with flowered wallpaper.
5. His love and devotion to liberty are well known.
6. The company claimed that over a hundred thousand entries were received in the contest and fourteen hundred prizes were distributed.

7. The old model is as good, if not better than, the new.

8. Christmastime, he traditionally goes to Sun Valley for the skiing.

9. In the package from our parents, we found a broken and unbroken phonograph record.

10. He's such a surgeon!

29 Point of View

PV

Do not, without good reason, change the point of view.

Changes in point of view include changes in person, number, and tense. Such changes violate consistency and may produce awkwardness and confusion. (Incongruous changes in diction are treated in **Rule 22f**(4), and those in figures of speech in **Rule 22g**(3) note.)

29a. Subject, Person, Number

Do not unthinkingly switch from one grammatical subject to another or make other changes in person or number.

FAULTY: When *the accused* comes into court, *you* register at the desk and wait *your* turn.

IMPROVED: When *the accused* comes into court, *he* registers at the desk and waits *his* turn.

FAULTY: *I* read the book and *it* was very good.

IMPROVED: *I* read the book and [*I*] found it very good.

FAULTY: If *one* considers the alternatives, *they* will choose the less disagreeable.

IMPROVED: If *one* considers the alternatives, *he* will choose the less disagreeable.

OR: Anyone who considers the alternatives will choose the less disagreeable.

FAULTY: The *group gathers* in the park every Sunday, where *they play* stickball. [The verb *gathers* treats the collective noun *group* as singular, but *they* treats it as plural.]

IMPROVED: The *group gather* every Sunday in the park, where *they play* stickball. [*Group* is now treated as plural in both parts of the sentence. Treating it as singular—"where *it* plays stickball"—would create awkwardness.]

29b. Tense, Mood, Voice

Do not unthinkingly make changes in tense, voice, or mood; do not change a direct to an indirect question.

FAULTY: I *walked* along the path to the lake, and then I *see* the fallen tree. [Shift from past tense to present tense]
IMPROVED: I *walked* along the path to the lake, and then I *saw* the fallen tree.

FAULTY: Little Ira *went up* to the stage and *was given* his certificate of merit by the principal. [Shift from active voice to passive voice]
IMPROVED: Little Ira *went up* to the stage and *received* his certificate of merit from the principal.

FAULTY: His recipe for success was simple: *work* hard and *you should* always be kind to your mother. [Shift from imperative mood to subjunctive mood]
IMPROVED: His recipe for success was simple: *work* hard and always *be* kind to your mother.

FAULTY: He was asked *whether he was* qualified for the job and *would he take* orders gracefully. [Shift from indirect to direct question]
IMPROVED: He was asked *whether he was* qualified for the job and *whether he would take* orders gracefully.

29c. Perspective

Do not carelessly change the perspective. To correct the fault, recast the passage so that you either keep the same perspective throughout or provide a suitable transition.

FAULTY: Planes eat up the vast distances from Sydney to Perth and Melbourne to Cairns, and as you travel along the northeast coast of Queensland, you can see the Great Barrier Reef through portholes in undersea observatories. [Abrupt shift from air view to undersea view]
IMPROVED: Planes eat up the vast distances from Sydney to Perth and Melbourne to Cairns, where the Great Barrier Reef provides one of the most magnificent tourist attractions in the world. [Single perspective maintained]
OR: Planes eat up the vast distances from Sydney to Perth and Melbourne to the northeast coast of Queensland. *Alighting in Cairns*, you can see the Great Barrier Reef through portholes in undersea laboratories. [Perspective changed after suitable transition]

EXERCISE

A. Correct any inconsistencies in point of view:

1. It's amazing how much a worker can produce when they are offered an incentive.

2. The procedure is intended to help the children think for themselves, so that the child does not become overdependent on the teacher.

3. When you examine the chair closely, the workmanship is very good.

4. I wondered how many times I would have to retype the page and will they ever come out the way I want them.

5. Postage due is collected from the addressee by the mailman, and he turns it over to the Post Office.

6. I would take the same route from school every day and bought a hot dog from the vendor at the corner of Main and South.

7. From far out in the bay, you can see the wall formed by the New York skyline, and behind it the tangle of traffic in the maze of small, narrow streets.

8. Since the instructor doesn't check up on his students' work except through examinations, the responsibility to get the work done is entirely yours.

9. When Paul reached the terminal, he tries to find a skycap, but they are nowhere to be found.

10. Anyone who would drive in reverse gear without looking behind them should have their license revoked.

30 *emph*
Emphasis and Variety

Structure sentences to put emphasis where it is needed and to achieve variety and interest.

Just as a speaker can use voice and gesture to hold his audience and make his point, so the writer can use the rhetorical framework of the sentence for the same purposes. He can shorten or lengthen sentences, change from one sentence arrangement to another, repeat key words, and in other ways maintain the reader's interest and give force to important words and ideas.

Emphasis is aided not only by the methods explained here, but also by other means, as, for example, the choice of words **Rules 22g** and **22h**), sentence unity (**Rule 24**), and parallel structure (**Rule 27**).

30a. Sentence Length

Vary the length of sentences for variety and force.

(1) Sentences should never be so consistently short as to be monotonous, nor so consistently long as to be tedious. Rather, a composition should have a good mix of short and long sentences.

Average sentence length has tended to decline over the years, but a rough average of 20 to 25 words per sentence is common in nontechnical material prepared for college-educated readers. This average can be obtained with occasional sentences of perhaps thirty or forty words if other sentences are kept to half that number or less.

The sentence that follows is too long and cumbersome:

The title of the final version of the Declaration of Independence described the document as "the unanimous Declaration of the thirteen united [small *u*] States of America," but nowhere does the word nation appear and there was no one capital city against which the British could aim a mortal blow, which helps to explain why, during the first five years of the War for Independence, British troops occupied every one of the most populous towns (Boston, New York, Philadelphia, and Charleston) without decisive effect on the war's outcome.

Below is the same passage as it was originally written. It is far easier to read and to follow. Only slightly different in arrangement from the sentence above, it consists of four sentences of 11, 22, 15, and 33 words respectively—an average of 20 words per sentence.

Nowhere in the Declaration of Independence does the word nation appear. The title of the final version described the document as "the unanimous Declaration of the thirteen united [small *u*] States of America." There was no one capital city against which the British could aim a mortal blow. During the first five years of the War for Independence, British troops occupied every one of the most populous towns (Boston, New York, Philadelphia and Charleston) without decisive effect on the war's outcome. —DANIEL J. BOORSTIN[1]

(2) A series of short, simple sentences is usually to be avoided, especially if they are choppy or sound childish. Try to combine related ideas into single sentences, and vary both the length and structure of the sentences.

MONOTONOUS: The crash came. Asheville was one of the hardest-hit towns in the country. My father and hundreds of others were left with boxes full of worthless deeds. The mayor was unable to face the hopeless indebtedness of the city. He therefore killed himself. The population now is still less than 60,000 despite the expansion of the city limits. I left Asheville in 1959. There was virtually no major construction. The old and historic buildings had been preserved, however. The owners didn't really appreciate the past. They were just too timid about investing in change.

INTERESTING: When the crash came, Asheville was one of the hardest-hit towns in the country. My father and hundreds of others were left with boxes full of worthless deeds. The mayor, unable to face the hopeless indebtedness of the city, killed himself. The population now is still less than 60,000 despite the expansion of the city limits. Until about 1959, when I left Asheville, there was virtually no major construction. The old and historic buildings had been preserved more because of the owners' timidity about investing in change than out of appreciation of the past.—PERRY DEANE YOUNG[2]

(3) A short sentence following one or more long ones is useful for

[1] "America: Our Byproduct Nation," *Time*, 23 June 1975, p. 66.

[2] "Goodbye, Asheville," *Harper's*, March 1975, p. 63.

achieving emphasis through a change of pace. The following paragraph concludes an article on the work of comedians. The last brief sentence embodies the key idea.

Burlesque and vaudeville, the historic breeding grounds of comedians, have disappeared, but there's no need to worry about where our next generation of comedians is going to come from, or whether the supply will run so low as to bring about a laughter crisis. Society will continue to hone new comedians unless it ever reaches the point where everybody is happy and fulfilled and secure, and children grow up without seeing anyone who is greedy or pompous or despotic or mean or malicious or hostile. *Only then will the comedian vanish from our midst.*—CARL REINER[3]

The very short sentence in the middle of the following paragraph is useful in focusing attention on the key idea.

Students have been complaining about depersonalization for decades, of being subjected to poor or indifferent teaching for centuries. Now, however, the institutions themselves (which used to seem somehow impenetrable) are in trouble. *A sense of crisis prevails.* College presidents realize that the quality of the education they provide depends to a large extent on the money they have, that no money means no students, and vice versa. College faculty worry about their job security and the dropping academic standards of each incoming class.—KATHERINE BARRETT[4]

30b. Beginning and End

Begin and end sentences with important words.

(1) Be sparing in the use of the expletives *it* and *there* (sometimes also called "anticipatory subjects") in such expressions as "*it* is," "*there* is," and "*there* were," at the beginning of sentences. Connecting words and phrases like *however, therefore,* and *in other words* are also usually better placed within the sentence than at the beginning.

WEAK: *There are* a number of advantages to the new class schedule.
IMPROVED: The new class schedule has a number of advantages.

WEAK: The weak respect power more than the strong, who know its limitations. *However,* the crucial factor is domestic opinion.
IMPROVED: The weak respect power more than the strong, who know its

[3] "Let's Put Another Laugh in Here . . . ," *Travel & Leisure,* March 1974, p. 7. [Italics ours]

[4] "College: Sis-Boom-Bah-Humbug," *Harper's,* October 1975, p. 3. [Italics ours]

limitations. The crucial factor, *however*, is domestic opinion.—MILES IGNOTUS

WEAK: *For instance*, in Philadelphia the Centennial celebration did not need any fabricated reason for its existence.
IMPROVED: In Philadelphia, *for instance*, the Centennial celebration did not need any fabricated reason for its existence.

WEAK: *He said that*, far from dragging his feet, he considered himself a trail-blazer.
IMPROVED: Far from dragging his feet, *he said*, he considered himself a trail-blazer.

NOTE: This rule is to be applied with discretion. Sometimes you will find that an expletive at the beginning does not contribute to weakness, and sometimes a connecting phrase must be placed at the beginning either because it would be awkward in some other place or because it would not elsewhere so effectively establish the connection or provide the emphasis intended.

It is the President, not the Congress, that is now complaining about the usurpation of power.
There is a frown these days on the "grinning birds" of Pacific Southwest Airlines.—ROBERT LINDSEY
In short, if the use of military force is to be limited and therefore efficient, the real leverage [on the price of oil] must come from market pressures.—MILES IGNOTUS
Ricardo did not think that this state of affairs was desirable, only inevitable. *Nonetheless*, he and Malthus earned for capitalist economics a name that it has never shaken.—TIME

(2) Avoid a weak anticlimactic phrase at the end of a sentence.

WEAK: Nature is profligate, *above all*.
BETTER: Nature is, *above all*, profligate.—ANNIE DILLARD

WEAK: He will do the right thing, *I know*.
BETTER: *I know* he will do the right thing.

WEAK: The great innovator is self-interest, *in Smith's view*.
BETTER: *In Smith's view*, the great innovator is self-interest.

30c. Varying the Type of Statement

For variety and emphasis, change from declarative statements—the conventional sentence type—to a question, a command, or an exclamation.

QUESTION: Grant's failures? I know how much I am running against the tide of current historical opinion when I use such terms. Yet what other name can we give to the campaign of 1864?—D. W. BROGAN

QUESTION: Will I eventually change my mind and work for a doctorate? I think I'd like to get closer to my undergraduate degree before I make that decision.

EXCLAMATION: One expects such a gap between popular culture and personal taste. But such a gap! As an artist, Forsythe simply obeyed her instincts.

EXCLAMATION: Then and there I experienced a flash known as the Aha! phenomenon, and the buried life of contemporary art was revealed to me for the first time! The fog lifted! The cloud passed! The motes, the scales, the conjunctival bloodshots, and Murine agonies fell away!—TOM WOLFE

COMMAND: I'll tell you how to get through college. Just go to class and do your work. I don't know any student who has done that and failed.

COMMAND: The magic word, the same in English and Vietnamese, was *sponsor.* Find a sponsor and be saved; get free access to the Great PX. —LISTON POPE, JR.

30d. Varying Sentence Patterns

Avoid repeating the same sentence pattern to the point of monotony. Change the pattern to achieve variety and emphasis.

A sentence can be constructed in a number of different ways. The following description of some useful sentence patterns will suggest the choice you have.

(1) Loose and Periodic Sentences

A loose sentence is one that can be stopped at some point other than the end and still make sense. A periodic sentence is one that cannot, without loss of sense, be stopped anywhere but the end. (The two preceding sentences illustrate the type of structure they define.) Loose sentences are, as a rule, more natural than periodic sentences, but an occasional periodic sentence is a useful stimulant.

LOOSE: They were in Los Angeles to record an album/ and prepare for a twenty-four day tour to the States,/ their first appearance in this country in more than five years. [The sentence can be stopped at either of the points shown by the slant.]

PERIODIC: Very ill at ease with his liberalism, Mill was one of the first to recognize what was involved when the free self, an essentially romantic image, entered into relations with society.—WYLIE SYPHER [The sentence cannot be stopped at any point except the end without loss of sense.]

(2) Active or Passive Voice

A sentence (or clause) in the active voice makes the subject the performer of the action of the verb. A sentence in the passive voice makes the subject the receiver.

ACTIVE: *I hit* the ball.
PASSIVE: *The ball was hit* by me.

Sentences in the active voice are smoother, more direct, and more emphatic than those in the passive voice. They are usually predominant. However, the passive voice can also be useful, as the last two examples below demonstrate. (See also pp. 213–14.)

ACTIVE: In 1920, American women won the right to vote. [This is stronger than the passive, "In 1920, the right to vote was won by American women."]
ACTIVE: The parents complained about the problems in disciplining their children. [This is stronger than the passive "The problems in disciplining their children were complained about by their parents."]
PASSIVE: English was learned more quickly by the men and children than by the women.—OSCAR LEWIS [Emphasis on the grammatical subject *English*]
PASSIVE: The house was built by the Talcotts, after whom the town was named.—EDMUND WILSON [The alternative construction, "The Talcotts, after whom the town was named, built the house," puts the main clause in the active voice, but it is awkward and misplaces the emphasis.]

(3) Inverted Order

Any change from the normal order of words in the sentence will result in emphasis.

NORMAL: He stood there, and I stood there.
INVERTED: *There he stood,* and *there stood I.*

NORMAL: Home and housework are not for me.
INVERTED: *Not for me* are home and housework.

NORMAL: You become older, but not wiser.
INVERTED: *Older you become,* but not wiser.

(4) Balance

Emphasis is achieved by the pairing of contrasting ideas in parallel fashion. The balanced elements should have about the same length and rhythm.

I knew that I should never write as well as I could, but I thought with pains I could arrive at writing as well as my natural defects allowed. —SOMERSET MAUGHAM

Our dilemma, then, is not an absence of leaders, but a paucity of values that might sustain leaders; not a failure of leadership, but a failure of followship. —BENJAMIN BARBER

(5) Climactic Order

A sentence or series of sentences is arranged climactically when the units that compose it follow the order of increasing importance or emphasis. A letdown at the end is an "anticlimax," a device sometimes used to produce a humorous effect.

In the following paragraph, Emlyn Williams starts to describe his boyhood impressions of D. W. Griffith's film *Intolerance.* The first sentence is matter-of-fact, but the other two, separately and together, build up increasing force.

The film was as bold as the title. Four stories forged ahead like horses drawing a chariot; with the cradle the focus moved mesmerically from one to another, to and fro, till the tempo mounted in four crescendos to a triumphant dénouement. The old hypnosis crept up to my head; the Quay, my family, school, my secret thoughts, everything dissolved away and the only reality was my two eyes fixed on the flickering screen.[5]

In a later passage Williams acts out the fantasies aroused by his seeing the film. Note the effect of the anticlimactic last phrase.

Many an evening, a wanderer in Rubbishland might have been astonished to see a schoolboy, a book under his arm, leap to the battlement top of a grass-grown dump. The Chaldean air thick with smoke, out of the blood-red sunset advances the locust army, arrows whistle; just as he aims he is mortally struck, in a close-up. The face twitches, empties of expression, the knees give, the Mountain Boy rolls down the slope to oblivion, scrambles up, brushes himself off, picks up his Algebra and walks home to fish and chips.[6]

[5] *George: An Early Autobiography* (New York: Random House, 1961), pp. 174–75.
[6] Ibid., p. 176.

30e. Repetition

Repeat a word or phrase to achieve emphasis.

If the injustice is part of the necessary friction of the machine of government, *let it go, let it go:* perchance it will wear smooth. . . .—HENRY DAVID THOREAU

We are told that art is now *under attack.* Of course, it has often been *under attack.*—IRIS MURDOCH

Quantitative *change,* no matter how overwhelming, never completely invalidates philosophical and moral principles. Moreover, *change* brings with it the means of adjusting to *change.*—HENRY A. GRUNWALD

Do not, intentionally or not, repeat a word that should *not* be emphasized. Instead, find a suitable synonym.

INEFFECTIVE: The *smoke* from the burning leaves soon *smoked out* the squirrels from their hiding place in the tree.

IMPROVED: The *smoke* from the burning leaves soon *routed* the squirrels from their hiding place in the tree.

EXERCISES

A. The long sentences below tend to obscure the author's ideas. Break them up into smaller units that convey the sense more effectively.[7]

1. Covering the permafrost is an "active layer" which thaws slightly in summer, permitting a thin growth of mosses and other spongy vegetation and which, if removed or seriously damaged, would expose the permafrost to the degree that it would melt excessively, resulting in harmful erosion, but by using vehicles with special tracks, winter construction crews will be able to move lightly over the frozen tundra without greatly disturbing the protective insulation.

2. On the generally flat terrain of the North Slope, bears have difficulty finding suitable holes for dens, so when grizzlies find a comfortable home, they hang on to it for generations, and to make sure that bears will not be unduly disturbed by construction, research teams mapped every den along the right-of-way, enabling work crews to bypass these areas wherever possible.

[7] The sentences in this exercise have been adapted from Norman Kenyon, "Answer in the Wilderness," *Venture,* Spring 1975, pp. 2–5.

3. Until the studies were made, it had been assumed that Arctic rivers froze to the bottom and contained no fish in winter and for this reason a pipeline could be laid through the ice without harm, but the research revealed that some streams have small open areas in winter caused by warm mineral springs.

4. When certain fish congregate here, exposure to dissolved gases in the water causes their eyes to bulge, as in cross-bred goldfish, and as a result of the various fish studies, the pipeline will skirt all stream areas where construction might alter the balance of nature.

B. The sentences in the following passages have been deliberately chopped up into very small units. Recast the passages to provide a pleasant variety in the length and structure of sentences.[8]

1. (1) Americans do not admit their newspapers are a scandal. (2) They assure one another that their newspaper press is one of their signal distinctions. (3) They do not admit that in literature they have as yet produced little that is important. (4) They play at treating literature as if it were an independent power. (5) They reform the spelling of the English language. (6) In so doing, they are guided by the insight of the average man. (7) They have an American writer to match every English writer. (8) The Western States at this moment have a native author named Roe. (9) They are being nourished and formed on his novels. (10) They ignore Scott and Dickens.

2. (1) The born lover of ideas and of light could be found in England. (2) He could not but believe that the sky over his head is of brass and iron. (3) So I once declared. (4) I make the same comment about America. (5) One can find there the person who craves for the interesting in civilization. (6) This person requires from what surrounds him satisfaction for his sense of beauty. (7) He must have the same satisfaction for his sense for elevation. (8) He, too, will feel the sky above him to be of brass and iron. (9) The human problem is as yet solved most imperfectly in America. A great void exists in the civilization over there. (11) There is a want of what is elevated and beautiful. (12) There is a want of what is interesting.

3. (1) I have been quoting some stout champions of brag. (2) They belong to the old Eastern States. (3) The new West promises to beat even them. (4) The other day there was sent to me a California

[8] Adapted from Matthew Arnold, *Civilization in the United States: First and Last Impressions* (Boston: Cupples and Hard, 1888).

newspaper. (5) It calls all Easterners "the unhappy denizens of a forbidding clime." (6) It adds, "The time will surely come when all roads lead to California. (7) Here will be the home of art, science, literature, and profound knowledge." (8) I repeat. (9) This is hollow stuff. (10) There is next to no common-sense criticism of that hollow stuff in America. (11) There are plenty of cultivated individuals there. (12) They are also judicious and delightful. (13) They are our hope. (14) They are America's hope. (15) Improvement must come through their means.

C. Revise each of the following sentences in order to improve a weak beginning or ending.

1. There are several ways in which you can deal with a stubborn cold.
2. The Mayor will come around to our point of view, I am sure.
3. It is a generous donor who supplies funds for the program.
4. In response to your request, we are enclosing our latest stamp catalog.
5. Any man, if he is willing to risk death, can become a racing driver.
6. The President climbed the steps to the dais unsmiling.
7. For his decision to manufacture the company's telephone equipment, Vail had a strong managerial reason also.
8. On the whole, attempts to treat science in the mass media have failed.
9. Truth is the basis of all fiction, I believe.
10. After all, maybe the magic of the movies has not been lost, but only transformed into a more viable extension of the television age.

D. Write the paragraphs described below, using in each a variety of sentence types, such as declarative, interrogative, imperative, exclamatory.

1. Your feelings about Christmas
2. The climax of a hard day at school or work
3. Your anticipation of an event to come—a trip, a date, a social gathering

E. Refer to the following examples in the text, and comment on the ways in which each writer has achieved variety and interest. Relate your analysis especially to the methods discussed in this section (Rule 30).

1. The passage beginning, "A long fourth of July weekend," by Jonathan Schwartz, p. 69.
2. The May 7, 1944 entry in the diary of Anne Frank, pp. 73–74
3. The passage on rock climbing, by Nancy Lyons, pp. 91–92.

F. On topics related to college life, as you know it, write five sentences as follows:

1. A loose sentence
2. A periodic sentence
3. A balanced sentence
4. A sentence illustrating the use of climax
5. A sentence utilizing repetition for emphasis

G. Wherever you find the passive voice in the following sentences, change the construction to the active voice. Do you think that the revised sentence is an improvement over the original in each instance? If not, why?

1. Concentrated preparation for musical performances should be tempered with physical conditioning.
2. The night before, the car had been placed by Laura in the garage.
3. The real flowering of his career was delayed until he went to art school in the early fifties under the G.I. bill.
4. If you are patient, the gift can be wrapped very prettily in decorative paper and a satin ribbon by the salesperson.
5. George is known by most of his intimates to have come from somewhere in Florida.
6. An enormous burden has been removed from that country's balance of payments by her newly achieved self-sufficiency in oil.
7. Such critical esteem has been won by only a small handful of books in the last quarter-century.
8. Here and there the lone gray shacks on the cliff could be seen by us from the beach.
9. The Greek boy harbored the hope that he would be helped to get a visa by his uncle who lived in Danbury now.
10. A major program of industrial reconstruction was announced by the Wilson government in November.

H. Invert the order in the following sentences to gain emphasis.

1. The soldier went boldly, but not fearlessly, about the business of disarming the bomb.
2. The chef was a towering man, even without his starched white hat.
3. That evening the worst of the storm came.
4. He got an insult in return for his kindness.
5. Carroll did not budge an inch as he felt the lash.

31 Paragraphs

par

See that every paragraph has a central idea, coherently developed and closely connected to the related paragraphs in the composition. Indent the first line of each paragraph uniformly about a half inch (five spaces on the typewriter).

31a. Paragraph Length

Pay heed to the length of paragraphs.

Paragraphs consist of a number of related sentences. In a modern work they average perhaps ten or twelve typewritten lines (about 125 words), with some paragraphs consisting of fifteen lines or more and others of several lines or less.

In determining the length of paragraphs, the writer must balance the requirements of content against the need for reading ease. Relatively long paragraphs are needed for description, explanation, and reasoning—in fact, any type of deliberative writing requiring much detail. Short paragraphs are most useful in swift narrative, dialogue, and lists and enumerations. They are also used occasionally to mark a major transition, to emphasize a point, or simply to provide variety. A short paragraph is often desirable at the beginning of a theme—for interest—and at the end—for emphasis. In newspapers, with their narrow columns, the number of words to the paragraph is considerably less than in a book or periodical, in which lines run across the whole width of the page. Paragraphs also run to fewer words in popular magazines than they do in the "intellectual" magazines and professional journals, where the material treated is more detailed or technical, and the audience expects greater demands on its attention.

31b. Paragraph Unity

All the material in a paragraph should relate to a central idea. The first essential of a good paragraph is that it deal with a single facet of your subject. This facet, the central idea of the paragraph, is often expressed in a single sentence, called the *topic sentence.* When everything in the paragraph relates to the central idea, unity of content is achieved. Extraneous ideas should be diligently excluded.

NOTE: In its true sense, unity in the paragraph is a matter not only of relevance of content, but of consistency of style and point of view as well. The principles of consistency given for sentences (**Rule 29**) thus apply also to the paragraph as a whole. See also "Tone and Style," pp. 49–54.

(1) The Topic Sentence

Customarily, the topic sentence begins the paragraph, but occasionally it is found inside the paragraph or at the end. When a paragraph has no topic sentence, the central idea should be clearly implied.

The following paragraph begins with the topic sentence.

> The trouble with many industry-college conferences is that so little gets said. The very nature of such occasions, with their emphases on "communication" and agreement, leads the participants to devote themselves largely to the common denominators that everyone agrees on. This makes for good feeling, but the net effect is to suppress the real issues. The businessman and the educator may both agree that, say, general education is a good thing and yet have totally differing concepts of what they want. Such debate is in bad odor; the differences are not aired and everyone goes his way with the problem untouched.—WILLIAM H. WHITE JR.[1]

You will note that the idea of the topic sentence is echoed in the last clause, "the differences are not aired and everyone goes away with the problem untouched." Although such a conclusion is not essential, it reinforces the main point and helps to make the paragraph the tightly contained unit it is.

Below is another example of a paragraph with the topic sentence at the beginning and the supporting details following.

> The life-style of FBI agents is usually in keeping with their image as solid citizens. They tend to buy their own homes, preferably in the distant, newly developed suburbs, and to send their children to public or parochial schools. Except in cities like Miami, where the norm is different, they

[1] *The Organization Man* (New York: Simon & Schuster, 1956), p. 107.

generally dress conservatively, notwithstanding the repeal of Hoover's old white-shirt-and-black-shoes rules. Their hair is still relatively short, and anyone who starts growing a moustache will likely be teased as a "hippie" for a while before he is ultimately accepted. There are only a few rebels here, who, in contrast to the many in the military, feel tempted to make themselves test cases by growing beards. (It remains the official Bureau view that a beard and other manifestations of nonconformity are outside the average citizen's reasonable expectations of an FBI agent. But it is not absolutely forbidden, and there are probably about a dozen bearded agents these days—in many cases because of special undercover assignments.) —SANFORD J. UNGER[2]

When the thoughts in a paragraph move from the specific to the general, the normal position of the topic sentence is at the end.

Visit now the human city. Observe the elevator operators, workers with electric drills, accountants, cashiers, teachers, salesmen, actors preachers, policemen. What marks them? What happens in their lives? They, too, eat and move about. And they do something more. They live on and off the labor and achievements of the dead and the contemporary. They can gather and use the experiences of the past for their work in the present. They can accumulate. They can begin where others left off. They can learn from the agony and sweat of those who have gone before. They can produce artificially because others produced the instruments. Here, then, is a unique ingredient—the manipulation of what happens in time. Men can draw from the PAST, in and through the PRESENT, and make ready for the FUTURE. The experience of the race can be accumulated, worked over, magnified, and transmitted. This *time-binding capacity* marks the peculiar and characteristic feature of man.—IRVING J. LEE[3]

In the next example, the topic sentence is found in the middle, forming a bridge between the material before and after. At the same time, the more specific first and last sentences of the paragraph complement each other and form a fitting introduction and conclusion. Again, unity is well served.

Technique is hardly worth talking about unless it's used for something worth doing: that's why most of the theorizing about the new art of television commercials is such nonsense. The effects are impersonal—dexterous, sometimes clever, but empty of art. It's because of their emptiness that commercials call so much attention to their camera angles and

[2] "G-Men—1975 Style," *Atlantic*, October 1975, p. 67.

[3] *Language Habits in Human Affairs* (New York: Harper & Bros., 1941), pp. 3–4.

quick cutting—which is why people get impressed by "the art" of it. Movies are now often made in terms of what television viewers have learned to settle for. Despite a great deal that is spoken and written about young people responding visually, the influence of TV is to make movies visually less imaginative and complex. Television is a very noisy medium and viewers listen, while getting used to a poor quality of visual reproduction, to the absence of visual detail, to visual obviousness and overemphasis on simple compositions, and to atrociously simplified and distorted color systems. The shifting camera styles, the movement, and the fast cutting of a film like *Finian's Rainbow*—one of the better big productions—are like the "visuals" of TV commercials, a disguise for static material, expressive of nothing so much as the need to keep you from getting bored and leaving. Men are now beginning their careers as directors by working on commercials—which, if one cares to speculate on it, may be almost a one-sentence résumé of the future of American motion pictures.—PAULINE KAEL[4]

(2) Multi-paragraph Units

Although one paragraph ought not to elaborate on more than one point, it does not follow that every point must be introduced and concluded within the limits of one paragraph. In fact, considerations of interest and paragraph length often require that one thought be carried over to two or more paragraphs. In such instances, the several paragraphs may be served by a single topic sentence. The following passage provides an illustration of this point. The first paragraph begins with the topic sentence; however, the thought expressed in that sentence is not adequately concluded until the end of the third paragraph. The reference in the first sentence is to Princeton.

This quiet leafy New Jersey town, continuously troubled by the sound of bells, still keeps a sense of its past. In Nassau Hall the Continental Congress sat in threatened assembly, and behind the second hand furniture shops of Witherspoon Street are the graves of a half dozen Signers. All but the most indifferent students are aware that a barren acre of cornland to the east of the town is the battlefield of Princeton. It is the privilege of certain towns to mumble over their past. Edinburgh, for example, wears its age proudly and obviously; little of London, except to the bearers of Baedekers, seems older than the Crystal Palace or the Albert Memorial.

Princeton is older than the rocks upon which it sits, perhaps because it needs but four years to establish a precedent in antiquity, so that, since the middle of the eighteenth century, forty generations of youth, each with its stiff customs and cries of revolt, have passed through the town on their way to middle age and mediocrity.

[4] "Trash, Art, and the Movies," *Harper's*, February 1969, p. 68.

Tom D'Invilliers, the poetic feeder to the epigrammatic hero of *This Side of Paradise,* was aware of this when, with Amory Blaine, he crossed the campus on their last night before leaving for the war: "What we leave is more than this one class; it's the whole heritage of youth. We're just one generation—we are breaking all the links that seemed to bind us to top-booted and high-socked generations. We've walked arm and arm with Burr and Light Horse Harry Lee through half these deep blue nights."
—JOHN PEALE BISHOP[5]

31c. Paragraph Development

Flesh out your paragraphs with relevant details, illustrations, discussion, and the like.

Without adequate support, generalizations use up ideas very quickly and lead to underdevelopment of your subject. Clarity, interest, and persuasiveness suffer. Every good topic statement suggests the possibilities for development. Consider the following methods.

(1) Definition

When a vital term is named, it may be useful or necessary to define it so that the reader will have a proper appreciation of its significance. The definition, which may well extend over a paragraph or more, selects from or combines a number of forms. It may give the intrinsic meaning of the term, the etymology of the term, or the history of the concept it represents; or it may be an "operational definition," one that tells how the thing named is used. The definition that follows embodies all of these treatments.

The word *bankruptcy* has a nasty ring. It is derived from a practice in Italy in the Middle Ages. Back in those days, if an artisan was unable to pay for his leather or copper or silver or whatever it was he used in his craft, the creditors would break his workbench. He then became a man with a ruptured *banco,* or a bankrupt.

Today, bankruptcy is more civilized. If an artisan were to go bankrupt in the United States, he would in all probability be permitted to keep his workbench intact, as well as the other tools of his trade. However, he would have to turn over his money, securities, or other property of value to the court. The Italian creditors of the Middle Ages were seeking revenge against deadbeat artisans, but the thrust of the administration of bank-

[5] From "Princeton," in *The Collected Essays of John Peale Bishop* (New York: Scribner, 1948), pp. 391–92.

ruptcy now is more toward rehabilitation. Bankruptcy today makes it possible for people whose debts are overwhelming to wipe them out and start over.[6]

The paragraph below is interesting not only for its attention to the term defined, including the writer's subjective reaction to it, but also for the contrast it establishes with a synonymous term. The contrast helps to sharpen our understanding of the principal work under examination. The paragraph follows a description of the author's exhilarating experience in negotiating, in a kayak, the rapids of the Roaring Fork River in the Rockies.

All this has to do with feeling feral. Now feral is a word which makes me think of Teddy Roosevelt and Nietzsche and Sabu. But also Rimbaud and Rousseau (the painter) and the early Rolling Stones. To be feral is to exist in a natural state, as an animal or a plant; to revert from domestication to a wild state. To feel feral, one need not roar. One can be very shy and quiet, or whimsical like the dancer Twyla Tharp or the poet Gary Snyder. It is not the same thing as virility. Among athletes, football players do not seem feral to me, but basketball players do. Among entertainers, Bette Midler does not seem feral but Stevie Wonder does. The distinction lies in a quality of spontaneity and grace: to what extent does the performer seem to be in touch with his actual body and soul?—RICHARD GOLDSTEIN[7]

(2) Details

Important to the support of a paragraph's central idea is the use of specific details. The details may be facts and figures, historical background, particulars regarding the composition, construction, operation, or uses of an object, or any other specifics that relate to the subject under discussion.

This paragraph, dealing with poverty in New York City, uses facts and figures.

With all the emphasis on minority groups, it should not be forgotten that the absolute number of white families (other than Puerto Ricans) with low incomes is also substantial. In 1959, almost 200,000 (63 percent) of the 317,000 families with incomes under $3,000 were white. Of course, the great majority of families in the city in 1960 were white (88 percent). By 1969, the share was somewhat smaller. Nevertheless, it appears that over two-fifths of the impoverished families in the city today are white, while

[6] Sidney Rutberg, "Breaking the Banco," *Harper's*, November 1973, p. 89.

[7] "Adventure in an Age of Austerity," *New York* Magazine, 1 April 1974, p. 51.

roughly one-third are black and perhaps about one-fourth are Puerto Ricans.[8]

Historical details are the substance of this next paragraph.

Knowledge of the optical principle of the *camera obscura* can be traced back to Aristotle; its use as an aid to drawing, to Giovanni Battista della Porta. The photographic camera derives directly from the *camera obscura*, which was originally, as its Latin name implies, a dark room, with a small hole in the wall or window-shutter through which an inverted image of the view outside is projected on the opposite wall or a white screen. In southern climates where people darken their rooms in hot weather, this phenomenon may well have been noticed even before its underlying principle was described by Aristotle. He observed the crescent shape of a partially eclipsed sun projected on the ground through the holes of a sieve and the gaps between the leaves of a plane tree. He also noticed that the smaller the hole, the sharper the image.—HELMUT GERNSHEIN[9]

The details in the following paragraph consist of both instructions and their rationale.

The question of watering a lawn is full of complications, and "if's" and "and's." In very hot, dry areas of the country, watering is essential to keep the grass alive as a lawn—a situation which leads me to wonder why one even tries to have a lawn under such circumstances. Whenever grass is watered it must always be done very thoroughly and regularly. Once watering is begun, the grass roots rise near the surface to take advantage of the extra supply, and if it is withdrawn, say, when you go on holiday, the roots are by then too shallow to search for the deep-lying moisture; as a result, the grass will die. Sprinkling the lawn for half an hour in the evening may make you feel cool, but it is an open invitation to crabgrass, which loves slightly damp soil but does not flourish so well or move so quickly into deeply watered grass. New or weak lawns that were reseeded in the spring need regular watering all summer, for the roots have not yet gone deep enough to survive the heat. New or weak lawns that are reseeded in the fall may get safely through the next hot summer in a New England-like climate, even if watering is never started, for roots established during the late fall weather will run deep enough to search out whatever ground water is available. It's the on-and-off, inadequate sprinkling that does

[8] From *Profile of a City*, prepared by the members of the Economics Department of the First National City Bank of New York (New York: McGraw-Hill, 1972), pp. 24–25.

[9] *A Concise History of Photography* (New York: Grosset & Dunlap, 1965), p. 10.

the damage, and it is better never to start than to do a poor job of watering.—THALASSA CRUSO[10]

(3) Example

The central idea of the paragraph may be developed through the use of example or illustration. The example can be useful in demonstrating an operation or process, or in reinforcing an assertion or argument. The several paragraphs below provide a concrete example of the workings of bankruptcy procedure. They immediately follow the definition of bankruptcy quoted on pages 462–63 from the same article.

For example, take this typical case of personal bankruptcy (cases of corporate bankruptcy are handled somewhat differently):

A young secretary earning $7,000 a year opened charge accounts at various stores convenient for lunch-hour shopping. Though her bills were mounting, she took out a bank loan to pay for her summer vacation. Then, when her widowed mother died, she had to get a loan from a finance company to pay for the funeral. After several sleepless nights, she finally admitted to herself that she'd never in this world be able to pay everybody back—and she filed for bankruptcy.

There was one hearing before a bankruptcy referee. None of her creditors showed up (maintaining a fund for bad debts is less expensive for them than getting involved in court battles), so all she had to do was answer a few brief questions and pay $350 to her attorney and $50 as a filing fee.

The substance of her testimony before the referee was that she had no money or property, and she walked out of the proceedings with a bankruptcy discharge which barred her prebankruptcy creditors from legally enforcing their claims against her.[11]

In the following paragraph, a specific example is cited to support the contention that the Federal Trade Commission takes years to prosecute a case.

These cases are extreme examples of poor staff work, but they also illustrate what can result from time lags. And delay, unfortunately, is a way of life at the Commission, built into even the smoothest-run deceptive-practices case. One typical case provides an illustration. On April 4, 1962, the FTC field office in Chicago began to investigate the Vollrath Company of Sheboygan, Wisconsin, for "making false savings claims and misrepresent-

[10] *Making Things Grow Outdoors* (New York: Knopf, 1971), p. 116.

[11] Rutberg, loc. cit.

ing the construction, efficacy, and other features of stainless-steel cookware it sells." Among other things, the company advertised that its "Vacumatic cookware would prevent certain diseases and satisfy hunger with less food because of the retention of vitamins and mineral content." *Four years* later, on July 20, 1966, the case was given to the Bureau of Deceptive Practices for prosecution. Yet another year passed before a hearing examiner made the initial decision in the case, and still another year before the Commission made its final decision.—EDWARD F. COX, ROBERT C. FELLMETH, AND JOHN E. SCHULZ[12]

The example in the next paragraph uses specific facts and figures to provide convincing evidence of the initial assertion.

The strength of steel components is one of the factors that recommends the material for use in very large installations. For example, the U.S. General Services Administration warehouse for office supplies and furniture, located in Duluth, Ga., contains 1,064,144 sq. ft.—or an area larger than 20 football fields. Another extremely large building belongs to J. Ray McDermott & Co., Inc., at Morgan City, La. The building is 800 × 400 ft. and rises 80 ft. to the eaves to contain about 25.6 million cu. ft. The space is necessary for the construction of such equipment as offshore oil drilling rigs.[13]

(4) Analysis

Like the whole theme, a single paragraph can be developed through analysis—the division of the subject into its components, which are named and explained or described. Sometimes this procedure involves a comparison or contrast of two or more kinds or classes.

In the paragraph below, the reasons for the exclusion of Negroes from certain types of employment in the early part of this century are enumerated and explained.

Several factors combined to keep Negroes out of industry and trade—especially the skilled and semiskilled jobs. First, most employers were simply disposed against hiring Negroes so long as an adequate supply of white labor was available—and with open immigration from Europe there was seldom a labor shortage. These employers feared that their white employees would object to working with Negroes, and many believed that Negro workers were less efficient. Secondly, many Negroes with skills had

[12] *Nader's Raiders: Report on the Federal Trade Commission* (New York: Grove Press, 1969), p. 72.

[13] *Steel Facts,* Summer 1973, p. 7.

acquired them in the South and were often unable to meet Northern standards. Moreover, they were seldom able to acquire skills in the North: apprentice programs were usually open to whites only, and Negroes had little desire to learn a trade so long as its job prospects remained uncertain. Finally, the refusal of most trade unions to admit black workers on an equal basis kept Negroes out of many trades. Some unions completely excluded Negroes through clauses in their constitutions; others admitted Negroes, but then either segregated them in separate, subordinate locals, excluded them from specific projects, or simply made no effort to find jobs for them.—ALLEN H. SPEAR[14]

The following paragraph, by Ernest Hemingway, names three common traits of the Spaniards and treats each in turn.

If the people of Spain have one common trait it is pride and if they have another it is common sense and if they have a third it is impracticality. Because they have pride they do not mind killing; feeling that they are worthy to give this gift. As they have common sense they are interested in death and do not spend their lives avoiding the thought of it and hoping it does not exist only to discover it when they come to die. This common sense that they possess is as hard and dry as the plains and mesas of Castille and it diminishes in hardness and dryness as it goes away from Castille. At its best it is combined with a complete impracticality. In the south it becomes picturesque; along the littoral it becomes mannerless and Mediterranean; in the north in Navarra and Aragon there is such a tradition of bravery that it becomes romantic, and along the Atlantic coast, as in all countries bounded by a cold sea, life is so practical there is no time for common sense. Death, to people who fish in the cold parts of the Atlantic ocean, is something that may come at any time, that comes often and is to be avoided as an industrial accident; so that they are not preoccupied with it and it has no fascination for them.[15]

In the next selection, not only are whales classified, but the two kinds are also compared and contrasted.

As most of us have learned at some time, there are two kinds—those with teeth and those with a sievelike arrangement of baleen, or whalebone, in their mouths which enables them to strain small organisms from the water. The baleen whales, of which there are ten species, constitute the suborder Mysticeti of the order Cetacea, and the toothed whales constitute the

[14] *Black Chicago: The Making of a Negro Ghetto, 1890–1920* (University of Chicago Press, 1967), pp. 34–35. [Author's documentation omitted.]

[15] From *Death in the Afternoon* (New York: Charles Scribner's Sons, 1932, 1960), pp. 264–65. Reprinted by permission.

suborder Odontoceti. Toothed and baleen whales evolved separately from different land animals, which took to the sea independently of each other, and they are not believed to be closely related. The baleen whales are the most "whalelike." They make up the large majority of the so-called great whales—the leviathans. The blue whales, which may be a hundred feet long and weigh more than a hundred tons, and all the other huge whales except the sperm are baleen whales. The toothed whales, familiarly represented by the numerous kinds of dolphins and porpoises, are mostly small, the only really large toothed species being the sperm whale. (Moby Dick was, of course, a sperm whale.) Toothed whales make up a large and varied group, which includes the beluga, or white whale; the narwhal, which has a strange, twisted tusk; the friendly little pilot whale; and the killer whale, largest of the dolphins.—FAITH MCNULTY[16]

31d. Order in the Paragraph

Arrange the contents of the paragraph in an orderly and effective way.

If for no other reason than the fact that a paragraph usually consists of a number of statements in a number of sentences, attention must be given to the order in which the units of thought are expressed. A logical and systematic progression helps to make clear the relation between the units and emphasizes the controlling idea. The order a writer chooses for any particular paragraph is determined by the nature of the material and the effect to be achieved. Two or more orders are often used in the same paragraph to complement each other.

(Clues to order in the paragraph are also given in **Rule 31b**, "Paragraph Unity," and **Rule 31c**, "Paragraph Development." In addition, the methods suggested for organizing the paper as a whole (see "Organizing Ideas," pp. 25–28) are in many ways applicable to the individual paragraphs that compose the paper.)

(1) General to Specific

Also called the deductive order, the order of general to specific places the topic sentence—a statement of the central idea of the paragraph—before the supporting particulars. In explanation and argument, this is a common way to organize a paragraph, and often the most satisfactory. The generalization in the paragraph below

[16] "Lord of the Fish," *The New Yorker*, 6 August 1973, p. 40.

comprises the first two sentences; it is followed by a number of specific details, many of them included in a direct quotation.

The executive is very gregarious when he sees some practical utility to the gregariousness. But if he doesn't see that utility, good fellowship bores him to death. One of the most recurring notes in executives' complaints about their work loads is the uselessness of so much of the socializing they have to put up with—whether it is entertaining after hours or human relations during hours. One rather studious executive, who at the time was bucking for a vice-presidency, put it this way: "It is when you get where I am that you see the difference between the 'contributory' and the 'noncontributory' aspects of the job. You've got to endure a tremendous amount of noncontributory labor—this talking back and forth, and meetings, and so on. The emptiness and the frustration of it can be appalling. But you've got to put up with it, there's no mistake about that, and you just hope that you can keep your eye on the contributory phases which put you on the glory road."—WILLIAM H. WHYTE, JR.[17]

The paragraph below also moves from the general to the specific. After an introductory opinion about apple pie, the author provides the supporting details: a little history, some comparison and contrast, some baking instructions, and a description of the end product.

To go beyond prejudice into revolt, let me say that I believe the English have come closer to perfecting the combination of apples and crust than we have. After all, they have had a longer time to practice. Even though apple pie is regarded as an American institution, it was part of English cookery at least two centuries before we took it up. The English version has one crust, usually made of puff paste or rough puff paste, that is placed over cooled, lightly precooked apples, seasoned with butter, sugar and a bit of lemon. The shape is apt to be oval. During baking the crust rises and becomes crisp and dry. And if one obeys the rule, he removes the crust after baking and cuts it in "sippets" or little triangular pieces before serving. One helps oneself to a sippet and some of the apple mixture. No bottom crust, no sog.—JAMES BEARD[18]

(2) Specific to General

The order of specific to general, sometimes called the inductive order, puts the details before the generalization or conclusion obtained from them. This order is useful in engaging the attention of the

[17] *The Organization Man* (New York: Simon & Schuster, 1956), p. 153.

[18] "There's Only *One* Way to Make an Apple Pie," *Travel & Leisure,* September 1975, p. 32.

reader when the details have an intrinsic interest, and in holding in suspense a conclusion that is more effective at the end than at the beginning.

The paragraph that follows might have begun, "One of the worst experiences of my life was working for a choice New York women's magazine." But it does not. Instead, it begins with some very colorful details, and the generalization regarding the quality of the experience is left for the end. The resulting interest, especially at the beginning, is evident.

There was often someone crying in the ladies' room. Sobs or gasps (and sometimes retches) came jerking out of those grim cabinets, while others swiftly swallowed pills, choked, sighed, and recombed their hair—to prolong that moment known as "away from your desk." Due to some spasm of corporate economy, there were no towels of any kind, so we had to dry our hands on thin, dissolving toilet paper. My sense-memory of working at one of New York's choicest women's magazines has always been peeling those wet wisps of paper from my palms and fingers, as the notes of weeping receded down the hallway, while I reluctantly walked back to my office, bracing myself for a fresh burst of violence—plus collective confusion, paranoia, and fatigue. Recently, I admitted to a former colleague that the experience was the only one in my life which seems just as bad in retrospect as it did at the time. "Even worse," she said, in accents of awe.—NORA SAYRE[19]

In the paragraph below, the conclusion is contrary to what the reader might have believed. It gains strength by its position after the supporting facts.

One way to show the dedication of the independent schools to the ideal of equal opportunity is to show what they have been doing for the education of minorities as defined by the Department of Health, Education and Welfare—blacks, Indians, Orientals, and the Hispanic-surnamed. The education of these minorities is often thought to provide a special justification for subsidies in the state sector. If we limit our view to New York City, with its atypical combination of free tuition and open enrollment, there is merit in this assumption; but if we look at the country as a whole, we will see its falsity. In St. Louis, 7 percent of the undergraduates at the University of Missouri are from minorities, but so are 7 percent at "private" Washington University. And "private" St. Louis University outperforms both schools with 10 percent. Johns Hopkins and the University of Maryland enroll about equal proportions, and none of the branches of the University of

[19] *Sixties Going on Seventies* (New York: Arbor House, 1973), p. 199.

Connecticut approaches the minority proportion at Yale. In California, the two principal independent universities, Stanford and Southern California, enroll 15 percent and 18 percent respectively. The University of California overall enrolls 17 percent. The examples could be multiplied, but the conclusion would remain: the independent colleges, with limited resources, have set a standard in the education of minorities rarely equaled by the state sector.—JOHN R. SILBER[20]

(3) Time

The order of time, or the chronological order, places events in the order of their occurrence. It is an order followed in narrative writing, as well as in the description of a process or procedure.

In the following paragraph, film director Raoul Walsh tells an interviewer how, with a broken leg, he got his first job in motion pictures as a rider in D. W. Griffith's *The Clansman.* Interest here is derived not only from the movement of the story and the odd circumstances, but also from the use of direct quotation.

"This fellow walked by," Walsh told me once, explaining the roundabout way he'd got into pictures, "and I had my hat on, you see, so he stopped in front of me and he said, 'Cowboy, do you want a job?' I said, 'Yes.' He said, 'Come on down to the theater at seven o'clock.' Well, I had a cane, so I hobbled down there at seven o'clock, went backstage, and he looked at me. 'Oh, hell!' he says, 'you got to ride a horse—how the hell can you ride a horse with that leg?' So I said, 'Where's the horse?' Well, he told another fellow to bring him out, and I got on a chair and got on the horse—see? Then he says, 'Now, let's see you get on that treadmill out there.' So I got the horse on it and then they told the fellow to start the treadmill slow, and the horse started to go, you know, and I sat on the horse, see. He says, 'All right—' "—PETER BOGDANOVICH[21]

The paragraph below, also in the chronological order, is a continuation of an account of the career of Scott Joplin, the ragtime composer, who was born in Texarkana, Texas, probably in 1868. Note the wealth of detail as the narrative moves forward.

Then, in about 1894, he made a crucial move to Sedalia, Mo. Sedalia was a railhead, and contained one of the biggest red-light districts in Missouri. It also contained the George R. Smith College for Negroes, which had a music department. Joplin enrolled to study composition, counterpoint and ad-

[20] "Paying the Bill for College: The 'Private' Sector and the Public Interest," *Atlantic,* May 1975, p. 34.

[21] "Paul Revere and the Trolley Tracks," *New York* Magazine, 8 April 1974, p. 72.

vanced harmony, supporting himself by playing in the red-light district, especially at the leading club for blacks, the Maple Leaf Club. In 1895, he published two pedestrian popular tunes and then, in 1899, a piece called "Original Rags." He also offered the publisher who issued it a piece which he had named in honor of the Maple Leaf Club. The publisher rejected it, possibly because it posed difficulties for the unskilled pianist. But a piano salesman-cum-music-publisher named John Stark, a white man, heard Joplin play the piece, and he arranged to publish it. "Maple Leaf Rag" swept the nation. It was the first piece of popular music to sell a million copies of sheet music. It gave impetus to the burgeoning ragtime boom, and it made Joplin a celebrity.—JAMES LINCOLN COLLIER[22]

The use of the chronological order in the description of a process is illustrated in this paragraph on the making of gas transmission pipe.

High-quality pipe fabrication begins with the flat sheet steel. On entering the mill production line, it is cleaned of dirt and foreign particles. Ultrasonic measuring devices check for quality and dimensional alignment. Moving along on rollers, the pipe takes shape as it passes the high-pitched whine of milling machines and the crackle of arc welders. Along the way, electronic gauges and quality control devices monitor each phase of production.

The succeeding paragraphs continue the description of the process, including the loading and transportation, and its final destination, where we now pick up additional chronology.

That final destination, after a possible stop at a pipe coating contractor's plant, or a storage yard, will be the job site. The lengths of pipe are welded together into a continuous pipeline placed in a trench, and the earth backfilled. But before the valves are opened for natural gas, the line undergoes a final "hydrostatic" test. It is filled with water under extreme pressure and monitored for up to 24 hours to make doubly sure it can withstand lesser gas pressures.

This test in the field is the last major step in the overall pipeline quality control program which began back at the steel mill, and is designed to eliminate any pipe failures during operation which would be costly to correct.[23]

22 "The Scott Joplin Rag," *The New York Times Magazine*, 21 September 1975, pp. 22, 24.

23 "The Making of Pipe," *Venture*, Summer 1975, pp. 16–17.

(4) Space

The details in descriptive paragraphs involving space are best arranged from a particular vantage point, like the top of a building, a vehicle in motion, or—as in the following paragraph—the boardwalk in Coney Island, New York.

Coney Island is one of the few places in the city from which it is possible to look at the open sea. (The Battery affords a view only of Governors Island, Jersey City, and various landmarks of the harbor.) The Coney Island boardwalk, without its summer crowds, allows one to gaze on the vast expanse of water known as the Lower Bay, through which ships pass as they leave for other ports. To either side, appearing faint and bluish in the distance, are low masses of land—Rockaway Point to the left, Sandy Hook to the right. Between them, where the water meets the sky, is the horizon of the Atlantic Ocean—a flat, genuine horizon. On sunny, windless days at this time of year, old people like to sit in folding chairs on the beach, facing the sun and the sea. At times, the sun is blocked by clouds, or it may pierce through clouds at a point in the distance, making a patch of water dazzle. Ships leaving the harbor are small when they appear on the right, become smaller still as they move away and to the left, and are tiny as they disappear over the horizon.[24]

In this paragraph we are asked to make the boardwalk our vantage point, and from there we are permitted to look at either side of the Lower Bay, then straight ahead to the horizon, back to figures on the beach, and then again to the sky, the sea, and the horizon—the kind of sweep that would be natural to any viewer of the scene.

Spatial order is also observed in the following paragraph, which takes the reader on a walk through historic Philadelphia. Note the order of movement as the narrator directs attention to the points of interest.

Now approach historic Philadelphia on the south side of Market. If you start at the Bellevue Stratford Hotel on Broad Street, take Pine Street east toward the river. Pine is antiques row, and it will ease you down the years with charm and drop you gently into the 1780s. (There are good buys here. Philadelphians all, and not in business for their health, they mean to move their precious merchandise and make room for more.) Turn briefly north on Eighth Street. Note the handsome, formerly Episcopal, now Greek Orthodox church built in 1822. As many before you have, you will wish you lived

[24] "The Talk of the Town," *The New Yorker*, 7 April, 1973, p. 34.

in the Morris House (1786) at 225 South Eighth; it is privately owned. Pennsylvania Hospital at Eighth and Spruce is a quarter of a century older than the country itself, yet manages to have all the up-to-date problems of any other hospital. Behind it is the Sephardic Jewish cemetery in which are buried that other financier of the Revolution, Haym Salomon, and Rebecca Gratz (*Ivanhoe's* medically minded co-heroine).—CHRISTOPHER DAVIS[25]

(5) Importance

When a number of points are to be made, they can be arranged in either ascending or descending order of importance. The points may be advantages, disadvantages, causes, effects, or other kinds of data. In the following passage, the first paragraph is an introduction to the second, and it is in the second paragraph that the announced guidelines are arranged in the order of descending importance (the italics are the author's).

Copywriters have developed, at one time or another, a great variety of rules for deciding whether to reject or retain the ideas they come up with. Basically, they boil down to a set of guidelines something like the following, which comes from Bill Colihan, formerly of Young & Rubicam.

According to Colihan, the first thing to look for is *news*. This is always the most highly motivating kind of copy, and it is also good for attracting attention. If news is not available, then try for *appetite appeal* (or whatever the appropriate term is for the particular product)—that is, make the product seem enticing. When this is not feasible either, try to *relate the product to the society;* show how it fits into our complex world. As a last resort, try building advertising around a *user image*.

Since the italicized points are merely mentioned here and need explanation, a third paragraph is used to define each of the points, following the same order as in the paragraph preceding. Thus we have a logical correspondence of ideas—an essential element in good organization.

These rules for sorting ideas correspond closely to the principles discussed in the preceding chapter. Since news is by definition new and unique, it will attract attention. Making the product seem enticing is a matter of communicating with the audience empathically, or making them feel what it is like to use the product. Relating the product to society is a means of borrowing interest for the copy story and making an empathic communication about

[25] "A Walk Through Historic Philadelphia," *Travel & Leisure*, July 1975, p. 22.

the use of the product. Finally, basing advertising on a user image is an attempt to bring audience identification into play.—Kenneth A. Longman[26]

The paragraph below follows the order of ascending importance, or the order of climax. Note the rising force as the author begins by mentioning the minimal skill in expression needed by the soda jerker and leads the reader, ultimately, to the supreme importance of expression in the very large organization.

If you work as a soda jerker you will, of course, not need much skill in expressing yourself to be effective. If you work on a machine your ability to express yourself will be of little importance. But as soon as you move one step up from the bottom, your effectiveness depends on your ability to reach others through the spoken or the written word. And the further away your job is from manual work, the larger the organization of which you are an employee, the more important it will be that you know how to convey your thoughts in writing or speaking. In the very large organization, whether it is the government, the large business corporation, or the Army, this ability to express oneself is perhaps the most important of all the skills a man can possess.—Peter F. Drucker[27]

(6) Cause and Effect

A paragraph may deal with a particular phenomenon, explaining the cause, or causes, and the effects. Often the causes and effects are dealt with in separate paragraphs.

The emphasis in the following paragraph is on effects.

Irrespective of the nature of the fluoride, the effects from eating contaminated forage are the same—an abnormal calcification of bone and tooth structures termed fluorosis, owing to a large increase in fluoride in these structures. Milk production is also decreased. Animals lose weight, acquire a stiff posture, become lame, and the hair coat becomes rough. Phillips reports that cattle and sheep are the most susceptible to fluoride toxicosis of all farm animals. Swine occupy a second rank, although fluorosis of swine in the United States has not been a major problem. Horses appear to be quite resistant to fluoride poisoning, and authentic cases of fluorosis of horses in the United States are rare. Poultry are probably the most resistant to fluorine of all farm animals and present no problem so far as fluorosis is concerned.—Franklin B. Flower And James V. Feuss.[28]

[26] *Advertising* (New York: McGraw-Hill, 1971), p. 305.

[27] "How to Be an Employee," *Fortune,* May 1952, p. 126.

[28] From "Effects of Air Pollution on the Environment," in *Air Pollution and Industry,* ed. R. D. Ross (New York: Van Nostrand Reinhold, 1972), p. 43.

Causes as well as effects are treated in this next paragraph.

The impact of television on the nominating process was only part of the deeper impact of the new electronic world on politics. Together television, the public opinion poll and the computer began to devastate the traditional political structure. For a century a cluster of institutions—the political machine, the farm organization, the trade union, the ethnic federation, the trade association, the chamber of commerce—had mediated between the politician and the voter, interceding for each on behalf of the other and providing the links that held the party system together. The electronic age was severing these links. Television presented the politician directly to the voter; public opinion polls presented the voter directly to the politicians. The political brokers began to lose their jobs, and the mediating agencies, in so far as they had political functions, were confronted by obsolescence.—ARTHUR SCHLESINGER, JR.[29]

31e. Connection

Provide smooth transition between ideas within and between paragraphs. Use a connective of some sort whenever necessary.

In many instances, no special effort is needed to connect ideas because their sequence makes the connection apparent. In other instances, however, some connecting device must be used to take the reader smoothly from one unit of thought to another and to show clearly the relation between them.

Except for the *and* in the last sentence of the following paragraph, the need for connection is minimal because one idea leads naturally to the next.

We are driving through tight, turbulent Roman streets, swept along by a surging surf of automobiles. The sound of horns is as persistent as the shrill chatter of a cricket-crowded garden, mounting at times to a chorus of angry screams. The tranquillity is gone, *la dolca vita* is choked by the exhaust fumes, and the sweet music of the language is dimmed by the roar of the new times filling the narrow streets from wall to wall.—MILTON KRIMS[30]

In the following example, on the other hand, note the words and phrases used to bind sentences and paragraphs together.

[29] *The Coming to Power* (New York: Chelsea House, 1971), p. xviii.

[30] "Fellini's Rome," *Holiday*, January/February 1974, p. 36.

THE NEED FOR WEATHER DATA

In the past the greatest benefactors of weather forecasting have been the farmers, mariners, fishermen, and other outdoorsmen. People in the cities, with transportation perhaps not more complicated than horsedrawn wagons and with relatively short distances to travel, were not overly concerned by severe storms or snowfalls. Today, however, our heavily urbanized society is becoming increasingly interdependent. We have increased the number of machines in use in the last fifty years; people travel more by air, electric trains, buses, and automobiles. Despite our advances in communications, structures, and highways, even a slight snowfall can produce tie-ups in an urban system. In the south of England, for example, the Southern Region system of Britain's railroads comes to a screeching halt when less than half an inch of snow falls. Elsewhere, on very cold days automobiles may not start. If there is snow, they may get stuck, along with trucks and buses, to cause the familiar traffic messes. Almost all urban activities are to come degree sensitive to the weather, not least being sporting events. Others who need to know the possible state of the weather are the construction industry, the utility companies, urban planners, and works departments. Some years ago the city of New York had a recurring serious shortage of drinking water caused by a prolonged dry spell. This shortage might have been avoided had the municipal au-

Contrast in time

Contrary idea

Contrast in place

Example

Addition

Repetition

> thorities had warning of a year or two about the possibility of a dry spell.
>
> It is obvious, then, that financial savings, as well as great reductions in physical discomfort and downright suffering, would accrue from accurate long-range weather forecasting—if, and this is a big "if," people heeded the warnings.[31]

Summary phrase — Repetition

Some of the most useful methods of transition are described below.

(1) Transitional Words and Phrases

Certain words and phrases are commonly used to signal the relationship between ideas. The connectives in the list below can only suggest the possibilities for such transitions.

Relationship	Connectives
ADDITION	and, also, too
	besides, furthermore, moreover
	first, second, third
	one, other, another
EXAMPLE	for example, for instance
	to illustrate
CAUSE AND EFFECT	because, since, thus
	for this reason
	therefore, consequently, accordingly
COMPARISON	similarly, in the same way
	likewise, in a like manner
CONTRAST	but, however, in contrast
	on the other hand
	nevertheless, notwithstanding
	in spite of
	then ... now

(2) Pronouns

Since pronouns are substitutes for other words, any pronoun that relates to a close antecedent serves a transitional purpose.

[31] Kurt R. Stehling, *Computers and You* (New York: World Publishing, 1972), pp. 137–38.

The Horsefly was one of the largest of these [*streams,* the antecedent, is in the preceding paragraph] in terms of the number of fish it produced. It is part of the Quesnel River system in central British Columbia, forming about 500 miles from the mouth of the Fraser, and is a bright, short, shallow, crystal-clear little stream that springs from two branches on the slopes of Mount Perseus, a cone 8,361 feet high that the natives call Haycock Mountain. Its source is about a hundred miles west of the Canoe River. . . .—ROBERT CANTWELL[32]

(3) Repetition of Words and Phrases

An idea may be carried over from one sentence to another, or from one paragraph to another, through the repetition of a key word or phrase. The repeated element is often preceded by a demonstrative pronoun like *this* or *that,* and sometimes a synonymous word or phrase is substituted for literal repetition. Note, for example, the pattern of repetition in the following paragraph. The repeated or synonymous terms are indicated by identical numbers.

In summary, the conventional wisdom[1] that fails to see an effective role for science[2] in many countries[3] at their[3] present stage of development[4] misses the point in several respects. It[1] conceives development[4] only in immediate and narrowly material terms[5]. It[1] also thinks of science[2] in narrow terms[5], failing to appreciate the broad impact of its[2] problem-solving attitude and its[2] cumulative, optimistic, self-reliant spirit on the development[4] of a country[3]. This same conventional wisdom[1] underestimates the time and effort needed to plant science[2] firmly on new soil[3], and thus neglects the long-term task[6] of establishing an indigenous scientific infrastructure[2] in the less-developed[4] countries[3]—an objective[6] that should, in reality, have the highest priority.

—MICHAEL J. MORAVCSIK AND J. M. ZIMAN[33]

[32] *The Hidden Northwest* (New York: Lippincott, 1972), p. 177.

[33] "Paradisio and Dominatia: Science and the Developing World," *Foreign Affairs,* July 1975, p. 707.

In the passage below, the repetition of words is carried over to a second and third paragraph.

Sound[1] has two[2] fundamental characteristics—frequency[3] and intensity[4]. Both[2] are important in determining whether sound[1] is pleasant and helpful, or harmful and unwanted.

Frequency[3] . . . [Paragraph follows.]

Intensity[4] . . . [Paragraph follows.]

(4) Parallel Structure

The repetition of the grammatical structure in a series of sentences often provides sufficient connection, so that other connecting devices are not needed. The awesome effect achieved by the venerable Joseph Addison in the third example below is especially striking. (For the use of parallel structure within sentences, see **Rule 27.**)

A soldier home from war, what does he want immediately? I was twenty-one and what I wanted were a hot tub and clean sheets, thin pajamas and the luxury of sleeping late. I wanted home cooking, the chance to work up a good sweat at tennis, followed by cold beer. I wanted the leisure to read, white flannels, and some good-looking neckties. I wanted to drive the family car, a gun-metal Moon with a powerful motor, and I, too, wanted girls. Not just any girls.—EDWARD WEEKS[34]

In the days before assembly lines and multioperation plants, every employee knew what orders were received, who the big customers were, whether materials were in stock, and how much was produced. He knew whether the business was prospering and, of course, could see when new men were added, when slack work forced layoffs. He knew when he did a good job and whether the shop produced merchandise of quality sufficient to maintain its reputation among competitors. He knew whether prices met competition and whether his wages were in line with those paid by other employers for similar work.[35]

When I look upon the tombs of the great, every emotion of envy dies in me; when I read the epitaphs of the beautiful, every inordinate desire goes out; when I meet with the grief of parents upon a tombstone, my heart melts

[34] From *My Green Age* by Edward Weeks, by permission of Little, Brown and Co. in association with The Atlantic Monthly Press. Copyright © 1973 by Edward Weeks.

[35] *Communication in United States Steel,* United States Steel Corporation.

with compassion; when I see the tomb of the parents themselves, I consider the vanity of grieving for those whom we must quickly follow. When I see kings lying by those who deposed them, when I consider rival wits placed side by side, or the holy men that divided the world with their contests and disputes, I reflect with sorrow and astonishment on the little competitions, factions, and debates of mankind. When I read the several dates of the tombs, of some that died yesterday, and some six hundred years ago, I consider that great day when we shall all of us be contemporaries, and make our appearance together.—JOSEPH ADDISON[36]

(5) Connection Between Paragraphs

All the methods of linkage already described may be applied not only to the connection of sentences, but to the connection of paragraphs as well. In the following passage, the first two paragraphs

Linkage to preceding paragraph

Better than such a defense, however, would be a consideration of what modern science really genuinely is, and what its limits are.

Reference to material that follows

Repetition

Science, both ancient and modern, has, in the first place, three indispensable characteristics:

Connecting phrase

Lead-in to following enumeration

First, it is *methodical* knowledge. I know something scientifically only when I also know the method by which I have this knowledge, and am thus able to ground it and mark its limits.

Parallel structure

Second, it is *compellingly certain.* Even the undertain—i.e., the probable or improbable—I know scientifically only insofar as I know it clearly and compellingly as such, and know the degree of its uncertainty.

Repetition

Third, it is *universally valid.* I know scientifically only what is identically valid for every inquirer. . . .—KARL JASPERS[37]

[36] "Reflections in Westminster Abbey," *The Spectator*, No. 26 (March 30, 1711).
[37] "Is Science Evil?" *Commentary*, March 1950, p. 230.

utilize repetition and connecting words and phrases; they are succeeded by a series of paragraphs in parallel structure, aided by the enumeratives *first, second,* and *third.* The italics are the author's.

One of the most useful of paragraph connectives is the transitional sentence or paragraph—one that serves both as a reminder of what has just been said and an introduction to what follows. The first paragraph in the passage just quoted is an example of a transitional paragraph, although it consists of only a single sentence. Other transitional sentences may constitute only a part of the paragraphs in which they appear.

If the period of the Civil War could be considered the time of the rise of the two-party system, the period after the war was clearly that of the system's apogee.—ARTHUR M. SCHLESINGER, JR. Connects a discussion of party politics before the Civil War with those after the conflict.]

Enormous as the youthful population has been, however, it is not big enough to explain the even greater rise in youthful criminality.—TIME [Forms a bridge between a paragraph citing the rise in the number of youths fourteen to twenty-four and the subject of the present paragraph—the rise in crime committed by such youths.]

Often the transitional sentences are much shorter.

Outside the cities, conditions were not much better.
These developments will have a major social impact.
This is no mere theory.
What will motivate this new type of student?

EXERCISES

A. With respect to each of the paragraphs below,

(a) Does the paragraph have a central idea? Is that idea expressed in a topic sentence? If not, state the central idea in your own words.

(b) What methods of development are evident?

(c) What specific order or orders are used?

(d) Is the transition between ideas smooth? Point to some of the methods by which connection is achieved.

1. [New York Harbor] was not always so safe. Heaven, if not history, only knows how many shipbottoms the Colonial Dutch left

behind on the unfathomed shoals of the harbor. The English were somewhat more cautious. By 1694, it is recorded, there were men who claimed to know where the channels were, not to mention the wrecks; and soon they were signing themselves aboard visiting vessels as pilots. For 200 years—plus one, to be exact—piloting was a competitive affair in the harbor, with small family schooners racing one another to be the first to offer its services to any incoming ship. Then, in 1895, it occurred to a number of the competitors that it might be more efficient and profitable if they were to pool their resources, acquire a steam schooner large enough to carry 20 or 30 men at a time, and accept assignments on a rotating basis. Thus did the Sandy Hook Pilots Association come into being. Today, the Association's 130 licensed members are responsible for the safe passage of 95 percent of all shipping that enters or leaves the harbor.—JOHN MITCHELL[38]

2. Muskrats are the bread and butter of the carnivorous food chain. They are like rabbits and mice: if you are big enough to eat mammals, you eat them. Hawks and owls prey on them, and foxes; so do otters. Minks are their special enemies; minks live near large muskrat populations, slinking in and out of their dens and generally hanging around like mantises outside a beehive. Sometimes, however, whole muskrat populations explode, just like lemmings', which are their near kin; and they either die by the hundreds or fan out across the land, migrating to new creeks and ponds.—ANNIE DILLARD[39]

3. Québec differs fundamentally from all its neighbours in America, whether inside Canada or outside its borders: its population is French. Far from going unnoticed, this characteristic is responsible for a way of life that is unique. The atmosphere in Québec is French, which is not commonplace in America! The *Québécois,* whose ancestors came from France more than three centuries ago, have spread out across Canada and the United States, but their real stronghold in the 17th century was the valley of the Saint-Laurent river. They settled and moulded it and, hardy discoverers that they were, conquered the vast surrounding territory: a thousand miles (1,600 kilometres) from east to west and from north to south.[40]

4. In a curious way, there is a distinct continuity between colonial America's notion of what children ought to be like and our present-day "enlightened" and "emancipated" notion. The Puritans

[38] "Sandy Hook Pilots," *World,* Summer 1975, p. 12.

[39] From "The Muskrat Ramble," *Travel & Leisure,* March 1974, p. 27.

[40] *Le Québec Touristique,* Government of Quebec, n.d., p. 36.

saw evil everywhere, not excluding the minds of children. A child who obeyed his parents and spoke tactfully and courteously was a child whose behavior attested to his parents' Christian virtues. The parents had recognized sin in their boys and girls and fought it (relatively) and subdued it (mostly). By the same token, today's parents also strive hard to be found among the elect. That includes those who have read their Spock (in revolutionary days it was the philosopher John Locke who had all kinds of advice about child rearing) and have sought out the best psychological methods or techniques for handling their young children, the best "learning environments" for educating them—and having done so, been found winners. The children of these elect "cope" well, "adapt" well, are able to assert themselves without "anxiety," get along with others without too much "frustration." In both instances one detects at least a thread or two of Utopian thinking. Whether it be prayer and Christian piety or psychological "insight" and the "sensitivity" that is offered in "groups" or by individual experts, the point is to apply what one has been trying to obtain (God's grace, a psychiatrist's knowledge) to children. Thereby one builds something that lasts longer than a particular lifetime: the "New Jerusalem" or the "better, happier world" that several generations of people have hoped to build here in America.—ROBERT COLES[41]

5. Oscar Wilde's celebrated remark to André Gide, "I've put my genius into my life; I've only put my talent into my works" suggests why he has always been an attractive subject for biographers. Apart from the dramatic circumstances of his downfall, the trial and imprisonment that resulted from his notorious affair with the young Lord Alfred Douglas, Wilde's personality was an elaborate artifice deliberately fashioned to yield anecdotes. Where most authors expect their work to represent them, Wilde was aware that he would have to depend on memoirs and biographies to promote the self he had invented. So he spoke in "perfect sentences," as Yeats recalled in his "Autobiographies," "as if he had written them all overnight with labor and yet all spontaneous."—JAMES ATLAS[42]

6. One of the most terrifying tanker accidents involved the Polycommander, a 50,380-ton Norwegian vessel. In May, 1970, carrying a full cargo of crude oil, she ran aground and burst into flames at

[41] "Growing Up in America—Then and Now," *Time*, 29 December 1975, p. 29.

[42] From a review of H. Montgomery Hyde's *Oscar Wilde: A Biography*, in *The New York Times Book Review*, 21 December 1975, p. 6.

Mixieiro Point, near Vigo, on the Spanish Atlantic coast. The oil spillage amounted to about sixteen thousand tons, or a third of her cargo; it started burning on the sea, and the flames were so fierce that they caused a fire storm—a heat disturbance of such intensity that it raised winds of hurricane force in the immediate vicinity of the stricken ship. The winds whirled aloft a huge amount of oil as a fine mist, and bore it to high altitudes. The mist condensed into drops, and some days later a black rain began to fall upon the farmlands and upon the villages of Panjón and Bayona, on the coast. The damage to homes, gardens, and crops was extensive, and cattle died of eating oil-covered grass.—NOËL MOSTERT[43]

7. That television arrived simultaneously with the height of McCarthyism probably helped to narrow the parameters of journalistic freedom, but it was bound to happen anyway. Politically, television was simply too powerful a force, too fast, too immediate, with too large an audience, for the kind of easy journalistic freedom that radio and print reporters had enjoyed. Newspapers competed with each other for power and influence, but television was a virtual rival of the government. It was as if an unwritten law of American journalism had evolved, stating that the greater the institutional platform, and the more power it has to influence public opinion, the more carefully it must be used and the less it must wander from the accepted norms of American society. It is better to be a little wrong and a little late on a major sensitive story than it is to be too right too far ahead of the rest of the country. There were two reasons for this sensitivity. The first was timidity, a desire not to offend the audience's sensibilities, not to get too far ahead of the parade, plus an awareness of political pressures that grew in direct proportion to the success and influence of television. The second was more honorable, the perception that the medium was so powerful that personal journalism of any sort bordered on being dangerous, that no one journalist should be too powerful. So television journalism, far more than print or radio journalism, contemplated the political implications of every story it broadcast, considered what the reaction might be. A political figure could be damaged by a piece in a major newspaper, but a television report might destroy him. Television's important figures became prisoners of their power.—DAVID HALBERSTAM[44]

8. Here is a scientist investigating a contagious fever. He wants to find out how the disease is transferred from one victim to the next.

[43] "Super Tankers," *The New Yorker*, 13 May 1974, p. 100.
[44] "CBS: The Power & the Profits," *Atlantic*, January 1976, pp. 63–64.

First he browses around in the literature of contagious diseases. In due time he gets an idea that it *might* be conveyed by some bloodsucking creature. By prolonged and painstaking research in the field and in the laboratory, in which many bloodsucking creatures are examined and discarded, he finally verifies the hypothesis. The mosquito is found guilty. Any competent man can repeat the experiment and prove it. A conquest has been made far greater than that of Cortes.—STUART CHASE[45]

9. Elephants are a funny bunch. In the first place, they usually do come in bunches, and I had never thought of anything so big in a bunch before. If you see one, you're almost certain to see another, and another, and another: lots of tusks and trunks and huge wrinkled knees and incongruously measly tails, as if nature, when she got to that point, wore out. Elephants will emerge in droves from the forested places at sunset to drink at the watering holes alongside which the safari lodges often are situated to accommodate animal watchers. They keep coming, on into the night, in orderly lines, an elephant pecking order: the biggest first, daddys, mommys, then the babies tagging along, often neatly tucked underneath their mothers. They queue up, not only to drink but to bathe, splashing themselves gloriously with the red-mud water, and then to rub themselves dry on the massively proportioned boulders that God clearly put there for that purpose.—JANE VONNEGUT[46]

10. Several factors underlie the women's rush to law school. At least one of them is common to men as well: a growing belief that a legal career offers security and opportunity; total law-school applications tripled between 1959 and 1972, while the number of female applicants increased fourteen-fold. The rise of the women's liberation movement is most often cited as the number one factor propelling women to law school. "The movement" has worked in two ways. It has stimulated a newfound confidence and determination to enter traditional male preserves, creating what Berkeley law-school professor Herma Kay calls "a feeling among women that they really *can* carve out a serious career for themselves, and that they can make some money, do some good, and have some fun at the same time." Further, for the new breed of feminist, it has pinpointed the law as the most effective tool for furthering the female revolution. It is hardly a coincidence that the marked rise in women's law-school

[45] *The Tyranny of Words* (New York: Harcourt, 1938), pp. 122–23.
[46] "On Safari in Kenya, Curious Regression," *New York Times*, 7 July 1974.

enrollment began in the late Sixties, when "the movement" was picking up its first real momentum.—ROGER M. WILLIAMS[47]

B. With respect to each of the two passages below,
(a) In what respect can the passage be considered a unit?
(b) How can the division into paragraphs be justified?
(c) How is connection between the paragraphs achieved?

1. An ancient Chinese sage is said to have observed that it is easy to paint a goblin but hard to paint a horse.

It is hard to paint a horse, because ever since our first astonished view of one it has become more and more unlikely that there might again be a horse seen by us with eyes undimmed and undeceptive.

Just so, with each passing year it has become more difficult for us to recapture the first engulfing sense of "strange things happening" that we must have felt when we first spoke a word. As most of us toddled unsuspectingly into our second year of life, we still retained almost completely the enchanted point of view of the little child from Mars. So it was that when we found ourselves controlling others from a distance by making noises in our throats, surely we were seized by what could only have been an unrelenting wish to make words and to watch their fantastic effects. At any rate, in the adroitly unpoetic wording of the academic experts, between the ages of one and three years the average child undergoes a language growth that he will never again equal in any later period of comparable extent.

Like March, speech comes in like a lion—a bounding and untiring lion—and goes out like a lamb—an unwell and monotonously bleating lamb.—WENDELL JOHNSON[48]

2. Leases on Federal land are acquired through periodic sales conducted by the Bureau of Land Management of the Department of Interior. Unlike the sealed bidding on offshore Federal leases, which run into thousands of dollars an acre with the lease going to the highest bidder, a Rocky Mountain producer can get in on the action for $10.

The $10 entitles the producer to file a card on one tract. He can file for as many tracts as he wishes, as long as he pays $10 for each. Then a lottery is held, with the Bureau drawing three cards for each tract. The holder of the first card drawn gets the lease, unless it is rejected

[47] "Law Schools: The Big Woman Boom," *Saturday Review*, 21 September 1974, p. 51.

[48] *Your Most Enchanted Listener* (New York: Harper & Brothers, 1956), pp. 7–8.

for some mistake in the filing, in which [case] the second, then the third get their chance. The winner then must make an advance payment of 50 cents an acre for a 10-year lease, along with a one-eighth royalty on any gas or oil produced.

The hairy part of Federal leasing is that all the lease holders get are the mineral rights. The government may already have leased or even sold the surface rights to a farmer or rancher who gets nothing if gas or oil is discovered on the land he is using. This leads to confrontations with surface-holders who sometimes refuse to let the producer on the land or demand exorbitant fees for seismic exploration and damages. Some cases end up in court and delay exploration for months.—WILLIAM HUTCHINS[49]

C. Study the paragraph by Huxley quoted on pages 57–58. How do you account for the length of the paragraph? If the author had put essentially the same text in several shorter paragraphs, what would have been gained or lost?

[49] "ANG's 1-Million-Acre Piece of the Rockies," *Venture,* Autumn 1975, pp. 5–6.

Index

Boldface numbers signify rules in Part II, "Handbook of English." All other numbers are page numbers. Numbers immediately following a colon represent the pages covered by the rule. The *ex* means that exercises or suggestions for composition are included.

A

B

D

E

F

G

H

I

J

K

L

M

N

O

P

Q

R

S

T

U